SECURING YOUR ORGANIZATION'S FUTURE

A COMPLETE GUIDE TO FUNDRAISING STRATEGIES

MICHAEL SELTZER

THE FOUNDATION CENTER
1987

Library of Congress Cataloging-in-Publication Data
Seltzer, Michael, 1947-
    Securing your organization's future.

    Includes bibliographies and index.
    1. Fund raising—United States. 2. Fund raising—Law
and legislation—United States. 3. Corporations, Nonprofit—United States—Finance. I. Title.
HV41.9.U5S45   1987   658.1'5224   86-31843
ISBN 0-87954-190-3

To Ralph

And in loving memory of
Dorothy and Max Seltzer

"Each time a person stands up for an ideal, or acts to improve
the lot of others, they send forth a tiny ripple of hope. . . .
These ripples build a current which can sweep down the might-
iest walls of oppression and resistance." —Robert F. Kennedy

CONTENTS

ACKNOWLEDGMENTS

Helping America's nonprofit organizations prepare for the 90s is no simple task. The rigors of the 80s make one wish for a modern Marshall plan to ensure the future health of the nonprofit sector. Fortunately, the ingredients for long-term success can be found in the experiences of nonprofits themselves, and their staffs, board members, volunteers, and supporting network of consultants and technical assistance providers. I offer this book as one tool for nonprofit leaders to use as they build their roads to organizational self-sufficiency.

I have been extremely lucky to have had so many new and old friends to turn to for assistance in researching and writing this book. I am particularly grateful to the numerous organizations, from Amnesty International USA to Working Women Education Fund, that I have had the pleasure of working with in my twenty years as a consultant, technical assistance provider, executive director, and board member. My life has been enriched by these women and men who have so bravely carried the banner for the causes of our time. Their stories and successes fill this book and, I believe, portray the spirit and courage that inspires us all. Space does not allow me to thank them all individually, but this book is my gift to all of them.

I do want to single out those individuals who have been invaluable in writing this book. First, I would like to express my thanks to the various specialists who served as this consultant's consultants: Judith L. Bardes (Planned Giving), Dr. Winifred deLoayza (Government), Leon Haller (Budgeting), Rochelle Korman, Esq. (Planned Giving), Kate McQueen (Federated Fundraising Organizations), Sandra Tanzer (Direct Mail), and the late Mark D. Turkel, Esq. (Legal).

Additionally, I would like to acknowledge the following people, who gave graciously of their time in interviews and in reviewing specific chapters: Ira Berger, Thomas D. Boyd, Peter Buttenweiser, the Rev. John Cannon, Lori Cooper, Chris Cowap, Alex Douglas, Dee Elwood, Alice Evans, Sara Gould, Judy Hozore, Raymond Johnson, Ian Kramer, Laura Landy, Douglas Lawson, Robert Leaver, Alice-Ann Leidel, Dr. Reynold Levy, Willoughby Newton, Robert Pierpont, Carolyn Pope, Richard Ray, Lawrence Redmond, Marty Rogol, Tim Saasta, Rabbi David Saperstein, Jill Shellow, Steve Shaw, Edward Skloot, Pamela Stebbins, the Rev. Robert Stromenn, Carl Valentine, the Rev. Lou Walker, Anthony Ward, and Charles Ziff.

I also owe a tremendous debt of gratitude to the friends who aided me in editing and revising the manuscript. They provided tremendous moral as well as technical support. They are: Liam Brosnahan, Lilly Cohen, Jean Horan, Judith Sutphen, Marilyn Wood, and Lenora DeSio. Ellin Stein's contributions are easily recognizable in many of the case studies. Cheryl Reeves made her own lasting contribution through her careful annotation of the bibliography. Randy Gardull played the key role in collecting the photographs and other graphic materials.

Finally, I would like to single out for special acknowledgment three individuals. Each of them teaches me a little more each day about true generosity of spirit: Phyllis Goodfriend, who faithfully typed this manuscript from beginning to end; Lenora DeSio, again, who helped me with wise counsel at every critical juncture; and Ralph Tachuk, whose constant support made this project possible.

I hasten to add: Tom Buckman, Patricia Read, Rick Schoff, and Joyce Fenster, as well as all the wonderful librarians at The Foundation Center for all their assistance; Barbara Moffat and Asia Bennett of the American Friends Service Committee for their early support; Joan Flanagan for a healthy dose of encouragement when I needed it most; Howard Dressner and Louis Winnick and The Ford Foundation for serving as this book's "angels"; and all my other dear friends.

Michael Seltzer
October 1, 1986
New York, New York

A TALE OF
TWO ORGANIZATIONS

Separated by less than two miles of city streets on the Upper East Side of Manhattan in New York City, two very different nonprofit institutions are flourishing.

On Fifth Avenue, the Metropolitan Museum of Art has "provided to our people free and ample means for innocent and refined enjoyment" for over 100 years. Its world-renowned collections of art and sculpture attract more than six million visitors annually.

To the north, in Spanish Harlem, East Harlem Block Schools has been providing quality education to both children and adults in the immediate neighborhood since 1965. This institution has grown from an initial storefront nursery program to an educational complex that now includes an elementary school, a college-training program for parents and adults, and programs for teenagers and senior citizens.

What do these two dissimilar institutions have in common? What can be learned about fundraising and organization building from their respective histories? How did they achieve their goals, and how can other concerned citizens and organizations match their success? The following pages will attempt to answer these and other questions.

VISION

As with all charitable undertakings, the founders of the Metropolitan Museum of Art and East Harlem Block Schools were prompted to action by their sense of how the world could be improved. In both instances, the founders moved toward equally practical and idealistic goals.

The businessmen, artists, and civic leaders who issued the call for "the establishment in this city of a Museum of Art" in November 1869 wanted to give the public access to the art treasures of the world. They believed such access would provide a vital new kind of education to the burgeoning masses of people in New York. At the Museum's formal dedication ceremony in March 1880 in its new Central Park home, Joseph C. Choate, a member of the founding board of directors, expressed these sentiments in his speech: "[The founders] . . . believed that the diffusion of a knowledge of art in its higher forms of beauty would tend directly to humanize, to educate and refine a practical and laborious people."

Thus, Mr. Choate and his colleagues took one giant step forward. Art would no longer belong exclusively to the wealthy; now others could enjoy it, learn from it, and draw inspiration from it as well.

In the 1960s, a group of East Harlem parents discovered that they shared a concern for a good education and advancement opportunities for their children. Believing that a solid education would lead to a better life, these parents nonetheless felt powerless when confronted by the lack of interest in and sympathy for their problems expressed by the public school system of New York City. They wanted to know why *they* couldn't be in charge of their own children's education. Simply taking charge of it, they first opened a nursery school program. Within fifteen years, that program had expanded to include five hundred children, teenagers, and adults, even providing college training for the parents themselves. That initial sense of frustration, even anger, fueled this community's efforts to create an entirely new educational system.

SECURING FUNDS

Every nonprofit organization has the need to raise money. Even founders as privileged as those who began the Metropolitan Museum of Art were no exception. In 1869, the Museum's initial organizing committee set a first-year fundraising goal of $250,000. They established three classes of membership to elicit contributions:

Patron	$1,000
Fellow in Perpetuity	500
Fellow for Life	200

Ironically, even though many who belonged to New York's "establishment" were involved in launching the Museum, the organizers netted only $106,000 that first year.

Of course, looking back over its growth and expansion over the years, we can see that the Museum's capacity to attract financial support increased beyond the wildest dreams of its initiators. One gift alone in 1969 demonstrates how far the Metropolitan Museum of Art had progressed from its very modest beginnings: Robert Lehman donated his personal collection of 3,000 works of art to the Museum, estimated to be valued at $100,000,000.

The East Harlem Block Schools began with fundraising events similar to those used by neighborhood groups anywhere, such as cake sales and rummage sales. Parents became not only fundraisers *extraordinaires* but also the volunteer backbone of the early education programs. They soon learned about government grantsmanship and successfully applied for a $75,000 grant—the auspicious first of many other grants that followed from local and national foundations and from city, state, and federal public sources. By 1983 the parents behind East Harlem Block Schools could look with pride at their institution, which now controlled a budget of over $1.25 million. Moreover, they had also pioneered the first parent-run, parent-staffed day-care program in New York City that had ever received public support.

THE MORAL

Despite the obvious differences, the experiences of the Metropolitan Museum of Art and the East Harlem Block Schools do have something in common. In both instances the founders and their followers were inspired by a vision, a sense of purpose, that sparked their work. The central characteristic of those visions was a concern for others as well as for themselves. A certain nobility of purpose was inherent in their enterprise. Not surprisingly, then, their pursuits brought them in touch with numerous other constituencies, ranging from the general public to foundations to government, which were moved to provide support, financial and otherwise.

At the same time, the founders solicited, recruited, and hired people who contributed the skills needed to ease their daily work of management, budgeting, publicity, grantsmanship, and planning, as well as specialists to answer the particular needs of the two institutions.

Both institutions frequently learned their lessons the hard way, through their own mistakes. Sometimes luck created major breakthroughs—a chance encounter with a sympathetic government official or an unsolicited offer of a free building.

The initial vision of each institution's founders served as the North Star for those who followed, challenging them on to even greater heights in building new viable organizations. Through the work of their successors, both the major art museum and the neighborhood education institution have earned the right to be called "successful" in their respective fields of endeavor.

In similar ways, other nonprofit organizations have been formed throughout the United States since pre-Revolutionary times. Today, the more than 785,000 nonprofit groups include social service agencies, zoos, hospitals, universities, performing arts groups, social action organizations, and others.

The success of these groups, agencies, associations, and organizations lies squarely in the hard lessons that the people behind such efforts as the Metropolitan Museum of Art and the East Harlem Block Schools learned from their own experiences.

INTRODUCTION

Charting a steady course through today's financial waters is becoming increasingly difficult for the leaders of nonprofit organizations in the United States. They are buffeted by powerful forces from all sides. The 1980s brought government cutbacks in funding, and budget doctors everywhere are sharpening their scalpels for yet more drastic surgery. Corporations and foundations are witnessing increased competition for limited philanthropic dollars, and although individuals are giving more than ever before, the demand for charitable support far outstrips their generosity.

As a result, the nonprofit's search for funds to achieve its goals has never been more fraught with challenges. Board members, staff, and volunteers must plan how to expend their limited time and resources more effectively than ever.

This volume is a handbook and reference work for the leaders of America's 785,000-plus nonprofits to help them in securing the futures of their organizations. It will arm the reader with the knowledge to prevail in today's climate. The secret to surviving and transcending the harsh new realities has been gleaned from years of trial and error. Simply stated, each and every nonprofit needs to seek out support from a variety of sources to achieve fiscal strength. In other words, their long-term financial well-being is linked to finding the appropriate mix of funding sources most suited to them, thereby creating a network of support.

This book proceeds along this course in three sections. Section 1, "Starting Right," focuses on the founding and running of an organization, including chapters on deciding purpose, setting up an organization legally, building a board of directors, planning programs, and developing budgets. Each chapter outlines a step-by-step process that any nonprofit can apply to its own situation. A start-up checklist at the end of Section 1 provides the reader with a summary worksheet for personal use.

Except for Chapter 2 ("Making an Organization Legal"), all of these tasks are also ongoing during the life of an organization, and are intrinsic to successful fundraising.

Section 2, "Exploring the World of Money," provides a comprehensive overview of the range of sources of revenue available to nonprofits, as well as step-by-step information for securing the support of the various sources presented. Chapters 7 through 12 focus specifically on different ways to secure support from individuals, including face-to-face solicitation, direct mail, special events, planned giving, and earned and venture income. Chapters 13 through 18 lend perspective to the daunting array of institutional sources, including foundations, businesses and corporations, government, religious sources, federated fundraising organizations, and associations of individuals. The purpose of each of these chapters is to enable readers to decide which of these sources are appropriate for their organization to pursue, and to guide them in effectively doing so. Each chapter contains a worksheet that gives you the opportunity to collect pertinent information useful to your own organization in tapping any particular source. You are advised to complete these worksheets, so you will be able to gauge which mix of sources will constitute your own funding mix in Section 3.

Section 3, "Developing Your Overall Fundraising Plan," aids readers in designing a fundraising strategy that capitalizes on the uniqueness of their own nonprofit organization, and then in putting that strategy into action. Through a series of ten phases of activity, nonprofit leaders will learn how to evaluate their organizations' strengths and assets, choose their funding partners, set fundraising goals, design strategies to secure both individual and institutional support, and plan and implement their fundraising efforts. Again, by completing the worksheets in this section, you will be immediately able to apply what you have learned to your own situation.

As the numerous examples and case studies throughout this book illustrate, success in fundraising is within your grasp. Use this book as a workbook, a reference work, and a guide as you go forward to raise the funds necessary for your group's future.

STARTING RIGHT

INTRODUCTION

Fundraising for nonprofit organizations involves preparation and readiness. A captain of a ship would never commence a journey without making sure that his or her vessel was in tip-top shape. In the same sense, the leadership of a nonprofit organization needs to make sure that its own house is in order before embarking on any fundraising campaigns. Otherwise, its efforts will falter and, ultimately, fail.

The journey is the same whether an organization is long established or recently arrived on the scene. The veteran group may be aided by an existing body of experience, a usually hard-earned reputation, and an expanding network of supporters. The fledgling organization can draw on the credentials and connections of its founders and learn from the experiences of similar groups. Both the new and the old groups prepare themselves in similar ways for the fundraising ahead. What steps must the old and the new organizations take before they can raise funds successfully?

Section 1 of this book presents the major organizational tasks that need to be addressed *before* a nonprofit can begin to compete effectively in the marketplace for charitable dollars. Briefly summarized, these tasks are as follows:

1. *Creating a Statement of Purpose*

A statement of purpose provides the bedrock and source of inspiration for an organization's efforts, as well as for any later fundraising initiatives. A group must assess meticulously the needs of its community and constituencies and then develop a statement of intent that addresses these needs in a clear and direct way. Articulating and proposing a course of action to confront commonly perceived problems serves as a strong rallying call to a potential array of allies.

2. *Making Your Work Legal*

An organization has to either incorporate with a state government and file for tax exemption as a charitable endeavor with the Internal Revenue Service, or seek out affiliation with an organization that has already obtained that status. In addition, many state governments require nonprofits to register with them annually. In these ways, a nonprofit group is assured that its activities are operating within the law and that donors can receive tax benefits from their contributions.

3. *Building a Strong Board of Directors*

The board of directors provides leadership to any endeavor through its members' contributions of time, expertise, and money. Rarely can an organization "settle" for the phantom board of yesteryear, when individuals lent their names and attended meetings only occasionally. Today's boards are vital to the policy-setting and fundraising operations of successful nonprofits.

4. *Planning Solid Programs*

Expressing concern about a particular problem and indicating a willingness to do something about it is not enough. An organization's leadership must demonstrate precisely what it plans to do to really make a difference. It must plan its strategies in advance. It then can anticipate results and present them to its prospective supporters as evidence of its credibility.

5. *Developing Realistic Budgets*

Remember: the public discriminates. It wants to know not only what you plan to do with its contribution but how much your programs will actually cost. Budgeting is the tool that enables an organization to project both revenues and expenditures.

All five of these tasks are detailed in the subsequent chapters of Section 1. By satisfactorily completing them, the leaders of a nonprofit effort can proceed confidently to raise the funds necessary to support their work. Again, without doing so, both the fledgling and the established organization will be handicapped in their fundraising efforts and possibly denied ultimate success.

To the beginner, most of these tasks will appear new; to the veteran, they should be familiar. Regardless, all nonprofit leaders need to pay close attention to these organization-building steps. They can then approach the public with their requests for support. They will be "fundraising-ready."

CHAPTER 1

DEFINING A STATEMENT OF PURPOSE

A single vision unifies every organization.

Every organization should begin by articulating the central beliefs and values that are inherent in its vision. To find them an organization needs only to go to its immediate constituents.

Envisaging the society, or even the world, that you desire may seem like hard work initially, but your organization will reap bountiful rewards from this exercise.

When the delegates to the Second Continental Congress gathered in Philadelphia in July 1776, the majority knew that they were bound together by shared values—a desire for freedom from tyranny and for the right to self-determination. Acknowledging that, our founding fathers recruited Thomas Jefferson to draft the Declaration of Independence, the statement that would best express their single vision, their central belief.

In that statement, Jefferson chose not only to describe the goals of the Second Continental Congress—to declare independence from England—but to address the values by which he and his fellow delegates were moved to act. They are stated in the preamble of the Declaration:

> We hold these truths to be self-evident, that all men are created equal, that they are endowed by their Creator with certain unalienable Rights, that among

these are Life, Liberty and the pursuit of Happiness. That to secure these rights, Governments are instituted among Men, deriving their just powers from the consent of the governed. . . .

These familiar words provided America with the context for its government.

Similarly, every nonprofit organization must start by formulating its statement of purpose, putting into words the essence of its vision and values. That statement of purpose will provide the vital focus every group requires for smooth internal functioning and will also define the organization's place in the world, giving its efforts scope, meaning and direction. Only then will the central purpose of your undertaking become clear to others. The statement you choose, then, frames your organization's public image, identifying it much like a slogan.

That image should attract people to your organization. On the strength of those words, members, donors, and volunteers will choose to rally around your efforts or to ignore them. The statement you choose may well be short and simple, as long as it is clear and powerful enough to move others to support your cause actively. Often, to an organization's surprise, the chosen phrase or sentence may strike a resonant chord in the listeners who have been waiting to be swept up by a cause that articulates their concerns.

A well-honed statement of purpose is the most crucial element of any fundraising effort. You are sounding a rallying cry that will touch your potential donors' own desires and interests. If chosen wisely, your words, with the enthusiastic help of converts, can echo far beyond the ears of the individuals or groups you are targeting.

Every organization develops its own declaration announcing its creation. It may be stated in the bylaws or in the application for federal tax exemption, but the leaders of a fledgling effort don't always realize that they should also concern themselves with finding the best words to express these binding sentiments to the general public. Drafting a statement of purpose provides them with that opportunity.

For the older, established organization, the task is also an important and vital one. As conditions in society change, so do the forces that affect an organization's programs. The success that has resulted from your work may also suggest that it is time to move on to other issues, constituencies, or locales. The March of Dimes faced this challenge after the discovery of the vaccine to combat polio. The organization then moved into an entirely different area of health—birth defects—to make a new contribution to the relief of human suffering.

Existing institutions may occasionally experience the symptoms of a flagging purpose, such as declining membership and public interest or dwindling revenues, and yet not recognize that their statement of purpose may be outdated and in need of review. For these reasons and others, statements of purpose should be regarded as living documents, subject to continual change. In fact, for both old and new organizations, they provide a future blueprint for a group's activities.

Finding precisely the right words may seem difficult. Yet, they are on the tip of the tongue of anyone who has become involved with your undertaking. All you have to do is allow people to express what they already know and feel.

ELEMENTS OF A SOLID STATEMENT OF PURPOSE

Statements of purpose, or mission statements, are declarations of goals to the public. Those goals are grounded in an understanding of the problem(s) your organization is tackling and the possible changes your efforts can produce. Your choice of words should not suggest a biblical pronouncement or a political oration. This is not the occasion for rhetoric. On the contrary, your words should be simple expressions of why your founders have come together and what they hope to accomplish. The staff and board of an existing non-profit organization should review their operating purpose statement to determine whether their past expression is still relevant to the current state of affairs in the community and to the organization itself.

In brief, your statement of purpose should answer the three key questions discussed below.

What Do You Hope to Accomplish?

What are the end results you would like to see? What are the changes you would like to effect in the society around you? To what end are your efforts focused? In the simplest terms, what would you like to see happen as a result of your organization's efforts?

Answers to these various queries form the basic ingredient of any solid statement of purpose. Without it, an organization has no sense of vision or guiding force.

The following example illustrates this point. Contrast the following two statements.

> The purpose of Maple Tree Senior Citizen's Center is to provide older people in the community with a hot meal every day and an opportunity for recreation and social life.

> The purpose of Maple Tree Senior Citizen's Center is to enable older people to live fuller lives through adequate nutritional care and social and recreational opportunities.

While both statements certainly describe what programs the Maple Tree Senior Citizen's Center provides, only the second statement suggests what the goals of these programs are.

How Do You Plan to Accomplish Your Goals?

What activities, programs, or services will you undertake to accomplish your goals? How would you characterize these efforts? Are they service-related, advocacy-focused, or public education-oriented?

Simply put, you need to state the *means* you will utilize to accomplish your stated aims. In the previous example, the Maple Tree Senior Citizen's Center will enable older people to live fuller lives *by providing adequate nutritional care and social and recreational opportunities.*

For Whose Benefit Does Your Organization Exist?

Which constituencies does your organization either currently or in the future plan to serve? How specifically can you define your prime constituents —by age, sex, geography, minority group status, income, or any other category connoting special status?

While our operating statement for Maple Tree Senior Citizen's Center clearly states its prime constituency, it does not indicate either what precise age group is being defined as the "older people" it will serve or which particular older people are the prime constituents. The statement could therefore be strengthened as follows:

> The purpose of the Maple Tree Senior Citizen's Center is to enable people aged 65 and over in the town of Deercreek to live fuller lives through adequate nutritional care and social and recreational opportunities.

In drafting your statement, be as specific as possible in stating whom you plan to serve. Avoid such phrases as "serving the general public" (unless that is really true); instead identify the specific groups within the general population that you are aiming to reach.

Let's consider an actual statement of purpose in light of what we have just described.

> The primary focus of Working Women's Education Fund is to eliminate discrimination and upgrade the working status and working conditions of women office workers. WWEF conducts research, engages in educational activities and programs, and provides support to the growing working women's movement.

As you can see, this sentence provides the reader with information on *what* the organization hopes to accomplish, *how* it plans to do so, and *whom* it will serve.

WRITING YOUR STATEMENT

Who can best write a good guiding statement for your organization? You! You have been motivated by some concern or interest to become involved with a particular effort, as either a staffer, board member, volunteer, constituent, or outside resource person. Others have joined together with you toward a common purpose or goal, and you should take the time to express these concerns or interest in words.

Take this opportunity to involve some of the organization's members in a shared task. Each person has a contribution to make in drafting your statement of purpose. Spontaneous responses from those closely involved with your effort usually provide the best raw material for developing your final sentence or paragraph.

People outside your group can also play a part. On the basis of their experience or expertise, they can make valuable suggestions to strengthen your final statement. They will have their own perceptions of what is "doable" and what is critically needed.

How can these various individuals participate in the process?

Invite a number of them to a special meeting with the stated intention of developing a statement of purpose. At the meeting, ask each and every participant to answer the question, "What would you like to see this organization accomplish?" If you prefer, ask the people to work on this task before the meeting and then they can come together to develop one statement from the various ones submitted. A less desirable, but serviceable, approach is to ask one person to write a draft to be circulated among the others eliciting their comments, suggestions, and revisions. Besides being quite invigorating to all who participate, such a process of drawing from various sources will strengthen the final product.

A good statement usually reflects the contributions of the organization's key players. The group's leaders will ensure responses from people by making clear the importance of the task to the future well-being of their collective efforts. The following section illustrates one method an organization can utilize to draft its statement of purpose.

One Way to Draft a Statement of Purpose

1. Announce a special meeting open to a designated number of those you have identified as sympathetic to your pursuit and who seem willing to be involved. The meeting should be held at a time and location that is convenient for everyone. Since you want to have maximum attendance, be sure to check in advance whether daytime or evenings, weekend or weekday, are the best meeting times for those you would like to attend. Stress the importance of this gathering in your written notice and in your follow-up conversations with your invitees. Let them know that you are ready to put into words a pending statement of purpose to set the direction of the fledgling organization you've already talked about together and that you value their input in this process. Even offer some of them a lift to the meeting, if you sense that easy transportation might ensure their attendance.

Aim at meeting of five to fifteen people. Let them know that each of them has a unique contribution to make.

2. Select a meeting space that is accessible and comfortable. The walls should provide enough room for everyone to post with masking tape a sheet of paper fourteen by seventeen inches, to provide a writing space.

Make sure that you have a sufficient supply of poster-size newsprint, magic markers, and masking tape (all available from a local art supply or office stationery store).

3. At the start of the meeting, the chair takes charge and helps the procedure to move along smoothly by reviewing the task ahead. For example: "We hope to leave this meeting with a simple statement that puts forth what we hope to accomplish through the establishment of this organization." The chair asks each person to write a statement expressing what he or she believes is the purpose of the organization.

Ask people to think about the principles that strike them as crucial and to disregard for the moment the usual concerns of style and grammar. "Right now," you should explain, "we're searching for content. We want your own words, nothing more." Take some time for questions and then ask everyone to choose a section of wall space.

The process has begun. Each person is going to write his or her own statement on his or her own poster sheet. The instructions continue: "Write whatever comes to mind. Don't censor yourselves. Put as many thoughts as you like on paper." Allow twenty minutes or more, if necessary, for the group to complete this endeavor. Then give everyone the chance to read his or her own statements aloud, just as they were written. Again, no editing, no censoring.

4. At this point, the chair, using the blackboard or newsprint, records the most frequently mentioned sentiments. Everyone in the room helps the chair to arrive at these conclusions.

Ask the group to pick out the common phrases and even the uncommon phrases, those that may have been mentioned by only one individual, but that speak to everyone present. The chair's role here, needless to say, is crucial. He or she must use intelligence as well as insight and intuition as one group of words after another is tested on the audience in order to assess precisely which phrases convey the concepts the whole group perceives as central to the organization's purpose. After listing the words, expressions, phrases, and sentences that the group agrees are important, the facilitator asks for a collective effort to complete the sentence: "The purpose of (name of organization) is to _____."

Again, don't fuss about grammar and style at this juncture. Look for *concepts*.

5. The chair can now focus the group on strengthening their draft by answering the questions posed under "Fine-Tuning Your Statement of Purpose." The desired outcome of this meeting should have now emerged, and in more ways than one, for not only has a working statement of purpose evolved but a new sense of unity, as well. The final product should embody the major principles that the majority agrees represent the heart of the new organization.

Finally, after some careful polishing for style and grammar, you are ready to exhibit your organizational banner.

Fine-Tuning Your Statement of Purpose

Once you have what you think is a good draft of your statement of purpose, check and rework it again by asking the following questions:

1. *Is it realistic?*

A statement of purpose should suggest clear parameters with regard to geographic scope, targeted constituency, and programmatic thrust. It should answer the question, "What can we realistically expect to accomplish if we are successful in our pursuits?"

2. *Is it clear and concise?*

Others can be inspired and motivated to act by a minimum of rhetoric. Powerful messages often are best conveyed with very few words. The founder's statement of the Boy Scouts of America provides an example that is both brief and meaningful: "to help young people grow to responsible adulthood."

3. *Does it indicate for whose specific benefit your organization exists?*

A statement of purpose should identify which constituencies would be the prime beneficiaries of your activities and programs. Let's look at the statement of purpose of Working Women's Education Fund again as an example:

> The primary focus of Working Women's Education Fund is to eliminate discrimination and upgrade the working status and working conditions of women office workers. WWEF conducts research, engages in educational activities and programs, and provides support to the growing working women's movement.

4. *Does it accurately reflect the values and beliefs that sustain your efforts?*

Drafting a statement of purpose provides an opportunity to put personal beliefs and values to work in mobilizing others into action. These beliefs constitute an organization's value system, which might differentiate the work of one group from others in the same field, or reveal critical differences in approach or methods among similar efforts.

The stated purpose of Citizen's Advocates for Justice provides us with considerable insight into how they approach their work with women criminal offenders: "We provide comprehensive services to female offenders where their humanity is affirmed, where community is encouraged, and where appropriate resources for changing their life-style are made available to them."

The statement of purpose of the Family Service Association of Nassau County, Inc. (FSA), offers not only a sense of *what* FSA hopes to do and *whom* it intends to help but also some important insights into *how* they plan to assist people. The *how* can reveal some of an organization's deepest values.

> The mission of FSA is to assist individuals and families in Nassau County without regard to race, creed or economic standing who are experiencing social or emotional problems. Counseling, family life education and advocacy are provided as well as special programs which address the changing needs of high risk groups. Families in serious trouble are often so engulfed with feelings of helplessness that they don't seek help. FSA has a strong commitment to reach out to such families, particularly the poor, minorities, and youth and the aged.

5. *Does it demonstrate a commitment to serving the public good?*

To obtain and maintain federal tax-exempt status, which is akin to governmental approval for any charitable venture, an organization needs to show how its activities are charitable (see chapter 2 for more on federal tax exemption). The word *charitable* is used in a broad sense by the Internal Revenue Service. Nevertheless, when the IRS reviews applications for tax exemption, applicants must demonstrate how their work is deliberately designed to serve the public good.

Clearly, activities beneficial to the public interest are numerous. Treasury Department regulations give examples of types of organizations whose activities would be considered charitable, such as:

1. Relief of the poor, the distressed, or the underprivileged;
2. Advancement of religion;
3. Advancement of education or science;
4. Erection or maintenance of public buildings, monuments, or works;
5. Lessening the burdens of government;
6. Promotion of social welfare to accomplish any of the above, or
   a. to lessen neighborhood tensions
   b. to eliminate prejudice and discrimination
   c. to defend human and civil rights secured by law
   d. to combat community deterioration and juvenile delinquency.*

*Reprinted from Publication 557 (revised January 1982): Tax Exempt Status for Your Organization, Department of the Treasury, Internal Revenue Service.

This list, however, does not include all the activities that might be considered consistent with the IRS interpretation of *charitable*. Discuss your statement with a lawyer who is familiar with IRS requirements to determine whether it would meet with their approval.

6. *Is this statement suitably powerful?*

Finally, since one of the uses of a statement of purpose is to motivate and inspire others, you must assess whether your statement has presented your effort as strongly as possible. Some people confuse rhetoric with power. A strong and powerful statement captures the essence of an undertaking in language that has meaning to your prime audiences. Sometimes we are so close to our own work that we lose perspective on its importance to other people who are not involved in daily operations. What gives a statement its strength is your ability to capture in words the driving force or sentiments most espoused by those whose support you hope to obtain. In other words, does your statement contain the overriding reason that would move people to rally behind your cause.

Let's examine another statement of purpose in light of this criterion.

The Trust for Public Land (TPL) conserves land as a living resource for present and future generations. As a results-oriented organization, TPL works closely with urban and rural groups and government agencies to:
• acquire and preserve open space to serve human needs;
• share knowledge of non-profit land acquisition processes;
• pioneer methods of land conservation and environmentally sound land use.
TPL practices a land ethic by improving public access to public lands, by fostering community-owned parks and gardens, and by establishing local, community land trusts.

You will note that The Trust for Public Land has expressed in the very first sentence probably the strongest reason why many people support its programs: "TPL conserves land as a living resource for present and future generations."

PUTTING YOUR STATEMENT OF PURPOSE TO WORK

You will be able to find many uses for your newly minted statement of purpose. Its final sentences or paragraph will serve as a valuable, if not integral, part of all of your fundraising materials. You can use it in proposals to corporations and foundations, direct-mail appeals to prospective donors, and even on your letterhead! You may, on occasion, choose to vary the exact words, depending on the particular audience you are approaching. Your existing words will always provide you with a good starting-off point.

Also, your declaration will provide all the individuals associated with your effort a useful script that they can call on when they need to describe your organization to others.

Whether your efforts are one-month old or twenty-five years old, paying close attention to the way in which you convey your central belief and purpose to yourselves and to the public will ensure your own vitality and continued growth.

Worksheet
DEVELOPING A STATEMENT OF PURPOSE

1. Use the answers to the following questions as a guide to drafting an appropriate statement for your organization. If your group is already in existence and has an operative statement, jot it down below and then review it in light of these questions. **Our current statement of purpose (or mission) is:**

_____

_____

_____

_____

   a. What do you hope to accomplish as a result of your efforts?

_____

_____

_____

   b. How do you plan to accomplish these goals?

_____

_____

_____

   c. For whose benefit does your organization exist?

_____

_____

2. Weave together your responses to questions 1a, 1b, and 1c into a single statement:
   The purpose of (the name of your group) is:

_____

_____

_____

_____

3. Evaluate your statement in light of the following considerations:

   a. The statement is realistic.
     ☐yes   ☐no   ☐somewhat
   b. The statement is clear and concise.
     ☐yes   ☐no   ☐somewhat
   c. The statement relfects our values and beliefs.
     ☐yes   ☐no   ☐somewhat
   d. The statement demonstrates a commitment to serving the public good.
     ☐yes   ☐no   ☐somewhat
   e. The statement is powerful.
     ☐yes   ☐no   ☐somewhat

4. Jot down possible changes that you can make in light of the above responses.

5. Now, modify your statement in ways that would strengthen it.
    The purpose of (the name of your group) is:

_____

_____

_____

_____

6. Share this draft with three people outside your organization for their comments. Be sure to include at least one person who may not be at all familiar with your issues. List possible candidates below.

_____   _____

_____   _____

_____   _____

FURTHER READINGS

Gross, Susan W. *The Power of Purpose*. Washington, DC: Management Assistance Group. June 1983. 9 pp. 1 copy free to nonprofit organizations. (Order from: Management Assistance Group; 1705 DeSales St., N.W., Suite 401, Washington, DC 20036).

Shows how a clear sense of purpose shared by every member of the organization is the most important ingredient in organizational effectiveness. The dangers in not having or not adhering to this purpose, particularly when engaged in fundraising, are discussed.

Leaver, Robert, and Jay Vogt. *The Preferred Future Design Process*. (Order from Organizational Futures, 35 South Angell St., Providence, RI 02906).

A workbook outlining step-by-step how you can plan and design your organization, including establishing purpose and vision, analyzing your market and competitive position, etc.

CHAPTER 2

MAKING AN ORGANIZATION LEGAL

Now that you and your assembled group have defined the purpose of your new undertaking, you are ready to set up a new organization. If your group is new or if you have not yet addressed legal issues, this chapter will acquaint you with the steps involved in establishing your organization legally.

Both new and older organizations must have their legal houses in order before they can expect any source of revenue to extend support. Once its legal affairs are taken care of, an organization is able to provide one of its most attractive benefits to contributors: a charitable tax deduction. Donors not only have the pleasure of seeing their funds go to a nonprofit effort that reflects their concerns, but they also can deduct specified amounts from their gross taxable income.

BYLAWS

The first matter to resolve concerns establishing rules to govern the activities of your organization. These rules outline how a group will effectively conduct its affairs toward a stated purpose. Rules involve the nature and frequency of meetings, procedures for selecting officers, and other matters that relate to any group's functioning. Your statement of purpose provides you with a context for your work, but it does not suggest how you will organize yourselves to work toward a prescribed set of goals.

The author wishes to thank Mark D. Turkel, Esq., of Baer, Marks and Upham, for his invaluable collaboration on this chapter.

A group may choose to write its rules of operation into a certificate of incorporation and a set of bylaws, if it will ultimately be filing as a nonprofit corporation (see discussion on page 22), or more likely merely create a set of bylaws, if it is going to remain unincorporated (see discussion on page 20).

Drafting bylaws is the most common method organizations use to state the rules and policies that will govern their internal operations. Although bylaws are not always explicitly required by state governments, they are legally binding and must accompany any application to the Internal Revenue Service for exemption from federal taxes. Bylaws should reflect an organization's uniqueness and its particular needs. They traditionally include the following information in a numbered article format.

Bylaws should be carefully thought through by those who are most closely involved in launching the new organization. You may underestimate their importance since you feel an inherent trust for those friends and acquaintances you have recruited to work with you and to serve on the founding board of directors. However, you are writing bylaws to govern your organization for now and for the future, when you and your colleagues may no longer be involved. Bylaws define policies that can be invaluable during times of organizational crisis, such as staff/board conflicts or differences of opinion among the members of the board itself.

Thus you should draft bylaws with care and thought. Discuss them with a lawyer and other members of the organizing committee. Decide whether you are going to be a membership organization and which powers would rest with the members. (Note that in some states, nonprofit corporations must be membership organizations.) Also, weigh the role of officers in your projected efforts, such as president and vice president(s) or co-chairs, to determine what would best serve your long-term interests (see Chapter 4 for more on officers). Finally, don't let the newly adopted bylaws sit on the proverbial shelf collecting dust. Use them and update them when revision appears necessary.

The bylaws of existing organizations are a helpful reference. Request copies from other groups and/or check the samples provided in *Nonprofit Corporations, Organizations, and Associations* (4th ed.), by Howard L. Oleck (your local library should have a copy of this valuable reference book).

Bylaws can be as detailed and specific as you like, or you may prefer to be general at the outset to allow for flexibility as the developing organization seeks to define its operating procedures. In either case, bylaws will take on greater importance in the future, as more and more new people become active in the organization.

Important Provisions in the Bylaws of Any Organization

1. Purposes stated in the charter should be restated in somewhat greater detail.

2. Qualifications for membership, methods of admission of members, rights and privileges.

3. Initiation or admission fees, dues, termination of membership for nonpayment or otherwise.

4. Rules for withdrawal, censure, suspension and expulsion of members (including appeals).

5. Officers' titles, terms of office, times and manner of election or appointment, qualifications, powers, duties and compensation (for each office, respectively).

6. Vacancies in offices or on the board of directors: when they shall be deemed to require action, and the method of filling such vacancies.

7. Voting by the members, including what number shall constitute a quorum. This may include cumulative voting, voting by bondholders on the basis of the number of bonds held, and other such special provisions, in many states, but not in all. Voting procedures should be carefully detailed.

8. Meetings for elections and for other than election purposes, including notice, quorums and agendas (general and special meetings).

9. Voting qualifications, individually or by groups, proxies, etc.

10. Directors' qualifications.

11. Classification of directors into two, three, four or five classes, each to hold office so that the terms of one class shall expire every year.

12. Executive committee of the board of directors to exercise all (or certain) powers of the board between board meetings.

13. Directors' titles, terms of office, times and manner of election, meetings, powers and duties.

14. Convention and assembly rules.

15. Property holding transfer.

16. The seal: its adoption, custody and method of use.

17. Bank depository, and which officers may act for the organization.

18. Bonding of the treasurer and other officers and agents.

19. Fiscal details: fiscal year, regular (at least annual) audits of books.

20. Principal office and other offices.

21. Books, records and reports.

22. Amendment methods and rules for the charter as well as for the bylaws.

23. Principal committees.

24. Dissolution procedures.

25. Disposition of surplus assets on dissolution.

From the book, *Non-Profit Corporations, Organizations, and Associations*, 4th Edition, by Howard L. Oleck. © 1980 by Prentice-Hall, Inc. Published by Prentice-Hall, Inc., Englewood Cliffs, NJ 07632.

FORMS OF ORGANIZATION

Individuals organizing a group typically have three options to choose from:

1. Unincorporated association.
2. Nonprofit corporation.
3. Affiliation with an existing nonprofit corporation.

You need to review each of these options and to weigh their respective benefits and disadvantages. Only then will you be prepared to decide which choice makes the most sense for your group.

Unincorporated Association

Many associations are formed for limited or clearly prescribed volunteer efforts, for example, sports and social groups, parent-teacher associations, volunteer firefighters, block clubs, tenants groups, and so on.

If their members are not interested in raising substantial sums of money, hiring staff, or providing tax deductions for members' dues or contributions, they might opt to become unincorporated associations. These groups would still be governed by a set of bylaws and possibly even have a set of articles of organization, or perhaps a constitution. They would be spared filing a federal tax return as long as their gross receipts were less than $25,000 in a given year. In addition, as long as their deductible expenses equal or exceed their revenues, they would have no taxable income.

The major disadvantage of this form of legal organization is that an unincorporated association is not a legal entity separate from the individuals involved. As a result, members of an association may be personally liable for the acts of the organization, since legal liability is obscure and unclear.

Unincorporated entities can file for federal tax exemption under Section 501(c)(3) of the Internal Revenue Code as long as they have some form of articles of organization. If they do not file for and receive tax-exempt status they are not readily eligible for grants from private foundations, who most often provide support only to tax-exempt entities. Also, they will not be able to grant tax deductions to their contributors for their donations. Due to these two distinct disadvantages—very few nonprofits opt for unincorporated status.

Nonprofit Corporation

The *American Heritage Desk Dictionary* defines a corporation as "a body of persons acting under a legal charter as a separate entity with its own rights, privileges and liabilities distinct from those of its individual members." The corporation is one of the most common forms of legal organization for conducting business in the United States. The nonprofit corporation is the most common form of legal organization used specifically for charitable and other nonprofit pursuits. Most nonprofit corporations also seek exemption from federal taxes from the Internal Revenue Service. The reasons for securing incorporation and tax exemption are as follows:

1. *Limited Liability*. Incorporating ensures that the corporation, not the individual member, is liable for any legal actions brought against the organization. Thus, individual members of the governing body (usually called the "board of directors," or sometimes the "steering committee") are not likely to be held personally liable for the corporation's actions so long as they have acted prudently and responsibly. The reverse is equally true: without incorporation, individual members who join in a specific undertaking may be held personally liable as individuals in a court of law.

2. *Exemption from Federal and State Income Taxes*. Nonprofit organizations that are granted exemption by the Internal Revenue Service do not have to pay federal income tax on their income or receipts. IRS approval of an application for exemption from federal taxes usually ensures exemption from state income taxes as well.

3. *Charitable Tax Deductions for Contributors*. Individual contributors may take a tax deduction with respect to their charitable contributions to organizations that are tax-exempt under Section 501(c)(3) of the Internal Revenue Code (that is, charitable, educational, scientific, literary, and similar organizations). In addition, lifetime gifts to charitable organizations, as well as bequests made by will, are not subject to transfer taxes (gift, estate, or inheritance tax). The Better Business Bureau has published a useful pamphlet called "Tips on Tax Deductions for Charitable Contributions," which outlines in greater detail the deduction of contributions to nonprofit organizations. The pamphlet is available free from The Council of Better Business Bureaus, Inc., 1515 Wilson Boulevard, Arlington, Virginia, 22209.

4. *Eligibility for Foundation and Corporate Grants*. Foundations and corporations generally restrict their grants to organizations that have obtained federal tax exemption under Section 501(c)(3) of the Internal Revenue Code. Such status does not by any means ensure that you can successfully obtain grants, but lack of tax exemption does preclude, in the majority of cases, the possibility of receiving them.

5. *Exemption from State, County, and City Taxes*. Tax-exempt corporations may also be partially or fully exempt from certain state, county, or city taxes, including sales, property, and other forms of local taxation, depending on the laws affecting their specific locale.

6. *Annuity Program for Employees*. Employees of nonprofit organizations exempt under Section 501(c)(3) may take advantage of certain special tax-sheltered an-

nuities [commonly known as 403(b) plans] for which they are eligible. A non-profit organization can choose to establish one of these plans, thus making it possible for individual employees to set aside a certain percentage of their annual salaries into interest-bearing accounts. Those funds become subject to income taxes only when they are withdrawn by the employee. These plans differ from standard IRA and Keogh plans in that employees can withdraw funds from them *without a tax penalty* in the event of retirement, death, disability, hardship, separation from the job, or reaching the age of 59½. To set up the plan, the nonprofit organization must qualify it with the Internal Revenue Service through an initial filing and continuing report and disclosure obligations.

7. *Reduced Mailing Rates*. Preferred second- and third-class mailing rates are available through the U. S. Postal Service to charitable, educational, literary, scientific, and similar organizations.

Despite all of these significant advantages and others not mentioned, certain reasons might prompt a group not to incorporate and file for federal tax exemption. For example, the group may wish to engage in substantial electoral activities, which is prohibited completely by the Internal Revenue Service for organizations that are exempt under Section 501(c)(3). Tax-exempts can participate, however, in certain lobbying activities for the purpose of influencing legislation. These activities are outlined in the Tax Reform Act of 1976. For details, check any of the publications on lobbying in the "Further Readings" sections of this book.

As outlined, you can see why most groups will more than likely choose to incorporate as a nonprofit organization and to file for federal tax exemption or to seek out the same advantages by affiliating with an existing tax-exempt entity. Primary overriding factors are usually the desire to provide charitable tax deductions to individual contributors and to seek grants from foundations and corporations.

The Process of Application

Success in securing both state incorporation and federal tax exemption usually requires the assistance of a lawyer with prior experience in the area of not-for-profit corporate law and tax exemption. Proper legal counsel increases the likelihood that the process will move along smoothly and that the various governmental bodies will act favorably. Because governmental approval is vital to your ability to proceed in setting up an organization, be sure to seek competent help. In other words, resist the temptation to jump in and complete the forms yourself, or to use services offered free (pro bono) by a friend who is a lawyer but who is unfamiliar with these matters.

Securing Legal Counsel

The best solution, of course, is to find a lawyer among your existing circle of friends, acquaintances, and colleagues who would be willing to undertake these tasks in your behalf on a pro bono basis and who, to reiterate, has knowledge in this particular area of the law.

Failing that, there are several resources to turn to before you have to hire appropriate legal counsel:

1. Contact other similar nonprofit organizations in your community and ask them who completed their original applications and if it was done on a pro bono basis. At the same time, you can also request copies of their state incorporation and completed application for federal tax exemption which will help you and your prospective lawyer.

2. Contact your local Community Legal Services program. This federally funded program can provide pro bono legal assistance to organizations if at least one-half of your board of directors can satisfy their income guidelines as low income.

3. Contact local technical assistance or management support organizations that specialize in providing guidance to nonprofit organizations for suggested lawyers. A directory of such organizations is available from Lynn Helbling Sirinek, Nonprofit Management Association, 2777 Heston Court, Columbus, Ohio 43235.

4. Contact law firms by mail to request pro bono assistance. The American Bar Association requests that all of its members undertake some pro bono charitable or public interest work each year. These decisions are usually made by one of the partners of the firm, or by a special committee that screens such requests.

5. Last, contact the local county or city bar association for suggested lawyers. Both organizations generally maintain lawyer referral services specifically for this purpose. You should be prepared to pay for legal assistance; but don't hesitate to begin by asking for pro bono help.

In exploring these options, remember that you are a consumer, albeit one who is seeking something to be donated. Because final approval of tax exemption by the Internal Revenue Service is your organizational lifeline, be sure that you have identified appropriate legal counsel. If the IRS rejects your application, you may reapply, but your chances for success the second time around may be slimmer. Therefore, be sure you start off with qualified help. To gauge a prospective lawyer's capabilities, politely inquire about his or her past experience in the nonprofit field: Has he or she incorporated other organizations? How recently? You might even solicit the names of some of these organizations. Once again, your goal is to obtain a lawyer who has had successful experience in the nonprofit field.

The pro bono arrangement may well not be the best for you or your lawyer. Lawyers usually give first priority to their paying clients. But you are still a client and, thus, can express your wishes and expectations. Clarify in advance with your attorney when you can expect the work to begin and to be completed.

State Incorporation

To obtain incorporation as a nonprofit entity, you must submit articles of incorporation to the appropriate office within your state government. (Note: It is not required that you incorporate in the state in which you plan to conduct your affairs, but most nonprofits do.) That office may be the Secretary of State or Attorney General of your state. The form for articles of incorporation for a nonprofit corporation is available from large commercial legal stationery stores or from the relevant state government office. Remember: the form varies from state to state. Depending upon the state jurisdiction, a filing fee, usually under $100, may be required with the completed certificate of incorporation.

An organization hoping to be incorporated must apply for and receive state incorporation before submitting an application for federal tax exemption. The former is usually processed by the appropriate state department within a matter of weeks, while the latter may take months. A copy of your state articles of incorporation must accompany your application for Federal tax exemption (Form 1023). These articles should be signed by a principal officer and approved by the Secretary of State of your state.

Federal Tax Exemption

As mentioned earlier, both the unincorporated association and the nonprofit corporation can file for federal tax exemption. Fortunately, obtaining the necessary forms to complete your application for federal tax exemption is fairly easy.

The Internal Revenue Service makes available four different publications to assist you in applying for recognition of exemption under Section 501 of the Internal Revenue Code:

1. Package 1023, which includes the actual application form for Section 501(c)(3) organizations (Form 1023) and instructions on how to complete it.

2. Package 1024, which includes the actual application forms for most other exempt organizations.

3. Publication 557, *Tax-Exempt Status for Your Organization*, which details the application procedure and pertinent related matters.

4. *The Internal Revenue Service Exempt Organizations Handbook*, which discusses in even more specific detail requirements for receiving tax exemption.

The first three publications are free. Simply call the tax information number in the phone book listed under "United States Government, Internal Revenue Service," or contact your local IRS tax forms office. The fourth item is available for reading in any IRS Reading Room; it may also be purchased for $54.00 by writing to Internal Revenue Service, Attention: TX:D:P:RR, 1111 Constitution Avenue NW, Washington, D.C. 20224. No filing fee is required with this application.

There are over twenty categories of tax exemption that an organization can fall under in Section 501 of the Internal Revenue Code. Each category has been given its own classification number by the Internal Revenue Service.

Most organizations that plan to solicit grants from foundations and corporations will want to be classified as tax-exempt under Section 501(c)(3) of the Internal Revenue Code. To qualify under this section, your "organization must show that it is organized and operated for purposes that are beneficial to the public interest" (IRS Publication #557, p. 12).

For the purposes of illustration, this discussion will focus only on obtaining tax exemption under Section 501(c)(3), using IRS Form 1023. Most aspects of this discussion, however, are equally applicable to other organizations described in Section 501(c).

If your organization started up before filing for tax exemption, you must attach to your 1023 application a statement of receipts and expenditures and a balance sheet for the current year and the three immediate prior years (or however many years the organization has been in existence, if fewer than three). Finally, the IRS requests a signed copy of your bylaws.

Although you can, in fact, complete the application form for recognition of exemption (Form 1023) without any outside assistance, it is not advisable to do so. Form 1023 consists of eight parts containing over one hundred questions, as well as seven additional schedules (related forms) pertaining to different kinds of nonprofit organizations. This contrasts, for example, with only eight questions on the state articles of incorporation form for nonprofit corporations in Pennsylvania. Some of the information requested in the application form is:

1. Full name of organization;

2. Employer identification number (see page 26 for explanation);

3. List of the organization's current or projected sources of financial support and fundraising plans;

4. Brief narrative description of the present and future program activities of the organization. This summary is critically important, for you are presenting here those activities you believe deem your work charitable in the eyes of the Internal Revenue Service.

5. Pertinent data on your governing body.

While some of the questions in the application are fairly straightforward, others are very often unfamiliar to the lay applicant and underline the need for outside qualified legal counsel to complete the form successfully. In completing the 1023 application, it is particularly crucial that the description of your organization's activities be consistent with the Internal Revenue Service's viewpoint of what constitutes charitable activity. Your lawyer can best advise you on how to answer the pertinent questions on Form 1023 to this end.

Again, incorporation and tax exemption are vital to the success of any fundraising efforts that an organization may launch. You should thus approach the application process as a partnership between both your organizing committee and your lawyer. Don't divorce yourself from it. Your group will need to make a number of decisions on such matters as purpose, membership, and governance before both your articles of incorporation and your application for federal tax exemption can be completed. You should even ask your attorney to attend a meeting of your group to review the completed forms before their final submission and to answer any questions.

One last word of caution: your work to obtain approval of your application for tax exemption is not over until the actual letter granting exemption arrives from the Internal Revenue Service. The IRS reviewing agent may request additional information from you once the review process has commenced. Again, you will want to consult with your lawyer before providing any additional data.

Last Legal Steps

At this point your legal work will be almost over. A few more hurdles await, and clearing some of them will provide your organization with distinct advantages. Most states and many localities require nonprofit organizations that anticipate raising more than a certain amount of money annually from the general public (the figure varies from state to state), by direct mail, telethons, raffles, or other means, to register with the Charities Registration Bureau of the state or locality from which they'll be soliciting. (For specific requirements of each state or locality, check Appendix A).

Nonprofit organizations that are exempt under Section 501(c)(3) may qualify for exemption from state sales tax and property tax if they own property. Check with your State Department of Finance or Taxation to secure the necessary forms. For property tax exemption, apply to your local (county, town, or city) tax assessor's office. Your organization may qualify for a nonprofit bulk mailing permit which would reduce your cost for third-class bulk mailings (of no less than 200 pieces) to six cents per piece. You can obtain your permit by applying to the main office of your local post office. An annual fee of fifty dollars is required at the time of application. (These figures represent the fees in August 1985.)

To be prepared to hire staff, you should be aware of your legal responsibilities as an employer. You should obtain an "Application for Employer Identification Number" (Form SS–4) from the local Internal Revenue Service tax forms office. Filing this completed form with a regional IRS office will register your organization with both the State and Federal governments for the purpose of withholding employee income tax. You will subsequently receive an employer identification number (EIN). You will also regularly receive forms to accompany your quarterly deposits of withheld employees' taxes which you will use when you deposit those funds with an authorized commercial bank or a Federal Reserve Bank.

One final step: register with the State Unemployment Insurance Program and the State Workers' Compensation Program.

Case Study

HOW THE FIRST EAST COAST THEATRE AND PUBLISHING COMPANY, INC., DID IT

Back in 1978 when a few of us decided to open a small press, we had very definite objectives: to legitimize ourselves as a company, to publish for quality rather than quantity, and to devote time to individual publications and authors as opposed to working on a magazine-style format.

To our way of thinking, legitimizing the press meant legalizing ourselves as a corporation and, as we chose, in a not-for-profit category. The bureaucracy ahead of us proved considerable. We needed a Certificate of Incorporation (specifically for not-for-profit), Articles of Organization, By-Laws, an elected board of officers, a record of "minutes," an accounts ledger, a corporate seal, a post-office box to receive mail, office space (usually provided in someone's home), a corporate bank account, stationery, and a filing system. Certain tax forms had to be filed, and accounts had to be kept detailing officers' salaries, any donations, and any expenditures. Without funds to hire the necessary legal aid essential in completing many of the above tasks, we found several ways to bypass hiring a lawyer.

Most helpful and encouraging were the Volunteer Lawyers for the Arts, an organization based in New York City that offers free legal aid to groups and individuals involved in the arts who qualify financially. Before meeting with one of the lawyers, we did footwork at the law section of the New York Public Library. Also preparatory to our meeting with VLA and to sorting out the legal jargon, we obtained a copy of *McKinney's Consolidated Laws of New York, Book 37, Not-for-Profit Corporation Law*, which you can purchase, along with other publications of this kind, from West Publishing Company of St. Paul, Minnesota. Pamphlet-style updates to this book appear each year.

Applications, such as the one required for the Certificate of Incorporation, are printed on what are called "Blumberg" forms, and you can buy them at stationery stores. Once we had drafted the essential information for filling out the Certificate and By-Laws, a lawyer from VLA pounded out the fine details. Then, after choosing a name for the company, we submitted the form to the New York State Attorney General's office and the Justice of the Supreme Court, after which we submitted it to the Department of State, Bureau of Corporations in Albany. Our application was approved and there was no conflict regarding our choice of name for the corporation; we paid a $50 fee and incorporation was granted. Thus, our first fiscal year began October 1, 1979. Almost one year from conception to reality, The First East Coast Theatre and Publishing Company, Incorporated, became official.

—Karen Corinne Boccio

Source: Written by Karen Corrine Boccio. Reprinted from *Small Press* Magazine, published by R. R. Bowker Division of Reed Publishing, USA, by permission of the publisher.

Affiliation with an Existing Nonprofit Corporation

If your organization plans to raise funds in any substantial way from foundations, corporations, or individuals, then it is strongly advised that you become either incorporated and federally tax exempt or affiliated with an organization that is. In either case, the nonprofit should be designated as charitable under Section 501(c)(3) of the Internal Revenue Code by the Internal Revenue Service.

Affiliation can occur for a short period of time or on a permanent basis. Most commonly, groups affiliate with existing organizations in one of two ways:

1. *Fiscal Sponsorship.* A group seeking charitable tax deductible contributions or foundation grants before receiving its own tax-exempt status may enter into a relationship with an existing exempt organization, which would receive funds to support the group's work and which, in turn, would independently grant such funds to the group. The funds raised are contributed to the exempt organization with the understanding that they will be used as a grant to the nonexempt group, but the exempt organization must at all times retain discretion and control over the appropriate use of the funds by the ultimate beneficiary.

2. *Adoption.* Adoption is a more encompassing relationship than fiscal sponsorship for a group. Typically, a group would be adopted as a project by an existing organization. Under this arrangement, the latter assumes full financial responsibility for and legal control of the former. The project is "housed" within the organizational structure of the adopting entity. As a result, the parent organization has the potential power to influence program-related decisions that face their new project.

The reasons that a new, or even existing, nonexempt group might seek affiliation with a charitable organization are varied. For example:

1. The group may wish to undertake only a very time-specific, short-term project. As a result, it does not need the benefits of permanent organizational structure. For example, a filmmaker might be seeking grants to produce a film, or a group of artists might come together to produce one exhibition. (Possible choices: fiscal sponsorship or adoption.)

2. The group plans to file for state incorporation and federal tax exemption, but it wants to start fundraising immediately. Affiliation with an existing nonprofit charitable organization enables them to do so. (Possible choices: fiscal sponsorship or adoption.)

3. The group may wish to focus all its initial energies on program activities rather than administration. As a result, they turn to another organization to take responsibility for such tasks as bookkeeping, payroll, financial reporting, and so on. This frees up more of the core group's time for program development. (Possible choice: adoption.)

4. A group may be uncertain whether there is sufficient support for their efforts. Affiliations provide their work an organizational haven while they test out their ideas and programs. If they find that their work is positively received, they then can move out on their own. (Possible choices: fiscal sponsorship or adoption.)

5. A fledgling project may lack organizational visibility and credibility. Associating with an existing, already well respected and visible entity provides them with some of these attributes early in their development. (Possible choices: fiscal sponsorship or adoption.)

6. During their start-up period, some incorporated groups may wish to be spared the time and expenses involved in securing federal tax exemption. As a result, they may affiliate with another organization that already has its tax exemption. (Possible choice: fiscal sponsorship.)

7. Finally, the organizing committee of a new project or effort may be reluctant to set up a formal board of directors until it has established more of a track record. Affiliation enables it to take time to build a board, since the board of the parent organization is its legal governing body. (Possible choice: adoption.)

The particular approach of your group to an issue or a social problem may be unique and pioneering, but it is unlikely that your organization is the first to be concerned about the problem. Presumably, there are other nonprofits with values and interests that correspond to yours. The parent or sponsoring organization might be interested solely on the basis of the importance and value it attributes to your program plans. It may even anticipate that some distinct benefits may accrue to it as a result of an affiliation, such as enhanced reputation, increased public visibility, and outreach to new constituencies. At the same time, there are reasons that might discourage organizations from serving as fiscal sponsors or parents for your work, such as:

1. They may be wary of assuming responsibility for a new undertaking with an unknown ability to attract funds;

2. They may decide that their costs in staff time and other expenses may be too high to be sufficiently reimbursed by any administrative fees they would receive;

3. They may be concerned that association with your project could blur the image of their purpose in the public's eyes.

In considering an affiliation with an existing entity, you should consider some of the potential disadvantages for your group as well:

1. In the case of adoption, since the parent organization assumes all legal and fiscal responsibilities for your group or project, it ostensibly has some voice in any matters relating to those responsibilities. The parent organization

may exercise this prerogative in a wide variety of ways. After all, your project will be an integral part of the larger entity.

2. You may believe that a totally independent identity is valuable to you for a number of reasons and that any relationship with another entity will detract from that image.

3. You may have to pay a fee, usually a percentage of grants and contributions received, to the parent organization or fiscal sponsor to cover the costs of the administrative services they will be providing to you.

4. You may be restricted by the parent organization or fiscal sponsor in approaching certain funders for a variety of reasons. It may want to secure support from a particular funding source for its own program rather than yours. In fact, the grantor may have a policy that allows a prospective grantee only one grant request in any given year, and for just one project.

Therefore, to the greatest extent possible, the relationship between your group and the parent organization should be delineated in a written agreement that sets forth some terms of understanding between the two parties. You would be advised to do this before entering such a relationship. In addition, you can include in the agreement a provision for the two parties to dissolve the understanding at some specified future time and go their separate ways.

Fiscal sponsorship involves accountability on your part to the parent organization only for the funds that you receive under its auspices, such as a grant from a foundation for a particular program you will be implementing. In this case, a grant agreement serves as the legal document that delineates the relationship between the fiscal sponsor and the project, rather than between the fiscal sponsor and the funding source.

The grant agreement becomes the document that details what the grantee may or may not do with the funds it receives. Typically, the agreement will provide that the grant may be used only for charitable (as broadly defined in Section 501(c)(3)) activities, and not for partisan political activities or lobbying. In addition, the grant agreement will provide for periodic reporting on the use of the funds by the grantee to the fiscal sponsor.

How to Find an Appropriate Sponsor or Parent Organization

As already mentioned, the best sponsors or parent organizations are usually organizations whose purposes and activities are compatible with your own.

In seeking out a possible sponsor or parent organization, draw up a list of prospects before settling on a final choice. You can identify candidates for this list in a variety of ways:

1. Check any local directories of nonprofit organizations that are available. Your local library will usually have such directories in its collection, perhaps in a community services section.

2. Contact local citywide consortium-styled associations that correspond to your area of interest, such as United Way, arts councils, health and welfare planning bodies, federations, etc. Speak to their directors or public information officers and elicit their suggestions for possible sponsors.

3. Check national organizational reference books, such as the *Encyclopedia of Associations,* for other potential candidates.

Finally, the members of your organizing committee or board of directors probably already know of a number of existing nonprofits that would be good sponsors. To draw on their knowledge, devote a meeting of your group to identifying an appropriate sponsor or parent. Ask several members of your core group to explore potential sponsors or parents through the avenues already mentioned and to bring the results of their research to the meeting.

Start off your meeting with a listing of the groups your researchers have uncovered. Place them on a blackboard or flip chart paper. Then ask everyone to brainstorm a list of other possible candidates for a sponsor or parent with whom you might share an affinity by virtue of mission, issue, constituency, or location. Don't hesitate in the beginning to include institutions you may consider too large, too removed, or otherwise too formidable. Continue this exercise until no new suggestions are forthcoming. Then stop and take stock of your list. The following are some standard criteria against which you can best measure your candidates:

1. Strong congruence with your mission and values;

2. Excellent administrative capabilities, especially in fiscal matters and grants management;

3. A record of accomplishment among funders;

4. A history of innovation and risk taking, at least in terms of programs.

You will probably want to add some other criteria of your own. As you do, you will perhaps find that you will be eliminating some of the smaller, less established groups from your list and narrowing down your prospects. You may also find that, before proceeding further, you will need more information concerning some of your candidates before you can complete your list of prospects.

Plan to meet with representatives from your final list to determine who may be most interested in adopting or sponsoring your project. Usually, the best approach is a letter that carefully outlines what you would like to accomplish. In addition, the letter should request a meeting and should be followed up by a phone call to schedule an appointment. If you know people personally at the organization, you may want to contact them to ask their advice on how best to approach the person in charge. Bring along another person from your core group to the meeting, for that will show that others are seriously involved, too, in your undertaking.

During the meeting, probe gently until you find out how an affiliated arrangement might work on a daily basis. Ask whether any administrative fees would be charged and, if so, how much they would be. Find out, also, whether the institution has entered into similar relationships in the past.

After a series of such meetings, your core group should be able to reach a decision. If you've found "the perfect match," be sure to draw up a letter of understanding (if a parent) or a grant agreement (if a sponsor) setting out your mutually agreed-upon terms, to be signed by both parties.

If you do not find an organization that gets high marks on the basis of your criteria to serve as a parent organization, you may still want to consider one of them as a fiscal sponsor for a year or so. This will provide you with more time to focus energies on developing programs rather than engaging in the administrative tasks inherent in obtaining tax exemption.

FURTHER READINGS

Advocacy is Sometimes an Agency's Best Service: Opportunities and Limits Within Federal Law. Washington, DC: Independent Sector. 1984. 32 pp. $5.00. (Order from: Independent Sector, 1828 L St., N.W., Washington, DC 20036)

> Looks at lobbying for nonprofit organizations by comparing the new OMB A-122 rule with tax code definitions of lobbying. This includes who is and is not covered, what is and is not lobbying, amount of lobbying permitted, record-keeping and reporting, and penalties for violation.

Connors, Tracy D. *The Nonprofit Organization Handbook.* New York: McGraw-Hill. 1980. 757 pp. $36.75. (Order from: Volunteer: National Center for Citizen Involvement, 1111 N. 19th St., Arlington, VA 22209)

> Covers a wide range of topics from corporate principles to taxation. Particularly useful are sample bylaws, budgets and financial statements, a tax checklist, and tax instructions.

Hopkins, Bruce R. *The Law of Tax Exempt Organizations.* Fourth Edition. Garden City, NY: Hoke Communications, Inc. 1983. 748 pp. $65.00. (Order from: Hoke Communications, Inc., 224 Seventh St., Garden City, NY 11530)

> Provides lawyers, accountants and administrators of tax-exempt organizations with both an overview of the legal aspects and answers for specific problems. All relevant cases, regulations, and rulings are included along with commentary and perspectives. Annual supplements keep the guide up-to-date.

Hummel, Joan. *Starting and Running a Non-Profit Organization.* Minneapolis: University of Minnesota Press, 1980. 160 pp. $20.00 hardcover; $10.95 paper. (Order from: University of Minnesota Press, 2037 University Ave., S.E., Minneapolis, MN 55414)

> Discusses legal issues, development of boards, budgeting and accounting, community relations, staffing, etc. Includes a checklist of tasks to be done.

Oleck, Howard L. *Nonprofit Corporations, Organizations and Associations.* Fourth Edition. Englewood Cliffs, NJ: Prentice-Hall, Inc. 1980. 1251 pp. $59.95. (Order from: Prentice-Hall, Inc., Englewood Cliffs, NJ 07632)

> Reference volume on the statutory and case law relating to all types of nonprofit enterprises. Where there is no formal law, covers the standard practices of organizing, operating, merging, and dissolving nonprofit organizations. An extensive index and many model forms make this particularly useful.

Olenick, Arnold J., and Philip R. Olenick. *Making the Nonprofit Organization Work: A Financial, Legal and Tax Guide for Administrators.* Englewood Cliffs, NJ: Institute for Business Planning, Inc. 1983. 416 pp. in looseleaf notebook. $59.50. (Order from: Institute for Business Planning, Inc. Englewood Cliffs, NJ 07632)

> Provides a financial management system with key records and forms, sample budgets, financial statements and legal safeguards to satisfy all legal and accounting demands for nonprofit organizations. Illustrates the system using a hypothetical organization.

"Tips on Tax Deductions for Charitable Contributions." Arlington, VA: Council of Better Business Bureaus, Inc. 1983. Free. (Order from: Council of Better Business Bureaus, Inc., 1515 Wilson Blvd., Arlington, VA 22209)

> Small pamphlet which gives individual taxpayers information on the laws covering tax deductions for charitable contributions to eligible organizations.

Volunteer Lawyers for the Arts. *To Be or Not To Be: An Artist's Guide to Not-for-Profit Incorporation.* New York: Volunteer Lawyers for the Arts. 1982. 12 pp. $3.00 plus $2.00 postage and handling. (Order from: Volunteer Lawyers for the Arts, 1560 Broadway, Suite 711, New York, NY 10036)

> Discusses pros and cons of corporate status, legal responsibilities, and information needed to file for incorporation and to apply for tax-exempt status. Alternatives to incorporation are also covered.

Treusch, Paul E., and Norman A. Sugarman. *Tax Exempt Charitable Organizations.* 2nd Edition. Philadelphia: American Law Institute. 1983. 726 pp. $95.00. (Order from: American Bar Association Committee on Continuing Professional Education, 4025 Chestnut St., Philadelphia, PA 19104)

United States. Internal Revenue Service. *Application for Recognition of Exemption Under Section 501(a) or for Determination Under Section 120* (Package 1024), Washington, DC: Internal Revenue Service. Free. (Order from: local IRS Tax Forms Office)

> Includes the actual application forms for exemption from federal income tax for organizations covered under other parts of Section 501(c) besides Section 501(c)(3).

United States. Internal Revenue Service. *Application for Recognition of Exemption Under Section 501(c)(3) of the Internal Revenue Code* (Package 1023), Washington, DC: Internal Revenue Service. July 1981. 8 pp. plus forms. Free. (Order from: local IRS Tax Forms Office)

Application forms for tax-exempt status (Forms 1023 and 872-C) along with instructions for completing them.

United States. Internal Revenue Service. *Internal Revenue Service Exempt Organizations Handbook.* Washington, DC: Internal Revenue Service. $54.00. (Available in any Internal Revenue Reading Room, or order from: IRS, Attention: TX:D:P:RR, 1111 Constitution Avenue, N.W., Washington, DC 20224)

Detailed discussion of the specific requirements for receiving tax exempt status.

United States. Internal Revenue Service. *Tax-Exempt Status for Your Organization* (Publication 557). Washington, DC: Internal Revenue Service. February 1984. 44 pp. Free. (Order from: local IRS Tax Forms Office)

Discusses the rules and procedures for organizations seeking to obtain exemption from federal income tax under Section 501(c) of the Internal Revenue Code.

Webster, George D., and Frederick J. Krebs. *Associations & Lobbying Regulations: A Guide for Non-Profit Organizations.* Washington, DC: Chamber of Commerce of the United States. 1985. 75 pp. $9.00. (Order from: Publications Fulfillment, Chamber of Commerce U.S. 1615 H St., N.W., Washington, DC 20062)

Explains the 1946 Federal Regulation of Lobbying Act and the Tax Reform Act of 1976 as they affect 501(c) organizations. Includes definitions, IRS rulings, and Supreme Court cases, as well as information on record-keeping and reporting.

CHAPTER 3

BUILDING A BOARD OF DIRECTORS

People, not simply ideas, make organizations successful. Without the involvement of individuals with different talents and expertise, a nonprofit organization cannot expect to accomplish its mission. With that involvement, however, a group has the power to prosper, for only that harnessed energy can keep an organization on track. This is as true for the established as for the fledgling organization.

One person or several may have contributed the original inspiration to your cause. Many others are needed to turn that initial vision into reality. The founders have merely set the stage for the group's establishment and continued functioning.

If an organization is established by one person, that individual generally aspires to lead the effort, either as staff (i.e., executive director) or as an officer of the board of directors (i.e., president or chair). Sometimes he or she might choose to serve in both capacities or, alternately, to step aside once other leadership emerges.

Wise founders will move quickly to bring in new people as part of their effort. They may become members of the nascent organizing group, which can be referred to as a planning or steering committee or a "core" group. This structure serves as an interim step until a board of directors is formally established.

In this way, the founder(s) will have expanded the number of people who can serve in a leadership capacity of the new undertaking from the very beginning. Some of these individuals will continue their involvement as founding board members; others may continue to play a part in the life of the organization, but not necessarily on the board or staff.

The leadership of an established organization must also be constantly on the lookout for potential board members to serve its needs. Few organizations consistently have the necessary complement of skills on their boards of directors. Also, many boards have members who rarely attend meetings or are silent when they do attend or are looking for the opportunity to resign. Finally, there are two other major reasons why the established nonprofit should constantly be seeking prospective board members:

1. A board needs "new blood" to provide new energy and ideas to an organization.

2. As conditions in society change, so the needs of an organization change as well. For example, as groups shift from government support to increased individual and corporate support, they need to bring new people onto their board to acquire the benefits of expertise and experience in personal solicitations and corporate fundraising. But in seeking out new board members, organizations can fall into one of two traps:

Trap #1: They can choose only those people they perceive as being like-minded, assuming that anyone with specific expertise is not going to be sympathetic to their goals, beliefs, or values.

Trap #2: They can choose only experts who have the necessary skills, but lack fullhearted agreement and understanding of their goals.

The safe approach to board selection is to reach beyond one's immediate circle of friends and acquaintances and to include those experts you need within your pool of prospects. Seek to achieve a balance of skills and empathy among your board members. Leaders of both the new and the older organizations need to bring in new individuals to augment and to complement their own skills, thus increasing the overall level of expertise available to their efforts.

THE BOARD OF DIRECTORS: ITS PURPOSES

The board of directors provides you with a structure to channel the energies of others into your organization. The board serves as the governing body of an organization. As such, it is usually responsible for managing the affairs of a nonprofit corporation. A board sets policies and makes critical decisions, such as hiring key staff, approving the operating budget, and laying fundraising plans. The board exerts this authority at its regularly scheduled meetings, at which the chair guides the members through discussions of the issues before them.

The days are past when board members could satisfy their commitment to an organization solely by participating in board meetings. The challenges for the success of nonprofits in today's world demand that boards collectively and their members individually do more. More likely than not, boards now set up subcommittees to devote more attention to particular issues than a board meeting normally provides. Board members also make themselves available to staff to participate in a variety of fundraising and planning activities. Savvy executive directors may call on appropriate board members for their advice and their assistance on numerous occasions outside the board meeting.

In other words, in today's world the board is not only an occasional working body, regularly meeting to set and review policy, but also a collection of individuals who make themselves available throughout the year as volunteer advisers and workers.

With this expanding list of expectations of a board of directors, the question arises of how an organization can most effectively develop a "working board" of individuals who will contribute their time willingly and frequently.

FINDING POTENTIAL BOARD MEMBERS

Within each of the categories just discussed, you've found several suggestions for recruiting the qualified help you need. Here are some additional ideas for reaching out for help.

1. Try major corporations in your vicinity. Contact the department responsible for community relations, public affairs, or charitable contributions to see if it has an employee recruitment program to match employees with community service opportunities.

2. Approach your local Volunteer Action Council or its counterpart, or any other agencies that specialize in recruiting volunteers.

3. Seek out the advice of local funders, such as foundation staff, United Way officials, and government officials, who have an interest in your field of endeavor.

4. Contact executive directors and board officers of large, established nonprofit institutions in your community, as well as of those whose efforts are similar to yours, for their suggestions.

5. Speak to religious leaders, ministers, priests, and rabbis in your locale to see if they can recommend any candidates, particularly from their own congregations.

6. Include in any promotional and membership materials pleas for volunteers with the specific skills you are seeking.

7. Ask for volunteers at any canvassing efforts, open houses, special events, and benefits that your organization sponsors.

8. Check with local chapters of professional trade associations such as the Bar Association, Chamber of Commerce, and Public Relations Society.

9. Discuss your needs with representatives of civic groups, such as American Association of University Women, Soroptomists, Hadassah, Junior League, Rotary, Lions, Jaycees, National Organization for Women, Gray Panthers, etc.

10. Find out if any hospitality organizations, such as Welcome Wagon, exist in your community and, if so, inform them of your needs. Very often, they provide the first contacts for a community's newcomers, those who are potential recruits for civic efforts.

Two Board Recruitment Stories
(Successful and Otherwise)

CASE 1

Several years ago, I was invited by letter to join the board of a well-respected organization in New York City, my hometown. Accompanying the invitation was an extensive packet of literature about the organization. They even enclosed an addressed and stamped reply envelope. After weighing their invitation for a week, I declined. Why?

I was naturally flattered at first, and initially receptive to the idea. Then, I asked myself some practical questions: "How will I benefit from joining X's board?" Sounds heretical, doesn't it? I should have been willing to jump in for "the good of the cause." Yes, I would derive some satisfaction from the knowledge that X organization was working on a matter close to my concerns. However, I found that I was making a mental list of the reasons that would attract me to serve on a board of directors. Let me share with you my list:

1. Increase my own knowledge of issues.

2. Enjoy the company of like-minded people.

3. Serve in a leadership capacity among my peers.

4. Meet new people.

5. Broaden my experience to enhance my consulting skills.

In reviewing the invitation extended to me, I was unable to answer fully whether participating on the board of this organization would meet my needs. Also, no one from X organization took the trouble to contact me personally to ask if I had any questions. Working under the press of other matters, I chose not to contact them to suggest a meeting and merely declined their invitation.

CASE 2

Conversely, around the same time, I had the task of recruiting new fundraising committee members for an organization that I co-chaired. A fellow board member recommended someone who was skilled in areas that our organization currently lacked. As a first step, I called up our prospect to suggest a meeting to discuss our organization's work and to explore the possibility of her serving on our fundraising committee. Before the meeting, I mailed her a packet of organizational literature and invited the executive director to join us for the meeting. At the meeting, we discussed the organization and our goals and how she could make a valuable contribution to our work. She thanked us for our invitation and promised us a decision shortly. Within ten days, she decided to join us and became an active and hard-working member of our group.

Why did the organization that asked me fail at recruitment, while my organization succeeded? The approach in the second case was more personal than in the first. Our request was based on a statement explaining why we needed her specific contributions. She was left with a sense of the worth we placed on her abilities. She agreed to join our committee not only because she believed in what we were doing but also because she enjoyed meeting us and realized that she would derive personal satisfaction from her involvement.

The obvious lesson of these two stories is that thoughtful approaches to potential board or committee candidates pay off. A second lesson is that the hardest workers in an organization are those who know what benefits they derive from their involvement.

Michael Seltzer

MAKING THE BOARD WORK

As any experienced board member knows, board work at its worst can be either exasperating or boring beyond belief. You may be too upset and angry after a board meeting to sleep a wink, or you may instead fall asleep earlier than expected—during the meeting.

Naturally it's good when a board functions smoothly and efficiently. And it can, thereby ensuring the members some satisfaction from their work. For that to happen, the board, and especially its chosen leadership, the officers, need to pay strict attention to the ways in which the governing body properly deals with the business before it.

Recognizing Its Authority

A board of directors is not an advisory body. A board actually has the power to set major policies to govern the affairs of an organization—in fact, it is accorded this responsibility by state law.

A board also carries the ethical responsibility to make sure the organization does everything reasonable within its power to fulfill its mandate. For example, when an organization is delinquent in paying its employee withholding taxes to the Internal Revenue Service, the board, collectively and individually, is responsible for the full payment of those taxes. This has been a painful and unexpected lesson for many boards in the past. Faced with both the legal and ethical responsibilities placed at its doorstep, a board is behooved to exert its authority.

Focusing on Major Issues

Do you recall the last meeting you attended during which thirty minutes was spent discussing what kind of food should be served at the upcoming social event, leaving only five minutes to discuss how funds for the upcoming year would be raised? Certain issues deserve priority treatment from a board. They include:

1. Recruitment, selection, evaluation, and support of key staff.

2. Budget review and adoption, and ongoing monitoring of expenses and income.

3. Long-term planning and mission review.

4. The board's own renewal process: rotation of old members and recruitment of new ones.

Too often, however, boards fail to distinguish among the various issues that face them on the basis of their importance. This responsibility rests first with the chair of the meeting, who serves as the board's guide to the business at hand. The chair must also be alert to the situation in which the board may have insufficient information to reach an informed decision. In those circumstances, a chair can delegate the matter at hand to a board committee for further investigation. That committee can then report its recommendation to the board for final resolution.

If a board is devoting an inordinate amount of time to small details rather than to major policy issues, it has lost sight of the forest for the trees. Its energies need to be refocused.

Delegating Work

Even when boards recognize their responsibility to focus their time and energy on the major issues of the organization, they often find that they don't have the necessary time to complete their work in meetings as a full body.

Instead of scheduling additional meetings, a board can delegate some of its work to various subcommittees. Most frequently, a board empowers a smaller body of officers and other board members to serve as a decision-making body between regularly scheduled meetings of the full board. This new body is often called an executive committee.

Other committees can be created as an organization evolves. New bodies, called subcommittees or standing committees, are often needed for specific functions, including fundraising or development, staff support, budget and finance work, nominations, community relations, program, and so on. A committee can be composed of board members and newcomers to an organization. As a matter of fact, one major benefit of committees is that they provide a vehicle to bring new potential candidates for the board into an organization.

A word of caution, however: boards can too easily avoid difficult or emotionally charged issues by delegating them to a committee. A board should delegate major policy issues to a committee only when it believes that an issue warrants some investigation or review prior to a final decision by the entire board. In such instances, a standing committee should only frame recommendations, not make any final decisions.

The board that functions best knows two things: how to delegate to others and when to accept responsibility for final decisions.

Raising Money

In these days of increasingly scarce resources for nonprofit organizations, a description of the board members' responsibilities is not complete without addressing their role in raising funds to support an organization's programs. Not so long ago, I sat on the board of an organization that was experiencing financial problems. The director approached a large, well-known contributor to good causes and put our organization's case before her. The donor offered two thousand dollars if the board members could match her amount. She calculated that the twenty-five board members should not find it difficult to raise that sum among their ranks. The match was met, but not until some of the most committed board members expressed their displeasure. One said, "I give very generously of my time to this organization. Why should I be expected to give financial support as well?"

While it has always been expected among the charitable endeavors supported by wealthy patrons in a community that board members would also be donors, the notion only recently is becoming accepted among organizations with less privileged constituents. Increasingly, the principle of giving by those on every level of an organization is gaining credence. Even private colleges are actively turning to students, faculty, staff, and parents of incoming students for charitable contributions.

Board members should feel a special obligation to make contributions of money, as well as time and energy, to an organization. The principle is more important than the size of the gift. The bottom line is, if a board member asks others to give money, shouldn't he or she be willing to do the same?

Moreover, there are many other fundraising tasks a board member can undertake on behalf of an organization, such as selling tickets to special events; soliciting memberships; asking for contributions; participating in meetings with prospective funding sources; hosting benefits at their homes, ranging from cocktail parties to kaffeeclatsches; and speaking to gatherings of potential supporters.

Choosing Officers

Who guides a board in its work? Who makes sure that a board does its job? These tasks fall to the officers of a board, who are appointed, selected, or elected by their peers. Officers are usually referred to as president and vice president(s) or chair and co-chair(s), as well as secretary and treasurer. Since most states require nonprofit corporations to list board officers in their articles of incorporation and to enumerate their functions in a set of bylaws, organizations usually do have officers, if only in name, and provisions for their responsibilities in their bylaws. Surprisingly, some groups resist empowering these positions with actual authority. Enlisting officers provides a board of directors with the chance to choose from its own number its most capable and hard-working individuals to serve as leaders.

The most crucial function officers perform is to ensure that a board tackles its work efficiently and effectively. A good presiding officer sets the agenda in consultation with staff in advance of upcoming meetings. The officer then chairs the meeting expeditiously, elicits different opinions on the matters at hand, keeps the board on track in the discussion, and moves the discussion along to a point of resolution.

In addition, the officers presiding over the meeting gauge the level of participation of board members in the life of the board. If they perceive that certain board members are perpetually absent or silent at meetings, it is their responsibility to take corrective action, either by talking privately to the board members about their lack of participation or by bringing the matter to the attention of the appropriate body (that is, the nominating committee).

It is also the responsibility of the board officers to ensure that board members fulfill fundraising responsibilities. This includes not only soliciting them for individual contributions but being sure they carry out fundraising tasks.

Officers, as well as other board members, may also be called on to appear in public on behalf of the organization at fundraising events, conferences, rallies, seminars, and the like. The board's officers should demonstrate the talents and expertise within the nonprofit group, enhancing its public image.

Understanding Board-Staff Relations

The relationship between a board of directors and a staff is unequal. Yes board and staff work together to accomplish the same objectives but that relationship is hierarchical, for the board is ultimately responsible the the fulfillment of the organization's purposes. Board and staff roles can easily become clouded by such factors as proprietary feelings on the part of an executive director, particularly when one is the founder of a group; a passive or rubber-stamp board; a negative interaction of personalities; or a desire to avoid conflict. An effective organization is guided by a carefully crafted balance between staff and board authority. Most simply put, staff are responsible for day-to-day operations, while the board sets long-term policies.

IDENTIFYING WHO SHOULD SERVE ON YOUR BOARD

How does an organization begin to identify appropriate board candidates? And, once identified, how does it go on to recruit them for service?

The initial organizing committee might best begin by seeking out those whose involvement and participation promise to aid as fully as possible in accomplishing the tasks ahead. Just as a contractor secures the services of electricians, carpenters, plumbers, and bricklayers to build a house, the initial organizers behind any new nonprofit venture should first identify the various tasks before them. Once those are understood, the organizers can go ahead and identify people with the necessary skills, experience, background, and, equally important, commitment to the endeavor.

Take an inventory of the skills the work ahead will require by identifying three clusters of potential candidates:

1. The first cluster is composed of natural constituents, those with whom you are working in concert to bring about the changes that will directly improve their lives. Needless to say, this group has the greatest practical investment in the work and, as a result, may well provide the passion and the drive to inspire others to this same commitment. Additionally, such a group often brings the most time and energy to your goal, again because its stake in its success is central. Mothers Against Drunk Driving (MADD) is just such an example. In May 1980, Candy Lightner, whose daughter was killed by a drunk driver, formed a group to fight drunk driving with her friends and family—a natural constituency. Today, there are 258 MADD chapters across the United States with a membership exceeding 300,000.

2. The second cluster is made up of those possessing program-related expertise in your field of endeavor. If you are establishing a public-interest law center or a women's health program, you would want to use experienced lawyers or medical practitioners, respectively, on your board. For financial reasons you most likely won't be able to hire as staff all the experts you'll need. Thus, the presence of even a few program experts in the goverance of your organization is a considerable asset. Assuredly, you would pick those who sympathize with your mission and would be willing to support it. Again using MADD as an example, the Long Island MADD chapter has on its board a psychologist who also runs weekly victim support groups, doctors, political and civic leaders—all people who bring to the board a particular area of expertise.

As a beginning exercise, write out a list of those occupations that bear directly on your work. That will give you a place to start. If, for example, your field is public-interest law, your list should include not only lawyers but judges, law professors, and legal workers as well.

3. The third cluster consists of those with relevant skills and expertise pertinent to the general needs of nonprofit organizations. They include:

    a. Accounting and other knowledge in fiscal matters
    b. Law, especially nonprofit corporation law
    c. Fundraising
    d. Grantsmanship
    e. Marketing
    f. Public relations
    g. Personnel
    h. Management
    i. Planning.

Although this is just a partial list and other skills might be added, these nine specific areas of service represent the most common needs of a nonprofit organization for its board or directors. Let us explain them one by one.

Accounting and Fiscal Expertise

An organization's credibility can sink at once if its finances are poorly handled. Late payment of federal employees' withholding tax or incorrect expenditures from funds received from a foundation can result in serious repercussions financially and possibly even legally. Thus, a board of directors has an important overseeing function with regard to the financial and business affairs of a nonprofit organization. As a result, it's important that the board possess among its own membership the ability to understand financial matters, including budgets, financial statements, and other pertinent documents.

While most people can learn to understand the kind of fiscal matters that come before a nonprofit board, it's crucial that at least one member have sufficient grounding in financial management to serve as the board's guide. Logically, then, such a person would serve as treasurer. Prospective candidates for such a post are accountants, comptrollers, and others who have experience in finances, either in the nonprofit, corporate, or public sectors.

Once this competency is added to its ranks, a board finds itself in a better position to read its regular financial statements and to make decisions, such as approving the annual operating budget, assessing anticipated revenues, and approving new expenditures.

Nonprofit Law

How do you negotiate a lease with a prospective landlord if you are renting office space?

What kinds of activities constitute lobbying, according to the regulations set by the Internal Revenue Service?

What are permissible grassroots lobbying activities for nonprofit organizations under Section 501(c)(3) of the Internal Revenue Code?

What laws should a board of directors as an employer be aware of when firing an employee?

What types of fundraising activity require special reporting procedures to the state in which your organization is conducting its business?

The list of legal questions you may face during the life of your organization could go on and on. Some boards, unwisely, believe that ignorance is safety as well as bliss, or that occasional legal questions can easily be handled by a phone call to a lawyer friend. That might work sometimes, but it won't always.

The involvement of a qualified lawyer on a board ensures that all legal matters will be dealt with properly. Moreover, as in the area of financial management, prior legal foresight is similarly preventive; for here, too, problems can be eliminated before they occur.

Obviously, the need for professional legal help becomes abundantly clear during periods of crisis, when documents such as bylaws may provide the means to resolve thorny issues. On the other hand, the lawyer-as-board-member also stands as watchdog over such mundane matters as filing annually with the State Charities Registration Bureau or Attorney General, or informing the board what constitutes a quorum for decision-making purposes, when necessary.

Fundraising, Grantsmanship, Marketing, and Public Relations

These four areas of skill relate to the development and community relations functions of an organization. Without them, an organization cannot be effectively financed and sustained on a long-term basis. They involve not only how you raise the necessary funds to support your programs and activities but also how you project your image and mission to the public.

While the majority of nonprofit leaders today have probably learned these skills through their own direct experience, fortunately the various aspects of fundraising and public relations are being codified and taught via many workshops, seminars, and publications such as the one you are reading. No longer are these skills passed down solely by word of mouth through successive generations within an institution.

At the same time, the role of board members in fundraising has never been more sought. Increasingly, successful fundraising requires board members to solicit large donors, join staff in visiting prospective foundations and corporate supporters, and participate in planning fundraising and public relations campaigns. The proverbial well connected board member whose name alone opens doors has been joined by those who are not necessarily well connected but who have learned the art of raising private support and are willing to use that skill on behalf of your organization.

Prospective board candidates with these skills can be identified through other nonprofit organizations, including larger agencies, institutions, hospitals, universities, professional trade associations of fundraisers and public relations professionals, and even public relations and fundraising firms themselves.

While professionals in these fields certainly can strengthen your board of directors, you should not be deterred from these tasks if you are not able to engage them as board members. What is important is that any board members you do recruit to serve should be well disposed to learning about fundraising and be willing to commit some of their time towards that purpose. Fundraising from individuals and from philanthropic sources can be learned and can even become enjoyable and satisfying.

Personnel

Most nonprofit organizations are employers at one time or another. Nonprofit colleges and medical facilities may even be among the largest employers in a community. Since idealistic and altruistic goals are often the underlying forces in the nonprofit venture, some organizations, especially smaller ones, see traditional employer-employee issues as incompatible with those aspirations. After all, "Aren't you receiving significant psychological benefits by working for such charitable purposes, enough to outweigh any material benefits that we might give you, like salary increases and more benefits?" says the old-fashioned nonprofit boss to his staff. Unfortunately, that attitude still persists and leads to unnecessary conflicts and tensions.

Since the nonprofit's "products" are usually the services of their employees and volunteers, tending to their concerns is of paramount importance. The hiring, training, and evaluation of employees promotes in the most direct way an organization's ability to accomplish its work.

The board should include some members who have expertise in personnel matters. A nonprofit cannot hope to replicate the skills available in the human resources or personnel department of a large corporation. It can, however, enlist as board members personnel specialists or other professionals in the helping professions such as training, social work, and psychology.

Again, as demonstrated with the previously mentioned skill areas, foresight can prevent serious problems, such as employee dissatisfaction and corresponding low morale, inadequate hiring procedures, or the need to fire an employee.

Management and Planning

These two terms are not always associated with the nonprofit sector. Yet, they are indispensable to the effective implementation of programs. Management means guiding the available human and financial resources toward a smooth accomplishment of your objectives. While a board of directors does hire an executive director to serve as the manager of an organization, the board still needs to practice sufficient supervision to ensure that this function is being adequately carried out.

Planning is another one of those terms that may seem simple yet can cause a sense of awe or unease when applied to nonprofits. Planning itself refers to mapping out the programs and activities of an organization, so that it can advance toward accomplishing its mission and objectives in a coherent and focused manner.

Whether you are engaging in a short-term project such as a fundraising event, or a long-term one such as developing a new program area, you are probably, consciously or otherwise, engaging in some aspects of the planning process. (See Chapter 4 for a discussion of planning in more detail.) By careful attention to the managing and planning functions in an organization, a board in conjunction with staff can see to it that the organization moves along the best course possible to accomplish its mission.

Increasingly, college courses in management and planning, as well as workshops and seminars, are being offered to nonprofits. Board members and staff might seek out such programs for themselves or recruit individuals who have expertise in these fields from other nonprofits or businesses.

An organization should endeavor to amass on its board individuals who possess all the skills necessary for its progress. This is obviously the optimal scenario. Some groups may choose not to place a lawyer or an accountant on their boards, run the risks previously mentioned, or contract for those services to be rendered to the organization.

Unfortunately, too many nonprofit leaders do not recruit beyond their immediate circle of friends and acquaintances or do not go beyond the first cluster—natural constituents. They may have underlying suspicions that professionals and businessmen, in particular, will not be sympathetic to their pursuits or will show a direct antipathy to their goals. In response to these understandable concerns, you can only be encouraged to test these assumptions by seeking out likely prospective board candidates and discussing with them what your organization is about and what your needs are. You will then at least be in a position to judge whether your initial concerns were founded. By keeping the three clusters—constituents, program-related skills, and nonprofit-related skills—before you, you will have a shopping list of the human resources you need for your organization to grow and to prosper.

SUMMARY

Through the careful identification of the skills an organization needs, the recruitment of qualified individuals to serve in its governance, and the efficient operation of its central policy-setting body, a nonprofit accomplishes much in building a strong organization and in strengthening its fundraising capabilities.

FURTHER READINGS

Anthes, Earl W., Jerry Cronin, and M. Jackson. *The Nonprofit Board Book: Strategies for Organizational Success.* West Memphis, AR: Independent Community Consultants, Inc. 1985. 240 pp. $24.50. (Order from: Independent Community Consultants, Inc., Box 1673, West Memphis, AR 72301)

Chapters cover such topics as: recruitment and orientation, powers and limitations, committees, board/staff relations, financial management, public relations.

Conrad, William R., Jr., and William E. Glenn. *The Effective Voluntary Board of Directors: What It Is and How It Works.* Revised Edition. Athens, OH: Swallow Press. 1983. 244 pp. $9.95. (Order from: Ohio University Press, Athens, OH 45701)

Provides ground rules for effective boards of nonprofit organizations. Many charts and forms enhance the usefulness of this book.

Doyle, Michael, and David Straus. *How to Make Meetings Work.* New York: Jove Publications Inc. 1984. 298 pp. $3.95. (Order from: Jove Publications, Inc., 200 Madison Ave., New York, NY 10016)

Describes and illustrates an interactive method designed to improve the quality of meetings and to make participants more effective.

Gardner, John W. *The Nature of Leadership: Introductory Remarks*. Washington, DC: Independent Sector. January 1986. 20 pp. Single copy free. (Order from: Independent Sector, 1828 L St., N.W., Washington, DC 20036)
    Defines and analyzes leadership in terms of the kinds of leaders, settings for leadership, judgments of leaders, the leadership team, and leaders in history.

Hanson, Carline, and Carolyn T. Marmaduke. *The Board Member: Decision Maker for the Non-Profit Corporation*. Sacramento, CA: Han/Mar Publications, 1972. 40 pp. $6.85. (Order from: Volunteer: The National Center for Citizen Involvement, 1111 N. 19th St., Arlington, VA 22209)
    Workbook for developing and maintaining a nonprofit board, including sections on policy, planning, board/staff relations, fundraising, and volunteers.

Mahoney, Brooke W., ed. *The Role of the Board Chairman or President*. New York: Volunteer Consulting Group. 1985. 13 pp. $5.00. (Order from: Volunteer Consulting Group, 24 W. 40 St., New York, NY 10018)
    Proceedings of a seminar for directors, trustees, and executive directors of nonprofit organizations. The Board Chair's role in acting as a liaison between the Board and the Staff was of particular concern.

Mathiasen, Karl, III. *The Board of Directors Is a Problem: Exploring the Concept of the Following and Leading Boards*. Washington, DC: Management Assistance Group. January 1983. 12 pp. 1 copy free to nonprofit organizations. (Order from: Management Assistance Group, 1705 DeSales St., N.W., Suite 401, Washington, DC 20036)
    In nonprofit organizations, the Board of Directors is a problem for the staff who must deal with it as well as for the individual board members who must figure out how to serve on it effectively. Characteristics of two general categories of boards, the following board and the leading board, are examined.

Mathiasen, Karl, III. *The Board of Directors of Nonprofit Organizations*. Washington, DC: Management Assistance Group. November, 1977. 16 pp. 1 copy free to nonprofit organizations. (Order from: Management Assistance Group, 1705 DeSales St., N.W., Suite 401, Washington, DC 20036)
    Discusses the duties of the board of directors and its relationship to staff. Ways to put together an effective board and to keep it working well are included.

Mathiasen, Karl, III. *No Board of Directors Is Like Any Other: Some Maxims About Boards*. Washington, DC: Management Assistance Group. September, 1982. 9 pp. 1 copy free to nonprofit organizations. (Order from: Management Assistance Group, 1705 DeSales St., N.W., Suite 401, Washington, DC 20036)
    There are certain generalizations which apply to boards of directors which can help board and staff members identify the differences among the boards they serve or serve on.

Nordhoff, Nancy S., Jo Larsen, Putnam Barber, and Dorothy P. Craig. *Fundamental Practices for Success with Volunteer Boards of Non-Profit Organizations*. Seattle: Fun Prax Associates. 1982. 127 pp. $14.20. (Order from: Fun Prax Associates, 711 Skinner Bldg., Seattle, WA 98101)

> General framework for self-assessment and planning that can be adapted to the specific needs of a variety of organizations with volunteer boards. Lists seven fundamental practices and several indicators of achievement for each. Workbook format provides exercises, checklists, and worksheets.

O'Connell, Brian. *The Board Member's Book*. New York: The Foundation Center, 1985. 208 pp. $16.95. (Order from: The Foundation Center, 79 Fifth Ave., New York, NY 10003)

> Guide to the functioning of voluntary boards which covers such topics as the legal responsibility of board members; finding, developing, and recognizing good members; and the relationship of board and staff. Includes a large bibliography.

On Being Board—How Not to be Dead Wood. Lakewood, CO: RAJ Publications. 1986. 28 pp. $1.50 for single copy; bulk discounts available. (Order from: RAJ Publications, P.O. Box 15720, Lakewood, CO 80215)

> Handbook on board membership for nonprofit groups which covers all board responsibilities in detail. Appendix discusses "problem" and "no-problem" board members. (Revised version of a handbook originally prepared for Rocky Mountain Planned Parenthood which has been made applicable to a more general audience.)

Public Management Institute. *Board Member/Trustee Handbook*. San Francisco: Public Management Institute. 1980. 464 pp. $49.00. (Order from: Public Management Institute, 358 Brannan St., San Francisco, CA 94107)

> Provides information for board members and trustees about such topics as legal responsibilities, board/staff relations, decisionmaking, and fundraising. Includes guidance for staff members in assessing the performance of the board and improving weak areas.

Steering Nonprofits: Advice for Boards and Staff. Special issue of *Conserve Neighborhoods* no. 35 (February 1984): 332–350. $2.00. (Order from: National Trust for Historic Preservation, 1785 Massachusetts Ave., N.W., Washington, DC 20036)

> Discusses the dynamics and evolution of nonprofit organizations and provides some perspective on the tensions and crises which both the board and staff may experience. By combining the varied management skills of its members, the board can work with the staff to effectively manage such an organization.

Trost, Arty, and Judy Rauner. *Gaining Momentum for Board Action*. San Diego: Marlborough Publications. 1983. 104 pp. $10.50 plus shipping and handling. (Order from: American Council for the Arts, Dept. 230, 570 Seventh Ave., New York, NY 10018)

The four sections of the book cover how to: understand the basics of boards, accomplish tasks, work together, and continue to develop the board. Each topic area includes a general discussion, practical examples, and worksheets.

Volunteer Board Member in Philanthropy, The: Responsibilities, Achievements, Special Problems. New York: National Charities Information Bureau, Inc. 1984. 24 pp. $4.00. (Order from: National Charities Information Bureau, Inc., 19 Union Square West, New York, NY 10003)

    A handbook for board members which includes sections on what happens when boards fail, what good board members do and do not do, five fallacies of contemporary philanthropy, and questions for self-evaluation.

Weber, Joseph. *Managing the Board of Directors.* New York: Greater New York Fund, Inc. 1975. 21 pp. $1.25. (Order from: Greater New York Fund, 99 Park Ave., New York, NY 10016)

    Guidelines for organizing and managing voluntary boards including recruiting new members, orientation, and board-staff relations.

Wells, Theodora. *Keeping Your Cool Under Fire: Communicating Non-Defensively.* New York: McGraw-Hill. 1980. 373 pp. $12.95. (Order from: McGraw-Hill, 1221 Avenue of the Americas, New York, NY 10020)

    Provides an approach to communications and problem-solving in which personal feelings are recognized and put to work. Presents principles of non-defensive communication using real-life situations as illustrations.

CHAPTER 4

PUTTING YOUR PURPOSE TO WORK:
PLANNING YOUR PROGRAMS

Your legal structure is in place, your organizing committee or board of directors is taking hold, and your leadership has collectively articulated a working statement of purpose for your fledgling effort. You might think you are ready to raise funds at this point. But you are still missing one critical ingredient for effective fundraising: a program plan of action. You need to present to your prospective supporters not only a sense of what problem you are attacking but what you plan to do about it in concrete terms.

This is as true for the well-established nonprofit as for the fledgling effort. It is true that a longstanding organization has a past reputation that will dramatically affect how people will respond to its fundraising appeals. However, its financial success is predicated on the fact that it has already demonstrated an ability to deliver results. Its ongoing success will depend on its ability to continue to deliver results.

Thus, program planning is a necessary prerequisite before *any* organization can go out and raise funds.

Program planning for nonprofits is essential to success, for through that process you can create a blueprint setting out all the tasks you need to complete efficiently before your mission can succeed. Without adequate program planning, your efforts will be haphazard and your results unassured. What are some of the advantages of planning your program activities?

1. Planning forces an organization to set some priorities on how it can most effectively use limited resources. This challenges the notion that a group should do everything.

2. Planning enables an organization to ask and answer some long-term questions, such as:

    a. Why do we exist?
    b. Whom do we serve?
    c. How will we make a difference?

3. Planning gives an organization a blueprint to chart its own future.

4. Planning improves communication at all levels within an organization, generating greater participation and trust.

5. Planning involves a team effort to succeed and, yet, also defines specific roles of staff, board, and volunteers.

6. Planning provides staff and board with criteria to measure their effectiveness.

Nonetheless, planning does not take place in many nonprofit organizations for a variety of reasons. Some are listed below.

1. *Planning does not immediately solve today's crisis.* While planning can ultimately offer solutions to daily problems, it does not do so in the short run. As a result, it is difficult to think about planning when you are concerned about meeting this month's payroll, for example.

2. *Planning creates change.* Many people are comfortable with the status quo and resist change, even when it is for the better. Change can be threatening.

3. *Good program planning is time consuming.* Planning requires thought before action. Nonprofit leaders are usually doers and activists. They are impatient with the problems they see and anxious to take immediate corrective steps. To engage in program activity successfully, however, you must pause before you act to plan out what constitutes the most effective response to the problem that concerns you.

The benefits of program planning far outweigh these real considerations. Let's review two common examples of inadequate planning in organizational life.

1. An organization is established to provide services to low-income residents in the community while also advocating changes that would eliminate the need for those services. Since the need is severe, the staff quickly becomes overwhelmed in providing services, neglecting their advocacy work. The organization becomes preoccupied with responding to daily needs while the root problem remains intact.

2. An agency hears about funds available for a particular project. Eager to raise money, it submits a proposal despite the fact that the project does not fall within its stated purposes. It receives the grant and implements the project. After the project has been in operation for six months, the agency belatedly realizes that the program has sapped their energies for their primary work.

Without adequate planning, as indicated by these two examples, an organization resembles a ship afloat with no charted direction. Only planning can enable an organization to navigate through the waters of real life while paying appropriate attention to the external forces surrounding its passage. In short, planning is an organization's only assurance in its efforts to create and to control its future.

A STEP-BY-STEP PLANNING PROCESS

Program planning involves a sequence of logical steps that lead an organization along the road to effective action.

Step 1: Decide to Plan

To engage in program planning successfully, all of an organization's key players, including the board of directors and the professional staff, need to agree on its importance and to be willing to participate.

Step 2: Assign Responsibility

Everybody within an organization can play a role in program planning. Either the board can establish a committee to work with staff, or the executive director can set up a staff-level committee to make recommendations to the board. In either case, the committee can solicit input from others for its deliberations. The greater the involvement in the planning process, the greater will be the degree of investment in the plan itself and its subsequent implementation.

Step 3: Develop or Review Your Statement of Purpose

All programs should flow from your organization's mission. (See Chapter 1, on statement of purpose.) If your statement has not been recently updated before considering any new potential undertaking, you should engage in an organization-wide process to make sure that the operating statement does, in fact, still capture the essence of the prime purposes of your work. External conditions that affect a group's intention are constantly in flux. As a result, a timely review of its statement of purpose is always in order.

Step 4: Assess the Extent of the Problem

Program success requires a clear identification and detailed assessment of the problems your organization has set out to correct. It is necessary to immerse yourself in the problem so you can understand it thoroughly. Subsequently, you will be better equipped to design sound programs that will solve the problem at hand. Your information gathering might involve research into existing literature on the issues as well as interviews with both constituents and resource people. This stage of program planning is sometimes referred to as undertaking a "needs assessment." An excellent how-to guide to community assessment can be found in chapter 3 of *Community Impact: Creating Grassroots Change in Hard Times*, by William R. Berkowitz (297 pages, 1982, Schenkman Publishing Co., Inc., Cambridge, MA).

Remember, your problem assessment should both flow from your stated purposes and set the stage for the subsequent objectives and programs that you will develop. Also, your analysis should take into account other parallel efforts and organizations whose activities are also geared to solving the problems that concern you. If you do not include these groups in your appraisal, you will not be able to set a unique course of action for your own programs.

Step 5: Set Program Objectives

Your needs assessment provides data from which you can decide what particular changes you will try to accomplish. At this point, you are setting objectives to govern your work. An objective is the desired outcome of a program and provides a benchmark by which you will be able to gauge your progress and effectiveness. Objectives should be stated in the form of the specific changes you are seeking. Too often, objectives are confused either with broader goals that might be found in a statement of purpose or with the methods you utilize to accomplish your objectives. Examples of objectives are:

1. To increase the reading skills of school-age children in our community.

2. To decrease the incidence of juvenile delinquency in our neighborhood.

3. To lessen the loneliness and isolation of senior shut-ins in our town.

It's easy to evaluate the results of any programs flowing from these objectives, for they are measurable: How many school-age children have advanced their writing skills; how much has the rate of juvenile delinquency declined; and how many seniors have become involved in social activities?

Setting objectives forces an organization to focus its activities squarely. You can begin to choose from a number of varying priorities for action resulting from your needs assessment. Your choice will be informed by your sense of what you can realistically accomplish, rather than by what you hope you might be able to do.

Step 6: Design Programs

At this juncture, you can proceed to plan programs—those sequences of activities or events that will advance your objectives. Too often, people start the program planning process here and overlook the previous steps. Programs should not occur in an organizational vacuum. They should squarely fit within the parameters of an organization's stated purposes and be linked to its objectives. Otherwise they may accomplish some good, but not necessarily the specific results you seek.

In designing programs, be specific. During the design process answer the following questions:

1. *What* are you going to do? Enumerate all the tasks involved.

2. *How* are you going to do it? Do you need any special expertise?

3. *Where* is it going to take place? Locally? Nationally?

4. *Who* has the responsibility for implementation? Staff? Which staff? Others?

5. *When* will the program take place? When will it start, and when will it end?

6. How much is the program going to cost? In both staff and non-personnel expenses?

Sound and thorough planning provides answers to all of these questions. Obviously, the what, how, where, who, and when of any program would be determined at one time or another, whether you plan consciously or not. You cannot proceed otherwise. But conscious program designing lets you control the process from start to finish and, therefore, the end product. Think of your programs as strategies or maneuvers required to put yourself in the best position to accomplish your objectives.

Step 7: Develop a Work Plan

You now have the data you need to sketch out a work plan toward implementing your program or project. Your work plan serves as a checklist for the people assigned to a particular effort as well as an informal contract with your board of directors and your funders.

To develop a work plan, list all the tasks involved in carrying out your program. Organize these tasks by function. For example, group all printing or promotion or organizing tasks together. Next to each task list the name of the party or parties responsible for its successful completion. Then chart out the optimal timeline for the completion of the entire program, including all the tasks enumerated. The following charts provide illustrative examples of work plans for two particular programs.

Work plans provide organizations with useful tools to stake out their work in a systematic fashion. There is no single best way to develop a work plan. Once established, it serves the purpose of making clear to all the appropriate parties their roles in making a project happen.

Step 8: Monitor and Evaluate Progress

Common sense is the rule in this last step. If a certain set of tasks is not completed on schedule, find out why. Elicit thoughts and suggestions from the responsible individuals. Involve them in the monitoring and evaluation processes as partners. Ask questions such as: Did we underestimate the amount of time necessary to complete X task? What corrective action needs to be taken? Do we need to reset any deadlines for completion of the project? The thrust of monitoring the progress of a project is to enable all those involved to do their jobs most effectively. The intent is not punitive.

It is best to set in advance the criteria against which you will ultimately evaluate your work. Use clear objectives so that staff and volunteers will know how their work will be measured. Also, schedule in advance those times when the program will be evaluated (three months, six months, twelve months, etc.).

SAMPLE TIMETABLE FOR ORGANIZING A BLOCK PARTY

WEEKS BEFORE THE EVENT

ACTIVITY	10	9	8	7	6	5	4	3	2	1	2 days
SELECT CHAIRPERSON	■										
Steering Committee	■										
Committee Chairpersons	■										
Committees		■									
Theme & Dates		■									
Committee Meetings			■								
Print Newsletter telling											
neighbors about Party				■							
Solicit Vendors				■							
Solicit Merchants & Neighbors					■						
Prepare & Print Posters							■				
PERMITS											
Street Closing					■						
Merchandise							■				
Beer & Wine							■				
Sound									■		
Notify Sanitation							■				
Entertainment							■				
PUBLICITY											
Send Press Release to:											
Monthly magazines					■						
Weekly papers									■		
Radio & TV							■				
Daily papers										■	
Call Citizens Committee							■				

Source: This chart is reprinted with permission of Citizen's Committee for New York City, from their booklet, *Lend a Hand and Have a Block Party,* available from: Citizen's Committee for New York City, Inc., 3 West 29th St., New York, NY 10001.

Sample Work Plan
ESTABLISHING A PROGRAM TO MEET THE NEEDS
OF NEW IMMIGRANTS TO OUR COMMUNITY

Tasks	Who	When: Time-Line Sept O N D J F M A M J J A
1. Reviewing Mission Statement	Staff/ Board/ Committee	|------>
2. Undertaking Needs Assessment	Staff/ Volunteers	|------->
3. Setting Program Objectives	Staff/Board/ Committee	|--->
4. Designing Program	Staff	|-------------->
5. Seeking Financial Support for Program	Board/Staff	x----------x----->
6. Implementing Program	Staff/ Volunteers	x----------x----->
7. Monitoring and Evaluation	Board/Staff	|-------------->

Sample Work Plan
ORGANIZING A NATIONAL TOUR OF "X" THEATER GROUP

Tasks	Who	When: Time-Line (16 months)
		Sept O N D J F M A M J J A S O N Dec
1. Establish Purposes of the Tour	Board/ Staff	|-->
2. Map out Schedule of Appearances	Executive Directors/ Logistics Coordinator	|----->
3. Select Plays to be Performed	Artistic Director	|----->
4. Commence Fundraising	Board/ Executive Director	|--------->
5. Organize Tour Publicity	Publicity Coordinator/ Local Publicists	|-------x------------>
6. Organize Ticket Publicity	Local Contacts	|---------------->
7. Rehearse Performers	Actors and Cast	|--------------------> - - -
8. Arrange Tour Logistics	Logistics Coordinator	|---------> - - - - - - -

APPLICABILITY TO FUNDRAISING

You plan programs to ensure their success. At the same time, you are making some of your fundraising work easier. Funders are increasingly examining proposals to gauge how methodical and thorough an organization has been in its planning process. For example, you now have the substance of a program proposal to submit to funders for their consideration. The steps outlined in this planning process parallel some of the major components of a proposal: problem statement or needs assessment; program objectives; methods; and evaluation. An excellent reference tool that shows how the program-planning and proposal-writing processes can be integrated is *Program Planning and Proposal Writing*, by Norton J. Kiritz. It is published in reprint form by the Grantsmanship Center, Los Angeles, CA.

You will find that your work will also aid you in writing copy for promotional materials (brochures, direct mail letters, case statements, etc.). Both board members and staff will also be able to use some of the data gathered in presentations to inform prospective donors and others.

Finally, once reported, the results of your work will demonstrate to both your individual and institutional supporters the value of their assistance. They now can see the return on their charitable "investment."

As you can see, careful forethought to planning programs increases the likelihood of their success *in advance of their execution*, and aids the fundraising process as well.

Making the MOST of a Plan:
Mission, Objectives, Strategies, Tactics

Nonprofit managers who practice planning are often challenged by questions of cause and effect, of sequence and consequence, of the "where-does-it-fit?" variety. One useful way to keep clear about the level of a problem or opportunity, and to see how actions lead to results,   planning data and ideas into this

Mission. The mission is the big picture, the enduring purpose that motivates board, staff, volunteers, and clients—the raison d'être of the agency. You'll probably never accomplish it completely; it should be the condition, circumstance, or "fact of life" that draws you into action.

Objectives. If you'll never satisfy the mission, at least your agency can accomplish certain specific results, outcomes, products, and milestones. These are your objectives: targets as your organization moves along the road toward the ultimate achievement of mission. Naming them in advance helps avoid the "shoot, hit something, call it the target" syndrome.

Strategies. With a specific objective in mind, it's possible to "get ready for action" by putting yourself in the best possible position for success. Military planners talk about "maneuvering for advantage" when they choose strategies. Nonprofit managers, with less fearsome objectives, also try to set things up in their favor.

Tactics. Actions, pure and simple (or complex) are the tactics of a program, the day-to-day conduct of business. Once you've chosen a strategy, tactical choices are more varied and more obvious—do they *contribute* to the strategy?

This bare-bones outline can help nonprofit managers put questions and ideas in their proper place and helps raise questions about alternative means to the same end.

SOURCE: Tom Boyd of Thomas Detrich Boyd and Associates, New York, New York

FURTHER READING

Berkowitz, William R. *Community Impact: Creating Grassroots Change in Hard Times.* Cambridge, MA: Schenkman Publishing Company, Inc. 1982. 297 pp. $18.95; $9.95 paper (Order from: Schenkman Publishing Company, Inc., 3 Mount Auburn Place, Cambridge, MA 02138)

Provides information to encourage people to create small-scale community building activities, including low-cost ideas for strengthening community supports. Stresses a personal style of community work and the limits of change. Essays cover topics such as assessment, planning, program execution, and evaluation.

Craig, Dorothy P. *Hip Pocket Guide to Planning and Evaluation.* San Diego, CA: Learning Concepts, Inc. 1978. 148 pp. $11.95. (Order from: University Associates, Inc., 8517 Production Ave., San Diego, CA 92121)

A series of examples and exercises lead the reader to define and effectively state the problem, set objectives, generate and assess possible solutions, choose the best strategy, and evaluate the outcome.

Dale, Duane, and Nancy Mitiguy. *Planning for a Change: A Citizen's Guide to Creative Planning and Program Development.* Amherst, MA: Citizen Involvement Training Project. 1978. 88 pp. $48.00. (Order from: Citizen Involvement Training Project, c/o University of Massachusetts, 225 School of Education, Amherst, MA 01003)

Using an exercise format, groups learn to plan and develop ideas and strategies to deal with issues. Topics covered include analysis, generating program ideas, decision-making, implementing ideas, and evaluation.

Fitz-Gibbon, Carol, and Lynn Morris. *How to Design a Program Evaluation.* Beverly Hills, CA: SAGE Publications, Inc. 1978. 164 pp. $8.50. (Order from: SAGE Publications, Inc., P.O. Box 5024, Beverly Hills, CA 90210)

Introduces the logic underlying the use of evaluation design and its importance in obtaining relevant data. Through diagrams, step-by-step directions, flow charts and examples, shows how each design can be conceived and implemented.

Granger, C. H . "The Hierarchy of Objectives." *Harvard Business Review* vol. 42, no. 3 (May/June 1982): 63–74. Reprint $1.00. (Order from: Harvard Business Review, Graduate School of Business Administration, Harvard University, Boston, MA 02163)

Discusses how to analyze and prepare objectives. Includes information on tests for validating objectives.

Hayes, Roger, Isabel Malanet, and Alban Calderon. *Workshops in Organizing: 1. Introduction to Organizing; 2. Research and Power; 3. Issues and Strategy; 4. Leadership.* New York: Center for Community Organizing, Community Service Society. 1985. 17 pp. each. $2.00 each; $6.00 a set. (Order from: Center for Community Organizing, Community Service Society, 105 E. 22nd St., New York, NY 10010)

Set of training manuals outlining the kinds of organizing skills needed by organizers, leaders, neighborhood residents, and other activists who are working to improve their communities. Each manual covers a particular skill area: 1. *Introduction to Organizing* describes what community organizing is, why it is needed, and ten steps to effective organizing. 2. *Research and Power* presents the dynamics of power, the importance of research, and how to use these factors as important tools. 3. *Issues and Strategy* provides an insight into how to choose an issue, develop an organizing campaign, and choose proper strategy and tactics. 4. *Leadership* describes the qualities which make a good leader, the need for collective leadership, and how it can be developed.

Hennesey, Paul. *Managing Nonprofit Agencies for Results: A Systems Approach to Long-Range Planning.* San Francisco: Institute for Fund Raising. 1979. 256 pp. in 3-ring binder. $39.00. (Order from: Public Management Institute, 358 Brannan St., San Francisco, CA 94107)

Shows how to prepare goals, objectives, action plans, budgets and evaluation systems. Includes many forms, worksheets and checklists, and provides a seven-step system for charting an organization's future.

Horowitz, Laura, *et al. Community Action Tool Catalog: Techniques and Strategies for Successful Action Programs.* Second Edition. Washington, DC: American Association of University Women. 1978. 260 pp. $7.00. (Order from: American Association of University Women, Sales Office. 2401 Virginia Ave., N.W., Washington, DC 20037)

Thorough manual in a step-by-step format on how to plan and implement community improvement programs. Includes techniques for dealing with institutions, fact finding, publicity, and planning which would be particularly useful for low-budget, volunteer groups.

Kahn, Si. *How People Get Power: Organizing Oppressed Communities for Action.* New York: McGraw-Hill Paperbacks. 1970. 128 pp. $3.95. (Order from: McGraw-Hill, 1221 Avenue of the Americas, New York, NY 10020)

Resource on community organizations, with information on building political power and leadership.

Kiritz, Norton J. *Program Planning and Proposal Writing.* Los Angeles: The Grantsmanship Center. 1979. 48 pp. $4.00 plus $2.00 handling per order. (Order from: The Grantsmanship Center, P.O. Box 6210, 650 South Spring St., Suite 507, Los Angeles, CA 90014)

    A step-by-step guide to planning and proposal writing. Includes a summary worksheet "Proposal Checklist and Evaluation Form" which, while primarily designed to assist in the preparation of a proposal, can be used to evaluate such aspects of planning as needs assessment and objectives.

Linkow, Peter R. "Implementing a Long-Range Plan." *The Grantsmanship Center NEWS* no. 51 (January/February 1983): 18–27. Single issue $4.75 plus $2.00 handling per order. (Order from: The Grantsmanship Center, P.O. Box 6210, 650 South Spring St. Suite 507, Los Angeles, CA 90014)

    Discusses how to take a long-range plan and implement it by following three steps: (1) evaluate the plan from the standpoint of implementation; (2) design and put in place an appropriate management system; and (3) schedule, monitor and control the implementation process.

Management Support Services. *Strategic Planning Workbook for Nonprofit Organizations.* 1985. 96 pp. $25.00. (Order from: Management Support Services, Amherst H. Wilder Foundation, 919 Lafond Ave., St. Paul, MN 55104)

    A step-by-step guide for nonprofit organizations interested in strategic planning, a method of planning in which the organization determines *what* the organization intends to be in the future and *how* it will get there. Includes worksheets and a number of examples of typical nonprofit planning issues, methods and formats and of a completed strategic plan.

Morris, Lynn, and Carol Fitz-Gibbon. *Evaluator's Handbook.* Beverly Hills, CA: SAGE Publications, Inc. 1978. 160 pp. $9.95. (Order from: SAGE Publications, Inc., P.O. Box 5024, Beverly Hills, CA 90210)

    A broad overview of the evaluation process as well as a practical guide to designing and managing evaluation programs. Includes step-by-step guides for three kinds of evaluation—standard summative evaluation, formative evaluation, and classical experiment—presented for practitioners with relatively little experience.

Morris, Lynn, and Carol Fitz-Gibbon. *How to Measure Achievement.* Beverly Hills, CA: SAGE Publications, Inc. 1978. 160 pp. $8.50. (Order from: SAGE Publications, Inc., P.O. Box 5024, Beverly Hills, CA 90210)

    Focuses on the use of tests for program evaluation including evaluation and selection of an appropriate test. Presents an annotated list of resources for developing an in-house test.

Morris, Lynn, and Carol Fitz-Gibbon. *How to Measure Program Implementation.* Beverly Hills, CA: SAGE Publications, Inc. 1978. 140 pp. $7.95. (Order from: SAGE Publications, Inc., P.O. Box 5024, Beverly Hills, CA 90210)

    Presents: (1) step-by-step methods for designing and using measurement instruments to describe how a program looks in operation, and (2) arguments about why measuring implementation is important.

Newber, Keith A., W. T. Atkins, J. A. Jacobson, and N. A. Reuterman. *Needs Assessment: A Model for Community Planning.* Beverly Hills, CA: SAGE Publications. 1980. 107 pp. $7.95. (Order from: SAGE Publications, Inc., P.O. Box 5024, Beverly Hills, CA 90210)

Provides a step-by-step method for conducting a human services needs assessment with information about methods, training interviewers, and using the collected data. Includes a sample questionnaire, sample publicity releases and letters to key informants.

Newman, Harvey. *Self-Evaluation and Planning for Human Service Organizations.* New York: AMACOM. 1986. Price to be determined. (Order from: AMA, 135 W. 50th St., New York, NY 10019)

A how-to manual on a self-evaluation process which contributes to short- and long-term planning.

Raia, Anthony P. *Managing by Objectives.* Glenview, IL: Scott, Foresman and Company. 1974. 199 pp. $13.65. (Order from: Scott, Foresman and Company, 1900 E. Lake Ave., Glenview, IL 60025)

Describes one philosophy of management, a proactive approach which emphasizes accomplishments and results and encourages participative management by individuals at all levels of the organization.

Richards, A., ed. *Needs Assessment Handbook.* San Francisco: Public Management Institute. 1980. 246 pp. in 3-ring binder. $49.00. (Order from: Public Management Institute, 358 Brannan St., San Francisco, CA 94107)

Covers how to gather needs assessment data quickly, where to find public data, how to design questionnaires and surveys, how to conduct telephone surveys, and where to get funding for needs assessment projects.

United Way of America. *Needs Assessment: A Guide for Planners, Managers and Funders of Health and Human Care Services.* Alexandria, VA: United Way of America, 1982. 109 pp. $12.00. (Order from: United Way of America, 701 N. Fairfax Street, Alexandria, VA 22314)

Guide to assessing human needs in a community.

CHAPTER 5

DEVELOPING BUDGETS

L et's imagine the following scenario. You knock on the door of a prospective supporter and donor and ask for a contribution. Your donor candidate listens to your request with patience and interest. After you have finished, your prospects asks, "How much do you need to get this project off the ground?" You stammer and finally say, "Well, I guess we can use whatever you can give us." Suddenly, the prospective donor politely terminates the conversation. Crestfallen and certainly no richer than before, you leave.

Obviously, this is a scenario you want to avoid, and a simple budget, a description of your proposed program or project in financial terms, might well have saved the day! Prospective backers, both individual and institutional, respond most favorably to requests that are predicated on the concrete financial needs of an organization. Preparing a budget is a process that forces you to anticipate the expenses inherent in your projected programs and activities for the coming year. It also enables you to estimate how much revenue you need to raise to meet your program objectives. Doing your budget homework before meeting with a potential funder will help you next time the inevitable question is asked: "How much do you need?"

WHAT IS BUDGETING?

Budgeting is a management tool. It empowers an organization's board and staff to decide how to use limited financial resources most effectively.

You may dream about starting any projects you like, but budgeting brings you back to reality, forcing you to choose among the different program options that compete for the same pot of available funds. Good budgeting reflects organizational priorities.

Budgeting is a program tool. It helps you determine how much in funds will be needed to launch a specific program you may have in mind. If you raise less than your total projected budget but have established budget priorities, you can more readily decide upon the allocation of available funds.

Budgeting is a financial planning tool. It forces you to anticipate both the amount of expenses and the amount of revenues required on a regular basis. The question of when these amounts are needed becomes a cash flow problem, a secondary but important concern for the money manager, who may need to resort to short-term loans or additional fundraising.

Budgeting is a form of management control over expenditures. The processes of preparing, administering, attempting to adhere to, or revising a budget provide the organization with a continuous monitoring system. With increasing competition for scarce resources, funders look with more favor at the nonprofit organization with both a worthy cause and sound financial management practices.

The development of a budget involves many people in an organization—from the board of directors, to the executive director, to the program manager, to the treasurer, to the professional volunteers. The process touches on a wide range of decisions, such as hiring staff, purchasing a word processor, moving an office, initiating a new service, and so forth. Many executive directors limit their concerns to the mission or program of the organization and unwisely ignore money issues, or, at best, relegate them to a board treasurer, accountant, or bookkeeper. Such a course of action robs the organization not only of the value of a budget-making process but of the crucial role budgeting plays in rallying every member of that group around a particular set of financial goals. Moreover, a board takes on more of a commitment, individually and as a whole, to help raise money when its members have decided together how to spend it. In short, budgeting defines the financial obligations of a group in reference to what it says it will do.

A key responsibility of the board of directors of a nonprofit organization is to approve the organization's general and operating expense budgets, specific program budgets, and projected income budgets for the year. By actively engaging in the budget review and approval process, a board is stating the amount of money the organization is committed to raise in the upcoming year and how it is going to spend it. Those final projected budget figures represent the collective vision of both staff and board, demonstrating how they perceive their work in sheer financial terms and how their program and activity priorities are set. Once that budget for the year is approved, it takes on internal power, becoming the guiding reference point for spending decisions. Therefore, the budget-making process should never be shunted off to the sidelines.

It is central to the basic mission, program, and management of the organization.

ELEMENTS OF A BUDGET

The following budget worksheets represent the typical information a young organization should document in its first year of operation: an organizational expense budget; a program expense budget; and an organizational revenue budget, projecting income. Since these budgets are being prepared for the first time, data is based both on actual research and on good guesses. It is always easier to prepare a budget when there is some past history on which to base future projections.

Expense budgets consist of two parts: personnel items and non-personnel items. *Personnel items* include staff (salaried and volunteer), contracted assistance (consultants, accountants, lawyers, etc), short-term employees (interns, work/study students, temporary workers), and fringe benefits (workers' compensation, health insurance, pension plans, unemployment compensation). *Non-personnel items* include office rent, utilities; telephone; printing; duplicating equipment; office supplies; postage; travel, office, and liability insurance; membership dues; subscriptions and entertainment.

Worksheet A
ORGANIZATIONAL EXPENSE BUDGET

First Year of Operations

Personnel Costs

A. Executive Director

$ _____ × 12 months × 100% = $ _____

(Note: 100% denotes full-time employment)

B. Program Coordinator

$ _____ × 12 months × 100% = $ _____

C. Administrative Assistant

$ _____ × 12 months × 100% = $ _____

D. Fringe Benefits (Employee Benefits)

Note: Fringe Benefits can either be computed by itemizing all fringe benefits, or by computing a fixed percentage of the total payroll of an organization or of a project

1. State Unemployment Insurance

    _____% × $ _____ (total payroll) = $ _____

2. Worker's Compensation (   ) = $ _____

3. FICA/Social Security (   ) = $ _____

4. Health Insurance (   ) = $ _____

5. Life Insurance (   ) = $ _____

6. Pension (   ) = $ _____

7. Staff Training (   ) = $ _____

E. Outside Contracted Services
1. Bookkeeper

$ _____/day × _____ days/year = $ _____

2. Consultant

$ _____/day × _____ days/year = $ _____

**Total Personnel Costs for
First Year of Operations:** $ _____

Non-Personnel Costs

   A. Office space rental
   $ _____ × 12 months = $ _____

   B. Utilities (gas, electricity, etc.)
   $ _____ × 12 months = $ _____

   C. Telephone (monthly service.
   including long distance charges)
   $ _____ × 12 months = $ _____

   D. Printing (including newsletters, brochures,
   annual reports, program publications, etc.)
   $ _____ × 12 months = $ _____

   E. Duplication
   $ _____ × 12 months = $ _____

   F. Equipment (including rental, leasing and purchasing of typewriters, duplicating machines, etc.)
   $ _____ × 12 months = $ _____

   G. Office supplies
   $ _____ × 12 months = $ _____

   H. Postage
   $ _____ × 12 months = $ _____

   I. Travel (including _____ trips to attend conferences
   of _____ and _____, etc.)
   $ _____ × 12 months = $ _____

   J. Office and liability insurance $ _____

   K. Membership and professional dues $ _____

**Total Non-Personnel Costs for
First Year of Operation** $ _____

   Total Costs for First Year of Operation $ _____

Worksheet B
PROGRAM EXPENSE BUDGET

First Year of Operation

Personnel Costs

A. Project Director
$ _____ × 12 months × 100% = $ _____

B. Community Organizers (2)
$ _____ × 6 months × 100% × 2 = $ _____

C. Executive Director
$ _____ × 12 months × 20% = $ _____

D. Administrative Assistant
$ _____ × 12 months × 30% = $ _____

E. Fringe Benefits (Employee Benefits)
1. State Unemployment Insurance

_____% × $ _____ (total payroll) = $ _____
2. Worker's Compensation (   ) = $ _____

3. FICA/Social Security (   ) = $ _____

4. Health Insurance (   ) = $ _____

5. Life Insurance (   ) = $ _____

6. Pension (   ) = $ _____

7. Staff Training (   ) = $ _____

F. Outside Contracted Services:
1. Bookkeeper
$ _____/day × days/year = $ _____
2. Consultant
$ _____/day × days/year = $ _____

Total Personnel Costs for
First Year of Operation: $ _____

Non-Personnel Costs

A. Office space rental
$ _____ × 12 months × 25% = $ _____

B. Utilities (gas, electricity, etc.)
$ _____ × 12 months × 25% = $ _____

C. Telephone (monthly service,
including long distance charges)
$ _____ × 12 months × 25% = $ _____

D. Printing (including brochures, program reports,
promotional literature, etc.)
$ _____ × 12 months × 25% - $ _____

E. Duplication
$ _____ × 12 months × 25% = $ _____

F. Equipment (including rental, leasing and purchasing
of typewriters, duplicating machines, computers, etc.)
$ _____ × 12 months × 25% = $ _____

G. Office supplies
$ _____ × 12 months × 25% = $ _____

H. Postage
$ _____ × 12 months × 25% = $ _____

I. Travel (including _____ trips to attend conferences
of _____ and _____, etc.)
$ _____ × 12 months × 25% = $ _____

J. Office and liability insurance
$ _____ × 12 months × 25% = $ _____

K. Membership and professional dues
$ _____ × 12 months × 25% = $ _____

**Total Non-Personnel Costs for
First Year of Operation** $ _____

**Total Costs of Program "X" for First Year of
Operation** $ _____

Note: The budget projections for program "x" are based on a rough estimate that the activities involved in conducting this particular program constitute 25% of all the work of the organization during this 12-month time period. Each group has to make a similar calculation for their own programs and projects.

    You have just identified the expenditures you will need to make to carry out the work of your organization, or your special program. Now to the income side of budgeting. The following worksheet will help you project the sources and amounts of revenue required to proceed with your work.

Worksheet C
ORGANIZATIONAL REVENUE BUDGET

Projecting Income for First Year of Operation

Income Sources

A. Individuals

    1. Contributions/Memberships $ _____

    2. Bequests and other forms of planned gifts $ _____

    3. Large Donor Gifts $ _____

    4. Special Events $ _____

    5. Payroll Deductions $ _____

    6. Direct Mail $ _____

B. Foundation Grants $ _____

C. Businesses and Corporations

    1. Contributions $ _____

    2. Grants $ _____

    3. United Way $ _____

D. Government (city, town, county, state, federal)

    1. Grants $ _____

    2. Contracts $ _____

E. Religious Institutions

    1. Special Offerings $ _____

    2. Contributions $ _____

    3. Grants $ _____

F. Earned Income Ventures

    1. Sales of "x" product or service $ _____

    2. Miscellaneous program-related income $ _____

G. Other Income:

    1. _____ $ _____

    2. _____ $ _____

Total Income $ _____

Worksheet D
BUDGET AND CASH FLOW PLANNING SHEET

Income	Jan	Feb	Mar	Apr	May	June	July	Aug	Sept	Oct	Nov	Dec
(Cash on Hand as of First of Month)	$	$	$	$	$	$	$	$	$	$	$	$
Individuals												
Foundation Grants												
Businesses and Corporations												
Government												
Other:												
Total Revenue in Hand	$	$	$	$	$	$	$	$	$	$	$	$

Expenses	Jan	Feb	Mar	Apr	May	June	July	Aug	Sept	Oct	Nov	Dec
Personnel:												
Non-Personnel:												
Total Monthly Expenses	$	$	$	$	$	$	$	$	$	$	$	$
Cash on Hand as of End of Month	$	$	$	$	$	$	$	$	$	$	$	$

THE BUDGETING PROCESS

Preparing a budget involves most staff members, the executive director, the executive committee of the board, the whole board of directors, and the treasurer or chief financial officer of the board. Staff members who are most familiar with daily activities may be in the best position to estimate costs such as telephone, postage, and office supplies. They may also be accountable for putting together individual program budgets. The executive director, however, is ultimately responsible for compiling all the program budgets and other available information and preparing a total organizational budget for submission to the board of directors. The executive director also monitors the organization's expenditures on a regular basis. If the organization is large enough or fortunate enough to have an active treasurer, this person can play a key role in preparing the required figures for review and analysis by the board, and in monitoring overall financial performance.

By law, the board of directors has financial responsibility for the nonprofit organization. As the accountable body, it must decide before approving the final budget whether overall estimates on expenditures and fundraising projections are realistic and sound and whether revenue projections are sufficient to match anticipated expenses. The board may find it necessary to modify staff recommendations. After the review process, which may take more than one meeting, the board is ready to adopt a general operating budget for the upcoming fiscal year. The monitoring process now begins; expenditures must be reviewed regularly against budget estimates.

Staff members must maintain expenses within the amounts designated for each budget category. Should they find later in the year that they cannot stay within budget ceilings, they must return to the board for permission to raise the limits on the expenditure category in question.

The treasurer's role in a nonprofit organization is vital to its financial management and integrity. According to Leon Haller, author of *Financial Resource Management for Non-Profit Organizations*, the treasurer, executive director, or other manager who fills this role on a daily basis must:

1. See to it that all financial transactions are recorded

2. Control use of the organization's assets

3. Assure preparation of accurate financial reports

4. Anticipate financial problems

5. Comply with state and federal reporting requirements.

The treasurer, or the person who assumes this role if there is none, plays a key role in the budgeting process by advising the board and working with the executive director. He or she may serve as a counselor to the executive director, or provide the vital checks and balances, or serve as a coach to board members who are less familiar with finances.

Guidelines to Budgeting

To reiterate, budgeting is the process that helps an organization estimate its possible expenditures within a projected future period of time—usually the next fiscal year—and also projects the revenues needed to cover those expenses. Sound budgeting should take into account the following guidelines:

1. **Be concrete and specific in making projections.** Base projections on the costs of carefully itemized resources, services, and personnel expected to be needed for program activity.

Try to break down your categories of expense and income in as much detail as possible. The following worksheets can help you. The more specific you are, the more accurate your projections will be. For example, all personnel expenses can be listed by the following formula:

(Title of Staff Position)

$ ___,___ / month x ____ months x ____% x ____ positions

"$" denotes the salary allocated to this position on a monthly basis; "months" indicates exactly how many months that position will be filled during a given year; and "%" tells whether the position is full-time, which would translate to 100%, or half-time, which would translate to 50%, etc. If there is one such position within your organization, you would multiply these figures by 1; for two such staff positions, multiply these figures by 2; and so forth.

No possible expense category or revenue source should be overlooked. In itemizing telephone costs, for instance, you can make separate projections for local and long-distance calls, as well as for purchase of phone equipment and use of long-distance service operators. When an expense is expected to vary from month to month, such as long-distance telephone charges, you can project a monthly unit cost on the basis of averaging out yearly use over twelve months. On the other hand, you do not need to take this principle to its extreme by projecting how many pencils you might need to buy each month. Look first at categories of expenses, and then at major subcategories, if they exist. If, during the year, you need to conserve your funds by decreasing your regular expenses, such detailing in advance will help you decide where best to cut corners.

2. **Be conservative in your projections.** In making estimates you should try to err on the high side for expenditures and on the low side for revenues. It is far better to be surprised with unanticipated revenues than with unpaid bills. Oddly enough, many organizations tend to do just the opposite.

When projecting income, for example, from special events that you have conducted in the past, you may project the same net income for the following year, even if you anticipate doing better. That way you will be erring on the safe side. After all, your income from that special event might rise, but so might your costs in organizing the event, resulting in no greater profit.

3. **Ascribe value to key volunteer labor** (see sample). Suppose your organization is composed totally of volunteers. No one has yet been placed on salary

to carry out the work of your group. Still, you and several others are putting in long hours of work, accomplishing tasks that would normally be done by salaried staff. How can you reflect this vital volunteer labor on the budget attached to a foundation proposal you submit?

It is important to ascribe a value to the labor of key volunteers for the following reasons: (a) Positions that volunteers currently fill are critical to the work of your group, as described in the body of the proposal. Without their labor, the project could not proceed. Therefore, excluding them from the budget would be inadequately representing your personnel resources. (b) Prospective supporters, especially funders, frequently attach significance to the scope of your efforts according to the size of your budget. Therefore, by presenting a less then total picture of your personnel power, unsalaried as well as salaried, you are in essence minimizing the labor it takes to run the organization, as well as minimizing the organization itself. (c) By adding your key volunteer staff to the budget under the "Donated" column, you show both your staff and your organization, and prospective funders as well, the importance you attach to their work.

A cautionary note: it does not necessarily follow, then, that you should place all of your volunteers on your budgets. Simply follow this rule: include in your program and general operating organizational budgets all those whose labor is vital to a specific project's operation, or to the organization as a whole. Exclude volunteers whose efforts, while important, may nevertheless be ancillary.

SAMPLE OPERATING BUDGET FOR
SHADY VILLAGE COMMUNITY ASSOCIATION

January 1989 to December 1989

	Requested	Donated	TOTAL
Personnel			
A. Coordinators (2) ($1,000 × 12 months × 100% × 2)		$24,000*	$24,000
B. Block Captains (5) ($500 × 12 months × 25% × 5)		$ 7,500*	$ 7,500
Total Personnel Expenses		**$31,500**	**$31,500**

*These positions are currently filled by unsalaried volunteers. We have ascribed salaries to them concurrent with those being paid to employees with comparable responsibilities at similar organizations.

4. **Ascribe value to donated nonpersonnel items as well** (see next sample.) An organization should also present on its budget nonpersonnel items that may have been donated, such as office space, telephones, furniture, printing, and other in-kind contributions.

Although donated items don't represent a direct cost to the organization, they do have a value to you and in the marketplace. They have a value to donors who can claim deductions for such gifts on their tax returns. Listing donated items in your budgets conveys to other prospective donors, such as individuals and corporations, your appreciation of the worth of in-kind donations. Also, you are illustrating the array of support you receive beyond dollar contributions.

You can also list in the "Donated" column those expense items that have already been funded by either another funder or your own organization. In either instance, annotate the sources of these matching funds. Should you ever seek a matching or challenge grant, this method of budgeting will enable you to document how assiduously you are, in fact, living up to the terms of your grant agreement.

SAMPLE OPERATING BUDGET OF HIGHLAND COUNTY TEEN HOTLINE, 1989–90

	Requested	Donated	TOTAL
1. Non-Personnel Operating Expenses			
A. Office Rent ($200/month x 12 months)		$2,400*	$2,400
B. Telephone Answering Machine		175**	175
Basic Service (3 lines x			
12 months x $35 = $1,260	$1,260		1,260
C. Printing			
1. 5,000 brochures		800***	600
2. 10,000 palm cards		600***	600
Total Requested from "X" Corporation	$1,260		$1,260
Total Donated		$3,975	$3,975
Total Budget for Non-Personnel Expenses			**$5,235**

* Office space donated by First United Methodist Church
** Answering machine donated by Barney's Hardware Store
*** Printing donated by Highland Savings Bank

5. **Make your proposal budgets realistic**. Don't ask for the moon when preparing budgets for proposals, and don't approach the budgeting process as you would approach spending the winnings from a lottery ticket. Inevitably, the reader of your budget is looking for evidence of some hard-nosed estimates of the expenses you plan to incur and relating them to results you expect to achieve.

Set salaries for your staff positions on the basis of salaries for comparable positions of responsibility at similar organizations. Contact your local United Way, health and welfare planning organization, or relevant trade organization for information on salary scales. If you cannot pay your staff "market" salaries, you should still be aware of what they are so you can consider giving raises when your future finances permit it. For nonpersonnel costs, be thrifty by getting competitive estimates from several vendors for different expenditures. Keep your consumer instincts operative as you shop for a typewriter or a computer or a long-distance telephone service. Your prospective funder will appreciate your care in maximizing the use of the dollars you receive. A non-profit organization need not have an outmoded, inefficient office, nor should it try to compete with a major corporation's offices in decor, accoutrements, and other cosmetic attributes.

6. **Establish minimum internal budgets**. Too often budgets are determined by the amount of money that has been raised to carry out a project, rather than by the minimum actually needed to carry out the project with some measurable success. Every organization should strive to establish a minimum budget for its programs by which it can reasonably expect to accomplish pro-jected goals to the satisfaction of its supporters, whether they are individuals, corporations, government, or foundations.

Your fundraising budget is your optimal operating budget. It should reflect all the expenses your work would require if you were to secure as much funding as you could reasonably expect in addressing the problem outlined in your proposal. If you do not secure all the funding outlined in your optimal budget, your funders will certainly understand a modified budget, so long as the pro-gram now associated with this budget still seems possible. This modified budget should represent no less than the minimum budget required to make a difference in the problems your organization is now addressing. If, however, you manage to raise only a percentage of the minimal operating budget, you should consider abandoning the project, and even returning its specified funds to the donor. At best, try for the donor's agreement to use the funds for another purpose or program that costs less.

On the other hand, if you succeed in raising *more* funds than projected as necessary in your optimal budget, you can either return the additional money to the funder or ask for the funder's agreement to expand the project or to distribute the funds to another project.

7. **Distinguish between organization budgets and program budgets**. An organiza-tional budget entails all the expenditures and all the receipts or revenues of

that body. It presents the group's entire financial picture. A program or project budget reflects only those expenses and revenues unique to a particular undertaking of the organization. Most groups need both types of budgets, because organization management functions such as overall administration, bookkeeping, fundraising, and public relations are as much a part of operations as the direct production of programs, services, and events are.

If an organization sends a proposal to a funder for general support or unrestricted support (in other words, for whatever activities a group might undertake consistent with its stated purposes and programs), it would submit an organizational budget. If, on the other hand, it were asked to submit a proposal specifically to cover the expenses of a particular project, it would submit a project budget.

8. **Don't underestimate your overhead or indirect costs in your program or project proposal budgets**. Considering the shift by many funders from general support to targeted program grants, it has become even more important for nonprofits to take special pains to calculate as accurately as possible all inherent costs in any specific project or program. There are two kinds of costs: (a) *direct costs*, representing all expenditures required by the specific program or project activities; and (b) *indirect* or *overhead costs*, including such expenditures as administrative and secretarial salaries, rent and utilities, telephone and duplicating, accounting and legal services, which an organization absorbs while supporting a program.

In preparing a budget, organizations sometimes make the mistake of overlooking indirect costs and present only direct costs as the total expense of a project. This is not only faulty but dangerous budgeting that leads to financial crisis. The "real" costs of a program will continue to exceed the revenues received, and a financial shortfall will begin to build. If unchecked, it will result in a serious debt situation or, at best, a serious drain on your revenues from unrestricted sources—that is, individuals and other means of general support. A project can potentially become a financial drain on an organization rather than an asset.

Indirect costs can be substantial. Some federal agencies allow their grantees as much as 40 percent of a project's overall costs as indirect costs or overhead. In other words, if the direct costs of a project total $20,000, the grantee would budget $8,000 (40 percent of $20,000) for indirect or overhead costs, for a total project budget of $28,000.

In preparing a project budget, it may be preferable to itemize all indirect costs and enumerate them in your budget. Some funders, however, permit only a fixed percentage of the project's total budget (personnel plus non-personnel) as a recognition of overhead cost. If their requirements are not made clear in their pre-grant application literature, ask your prospective funders if they have any preference.

Budgeting Forever

Budgeting is not simply an activity to be carried out once a year for the board or whenever a funding proposal is being prepared. To the contrary, a budget is a working document for staff's and board's continued use throughout the year; actual expenses and receipts should be regularly measured against it, usually on a monthly basis. Since neither income nor cash outlays can usually be predicted with total precision, budgets provide the only means for measuring your actual receipts and expenditures against your projected figures. You will then be able to guard against unexpected deficits and to take any necessary corrective action. You are also able to assure your prospective and current supporters that their dollars will be used wisely. This will further result in a strengthening of your overall credibility.

Summary Work Sheet
SECTION I CHECKLIST:
Getting Your House in Order

Name of Your Organization: _____

_____

1. Statement of Purpose
The purpose of this organization is:

_____

_____

_____

_____

(See Chapter 1 if you need assistance)

2. Structure
Our organization has: (Check the appropriate boxes)
   a. INCORPORATION
      ☐ filed for incorporation as a not-for-profit corporation with the State
        of_____, and expects to have a response by _____.
                                             (date)
      ☐ received notice from the State of _____ that its application for
        incorporation has been accepted as of _____.
                                     (date)

   b. FEDERAL TAX-EXEMPTION
      ☐ filed for exemption from Federal Income Tax with the Internal Revenue
        Service, and expects to have a response by _____.
                                       (date)
      ☐ received notice from the Internal Revenue Service that it has been awarded
        a exemption from Federal income tax under section 501 (c) (3) of the IRS
        Code as of _____.
             (date).
   c. ADOPTION
      ☐ been adopted as a project of _____, which is incorporated within the
                          (name)
     State of _____, and is federally tax-exempt under section 501 (c) (3) of
     the Internal Revenue Code.

   d. FISCAL SPONSORSHIP
      ☐ secured _____ as a fiscal sponsor
              (name of non-profit organization)
     of our activities.

   e. UNINCORPORATED ASSOCIATION
      ☐ decided to operate as a unincorporated association.
                     (See Chapter 2 if you need assistance)

3. Governance

a. We have written a set of by-laws that designates the
_____ as the prime decision-making body within our organization.
(board of directors, steering committee, etc.)

b. We have decided (to be, not to be) a membership organization.

(See Chapter 3 if you need assistance)

4. Programs

a. We are currently conducting the following programs:

1) _____

2) _____

3) _____

4) _____

b. We would like to establish the additional following programs:

1) _____

2) _____

3) _____

4) _____

(See Chapter 4 if you need assistance)

5. Budgets

a. The total operating budget for our organization for the upcoming year is:
$_____ (198_ to 198_)

b. The estimated budgets for our projected programs for that year are:

Programs	12-Month Budget
1) _____	$_____
2) _____	$_____
3) _____	$_____
4) _____	$_____
5) _____	$_____

(See Chapter 5 if you need assistance)

FURTHER READINGS

Bennett, Paul. *Up Your Accountability: How to Up Your Funding Credibility by Upping Your Account Ability*. Washington, DC: The Taft Group. 1980. 66 pp. $15.95. (Order from: The Taft Group. 5130 MacArthur Blvd., N.W., Washington, DC 20016)
> Covers the basics of accounting for non-professional managers of small non-profit organizations including a chapter on budgeting. Discusses how to set up bookkeeping and prepare financial reports.

Bowe, Gerald G., Jr., *Where Do All the $ Go? What Every Board and Staff Member of a Non-Profit Organization Should Know About Accounting and Budgeting*. Concord, NH: The New Hampshire Charitable Fund. 1975. 40 pp. $3.75. (Order from: The New Hampshire Charitable Fund, P.O. Box 1335, Concord, NH 03301)
> Provides a simple explanation of the basic principles and vocabulary of accounting, budgets and internal control. Includes useful charts and tables.

Braswell, Ronald, Karen Fortin, and Jerome S. Osteryoung. *Financial Management for Not-for-Profit Organizations*. New York: John Wiley and Sons. 1984 419 pp. $29.95. (Order from: John Wiley and Sons, 605 3rd Ave., New York, NY 10158)
> A fairly technical source on such aspects of financial management as financial analysis, management of working capital, and investment in long-term assets. Covers the key concepts and applications relevant to financial decision-making for nonprofit organizations.

Finance and Management (Special Reprints Package 3). Los Angeles: The Grantsmanship Center. $19.95. (Order from: The Grantsmanship Center, P.O. Box 6210, 650 S. Spring St., Suite 507, Los Angeles, CA 90014)
> Reprints of 8 articles from *The Grantsmanship Center NEWS* on such topics as the annual report, cost accounting, program evaluation, and the IRS and charities.

Frederiksen, Christian P. *Budgeting for Nonprofits*. Second Edition. San Francisco: Public Management Institute. 1980. 321 pp. $59.00. (Order from: Public Management Institute, 358 Brannan St., San Francisco, CA 94107)
> Emphasizes how to avoid overspending and better utilize shrinking resources. Provides a simplified budgeting system with many forms, worksheets, checklists and model budgets.

Honig, Lisa. "Fundraising Events, Part Three: Budgeting." *Grassroots Fundraising Journal* vol. 1, no. 4 (August, 1982): 8-11. Single issue $2.50. (Order from: Grassroots Fundraising Journal, P.O. Box 14754, San Francisco, CA 94114)
> Discussion of when and how to budget for specific fundraising events. Provides a sample budget form for one type of event, a concert.

Gross, Malvern J., and William Warshauer, Jr., *Financial and Accounting Guide for Non-Profit Organizations*. 3rd Edition. New York: The Ronald Press. 1979. 568 pp. $49.95. (Order from: The Ronald Press, 605 Third Ave., New York, NY 10158)
> Covers financial reporting, accounting and control as well as the federal and state reporting requirements for nonprofit organizations. Includes extensive sample worksheets and forms.

Haller, Leon. *Financial Resource Management for Nonprofit Organizations*. Englewood Cliffs, NJ: Prentice-Hall, Inc. 1982. 191 pp. $8.95 (Order from: Prentice-Hall, Inc., Englewood Cliffs, NJ 07632)
> Guidelines for managers to carry out planning and decision-making activities to: project costs of activities; purchase goods and services; control expenses; organize records and reports; and manage team members.

Macleod, Roderick. "Program Budgeting Works in Nonprofit Institutions." (Reprint 71510) *Harvard Business Review* vol. 49, no. 5 (September-October, 1971): 46-56. Reprint $1.00. (order from: Harvard Business Review, Graduate School of Business Administration, Harvard University, Boston, MA 02163)
> Instructions for establishing a planning and accounting system for nonprofit organizations which will allow them to have better control over the expenditures of money, materials, and person-power.

Nonprofit Management Association. *Financial Management of Nonprofit Organizations*. Los Angeles: Nonprofit Management Association. (1984). 16 pp. + 26 pp. $5.00. (Order from: Nonprofit Management Association, Box 2350, Minneapolis, MN 55402)
> Outline of a day-long seminar on financial management for board members, senior non-accounting staff and financial managers. Highlights the differences between business and the nonprofit environment. Includes articles written for non-accountants.

Olenick, Arnold J., and Philip R. Olenick. *Making the Nonprofit Organization Work: A Financial, Legal, and Tax Guide for Administrators*. Englewood Cliffs, NJ: Institute for Business Planning, Inc. 1983. 416 pp. $59.50. (Order from: Institute for Business Planning, Inc., Englewood Cliffs, NJ 07632)
> Provides a financial management system with key records and forms, sample budgets, financial statements and legal safeguards to satisfy all legal and accounting demands for nonprofit organizations. Illustrates the system using a hypothetical organization.

United Way of America. *Budgeting: A Guide for United Ways and Not-for-Profit Human Service Organizations*. Alexandria, VA: United Way of America. 1975. 55 pp. $10.00. (Order from: United Way of America, 810 N. Fairfax St., Alexandria, VA 22314)
> Presents details on the techniques and processes of budgeting. Includes a number of tools for carrying out this process in nonprofit organizations.

Vinter, Robert D., and Rhea K. Kish. *Budgeting for Not-for-Profit Organizations*. Macmillan Free Press. 1984. 390 pp. $22.95. (Order from: Macmillan Free Press, 866 Third Ave., New York, NY 10022)

GENERAL FURTHER READINGS FOR SECTION 1

Flanagan, Joan. *The Successful Volunteer Organization: Getting Started and Getting Results in Nonprofit, Charitable, Grass Roots, and Community Groups*. Chicago: Contemporary Books, Inc. 1981. 376 pp. $13.95 (Order from: Contemporary Books, Inc., 180 N. Michigan Ave., Chicago, IL 60601)

How-to manual for volunteer organizations discusses getting started, getting results, getting organized, and getting advice. Principles for strengthening organizations include how to conduct productive meetings, do fundraising and publicity, and build a stronger membership and board of directors. Includes an annotated bibliography.

Gray, Sandra Trice. *Resource Directory of Education and Training Opportunities and Other Services*. Washington, DC: Independent Sector. 1985. 215 pp. $18.00. (Order from: Independent Sector, 1828 L St., N.W., Washington, DC 20036)

Directory of training programs in nonprofit management including degree programs, workshops, and seminars. Information on program concentrations and objectives; entrance and exit requirements; courses, workshops and seminars offered; salaries, stipends and scholarship awards; locations available to lease for training and meetings.

National Center for Charitable Statistics. *Non-Profit Service Organizations: 1982*. Washington, DC: National Center for Charitable Statistics. 1985. 276 pp. $25.00. (Order from: National Center for Charitable Statistics, 1828 L Street, N.W., Washington, DC 20036)

Brings together the textual and tabular materials about tax-exempt service organizations as compiled in the 1982 Census of Service Industries done by the U.S. Bureau of the Census. Includes data for the whole United States as well as for each state.

Powell, Walter W. *The Nonprofit Sector: A Research Handbook*. New Haven, CT: Yale University Press. Anticipated publication Spring 1987. Approx. 1450 pp. Estimated cost $60.00. (Order from: Yale University Press, 92A Yale Station, New Haven, CT 06520)

Collection of articles on the political, economic, sociological, legal, policy, and business aspects of nonprofit organizations of all types, both in the U.S. and abroad.

Zaltman, G., ed. *Management Principles for Nonprofit Agencies and Organizations*. New York: AMACOM. 1979. 584 pp. $34.95. (Order from: American Management Association, 135 W. 50th St., New York, NY 10020)

Collection of articles on a variety of management topics such as leadership, human resource management, managing change and problems, strategic planning, information systems, marketing and financial management.

Zehring, John William. *How to Work Smarter—Not Harder*. Cleveland, OH: Third Sector Press. 1986. 1 volume looseleaf. $75.00. (Order from: Third Sector Press, P.O. Box 18044, Cleveland, OH 44118)

Handbook of management tips for development officers. Includes advice on such topics as managing time effectively, hiring and nurturing staff, and using computers.

EXPLORING THE WORLD OF MONEY

CHAPTER 6

THE MANY SOURCES OF FUNDING

A shopkeeper just starting out must decide what products and services the store will feature, find an attractive location, put out a sign, and open for business. Revenues result from product sales. If only procedures were as simple for the person running a nonprofit organization!

But they are not. Once an organization decides what services to provide to improve the community's quality of life, it has to figure out how to underwrite those services financially. In other words, the services provided by a nonprofit program do not usually produce revenues that will cover the costs of their delivery. There is no profit inherent in providing hot meals to senior citizens. There is no profit inherent in giving the public an opportunity to explore a wilderness area. (The exceptions to this premise, are discussed in Chapter 12.)

As a result, nonprofit "shopkeepers" must ready their wares (programs), and then find philanthropic sources to make them available to the public. These sources are institutions and individuals who are motivated by a sense of *philanthropy*, which is defined in the *American Heritage Desk Dictionary* as "the effort or desire to increase the well-being of mankind, as by charitable aid or donations." Philanthropy's roots lie in the ancient traditions of charity that date back three thousand years, *charity* being defined as particular concern for the individual.

In recent years, the word *charity* has often been replaced by *philanthropy* to reflect an interest not only in the welfare of the individual but in the larger community as a whole—neighborhood, community, town, city, nation, and world. Whereas in the past an act of charity was best exemplified by giving alms to the beggar, today an act of philanthropy is to help many people, usually through the work of a nonprofit organization.

The philanthropic instinct pervades modern America, as evidenced by the vast numbers of individuals and institutions that support nonprofit initiatives. Individuals extend their support in myriad ways: at home, through direct mail as well as through telethons and door-to-door canvasing. They give at their offices through workplace solicitation and payroll deductions. They give in their communities through special events and by purchasing goods and services from nonprofits, ranging from gifts, cards, and theater tickets to school tuition and hospital care.

Institutions that lend assistance to nonprofits run the gamut from local, state, and federal governments to foundations to businesses and corporations to religious institutions. Additionally, thousands of local and national associations, usually nonprofit themselves, also extend some kind of aid to charitable and philanthropic undertakings.

The mere existence in this country of thousands of nonprofit organizations illustrates the breadth and depth of American philanthropic traditions.

Tapping these philanthropic resources is the continuous assignment of those who must pursue dollars to finance their nonprofit activity—a process popularly referred to as fundraising.

Fundraising might appear to some like charting unknown waters or, at best, like a lot of hard, often thankless, labor that may or may not lead to success. It need not be either aimless or fruitless. Wisdom gleaned from the experience of others in the nonprofit world provides us with guidance and counsel. Nonprofit leaders who have too little time, too much to do, and too few other people to help out can draw some comfort from the shared experiences of their predecessors and their contemporaries in the nonprofit sector.

The first principle to keep in mind is that successful fundraising requires careful forethought and adequate planning. Some of the exciting and innovative ventures of the 1960s and 1970s did not make it into the 1980s—because they did not plan beyond the major government grants that they enjoyed in those early years. In the 1990s, perhaps more than ever before, the world of non-profit financing is vast and complex, requiring more careful advance preparation and follow-up.

Wise money-seekers quickly learn to diversify by seeking funds from several sources. This is the next most important principle. Imagine your funding as a multilegged stool. If one leg is removed, the stool will continue to stand. In the same sense, that's how the funding base of your organization should be. Each leg represents a different major source of revenue for your organization. If, for any reason, one source ceases to exist, your organization will become slightly handicapped, but it will still be able to persevere on the basis of income from the remaining sources.

Thus, an organization totally dependent on federal grants and contracts for its revenues is extremely vulnerable. The group that receives support from foundations, a federated fundraising body, and a pool of individuals, in addition to the federal government, is clearly stronger and more secure. In 1869 the Metropolitan Museum of Art turned to New York City's wealthy citizens for support; today, the Museum's leadership turns also to the local, state, and federal government, corporations, foundations, as well as to large numbers of individuals. Today, diversification is vital. You cannot hope to finance your work successfully from any one source, for even if you do succeed in obtaining that one large elusive grant, your future will be insecure.

Where does the uninitiated as well as the veteran fundraiser begin?

Most simply, you must acquaint yourself with the entire array of philanthropic resources available, so that you can select those sources most appropriate to your own organization. By reviewing the chapters in this section and completing the worksheets at the conclusion of each chapter, you can pinpoint those funding sources that are most likely to extend support to your organization. Remember that it is highly unlikely that every available source is suited for your efforts. You need to choose your "best bets." This is the focus of Section 2. You will then be able to proceed to Section 3, where you will narrow down your list to those funders that will constitute your particular funding "mix." Then you will be able to map out your fundraising plan of action.

INDIVIDUALS

American philanthropy can trace its origins to individuals rather than to governments, businesses, or foundations. Our "founding" philanthropists were individuals such as Benjamin Franklin, whose generosity led to the creation of several of Philadelphia's earliest nonprofit institutions. Even in colonial times, however, charitable giving was common among individuals from all walks of life, not the exclusive province of the wealthy.

This tradition predates, of course, American colonial history. During the Middle Ages, Europe's greatest cathedrals were built not only through the largesse of kings, queens, and other nobility but also through the charity of the tradespeople and artisans of the time. The famed Gothic cathedral in Chartres, France, can thank various merchant and guild associations, including bakers, carpenters, weavers, shoemakers, butchers, masons, fishmongers, furriers, and others for the funds that helped create many of its breathtaking stained glass windows.

Today, individuals are actually the biggest source of nonprofit philanthropic funding. They regularly provide over 80 percent of all philanthropic gifts in a given year. In 1985, for example, individuals contributed $66,060,000,000 in direct donations and $5,180,000,000 in bequests to nonprofit organizations, given year. In 1987, for example, individuals contributed $76,820,000,000 in direct donations and $5,980,000,000 in bequests to nonprofit organizations, according to estimates made by the American Association of Fund-Raising Counsel, Inc. This averages more than $300 for every man, woman, and child in the United States. Contrary to a popular notion, half of all charitable dollars come from families with yearly incomes below $25,000, and people with incomes under $10,000 contribute about three times more of their income than do people with incomes of $50,000 to $100,000, according to "Origins, Dimensions and Impact of America's Voluntary Spirit," by Brian O'Connell.

America's philanthropists today are each and every one of us. Whether we are responding to a direct mail solicitation or attending a special event, our dollars are making nonprofit endeavors possible.

What may distinguish individual philanthropy today from that of previous eras is that its depth and variety are unmatched. Never before have nonprofit leaders been more creative in their approaches to individuals. Some of the more popular current methods that nonprofits use to approach individuals for support are discussed in Chapters 8 through 12.

FOUNDATIONS

Foundations are relatively recent arrivals on the philanthropic scene. The modern foundation can trace its origins to the late nineteenth century, when industrialists such as John D. Rockefeller and Andrew Carnegie established foundations to distribute portions of their huge fortunes for charitable purposes.

The purpose of a foundation is to make grants and contributions to other nonprofit organizations. While some have been created through the gifts of one wealthy individual or family, others, like community foundations and certain public charities, receive their income from a number of different individuals and families. Additionally, some corporations choose to create foundations to distribute some of their profits to charitable causes.

The assets of individual foundations may be impressive, but their collective annual grantmaking usually represents less than 7 percent of all philanthropic giving in any particular year. Currently, there are more than 24,000 foundations in the United States, ranging in size from small, unstaffed local foundations to large, professionally staffed ones. In recent years, there has been a growth in non-endowed grantmaking institutions. They are legally defined as public charities and usually derive their income from a large number of individuals. Examples of these include the Ms. Foundation for Women, which supports grassroots women's groups; the Film Fund, which funds social issue media; and the Funding Exchange, which makes grants to social change initiatives.

As a result of federal government cutbacks in social programs in the 1980s, foundations are receiving a greater volume of requests than ever before. Since their grantmaking budgets do not usually increase significantly from year to year, their ability to respond to new inquiries is severely curtailed. In response to this problem, more and more foundations are looking for creative ways to increase the impact of their dollars. Some make challenge or matching grants, which have to be matched by other sources. Others provide supporting programs to enhance a group's fundraising capability, such as funds for direct mail efforts or for computerization.

Chapter 13 offers more information on how foundations operate and on how to approach them effectively for support.

BUSINESSES AND CORPORATIONS

It is a given today that the business sector, from the neighborhood mom-and-pop store to the giant corporation, are supporters of nonprofit organizations. Local merchants have probably always played a role in enhancing the quality of life in their surrounding communities, but corporations are relative newcomers to the philanthropic scene. Corporate giving in the United States started in the late 1800s, when the railroads began their long association with the Young Men's Christian Association. As the railroads expanded westward, there arose the need for inexpensive and temporary housing for the employees. To meet that need, the railroad companies helped build "railroad YMCAs." Hence, from its very beginning, commerce found that it could serve its own interest through charitable activities.

Today, corporate giving rivals foundation giving in total size, exceeding $4.5 billion in 1987, according to *Giving USA*, published by the Conference Board, a business research organization. In 1977, according to *A Profile of Corporate Contributions*, by Hayden Smith, a total of 525,122 corporations made charitable contributions in the United States. This figure is based on information provided by the Internal Revenue Service.

What distinguishes corporate philanthropy is the extensive variety of ways that businesses can assist nonprofits, aside from cash grants and contributions. Companies, especially large ones, have vast human and material resources that they can make available to groups. A neighborhood store can place a canister next to its cash register to collect contributions, put flyers and posters in its window, and sponsor a special event. In New York City, the Third Avenue Merchants' Association (TAMA), whose members line Third Avenue in Manhattan from 14th to 34th Streets, have donated part of the proceeds from their annual street fair to community projects for each of the past ten years. Corporations can donate materials, office equipment, and products; provide free quality printing of newsletters, ad books, annual reports, raffle tickets, and other promotional materials; and serve as a source of volunteers. They can directly promote nonprofit activities through joint promotions. As long as there is interest, businesses and nonprofits can work together in boundless ways.

Just as foundations cannot accommodate the increased volume in requests they have received as a result of federal government cutbacks, neither can corporations. Corporate giving has steadily risen in the 1980s, but nowhere near enough to respond to a large percentage of the requests they regularly receive. As a result, nonprofits are well advised to explore also non-cash support from business, as well as to develop creative projects in which they can work collaboratively with businesses.

Chapter 14 provides further insights into corporate philanthropy, and on how nonprofits can succeed in securing business support.

GOVERNMENT

Government's responsibility for promoting social welfare in the United States has progressed a great deal since the nineteenth century, when care for the destitute was not always seen as part of government's mandate. Many of today's civic functions, such as fire departments and libraries, were previously operated by nonprofit associations rather than by a governmental body, and some even continue to be. In many cases, nonprofits have been the trailblazers for later government involvement. Even as well known a program as the Peace Corps took its philosophy from nonprofit precursors like Operation Crossroads Africa, which continues to send college students to African countries each summer to work on development projects.

Today local, state, and federal government are well-entrenched partners with the nonprofit sector in protecting and promoting the well-being of its citizens. That alliance remains intact despite the Reagan administration's efforts to shift some of this responsibility from the federal government, but this relationship has been severely strained by the passage of the Gramm-Rudman-Hollings Act in 1986. The budget cuts dictated by this legislation raise new difficulties for nonprofits. Not only do they have to seek out new revenues to compensate for lost federal dollars, but they also have to respond to the increasing needs for assistance from those constituencies affected by the cutbacks.

However, in spite of these reductions in federal support, all units of government will continue to look regularly to the nonprofit sector for services in a variety of fields, including social services, health, housing, education, the arts and humanities, and employment, to name a few.

It is hard to calculate the total sum of annual financial support that government provides to nonprofits through grants and contracts. New York City alone awards over one billion dollars annually in grants and contracts to nonprofits to perform services for New Yorkers. Given the immense resources of government, suffice it to say that it is the largest underwriter of nonprofit endeavors in general. It is common for governmental units actually to "contract" for services with nonprofit entities. A contract involves a much more clearly defined relationship between two parties than does a grant. In contracting, government seeks agencies to carry out services that it has decided merit rendering.

Probably no other segment of nonprofit financing will continue to undergo so much change in the near future as government. Conservative pressures for cutbacks in social spending will continue to wreak havoc on the established system of governmental responsibility for human services that reached its peak in the 1970s. However, government will continue in the directions that were clearly established over fifty years ago during the Great Depression. Whatever realignment occurs between federal, state, and local units of government in the future will still leave intact government's preeminent role in financing nonprofit providers of human services.

See Chapter 15 for more information on government support and on how groups can secure such assistance.

RELIGIOUS INSTITUTIONS

Close to 50 percent of the charitable dollars donated each year by individuals goes to religious bodies and their related institutions and agencies. Organized religion has served as the transmitter of charitable traditions from one generation to the next. And it is religion that provides some of the moral imperatives behind charity and philanthropy.

It is hard to estimate how much financial support religious structures in turn provide to other nonprofit initiatives, but some of the evidence is impressive. For example, each year the Campaign for Human Development of the United States Catholic Conference gives out grants exceeding six million dollars to social change and economic development projects nationwide. Religious bodies, from the local parish to the national governing body, provide a range of resources extending beyond the financial, including office and meeting space, volunteers, and advocacy support, among others.

Giving, of course, is not the province of any one particular religion. It pervades all religions and is expressed in many different ways. Some religious groups prefer to establish their own nonprofit organizations, while others prefer to make grants to other nonprofit entities. Some may actually undertake both roles—direct provider of service as well as grantmaker.

Today, when foundations and corporations are experiencing greater demands for aid and when the federal government is drastically cutting back its social welfare expenditures, religious funding is becoming more visible and appreciated for its breadth and purpose.

Chapter 16 guides the reader through the world of religious philanthropy and provides suggestions on how to work most effectively with religious bodies.

FEDERATED FUNDRAISING ORGANIZATIONS

Federated fundraising organizations are nonprofits that are usually organized along geographic or constituency or issue lines for the purpose of raising funds from the general public and distributing them to designated nonprofits. Preeminently, they organize annual fundraising campaigns in the workplace to solicit contributions from employees in the form of payroll deductions at regular intervals. Thus, individuals stretch their contributions over fifty-two weeks, which often enables them to consider larger gifts than they would if they wrote one single check. This is the simple ingredient behind much of the success of federated fundraising.

Federated fundraising was once associated exclusively with one term: the community chest. While United Way, today's successor to the community chest, still dominates the field, there are increasing newcomers to the field each year.

In local communities across the country, nonprofits have discovered that they can maximize their fundraising potential by banding together in some form of fundraising coalition. This phenomenon has led to the creation of more than 100 "alternative" funds that embrace women's and minority issues, housing, health care, the arts, neighborhood development, the environment, and other areas of nonprofit concern.

Revenues raised by federated fundraising organizations show it to be a very lucrative approach. In 1988, the United Way of America reported pledges of $2.78 billion to its 2300 autonomous locals across the country. Thirty-eight alternative funds, according to the National Committee for Responsive Philanthropy, raised a projected $22 million in 1988. The bulk of these funds are then distributed as grants to local nonprofits. In the years to come, more nonprofits will be knocking on the doors of their local United Ways, while others will be joining their counterparts in the establishment of new fundraising federations in their communities.

For more information on federated fundraising organizations, turn to Chapter 17.

ASSOCIATIONS OF INDIVIDUALS

Individual desire for community with others often expresses itself in the form of associations. People with like-minded interests band together to work for a common good. Today, more than 40,000 such formal bodies exist. Additionally, there are countless numbers of local grassroots self-help groups. As Mark Twain once noted, "when two Americans meet on a street corner, an organization is bound to be started."

While the prime motivating force behind such efforts is not necessarily philanthropic, it is quite common for associations to embrace some charitable activity as part of their mandate. They may choose to administer such activities themselves, or to work in partnership with other nonprofit organizations. The Junior League is an example of an association that does both. Local service clubs, such as the Lions, Rotary, or Soroptomists, often organize special events to benefit local charities.

Associations can be a prime source of volunteers, and also serve as partners in advocacy programs. Some groups, such as the League of Women Voters, have been active in issues like voter registration and international affairs for a long time.

There is no end to the list of efforts undertaken by associations toward higher goals. The key for the nonprofit is to explore which associations might share their concerns and to be willing to act together with them on some issue or activity. During the current period of increased competition for financial support, nonprofit organizations can enhance their success rate by demonstrating the support of associations in their communities.

Chapter 18 presents the world of associations in greater detail and describes how nonprofits can seek their support.

SUMMARY

Sound fundraising involves reviewing all potential revenue sources and subsequently selecting those appropriate for a particular nonprofit undertaking.

Make choices strategically. In the search for funds, you can inadvertently begin in any of a number of places; however your time and available energies are limited, so you need to decide in advance how you can make the best use of your resources. Once you have selected the mix of revenue sources that is most suited to your work, you will be able to develop a fundraising strategy and plan to guide you.

The chapters in this section detail the range of financial resources available to nonprofits and aid you in selecting those most appropriate for you to approach. Complete the worksheets at the end of each chapter. Then, you can proceed confidently to Section 3, where you will be able to develop a fundraising plan suited to your chosen mix of funding partners.

Part A
APPROACHING INDIVIDUALS FOR SUPPORT

CHAPTER 7

APPROACHING INDIVIDUALS FOR SUPPORT

GIVING FROM INDIVIDUALS: AN OVERVIEW

Individual donors are persons or families who give to organizations of their choice for personal reasons. They represent no group or institution, only themselves. Individuals consistently provide the greatest percentage of the charitable dollar to nonprofits each year. In 1987, for example, individuals gave $76.82 billion to nonprofit organizations, accounting for 82 percent of all charitable contributions that year, according to *Giving USA, 1987 Annual Report.*

According to a Gallup survey conducted in 1982 at the behest of Independent Sector, National Society for Fund Raising Executives, and the 501(c)(3) Group, 86 percent of all Americans reported making a charitable contribution in 1981. That suggests that over eight out of every ten Americans, including children, were philanthropists that year.

Equally impressive is the data on the income of these donors. "Lords and Ladies Bountiful" still do exist (as evidenced by a gift in 1982 of $1.3 billion by J. Paul Getty to the museum bearing his name in Los Angeles, California), but all the giving isn't by the Gettys of the world. In fact, estimates of giving by households suggest that in 1981, one-third of individual charitable donations came from households with incomes below $20,000, approximately one-half from households with incomes between $20,000 and $50,000, and between 15 and 20 percent from households with incomes greater than $50,000 (*Dimensions of the Independent Sector, A Statistical Profile,* published by Independent Sector,

1984). The following table provides a capsule overview of giving by individuals over an 18-year period.

	Amount (billions)	Personal Income (billions)	Percent of Income
1970 . . .	$16.19	$ 831.8	1.95
1971 . . .	17.64	894.0	1.97
1972 . . .	19.37	981.6	1.97
1973 . . .	20.53	1,101.7	1.86
1974 . . .	21.60	1,210.1	1.79
1975 . . .	23.53	1,313.4	1.79
1976 . . .	26.32	1,451.4	1.81
1977 . . .	29.55	1,607.5	1.84
1978 . . .	32.10	1,812.4	1.77
1979 . . .	36.59	2,034.0	1.80
1980 . . .	40.71	2,258.5	1.80
1981 . . .	46.42	2,520.9	1.84
1982 . . .	48.52	2,670.8	1.82
1983 . . .	53.54	2,838.6	1.89
1984 . . .	58.50	3,108.7	1.88
1985 . . .	65.94	3,327.0	1.98
1986 . . .	72.03	3,534.3	2.04
1987 . . .	76.82	3,745.8	2.05

Reprinted with permission from *Giving USA:* Estimates of Philanthropic Giving in 1987 and the Trends They Show, a publication of the AAFRC Trust for Philanthropy.

As the table demonstrates, giving by individuals is not only substantial, but also is steadily increasing. To give you an idea of how much individuals of varying incomes actually give each year charitably, review the table on *Preliminary Itemized Deductions—1982 Individual Tax Returns*.

Preliminary Itemized Deductions—1982 Individual Tax Returns

Adjusted Gross Income	Medical, Dental	State, Local Taxes	Interest Paid	Charitable Contributions
$ 10,000–$ 12,000	$1,638	$ 1,063	$ 2,589	$ 595
$ 12,000–$ 16,000	1,236	1,263	2,455	753
$ 16,000–$ 20,000	890	1,478	2,549	662
$ 20,000–$ 25,000	909	1,831	2,966	721
$ 25,000–$ 30,000	752	2,058	3,195	732
$ 30,000–$ 40,000	687	2,576	3,596	859
$ 40,000–$ 50,000	843	3,238	4,483	1,149
$ 50,000–$ 75,000	897	4,575	6,242	1,551
$ 75,000–$100,000	972	6,919	8,719	2,523
$100,000–$200,000	1,557	10,120	13,915	4,647

SOURCE: Internal Revenue Service

Individuals extend financial support to nonprofit organizations in a number of ways:

1. They give cash to door-to-door canvassers who are helping out the local volunteer fire department, a public interest campaign, or a health charity.

2. They attend movie premieres, theater parties, dances, dinners, or any of the other numerous special events organized as benefits.

3. They respond to letters (direct mail appeals) and telephone calls (phonathons) that reach them at their homes.

4. They write their favorite organizations into their wills, and even designate them as recipients of their property after their death.

5. They purchase second-hand or homemade clothing or household items at thrift shops, bazaars, tag sales, garage sales, or auctions, and they purchase greeting cards, calendars, cookies, and other products sold by nonprofits. (These methods will be further discussed in Chapter 12.)

Probably no country in the world has been as ingenious as the United States in thinking of ways for its citizens to support its charitable endeavors. The U. S. government also encourages charitable giving by providing individuals with specific tax deductions for their contributions. The current tax laws allow distinct tax benefits to both the small and large giver, although, needless to say, the advantages increase with the size of the gift.

Since 1981, those individuals who do not file itemized income tax returns (over 60 million Americans) had been able to deduct their charitable contributions. The provision of the tax law which made this possible, however, expired at the end of 1986.

WHAT INDUCES AMERICANS TO BE GENEROUS?

There is no one simple answer. People's charitable patterns are as varied as their shopping habits. What is clear is that people derive considerable satisfaction from participating in this strictly voluntary activity, one, moreover, that does not pertain directly to their own basic needs for food, clothing, and shelter. Sheer altruism may well be a good part of what motivates individuals' charitable actions, but common sense suggests there is more. Individuals can receive many benefits in exchange for their charitable contributions: recognition, a sense of belonging, personal satisfaction, self-esteem, appreciation, as well as whatever concrete benefits the recipient organization might offer in return, such as gifts, membership benefits, and opportunities to attend special events.

Let's first examine why individuals are moved to become philanthropists. Remember, too, that the struggling low-income family that manages to give away a Thanksgiving turkey to a less fortunate family is as philanthropic as J. Paul Getty.

Values and Benefits

Primarily, individuals are motivated in daily actions by their own value systems, which usually emerge directly from their own life experiences. If you encountered discrimination as a result of your minority group status, you know too well the personal costs of bigotry and may be motivated to do something to make life easier for others who do and will face similar situations. If you grew up in a poor neighborhood that offered few opportunities for exposure to knowledge and yet you managed to enrich your life at the local library, you will probably never forget how valuable an education that library provided. That experience is precisely what moved Andrew Carnegie in the 1800s to give away millions to the founding of libraries throughout the land. Similarly, if you experienced the loss or disability of a loved one as the result of a disease, you have become tragically familiar with that pain. You may come to value life and health more and thus be moved to support organizations that work to reduce the incidence of the particular affliction that you witnessed, with all its accompanying pain.

Not surprisingly, these same experiences, values, and beliefs are what moved the founders of organizations to create them. Some health charities in the United States were begun by individuals who had directly suffered in their lives from the disease, and they then set out determined to cure it. One of the more famous examples, of course, is the founding of the March of Dimes, then known as the National Foundation for Infantile Paralysis, by Franklin D. Roosevelt, himself a victim of polio in 1938.

Sense of Community

The America of the past, consisting of a series of geographically prescribed communities, offered everyone a sense of status as a member of a specific community. You knew all your neighbors and saw many of them in your daily life. Many small towns in America still enjoy these connections.

For most of this country's residents, however, a sense of belonging comes less easily. Life in crowded urban centers or sprawling suburbs cannot provide a feeling of relatedness. In these settings, that natural yearning to belong may be satisfied through voluntary association with any one of countless organizations, ranging from block clubs, tenant groups, co-ops, social groupings, adult educational programs, self-help efforts, and many other organizational forms that are generally nonprofit. In addition, local and national organizations that speak out on issues ranging from the equality of women to the protection of civil liberties to saving the whales provide a means for like-minded people to seek each other out for friendship and camaraderie. By attending the local symphony or ballet, you often meet others who share your passion for the arts. This same dynamic supplies the fuel for many fundraising special events.

Sense of Personal Worth

People need self-esteem. Yet, contemporary life can too frequently rob individuals of that precious commodity. Too often, the workplace does not reinforce a sense of worth but, instead, devalues individuals through the tedium of the work and a sense that they are readily interchangeable. As a result, people look elsewhere for the recognition that can nurture and challenge them. Sometimes, too, people become stymied in their struggle for leadership on the job and, consciously or not, seek other arenas where their efforts might be appreciated.

People may enjoy material success as a result of their work, but still feel somewhat inadequate, unappreciated, or alone. In these instances, one might look toward philanthropy and offer oneself as a volunteer, a board member, or a donor, hoping to receive recognition and validation from peers.

Posterity

Few of us get the chance to have a building named after us. Nonetheless, the motivation that inspires a millionaire to endow a wing of a hospital abides within us all. Just as parents often see their children as extensions of themselves into the future, individuals are moved to make contributions—with or without personal recognition— to the causes and organizations that most touch their own lives. It is their stake in the future. Such wishes undoubtedly influenced those who left a total of $5.98 billion in bequests in 1987—contributions that may represent a grasp at immortality.

Sheer Fun and Pleasure

For many people, donating, volunteering, and attending fundraising events gives them some pleasure in life. Attending a gala movie premiere or a theater party or a walkathon is fun. If they weren't, these events would cease to attract the large numbers of people they do each year.

Feeling Good

If there weren't donors, there wouldn't be beggars. How many times have you seen someone smile in satisfaction after giving some coins to the perennial Santa Claus in front of department stores at Christmas time? The donor was probably moved by long-stored memories into a reflexive behavior, enabling him or her to walk away feeling a little bit better through a very small gesture.

Affirmation of values and beliefs, community, personal worth, posterity, fun, and feeling good—with so many possible benefits, it is no mystery that so many people behave philanthropically each year. A fundraiser once told about how he'd asked a wealthy prospect for a gift. In reply, the donor-to-be first expressed that he felt it was an honor to be asked.

Add to this list the factors that ring true to you and others around you. You should be able to gain a sense of what will motivate others to be generous.

CAN ANY NONPROFIT ORGANIZATION SUCCESSFULLY RAISE MONEY FROM INDIVIDUALS?

Certainly. Of course, the number of potential prospects will vary greatly, depending on the identity of the asking organization. For example, groups working to rebuild the South Bronx in New York City into a viable and economically sound community had limited attraction to those living outside New York City. It was President Carter's dramatic visit that turned the South Bronx into a symbol of urban decay throughout America;   then things changed. The South Bronx became a rallying cry for everyone in the nation who was committed to stemming the decline of our cities' older sections and to providing equal economic opportunity to this country's low-income and minority citizens. Overnight, the number of potential contributors to South Bronx redevelopment efforts skyrocketed.

IDENTIFYING YOUR OWN INDIVIDUAL SUPPORT BASE

Each organization has its own universe of potential contributors to approach for donations. The ability to secure dollars successfully from them is dependent upon a number of factors, including people power, time, promotional materials, and the money to pay for the expenses involved in making solicitations. But let's put those considerations aside now, however briefly, and proceed to identify our supporters.

Tom Boyd, a trainer and consultant to nonprofits based in New York City, offers a very useful tool in this regard. It's the "concentric circles" model. Assemble a core group of your organization (board of directors, steering committee, fundraising committee, staff, etc.), and ask them to brainstorm a list of potential individual constituencies who would be willing to extend support to your organization if approached. One way to elicit the needed response is to ask those assembled the following question: Which individual constituencies are the most committed to our organization's purposes and goals?

In answering this question, you will be listing categories of individuals as well as perhaps particular people. Let everyone in your group contribute suggestions before you stop. Then organize the responses. Take a compass, and on a piece of poster-size paper or a blackboard draw one large circle and then three circles within that circle, all emanating from the same point (see worksheet for this chapter).

In your first circle, the bull's-eye, list individuals who have the *greatest stake* in the success of your undertaking. Who are your most likely supporters? First, those whom your work will most directly benefit. They understand the value of your work, for they are its direct recipients. Some, to be sure, may not be able to make large donations, but we are not talking about the size of gifts yet. Simply start with your own constituents, whoever they may be.

Are there other candidates for the first circle? Well, yes, we forgot ourselves. How can we ask our friends to contribute to something that we don't already give to? Add the members of your board of directors, your volunteers, and even your staff. Again, the amount of expected contributions is not important yet, but the principle is.

If you are running a day-care center, you know that all of the parents using your facility are likely to make contributions. How about their older sons and daughters? Don't they benefit from the existence of your center by being freed from the responsibilities of child care? How about the children's grandparents? Don't they also appreciate that their grandchildren are receiving quality care when their own son or daughter is at work? These three constituents are good candidates for the first circle of contributors to your day-care center. Let's define those who were selected for the first circle as your *internal constituency*. They are really the insiders of your organization.

Everyone in the first circle has a direct self-interest in the success of your effort. In making choices for the second circle, select those constituencies already known to this internal constituency—that is, friends, colleagues, and acquaintances.

A new theater group for example, when trying to get off the ground, realized that the personal friends of all the actors, directors, and others involved in the venture were likely supporters. They amassed the Christmas and holiday mailing lists of the members of their organizing committee, developing a mailing list of 2,700 names. Then, their members wrote personalized notes with each appeal letter. They netted $15,000 in contributions! Begin to place in the second circle individuals and constituencies who are kindred souls. Ask yourselves, "Who do we know who has an interest in our work?"

Once you've exhausted choosing candidates for your second circle, turn to those individuals with whom you do not have existing or prior personal contact, but whom you presume would be responsive. Let's call these people your *prospective supporters*, and place them in the third circle.

For example, when Mothers Against Drunk Driving (MADD) first formed in Fair Oaks, California, the founders knew that they could appeal not only to mothers who had lost a child in an alcohol-related accident in their own community but to mothers throughout the country who had experienced or could experience a similar loss.

If you are establishing a mothers' center, for example, which helps new mothers raise their infants, you might add to your third circle local pediatricians, nurses, social workers, family counselors, and others whose professional lives bear on your work's activities. The third circle will help you begin to make generalizations about the types of individuals who might be receptive to your cause. If you've found that you had a significant number of pediatricians on your list, you may want to target all the pediatricians in your community as prospects. Continue to ask yourselves, "What other categories of people might respond to a request for contributions?" This is a good opportunity to brainstorm; consider all possibilities, even if at first they seem remote.

Finally, ask yourself which individuals or categories of individuals that have not yet surfaced through this exercise might respond to a request. Again, using the mothers' center as a model, how about senior citizens or even single people who enjoy children? Clearly, these two groups are not the likeliest prospects nor are they particularly easy to identify, but still they are prospects.

By completing this exercise with other members of your group, you can begin to identify individuals and types of individuals who are your most likely contributors.

Worksheet

for

_____

(name of your organization)

APPROACHING INDIVIDUALS FOR SUPPORT

1. Building on Individual Support to Date

a. Have any individuals ever supported your work in the past?

☐ yes   ☐ no

b. If yes, how many?

_____

c. What characteristics do these individuals share? How do their interests correspond to each other?

Comments:

_____

_____

_____

_____

d. What is _your_ sense of what they valued in your organization's work?

Comments:

_____

_____

_____

_____

e. How did you approach them for financial support in the past? Check appropriate boxes.

☐ Face-to-face solicitation   ☐ Planned giving
☐ Direct mail   ☐ Earned or venture income projects
☐ Special events   ☐ Other

2. Targeting Your Prospective Individual Supporters

Complete the accompanying "concentric circles" chart to target your own individual prospects. Remember that you should fill in the circles in the following manner:

First Circle—your most likely contributors (your internal constituency: members of the board of directors, clients, current donors and members, staff, volunteers, etc.).

Second Circle—other individuals you know who have a direct self-interest in the success of your efforts (friends, colleagues, acquaintances).

Third Circle—prospective supporters who are new to you.

Fourth Circle—remaining individuals and categories of individuals who conceivably would respond positively to a request from your organization. Pay particular attention here to unusual possibilities that may not have occurred to you initially.

3. Making the Match

For the previously identified constituencies, complete the following exercises (use your own blank paper).

a. Write whatever thoughts immediately come to mind about why X individual or constituency would be interested in supporting your work.

b. Develop one or two sentences relating your work to the interests of the individuals you are approaching.

4. Assessing Potential Individual Support

On the basis of what you have determined, how would you rank your chances of securing support from individuals?

☐ Very Good   ☐ Possible   ☐ Unlikely   ☐ Still Unknown

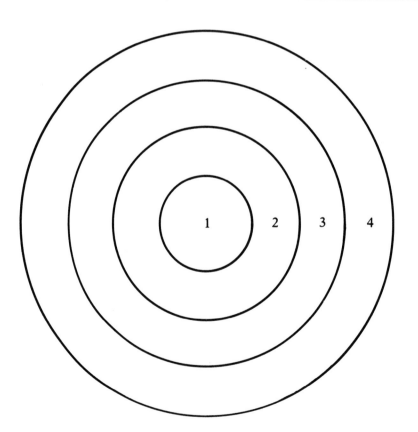

FURTHER READINGS

American Association of Fund-Raising Counsel, Inc. *Giving USA: Estimates of Philanthropic Giving in 1987 and the Trends They Show.* New York: American Association of Fund-Raising Counsel, Inc. 1988. 135 pp. $5.00. (Order from: American Association of Fund-Raising Counsel, Inc., 25 West 43rd St., New York, NY 10036)

> Annual compilation of facts and trends in private philanthropy. Includes information on sources of philanthropy and categories of philanthropic activity such as hospitals, educational, religious, etc. Numerous charts and tables. (Includes subscription to bimonthly newsletter *Fund-raising Review*.)

Bergen, Helen. *Where the Money Is: A Fund Raiser's Guide to the Rich.* Alexandria, VA: BioGuide Press. 1985. 101 pp. $12.95 plus $1.00 postage. (Order from: BioGuide Press, P.O. Box 16072-M, Alexandria, VA 22302)

> Step-by-step guide for the donor research process to help fundraisers and development officers identify potential wealthy donors in any locale and find relevant biographical information about them.

The Charitable Behavior of Americans: Findings from a National Survey. Washington, DC: Independent Sector. 1986. 54 pp. $14.00. (Order from: Independent Sector, 1828 L St., N.W., Washington, DC 20036)

> Results of a national survey by Yankelovich, Skelly and White commissioned by the Rockefeller Brothers Fund to look at charitable behavior of individuals. Provides details on who gives to whom and how much, including such influences as marital status, educational level, religious activity, etc.

Charitable Gift Planning News. Monthly. Boston, MA: Little, Brown and Company. $80.00/yr. (Order from: Little, Brown and Company, 34 Beacon St., Boston, MA 02106)

> Periodical provides information on all aspects of gift giving for directors of development, tax lawyers and estate planners.

Conrad, Daniel Lynn. *Successful Fund Raising Techniques.* Second Edition. San Francisco: Public Management Institute. 1977. 351 pp. in 3-ring binder. $39.00. (Order from: Public Management Institute, 358 Brannan St., San Francisco, CA 94107)

> Within this book on general fundraising methods is a chapter on donor motivation.

Flanagan, Joan. *The Grass Roots Fundraising Book: How to Raise Money In Your Community.* Chicago: Contemporary Books, Inc. 1982. 344 pp. $11.95 (Order from: Contemporary Books, Inc., 180 N. Michigan Ave., Chicago, IL 60601)

> Classic guide for raising money from interested people in ways that also build the organization.

Grambs, Marya, and Pam Miller. *Dollars and Sense: A Community Fundraising Manual for Women's Shelters and Other Non-Profit Organizations.* San Francisco:

Western States Shelter Network. 1982. 135 pp. $22.00. (Order from: Western States Shelter Network, 870 Market St., Suite 1058, San Francisco, CA 94102)
   Covers a variety of fundraising techniques, but the discussion of attitudes about asking for money is particularly relevant in looking at raising money from individuals.

Hodgkinson, Virginia Ann, and Murray S. Weitzman. *Dimensions of the Independent Sector: A Statistical Profile.* Washington, DC: Independent Sector. 1984. 79 pp. $35.00. (Order from: Independent Sector, 1828 L St., N.W., Washington, DC 20036)
   Section 1 provides an overview of the independent sector including income, types of organizations, etc. Section 2 discusses support and use of resources. Many charts and graphs make the information accessible.

Klein, Kim. *Fundraising for Social Change.* Washington, DC: CRG Press. 1985. 208 pp. $20.00(Order from: Kimberly Klein, 517 Union Ave., Knoxville, TN 37902).
   Strategies to help low-budget organizations (budgets under $500,000) establish, maintain, and expand community-based fundraising programs, particularly in raising money from individuals.

Levin, Nora Jean, and Janet Dempsey Steiger. *To Light One Candle: A Manual for Organizing, Funding and Maintaining Public Service Projects.* 1978. 162 pp. $6.00. (Order from: American Bar Association, Division of Bar Services, 1155 E. 60th St., Chicago, IL 60637)
   While it was written to help state and local bar associations raise money from lawyers, would be useful to any organizations that want to raise money from professionals of high salary.

Lord, Benjamin. *America's Wealthiest People: Their Philanthropic and Nonprofit Affiliations.* Washington, DC: The Taft Group. 1984. 78 pp. $57.50. (Order from: The Taft Group, 5130 MacArthur Blvd., N.W., Washington, DC 20016)
   Biographical profiles of 8,000 people who either give or control a major portion of the $60 billion of private giving. Includes information about their philanthropic connections, nonprofit involvement, corporate affiliation, employment, educational background, birthplace, etc.

Patterns of Charitable Giving by Individuals. II. A Research Report. Washington, DC: Independent Sector. December, 1982. 6 pp. $2.00. (Order from: Independent Sector, 1828 L St., N.W., Washington, DC 20036)
   Summary of the results of a survey conducted by The Gallup Organization for the Independent Sector to look at the giving patterns of Americans. Copies of the full survey, *Survey of the Public's Recollection of 1981 Charitable Donations*, is available from the Independent Sector for $15.00.

Social Register. New York: Social Register Association. Two times a yr. Approx. 990 pp. $75.00 (1986). (Order from: Social Register Association, 381 Park Ave. South, New York, NY 10016)

Information on the prominent older families in the United States including address, names of clubs, colleges, etc.

Standard and Poor. *Poor's Register of Corporations, Directors and Executives.* New York: Standard and Poor's Corporation. Annual. Approximately 2660 pp. in vol. 1; 1485 pp. in vol. 2; 1110 pp. in vol. 3. $140.00. (Order from: Standard and Poor's Corporation, 25 Broadway, New York, NY 10004)

Volume 1 alphabetically lists approximately 45,000 corporations with the names, titles, and functions of officers, directors, and other principles. Volume 2 alphabetically lists 72,000 individuals with their business affiliations, titles, business and residential addresses plus such information as place of birth, college, and memberships. Volume 3 is a series of indexes to the first two volumes including those by geography, family, and industrial classification.

Taft Group, The. *People in Philanthropy: A Guide to Philanthropic Leaders and Funding Connections.* Washington, DC: The Taft Group. 1984. 361 pp. $187.00. (Order from: The Taft Group, 5130 MacArthur Blvd., N.W., Washington, DC 20016)

Profiles of over 500 of America's richest people with biographical data as well as information on their philanthropic activities.

"Tips on Charitable Giving: How to Give But Give Wisely." Arlington, VA: Council of Better Business Bureaus, Inc. 1982. Free. (Order from: Council of Better Business Bureaus, Inc., 1515 Wilson Blvd., Arlington, VA 22209)

Small pamphlet with information for potential donors on how to give wisely provides useful tips for soliciting organizations on how to approach donors effectively.

"Tips on Tax Deductions for Charitable Contributions." Arlington, VA: Council of Better Business Bureaus, Inc. 1982. Free. (Order from: Council of Better Business Bureaus, Inc., 1515 Wilson Blvd., Arlington, VA 22209)

Small pamphlet provides information for taxpayers on the laws covering tax deductions for charitable contributions. Helpful for organizations who may want to use tax incentives in soliciting contributions from individuals.

Who's Who in America. 43rd Edition. Chicago: Marquis Who's Who, Inc. 1984–1985. 3627 pp. in 2 volumes. $265.00 plus shipping. (Order from: Marquis Who's Who, Macmillan Directory Division, 3002 Glenview Rd., Wilmette, IL 60091.)

Biographical data on approximately 77,000 prominent Americans. Often includes both home and business addresses.

CHAPTER 8

APPROACHING INDIVIDUALS FOR SUPPORT

FACE-TO-FACE SOLICITATION

Face-to-face solicitation—meeting potential contributors in person and asking them for money—is the most effective way to enlist support from people outside an organization as contributors, volunteers, or both. No soliciting attempt works as persuasively as the personal visit or meeting. Sending an appeal through the mail is secondarily effective, compared with the one-to-one, in-person contact. The maxim in fundraising from individuals is clear: the more personal the contact, the more likely a positive response. This principle remains as true for the trustee of the local museum who pays a visit to a wealthy patron as for the public interest canvasser who knocks on all the doors in a neighborhood.

HOW DOES FACE-TO-FACE SOLICITATION WORK?

Remember "Trick or Treat for UNICEF"? And the original March of Dimes during the 1950s, for which mothers scoured neighborhoods on a door-to-door basis to solicit contributions? The stereotype for this kind of fundraising is usually the arts patron and the humble trustee at the doorstep, but the fact is that Americans of all ages and all walks of life at one time or another participate, in person, in asking someone else to give to a charitable organization. Similarly, nonprofit organizations of all shapes and sizes engage in some form of personal solicitation.

As mentioned earlier, individuals gave $66 billion in 1985 to nonprofit organizations. If personal, face-to-face solicitation is the most effective way to net results, we can only presume that a healthy percentage of that total comes about in that fashion.

It sounds simple—it *is* relatively simple—yet, to be honest with ourselves, we must face up to the built-in reluctance we frequently feel when asking friends or strangers for a contribution of money, whatever the cause.

Understandably, your resources in time and in money are limited, and you will need to set some priorities.

To begin, look at the results of your "circle exercise" (see Chapter 7) and count the number of people you listed in your first circle. At the same time, keep in mind your own group's resources, such as how many people can actually be counted on to knock on doors or call on others to make contributions (your "askers"). If you identified 50 individuals in your first circle and also have 10 volunteers willing to be "askers," then it is realistic to think that each of those 50 might be personally approached.

If you identify lawyers as strong prospects in your third circle, you would immediately want to ascertain how many lawyers live or work in your community. If you find that they number in the thousands, perhaps from reviewing the local bar association directory, you might decide to approach them through a direct mail appeal rather than face-to-face. Or you might seek an opportunity to address a local meeting of lawyers to lay the groundwork for a later appeal by mail. (See Chapter 18 for more information on approaching associations for support.)

It's vital to remember our first guiding principle: the more personal, the more successful. If you are approaching your personal friends and acquaintances, you will more than likely net favorable responses to an appeal. This is one of the primary reasons for the success of walkathons, runathons, bikeathons, and the like. Because the participants in these events are sponsored by friends and family, the event is more likely to raise money than would an event without that personal connection.

Our second guiding principle flows from the first: People are likelier to give to individuals whom they respect, or with whom they identify, or both. Lawyers respond to other lawyers, to judges, and to others in the legal profession whom they admire. They also respond to individuals associated with organizations they respect. So, even if most local lawyers do not know your name, if, for example, you are an officer of the local chapter of the American Civil Liberties Union, that connection might increase the lawyers' willingness to contribute. This explains why so many organizations list on their letterheads a number of individuals together with their affiliations as sponsors, patrons, or advisers, even though a disclaimer may appear at the end of the list, saying "organizations listed for identification purposes only."

Look at yourself first and ask, "Whom do I respect and look up to in my community?" Is it a local religious leader, an elected official, an artist, a writer?

Your own responses will not be considerably different from those of the people you will be approaching.

You might now recruit some of these local celebrities or influential people to join your efforts, either as askers or sponsors. If a person chooses to become a sponsor, inform other prospective supporters (donors) that "so-and-so" has signed on as a sponsor of your organization, and ask them to consider joining him or her as a member.

Undoubtedly, becoming an "asker" is not always easy. As with almost everything else in life, one learns best by doing. It might help to remember that you are not asking someone merely to give you money; you are asking for help in supporting something you believe in, and that you think they will, as well.

You may prepare yourself in several ways: by role playing different situations with your other askers; by inviting a veteran asker from another organization to talk about asking; and finally, by first asking someone who is a friend. You might even tell your friend that you are practicing. Use a "buddy system"; ask another member of your askers' group to come along, and work as a team. Afterward, you will have the chance to debrief together. Your donor might even give you some valuable feedback on the meeting. Also, don't hesitate to be direct when you are writing the letter or placing the phone call to set up an appointment. Explain why you are seeking the opportunity to meet with the other party; for example: "I am involved with a new organization which is currently doing critically important work. Since I know that you share my interest in ＿＿＿, I would like to get together to tell you what we are doing and to ask for a contribution."

Now for the third guiding principle in individual fundraising: *Know your donor*.

Know why you think each potential donor will be interested in your organization. Jot down some notes before the meeting to remind yourself why you've decided to approach this particular person. It may be no more than the fact that your friend has always shown an active interest in whatever activities you two have shared in the past. Or it may be that you know from your previous social contacts that he or she shares your passion on a certain issue that your new group is now addressing. If so, you'd probably want to allude to this shared interest in your letter or phone call when requesting the meeting.

Do I Ask for a Specific Amount?

The answer is unequivocally yes. Prospective donors should know how much you need. You should tell them.

You might begin by saying, for example, "We need to raise $3,000 by December 1st so that we can rent an office and purchase the supplies we need to open our doors for work. I am giving $100. Would you consider giving a similar amount?"

Remember, people are free to refuse or to ask for some time to make a decision. Be sure to wait thirty seconds for a response. And, whatever the response, at least you've been clear about the specific sum of money your purpose requires.

How do you decide how much to ask for? Obviously, you would decide that in advance by considering not only your needs but what you already know about your prospective supporter. In our society, money is both a complex and a personal matter, as we are reminded every time we go out for dinner with friends. The moment the check arrives, we begin to stumble: Who will pick it up? How is it going to be paid? Frequently a prospective donor needs some help, and you might indicate a number of options and a range of possible gifts. The prospective donor, then, can think within that range and come to a decision.

WHAT ARE THE ADVANTAGES OF RAISING MONEY BY FACE-TO-FACE SOLICITATION?

To repeat, face-to-face solicitation is the most vital key to securing support from people with the means to give it. Learning how to engage others successfully in lively discussions of your work, endeavoring to win them over as supporters, paves the way for your organization to become a potential recipient of both small and large donations. More often than not, the return for your efforts will more than compensate for the time and energy expended.

If you need to enlist the support of a large number of people—as contributors, petition signers, leafleters, and so on—personalized approaches, whether through tabling at a busy shopping center or at a well-traveled street intersection, or through a meeting at someone's home, can be very effective. 9 to 5, the national association of working women, undertook an extensive canvassing campaign not only to increase their coffers, but to spread the word, as it were, to folks they normally might not have encountered.

Moreover, these experiences, for many people, may also be the most rewarding, for they involve contact with others.

WHAT ARE THE DISADVANTAGES OF RAISING MONEY BY FACE-TO-FACE SOLICITATION?

1. Identifying prospects, training your volunteer askers, and making appropriate approaches are all tasks that require time and effort. Therefore, your rate of positive return in relation to effort needs to be high.

2. Constancy of effort is mandatory. Personal fundraising requires you to keep your supporters abreast of your work with some regularity, not only when you need money. Success flows from sustaining the relationship between you and the individual donor. The rewards lie in the support that your contributors will continue to provide over the years.

3. Your staff, volunteers, and board members will probably need some training, such as role playing, to be comfortable enough to approach others to ask for contributions and to become successful askers.

HOW DO I DECIDE WHETHER TO TRY
FACE-TO-FACE FUNDRAISING FOR MY ORGANIZATION?

Again, every nonprofit organization, from the smallest to the largest, can learn how to raise funds successfully from individuals face to face. This holds true regardless of the incomes of your constituency, and regardless of whether you choose to canvass a neighborhood rather than to call on wealthy patrons to elicit donations. In either case, you will find that you have a constituency ready to respond to your requests.

To decide whether personal soliciting will prove worthwhile, consider the effort it will take in time and money and the results of past experiences, if any. Your own experience will be your best guide. Beyond that, look at some other considerations in the following list and the summary worksheet at the end of the chapter.

1. Can you demonstrate a real need for individual charitable dollars? If you are currently receiving the bulk of your income from public sources—city, county, state, federal—you may have to overcome a certain image in the minds of your constituents that the government provides for all your needs. It then becomes incumbent on you to present clearly not only your financial status but also your programs, so that a prospective donor can understand which programs receive public underwriting and which do not.

2. Similarly, if you are not receiving and don't anticipate receiving grants and contracts from government or foundations or corporations, you will be able to make a stronger case for why individuals should give you support.

3. Do you have a potential constituency to approach? Check your circle exercises again to determine whether you are close enough to your prospective supporters for personal contact. If your mission is to save a species of butterfly in remote Brazil from extinction and your possible supporters are scattered in different corners of the world, your chances of meeting them all personally are decidedly limited. If, however, your purpose is not so rarefied, as with most nonprofit organizations, you will probably have identified in your circle exercise different prospective constituents who can surely be approached, one-to-one, for support.

4. Will the return in dollars justify the time expended? Your own past experiences, and those of other organizations, will serve as your best guide. Keep in mind that making requests for money in person is the most effective way to elicit support from individuals. As a result, most organizations should include personal solicitation among their mix of approaches.

Face-to-face solicitation should provide a donor base that can be depended upon for ongoing support. The more personal the relationship between the donor and the organization, the more assuredly you can expect the donor's continued involvement and support.

Case Study
MASSACHUSETTS COALITION OF
BATTERED WOMEN SERVICE GROUPS

Since 1981, the Massachusetts Coalition of Battered Women Service Groups (MCBWSG) have taken their message door-to-door in numerous neighborhoods around Boston. Just as women in the 1950's knocked on doors in behalf of the March of Dimes efforts to fight polio, women are again taking to the streets to draw attention to and raise funds to combat another pressing social concern— domestic violence.

In less than five years, the Coalition has raised hundreds of thousands of dollars through canvassing, today's popular term for door-to-door solicitation. In the process, they have also educated countless Massachusetts residents to the fact that every eighteen seconds a women is beaten in the United States.

Why did the women of the Coalition choose canvassing as their prime vehicle for grassroots education and fundraising? How did they succeed in their efforts?

Canvassing replaced grantsmanship as a fundraising strategy for the Coalition in 1981. Like many nonprofits, MCBWSG found the winter of 1981 to be particularly cold. Their original federal grant of $100,000 had run out, and the new administration was not inclined to renew it. As a result, staffing was reduced from eight to two, and MCBWSG was back to square one financially.

The Coalition had been formed in 1978 when the staff of 11 shelters for battered women from all over the state came together for their first meeting. They formed the Coalition "to share information and skills, to strengthen and support each other locally and statewide, and to work jointly on mutually necessary projects." In addition, they wanted to strengthen their collective position to receive funding.

After conducting negotiations with the State government to secure funds for their members, the Coalition successfully obtained $100,000 from the Community Services Administration in Washington, D.C. for an education and training project. Thus, in the spring of 1979, MCBWSG was able to hire its first staff to facilitate regional networking and to provide training in legal advocacy, community education, and peer support and empowerment. While this federal support lasted two years, it was the Coalition's sole source of support. When those funds dried up, staff and board were interested in finding new sources of revenues that were both ongoing and predictable.

That was when the Coalition decided to take their case to the streets. They reviewed an array of methods of raising funds from the general public, including sales of products, large scale direct mail, personal appeals to major donors, special events, and finally, canvassing.

Canvassing seemed the most attractive alternative for many reasons: (1) minimal start-up capital was needed; (2) the financial return was more immediate than other methods of solicitation; (3) it provided an excellent vehicle for community education, a major Coalition goal; and (4) canvassing had proven effective in the Boston area, since there were eight operating programs, two of which were especially successful.

The actual canvass appeared simple enough. Trained, paid workers would go door-to-door in predetermined sympathetic neighborhoods, enlisting people's sup-

Canvassers use this brochure in their door-to-door solicitation.

Source: Logo, brochure, Massachusetts Coalition of Battered Women Service Groups, Boston, MA. Reprinted with permission.

port for an issue. But initial appearances belied the complexity of canvassing.

Board and staff soon learned that mounting a successful canvassing operation required proficiency in long-term planning, administration, budgeting and fiscal management, and personnel matters. Many of these skills had to be acquired through trial and error. For example, recruiting qualified canvassers was not simple. Candidates had to be willing to work in all kinds of weather, be adaptable, be able to deal with rejection, and believe in the Coalition's goals. According to Sue Doucette, the current canvass director, "good candidates are hard to find." First, they had to make it through a phone interview, and then, an extensive personal interview.

Before canvassers go out in the field, they participate in training and strategy sessions, covering such topics as how to get into apartment buildings and how "to educate not debate" someone who wants to give the canvasser a hard time. The trainees also learn about eye contact, body language, and developing their "rap" so that the "who, what, and where" of the organization comes across in the first minute of conversation. To assure their personal safety, they are urged to leave any situation the minute they feel uneasy. They are also taught self-defense techniques. Before they go into any neighborhood, the canvass director gives the local police a list of their names and sends a press release to the local newspaper to let people know they're coming. Finally, they review last year's map and donor list, and discuss the targeted community's political and socio-economic make-up.

The Coalition learned many skills in the course of running their canvass six days a week all year around. Fortunately, for others who are considering canvassing, the Coalition wrote and produced an excellent 65 page manual, based on their experiences. Copies are available for $5.00 from MCBWSG, 20 East Street, Boston, Massachusetts 02111.

Today, after four years of experience, the Massachusetts Coalition of Battered Women Service Groups grosses over $200,000, and nets $60,000, from its canvassing efforts. They contact 40 to 60 people each night, and a total of 50,000 to 60,000 each year. The coalition is on stronger financial footing than ever before, and has successfully trailblazed a new form of fundraising for the battered women's movement.

by Ellin Stein and Michael Seltzer

Case Study
EQUITY LIBRARY THEATER

FEVER PITCH—At Equity Library Theater fundraising
is a science and an art

Many hard-pressed arts groups have refined the art of fundraising to a science but few, if any, do it with as much energy and drama as the Equity Library Theater in New York City does. But then, few arts organizations use their cast members to present their fund appeals in music and dance. The Equity "pitch," an original 10- to 12-minute mini-musical which takes place between the first and second acts of ELT musicals has become a time-honored tradition that audiences anticipate eagerly despite its somewhat "biting" finale, featuring cast members marching up the aisles to pass the hat around. The pitch, which sometimes uses original compositions, frequently incorporates music from the evening's regular production or from other works by the same composer, with special lyrics underscoring the funding needs of the much-honored showcase theater. ELT, beginning its 42nd season, has probably introduced more theater greats to audiences at the beginning of their careers than any similar group.

Between acts of a recent production of Sigmund Romberg's *Up in Central Park,* the pitch, a parody of "Serenade" from *The Student Prince,* began with the immortal words, "Overhead the floor is leaking, once we had to stop the show," while a hit from *The New Moon* plaintively pleaded, "Wanting you, to contribute a bill or two, to the actors who pass by you." If audience enthusiasm continues and the bucks keep flowing in (several patrons have volunteered to write original pitches), ELT might be tempted to present a different kind of revival, one showcasing the best pitches of the past. Then audiences, once again, might have the opportunity to hear the immortal 1972 rejoinder to an arts agency which denied the theater a grant—"I've got the New York Council on the Arts blues/Can't lose 'em/Because the New York Council canceled their dues."

by Alvin H. Reiss

Summary Worksheet

for

_____

(name of your organization)

APPROACHING INDIVIDUALS FOR SUPPORT: FACE-TO-FACE SOLICITATION

Building on Efforts to Date

1. Are you already approaching individuals directly for support?

_____ yes   _____ no

2. If yes, which of the following approaches have you used?

_____ Personal Visits

_____ Canvassing

_____ Phonathon

_____ Other _____

3. How can you enhance the income potential of any of these approaches?

Additional Actions Needed

a. _____   _____

_____

_____

b. _____   _____

_____

_____

_____

c. _____   _____

_____

_____

4. Which of these approaches are "proven" successful traditions (i.e., revenues exceed costs, people continue to respond affirmatively to requests, etc.)?

a. _____   _____

b. _____   _____

c. _____   _____

5. Which approaches should be discarded or overhauled?

a. _____ _____

b. _____ _____

c. _____ _____

Planning New Efforts

6. Has any other organization in your community engaged in face-to-face solicitation? What has been their experience? Have you approached them for advice?

Name of Organization

a. _____

b. _____

c. _____

Rating Your Face-to-Face Solicitation Potential

7. On the basis of what you have learned, how would you rank your capability to elicit support from individuals through face-to-face solicitation?

☐ Very Good   ☐ Possible   ☐ Unlikely   ☐ Still Unknown

FURTHER READINGS

"Asking for Money: Getting Over the Fear of Asking." *Grassroots Fundraising Journal* vol. 2, no. 2 (April 1983): 1–4. Single issue $2.50. (Order from: Grassroots Fundraising Journal, P.O. Box 14754, San Francisco, CA 94114)
> Discusses some of the reasons that asking for money is hard and provides some exercises to help groups get over the fears of asking for money.

Conrad, Daniel L. *How to Solicit Big Gifts*. Revised Edition. San Francisco: Public Management Institute. 1978. 250 pp. in 3-ring binder. $49.00. (Order from: Public Management Institute, 358 Brannan St., San Francisco, CA 94107)
> Provides information on how to locate prospects, train solicitors, phrase requests and do follow-up to solicit big gifts.

Cover, Nelson, comp. *A Guide to Successful Phonathons*. Revised Edition. Alexandria, VA: CASE Publications. 1984. 95 pp. $14.50. (Order from: CASE Publications Order Department, P.O. Box 298, Alexandria, VA 22314)
> Shows how to raise money through phonathons including how to set a timetable, secure facilities, recruit and train volunteers, and do follow-up.

Massachusetts Coalition of Battered Women Service Groups. *Canvass Manual*. Revised Edition. Boston: Massachusetts Coalition of Battered Women Service Groups. 1984. 67 pp. $5.00. (Order from: Massachusetts Coalition of Battered Women Service Groups, 20 East St., Boston, MA 02111)
> Explores the concept of canvassing as a method of fundraising based on the organization's three years of experience. Includes discussion of the positive aspects of this approach in outreach and education in addition to the money raised. Also discusses such aspects as potential problems, management, and training.

Seymour, Harold J. *Designs for Fund-Raising: Principles, Patterns, Techniques*. New York: McGraw-Hill Book Co. 1966. 210 pp. $37.50. (Order from: McGraw-Hill Book Co., 1221 Avenue of the Americas, New York, NY 10020)
> Information on designing and carrying out a campaign to ask for money in person from large donors. Includes ideas on motivating volunteer fundraisers and potential donors.

CHAPTER 9

APPROACHING INDIVIDUALS FOR SUPPORT

DIRECT MAIL

Direct mail is the most personal medium of raising funds after face-to-face and telephone contact. Direct mail fundraising—the mailing of appeals to individuals for financial support—differs from other forms of fundraising from individuals in that you are soliciting large numbers of people for reasonably small donations, under $100. It can range from a few handwritten pleas sent out to friends, to a mimeographed or photocopied letter sent to a few dozen supporters, to a slick, multifaceted printed packet sent to tens or hundreds of thousands of people whose names are on mailing lists.

Traditionally, large national nonprofit organizations, such as CARE, Smithsonian Institution, National Audubon Society, National Organization for Women, and Planned Parenthood, utilize direct mail. Increasingly these days, local nonprofits of all sizes have been systematically using direct mail to seek out contributors as well.

Depending on your initial investment of funds to cover your start-up direct mail costs, such as printing, postage, and purchase of lists of potential donors, you may realize anywhere from several hundred to tens of thousands of dollars from a direct mail effort.

A cautionary note: Direct mail is really an investment in your financial future. The first-year costs of establishing a direct mail program may exceed the actual dollars that you will raise. However, don't despair, for carefully planned

The author wishes to thank Sandra Tanzer for her invaluable collaboration on this chapter.

direct mail efforts in the subsequent years will produce greater profits, and thus, justify the initial investment.

WHAT ARE THE ADVANTAGES OF RAISING MONEY BY DIRECT MAIL?

1. Direct mail is a highly personal medium and an effective way to get your message across. Letters arrive at the homes of potential supporters, where they can be read in private. In spite of some popular notions about direct mail, people on the whole are responsive to it.

2. It can be an efficient use of your organization's time and money, for successful mail appeals bring in new supporters to an organization as well as identify prospective larger supporters of your work. For example, if someone responds to your organization's first mail solicitation by sending a check, that person is likely to contribute again. People who contribute $100 or more might well be responsive to other forms of solicitation. Compiling a direct mail list can be *easy.* Consider the example in an earlier chapter of the fledgling theater group that asked its actors to bring in their Christmas card list for their first appeal.

3. The results from direct mail are measurable. You can count the number of separate letters mailed out and the exact costs of any particular appeal. Finally, you can also determine the number of responses, the total dollars received, and the names and addresses of the contributors (see accompanying explanation). As a result, you can measure whether your direct mail efforts have been profitable.

4. Direct mail can educate new and old constituencies to your issues. Newcomers, your "prospects," might read just the message on the outside of your envelope, or the contents within. They may not all respond immediately with a contribution, but they may become more sensitive to your issue. In the same sense, your existing constituencies can become better informed about issues of mutual concern through your direct mail appeals and be moved to give again and/or to give more.

WHAT ARE THE DISADVANTAGES OF RAISING MONEY BY DIRECT MAIL?

1. Direct mail is an expensive form of communication, particularly when compared with newspaper, radio, and television advertising. To reach ten thousand people by direct mail, you need to pay printing, postage, and mailing costs (and perhaps some fees for artwork and computer services).

Finding those vital names and addresses requires time and, more important, money. Direct costs are incurred through printing, postage, and, perhaps, the purchase of prospective donor lists.

Indirect costs are also incurred through direct mail solicitation. These costs include the time it takes your salaried staff to prepare and coordinate the mailings and, possibly, to organize volunteers to stuff your appeals ("stuffing parties").

2. There is also an element of risk inherent in direct mail. You can estimate only roughly how much money you might net, based on your previous experiences. If you're approaching individuals for the first time—"cold prospects"—you are even more in the dark about their possible responses.

Your total costs could be anywhere from $50.00 to $300.00 per 1,000 people reached. By contrast, some television or radio spots are available free as public service announcements. Some free space can also be secured in newspapers. Of course, TV, radio, and newspapers reach thousands and even millions in a single exposure. As a result, direct mail does cost more than other forms of communication; however, you are likely to net more with a carefully planned direct mail effort.

3. With direct mail, you have to spend money to make money. If you are approaching individuals for contributions for the first time, the process is fraught with risk. Choosing unlikely lists of contributors initially will cost you money that you will never recoup. A response of between 0.5 and 1.0 percent (50 to 100 people from a mailing of 10,000) is considered acceptable for first-time mailings to cold prospects.

How to Determine If a Direct Mail Campaign Is Profitable

Ultimately, profitability is measured by income minus expenses. But there are other critical indices in assessing the success of a direct mail appeal.

1. Response Rate. The number of letters mailed relative to the number of contributions received is called the response rate. For example, if you mail out 1,000 letter appeals and receive 55 contributions in response, your response rate is 55 ÷ 1,000, which is 0.55 percent.

2. Average Gift Size. The size of the "average" contribution or gift is calculated by the total dollars raised divided by the number of contributions. For example, if you received $825 from 55 donors, the "average" gift would be $15.00 (825 ÷ 55).

The response rate and average gift size are important in computing your profitability. By determining each of them, you can then compare the results of different mailings in a very objective and easy manner.

3. The Average Cost. The average cost of obtaining this response/contribution is determined by dividing the total cost of the mailing by the number of positive responses received. For example, if you mail out 1,000 letters at a total cost of

$330.00, netting 55 positive responses, the average cost is $6.00 (330 ÷ 55). The cost of obtaining one contributor is $6.00.

4. By computing your average gift size and the average cost, you can then figure out how much you spent on the average to raise your average gift. Using our example, the average gift is $15.00 and the average cost is $6.00. Each contribution of $15.00 cost you $6.00, yielding an average *net* contribution (or profit) of $9.00.

HOW TO DECIDE WHETHER TO USE DIRECT MAIL SOLICITATION FOR YOUR ORGANIZATION

Practically every kind and size of nonprofit organization can use direct mail. Almost all nonprofits use the mails for communicating with donors anyway. The potential to net contributions, however, varies considerably, depending upon a number of factors, such as start-up funds, the appeal of your issues to individuals and the persuasiveness of your case.

Deciding whether direct mail solicitations will prove worth your effort in time and money is not easy to determine, but let's examine some of the considerations involved.

1. Can I afford to put my organization into the direct mail business? Every group can afford a low-cost direct mail effort, as described below. Of course, if you have an existing list of supporters to whom you are already mailing newsletters or literature, the cost of adding an appeal for funds to any of these mailings would be minimal. You certainly can and should be asking your existing contacts or readers for money. If, on the other hand, that list is relatively small and does not really encompass your universe of potentially interested individuals, it is really not your best source of income.

It is obviously more expensive to approach "untested" groups of individuals for contributions, since you have no first-hand prior experience with these prospects. If you are approaching totally new prospects and/or will have to cover all of the costs of a pilot mailing, you will need to gauge in advance your relative costs versus your potential income. The worksheet below can serve as a guide for this computation.

2. Does your organization already have mailing lists of supporters that might be used for direct mail purposes? Do you collect names and addresses of people who attend your special events or who sign petitions circulated by your group? Do you maintain a list of people who have written to you to request information on your work? Have you a list, too, of individuals to whom you may have provided services?

Any of these lists can be used for direct mail purposes. In fact, these lists contribute to what is known in direct mail circles as an organization's "house list." A house list is made up of individuals who have some previously established relationship with your organization. Of course, there is no guarantee that you will receive X number of positive responses from such a mailing; a list of that sort, however, does say you've got some names of people who have already expressed an interest in your work and they are your most likely supporters.

3. Are there other organizations similar to your own that have been successful in raising money through direct mail appeals? If so, they have already determined for you that direct mail can be effective in eliciting contributions from potential supporters.

4. If you have no lists of your own, do you have access to the mailing list of similar organizations? Those which have attracted people to their ranks might also respond affirmatively to yours. You can check this simply by contacting these organizations directly and asking if you could do a mailing on their list.

You may find that some organizations are unwilling to give you their list for a mailing. Or some will make their lists available only for a fee or on an exchange basis with your own list.

If you are approaching a national organization but your work has only local appeal, you will want to request only the names of people who live in nearby zip code areas. You can also purchase mailing lists of potential sympathizers from direct mail list brokers (check for listings in your local telephone Yellow Pages). And don't forget how to be a smart shopper. Check for references from other nonprofit organizations that have used a specific list broker. Call them up and find out what their experiences were.

If you have responded affirmatively to any of the above items, you certainly should consider direct mail as part of your overall fundraising effort. Check the summary worksheet at the end of the chapter.

Worksheet
ESTIMATING THE POTENTIAL INCOME OF
FIRST-TIME PROSPECT MAIL APPEALS

1. Set a range of gifts for the solicitations. Estimate roughly the average dollar response that mailings to these individuals have netted for other organizations. You can sometimes obtain this data by asking the organization whose list you are utilizing. Look at past direct mail appeals of that organization and see what the range of gifts requested is. The lowest category often represents the average level of gift. For example, if an organization is asking for contributions in the range of:

☐ $25   ☐ $50   ☐ $100   ☐ $_____ (Other)

$25 represents the average gift anticipated.

Your Anticipated Average Gift = $_____.

2. Now, set the top possible gift, which is frequently $100. The "Other" category is for those who wish to give less than $25, more than $100, or some unlisted amount in between.

Your Top Average Anticipated Gift = $100.

3. Fill in the rest of your range of gift sizes. Usually, you give your potential supporters four to five possible options, including "Other" as the last option listed.

1. _____   4. _____

2. _____   5. Other _____

3. _____

4. Using the accepted reference of 0.5 to 1.0 percent return on initial mailings, calculate the potential range of income. For example, if you mail out 10,000 pieces asking for $25 as the lowest gift,

0.5% × 10,000 = 50 people
50 people × $25 = $1,250

1.0% × 10,000 = 100 people
100 people × $25 = $2,500

Your gross potential range of income for this mailing is: $1,250 to $2,500.

Comparing Projected Income Against Projected Expenses
Total Expenses $_____
minus
Potential Range of Income $_____
equals
                                  Net $_____   to $_____

If your income exceeds your expenses, then clearly your direct mail effort is profitable.

If your income equals your expenses, you have not wasted your time, for you have acquired up to 100 potential new donors who can be approached a second and a third time for contributions.

If your income is substantially or alarmingly less than your expenses, you need to find a less expensive way to reach those 10,000 prospects. For example, cut your production costs by seeking out donated printing or artwork, or using volunteer labor, or swapping prospect lists instead of buying them. You might also start your gift table with a higher gift to raise your anticipated income.

HOW CAN YOUR GROUP ORGANIZE A DIRECT MAIL EFFORT?

Direct mail should not be a single event but rather a sustained effort throughout the year to present your organization to potential supporters through the mail on a regular basis. In many cases, the more times you mail out to a list of supporters (particularly your "house list"), the more money you will ultimately raise. Some organizations successfully mail once a month to their regular contributors, and others may mail two or three times each year with equal success. There is no fixed number of times an organization "should" mail.

Direct mail can very nicely fit into your overall fundraising program. For example, the donors you acquire through direct mail ("prospecting") become possible candidates for major contributions, or participants in special events, or sources of volunteers, or consumers of any products that you might market (such as calendars, gift cards, or posters). The following steps outline the procedures to follow in organizing a direct mail campaign.

Step One. *Identify Your Audience of Prospective Supporters.* Refer back to the circles exercise in Chapter 7. Select the people with whom you have already established some contact through the mail as candidates for your first mail appeal for contributions. Of course, include anyone who has already given you unsolicited contributions of any size. If the list of those individuals is modest in size (less than 500 names), you might consider augmenting it with other names. Even if your initial list is a good size, you may still consider getting additional names and undertaking an expanded mailing.

Step Two. *Augment Your Initial Mailing List.* Presuming that you want to augment your initial list, you can do so in a number of ways.

1. "Swap" your current list with groups who have similar constituencies. Exchanging one name (and address) with that of another organization expands your potential list without incurring any costs. Of course, some groups may be protective of their mailing lists and refuse to exchange or even sell their lists, due to factors of confidentiality or protectiveness.

2. Compile a list of the friends, relatives, colleagues, co-workers, business associates, vendors, neighbors, and so forth already on your list. If each of your principal supporters gives you ten new names and addresses, you have increased the size of your list tenfold.

3. Beg for or borrow lists from organizations. Convince them of the value of your work and ask for a one-time loan of their list.

4. Make use of the free publicity outlets in your community, such as notices in local newsletters, public service announcements on radio, and other ways to spread the word about your work and to encourage inquiries. Once you get the name and address of an interested individual, you have a candidate for your direct mail efforts. Your initial investment in labor may consist of only a press release mailing to local media.

5. Purchase (or "rent") existing lists of donors from groups who have similar constituencies. The average list of contributors available for rental ranges in price from $45.00 to $75.00 per thousand names. Sometimes you can rent directly from the organization; but more likely you will have to rent from a professional list broker.

Once you know to whom you are mailing, you can then determine what you are mailing.

Step Three. *Develop the Mailing Piece (or Package).* Tradition dictates that a direct mail package be comprised of the following:

1. Outside envelope which can include a "teaser" (a slogan or quotation to compel people to open the envelope);

2. Letter, which can range from one to six pages (most frequently one 8½-by-11 inch sheet printed on both sides);

3. Reply device (card restating the request for money) which fits into the reply envelope;

4. Return envelope (with or without a postage imprint).

Mailings, however, can also consist of a self-mailer—a flyer with a coupon —or even a postcard, depending on the circumstances and money available. You can also include other items in a mailing, such as a brochure, a newsletter, a cover note from your president or a local celebrity, or a calendar of events.

Within certain postal guidelines, you can mail anything you want. The best way to engage in direct mail is to limit your enclosures to those really pertaining to the request for a contribution. You should concentrate on your written copy for the letter, envelope, reply device, and, even possibly, the return envelope. Also, you should pay attention to artwork, color, and typeface style. The presentation of your message does influence your chances of success.

Step Four. *Write Copy for the Mailing.* Through your copy, you need to establish in the most definitive terms the reason(s) recipients should support your work. You might present only one reason and support it in your letter. Stress why your cause or program is unique. Tell about your mission and what the money will be used for without being too wordy. Highlight key points. Make it easy to read. If possible, build a story around your central idea, or recount a history of the issue or cause you represent. Set a tone for your writing. It can be whimsical, dramatic, serious, emotional, or otherwise, but whatever tone you choose has to be consistently conveyed throughout the mailing package. Finally, your copy must inform the reader how to mail in a contribution to support your work, such as, "Use the enclosed reply card and envelope to let me hear from you today."

The letter is heavily weighted with copy and all the other mailing pieces should support it. For example, you should use the same type style in each piece of the mailing. Your copy should always offer something to the recipient of your appeal. That something can be intangible, such as an offer to protect your constitutional rights with your contribution. The donor might derive some sense of protection or well-being from the gift, as well as a sense of participation in a cause. Membership in an arts organization, for example, might provide a sense of social cachet to members.

Your offer can also be tangible, such as providing a newsletter or a schedule of events or even a magazine or a membership with or without specific benefits. In any case, the reader should be aware that there is something available in exchange for a contribution. The various components of the mailing piece should all mention one of the offers. For example, the reply card can start off with a statement like, "Dear Ira, You can count on me to help ACLU resist this historic swing against individual liberties." (Note the fact that the reply is personalized ("Dear Ira") and uses the pronoun *you*.)

Usually, it is recommended that the minimum gift amount be mentioned somewhere in the letter to encourage at least that level of gift. In addition, your reply card will generally list four or five categories of giving levels, including "Other." You can set an overall financial goal in the letter itself, such as, "We need to raise an additional $2,500 to open the doors of our second shelter. If 100 readers of this appeal each give us $25, we will meet our goal."

Minimally you want to cover the costs of the mailing itself, so that you don't lose money. You hope to net more. Generally, people who give will contribute the amount you have asked them to give. Also, identifying levels of giving with appropriate names, such as *patron* or *benefactor* for your highest category of gift, helps stimulate higher giving. Categories also provide a vehicle to encourage givers to aspire to a higher category of giving in the future.

But no matter how good the soliciting letter is, the recipient must first be enticed to open the envelope. A "teaser" on the envelope will encourage a prospective donor to read on. The Southern Poverty Law Center in Montgomery, Alabama, for example, included a photograph in its package. On the envelope was a bright yellow sticker reading "Photo Enclosed, Please Do Not Bend." In a direct mail solicitation for members, the Smithsonian Institution in Washington, D.C., used this teaser: "Postmaster: Please deliver this official invitation promptly." Both of these methods are very effective.

A NOT-FOR-PROFIT COMMUNITY-SPONSORED CENTER FOR THE PERFORMING ARTS

Dear Friend,

We're looking for backers. Wanna be an angel? Here's a new
script.

<u>"NINETY-FIFTH STREET"</u>
A Real-Life Drama in One Significant Act

(LIGHTS COME UP ON A CONCERNED NEW YORKER opening
yet another piece of direct mail advertising.
MUSIC UNDER: "The Unfinished Symphony")

CONCERNED NEW YORKER
(Reads:)
"We'd like you to consider becoming a member of Symphony Space."
(sighs:)
Who's got the time? What's Symphony Space?

(Suddenly, as if by magic, a STILL, SMALL VOICE is heard)

STILL, SMALL VOICE
Wait! Don't throw away that expensive mailing piece. You know,
you really should become a member...

CONCERNED NEW YORKER
I should? Why?

STILL, SMALL VOICE
Symphony Space is a place where they do all kinds of things in
music, theatre, dance, film, and literature. They are very
interesting. And exciting.   And innovative.   And
inexpensive...sometimes free.

CONCERNED NEW YORKER
Good! Whenever they have something I'm interested in, I'll buy
tickets and go. Why do I have to bother about membership?

STILL, SMALL VOICE
(MUSIC SEGUES: "Pathetique Symphony")
They really need you. What they've accomplished is remarkable,
but did you know they have to raise a vast percentage of their
budget through contributions?

CONCERNED NEW YORKER
How come? Why don't they just charge more for tickets?

Symphony Space, Inc. ☐ 2537 Broadway at 95th Street ☐ New York, NY 10025 ☐ 212-864-1414

STILL, SMALL VOICE
(getting more impassioned)
They can't do that! Symphony Space has been devoted to providing New Yorkers with excellent artistic events at the lowest possible prices. They've helped to revitalize the Upper West Side community. They've given a break to countless numbers of minority artists. And have served all kinds of performing groups who use the place at the most advantageous subsidized rental rates.

CONCERNED NEW YORKER
(growing interested)
Oh, Symphony Space does all that?

STILL, SMALL VOICE
That's one part of it. Symphony Space also creates their own wonderful events. They invented the Wall-to-Wall free marathon concert and created Wall-to-Wall Bach, Beethoven, Schubert, Copland, Cage and Rodgers, among others.

CONCERNED NEW YORKER
Oh yeah...I've heard about those. Thousands of people waiting on line in the street to get in.

STILL, SMALL VOICE
Not if they're members! They receive priority admission to all free events. Why not become a member today and take advantage of all their membership benefits. Why are you hesitating?

CONCERNED NEW YORKER
(agitated)
I just want to be sure that I'll be doing something significant with my money. Something that will make a difference.

STILL, SMALL VOICE
Oh, you will be! membership support opens up doors for further funding from foundations, corporations, and the government. Why, it's a vote of confidence for one of the good things in life!

(MUSIC CRESCENDO: "New World Symphony")

CONCERNED NEW YORKER
(inspired)
O.K., I'll do it! This will be...my SIGNIFICANT ACT!

(THEY embrace and send in their membership forms as the MUSIC SWELLS and the)

LIGHTS FADE

How about it?   *Allan Miller   Isaiah Sheffer*
                  Allan Miller   Isaiah Sheffer
                  Artistic Directors

Direct mail letters can use a humorous approach.
Source: Symphony Space Inc., New York, NY. Reprinted with permission.

Step Five. *Design the Mailing.* Once you have a rough copy of your appeal, you can proceed to the design stage. Some kind of artwork is always desirable, no matter how limited your budget. It may mean only paying attention to an organizational letterhead and a uniform type style to produce a standard 8½-by-11 inch two-sided letter. Photographs are a boost to a mailing. Very often, you will find them on the reply card or in an enclosed brochure. You can also use parts of your letterhead for the artwork of other pieces of the mailing, since you do want the mailing to present a uniform grahic image. A brochure is a nice graphic addition to a mail appeal, but it is not necessary. A very good case for contributions can be made without one, if you are concerned about economy.

Check postal regulations about maximum and minimum size and weight for bulk and first-class mailings. This will help you decide the size and total number of your own enclosures. The most common approach is to use a No. 10-sized envelope.

Step Six. *Arrange Printing and Mailing.* Once you decide how many pieces your mailing will include—letter, return envelope, reply card, and outside envelope (the "carrier")—and their respective sizes, you should investigate local offset printing concerns. Obtain at least three bids before you select a company. Make sure that your three contacts are making bids on the basis of the same specifications and that they give you a detailed bid, including a paper sample. If a printer is a member of your board or of your family, your printing might be donated. (Unless you have a really strong personal relationship with a printer, it is unlikely.) Ascertain whether the price of the printing includes delivery. Be sure that the bid includes such factors as perforations, if any.

Typically, you will want your printer to fold your letters. You can plan a volunteer night to "stuff" your mailing and to bundle it appropriately for the post office. If you have more than 5,000 outgoing pieces, you should consider engaging a letter shop to affix labels, to stuff envelopes, and to bundle for mailing. If you have a large volunteer force, you can consider doing these jobs yourself.

After affixing labels on a bulk-rate mailing, you need to organize the mailing by zip code. Check the bulk-rate office of your main post office, or check with your local postmaster for details on bulk-rate mailing. There are nonprofit mailing houses and sheltered workshops that also do business by stuffing nonprofit mailings.

Step Seven. *Monitor Daily Returns to Your Mailing.* Plan on the necessary people power to open your mail, starting two to three weeks after a third-class bulk mailing and about one week after a first-class mailing.

As a rule of thumb, all contributions should be acknowledged as soon as possible. The acknowledgment builds goodwill, provides a receipt for a donation, and also can include a small envelope for an additional contribution. If you have stated in advance in your mailing that "your canceled check will serve as your receipt for tax purposes," you don't have to send an acknowledgment, but it's advisable to do so to promote goodwill.

You will be tabulating the number of responses and the dollar amounts so that the response rate and the average gift can be calculated. You will also want to note the number of responses received each day and gauge the trend of the responses to help future planning. This will help you predict cash flow in response to future mailings.

Step Eight. *Assess the Results.* In assessing your results, you will be looking perhaps at summarizations of weekly reports; you will be appraising the success or failure of the campaign in terms of total responses, total dollars earned, average gift, and dollars earned versus dollars spent.

Remember, if this was your first mailing to a list of names and your income roughly equals your expenses (you "break even"), you can think of yourself as fairly successful since you have now gained a number of donors who will respond again to your requests for support. If your expenses exceeded your income by a wide margin (more than 30 percent), then you may want to reassess the suitability of direct mail for you altogether, *unless* you can isolate the exact reasons why the mailing failed and correct them in your next attempt. A mailing might fail because of bad timing, high costs, or wrongly targeted lists.

Step Nine. *Schedule Future Mailings.* Nearing breakeven or profitability in your first mailing should inspire you to repeat the campaign. Although you should definitely schedule another mailing on the anniversary of your initial effort, you will not want to wait a year until your next mailing. Deciding when to mail again is your next task. Many organizations mail successfully at the following times:

- September 1 to October 15: Post-Labor Day Season
- November 7 to November 21: Year-End Holiday Period (Appeals at this time of the year reach people during a season of generosity and also afford them a tax write-off just before the end of the year.)
- January 1 to February 1: Post-Holiday Appeal (People are looking for opportunities to make themselves feel better.)
- March to April: Spring Appeal (It is sometimes good to mail out around tax time.)

There are really as many potential times for mailings as there are weeks in the year. A significant factor is your own seasonality, that is, when your own programs occur or when you experience a particular emergency. You usually plan a fixed mailing schedule of three to four mailings a year, with the opportunity for additional emergency appeals as the situation warrants. After engaging in direct mail for one year, you will be able to gauge what times of the year engender the best responses to your requests. Calculations based on average gift, response rate, and profitability (as measured by costs versus revenues) provide you with the data necessary to decide when to schedule your mailings. For example, you may reserve your mailings to new lists for the time of the year when you received the most responses previously. You can continue to mail out to your regular list at the other scheduled times.

Summary Worksheet

for

_____

(name of your organization)

APPROACHING INDIVIDUALS FOR SUPPORT: DIRECT MAIL

Building on Direct Mail Efforts to Date

1. Are you already using direct mail to raise funds?

     ☐ yes   ☐ no

If yes, when have you been sending out appeals? How many times each year?

a. _____   _____

b. _____   _____

c. _____   _____

d. _____   _____

e. _____   _____

2. What is the net income for each of these appeals?

a. $ _____

b. $ _____

c. $ _____

d. $ _____

e. $ _____

3. How can you enhance the income potential for any of these appeals?

                                      Additional Actions Needed

a. _____   _____

                                           _____

                                           _____

b. _____   _____

                                           _____

                                           _____

c. _____   _____

                                           _____

d. _____   _____

    _____

    _____

e. _____   _____

    _____

    _____

4. Which of those special appeals are "proven" traditions (i.e., more people respond, more funds are raised each time, etc.)?

_____   _____

_____   _____

_____   _____

5. Which appeals should be discarded (due to declining numbers of responses or lower receipts) or vastly overhauled?

_____   _____

_____   _____

_____   _____

Assessing Your Organization's Direct Mail Readiness

6. Have you identified the particular constituencies that you can approach for support by direct mail?

☐ yes   ☐ no

They are:

a. "house list"   _____

b. other: _____

c. _____

d. _____

e. _____

7. Does your organization already have mailing lists of these constituencies?

☐ yes   ☐ no

8. If not, do you have access to such mailing lists (through friends and colleagues, other organizations, etc.)?

☐ yes   ☐ no   ☐ untested

9. Have you determined the fixed costs versus potential revenues of a direct mail effort to gauge your potential net income?

☐ yes   ☐ no

Projected Costs $ _____

Projected Income $ _____

10. Does the anticipated return in dollars justify the time expended?

☐ yes   ☐ no

Finding Assistance and Counsel

11. Name three or more individuals who can advise you on starting or enhancing your direct mail effort.

a. _____

b. _____

c. _____

d. _____

e. _____

Rating Your Direct Mail Potential

12. On the basis of what you have determined, how would you rank your chances of securing individuals' support through direct mail?

☐ Very Good   ☐ Possible   ☐ Unlikely   ☐ Still Unknown

FURTHER READINGS

Andres, Susan. "A Primer on Mailing Lists." *The Grantsmanship Center NEWS* no. 49 (September/October 1982): 14–30. Single issue $4.75 plus $2.00 handling per order. (Order from: The Grantsmanship Center, P.O. Box 6210, 650 S. Spring St., Suite 507, Los Angeles, CA 90014)

Basic procedures for organizations getting into the mailing list market, either as a seller (renting your mailing list to other organizations) or as a buyer. Includes a glossary of mailing-list terminology.

Ballenger, Bruce, *Direct Mail on a Shoestring* (NRAG Paper vol. 4, no. 4). Helena, MT: Northern Rockies Action Group. Spring 1984. 24 pp. $7.50 prepaid. (Order from: Northern Rockies Action Group, 9 Placer St., Helena, MT 59601)

A guide for groups with limited budgets who want to explore the potential of direct mail fundraising. Includes principles to consider in determining whether to use direct mail as well as specific techniques.

Craver, Roger, Charlene Divoky, and Sanky Perlowin. *Evaluating Your Fund Raising Program.* Garden City, NY: Hoke Communications, Inc. 1981. Audio cassette, $10.00. (Order from: Hoke Communications, Inc., 224 Seventh St., Garden City, NY 11530)

Three professionals demonstrate the kinds of questions they might ask the executive director of a hypothetical organization which wants to start a direct mail campaign. Includes advice on goal setting, how to present the organization's cause, and how to ask for the largest possible gift.

Dermer, Joseph, editor. *America's Most Successful Fund Raising Letters.* Hartsdale, NY: Public Service Materials Center. 1981. 141 pp. $19.95. (Order from: Public Service Materials Center, 111 N. Central Ave., Hartsdale, NY 10530)

Examples of fundraising letters which were winners in a nationwide contest sponsored by Public Service Materials Center. Includes commentary by each author explaining the objectives and results and why it was written the way it was.

Direct Mail Fundraiser's Association. *A Guide to Direct Mail Fundraising.* New York: Direct Mail Fundraiser's Association. $12.00. (Order from: Direct Mail Fundraiser's Association, 28 W. 44 St., Suite 1215, New York, NY 10036)

This guide to fundraising using direct mail is published in a loose-leaf notebook for easy updating.

Divoky, Charlene. *Direct Mail—A Preliminary View.* Winchester, MA: Divoky & Associates. November 1981. 5 pp. Free. (Order from: Divoky & Associates, 100 Main St., Reading, MA 01867. Include self-addressed stamped envelope.)

Introduction to the objectives and methods of direct mail fundraising. Includes figures on costs and expected benefits of various size mailings over 30,000.

Ensman, Richard. "Building a Mailing List: An Introduction." *The Grantsman-ship Center NEWS* no. 53 (May/June 1983): 10–21. Single issue $4.75 plus $2.00 handling per order. (Order from: The Grantsmanship Center, P.O. Box 6210, 650 S. Spring St., Suite 507, Los Angeles, CA 90014)

> Discusses how an organization's mailing list should be organized and main-tained in order to get the most benefit from it. Includes suggestions on using both the house list (natural constituencies) and prospect list.

Huntsinger, Jerry. *Fund Raising Letters: A Comprehensive Study Guide to Rais-ing Money by Direct Response Marketing.* Richmond VA: Emerson Publishers. 1985. 400 pp. $135.00; $95.00 for nonprofit organizations. (Order from: Public Service Materials Center, 111 N. Central Ave., Hartsdale, NY 10530)

> Manual covering such aspects of direct response marketing as fundraising letters, creating the package, and creating special letters. Also includes sug-gestions for using television, radio and the telephone to raise funds.

Keller, Mitchell, ed. *The KRC Collection of Direct Mail Fund Raising Appeals.* New Canaan, CT: KRC Development Council. 1985. 123 pp. $37.50. (Order from: Public Service Materials Center, 111 N. Central Ave., Hartsdale, NY 10530)

> Examples of a wide range of appeal letters illustrating ways many nonprofit organizations are raising money by mail. Includes whole packages for these appeals with critiques of their strengths and weaknesses.

Keller, Mitchell. *The KRC Guide to Direct Mail.* New Canaan, CT: KRC Devel-opment Council. 1981. 207 pp. $39.50. (Order from: Public Service Materials Center, 111 N. Central Ave., Hartsdale, NY 10530)

> Guide to successful methods of fundraising using direct mail. Chapters cover strategies, writing and designing the package, mailing lists, using the com-puter, evaluation of results, and relevant legislation. Includes sample forms and records.

Lautman, Kay Partney, and Henry Goldstein. *Dear Friend: Mastering the Art of Direct Mail Fund Raising.* Washington, DC: The Taft Group. 1984. 300 pp. $47.50. (Order from: The Taft Group, 5130 MacArthur Blvd., N.W., Washing-ton, DC 20016)

> Step-by-step guide to direct mail fundraising.

Public Management Institute. *Direct Mail Fund Raising.* San Francisco: Public Management Institute. 1980. 400 pp. $49.00. (Order from: Public Management Institute, 358 Brannan St., San Francisco, CA 94102)

> Systems approach to successful fundraising via direct mail. Includes infor-mation on how to find mail lists, save on printing and mailing, and set up a revolving fund. Sample forms, checklists, and worksheets.

CHAPTER 10

APPROACHING INDIVIDUALS FOR SUPPORT

SPECIAL EVENTS

A special event is a specific occasion that a nonprofit organization plans and carries out to attract publicity, to gain new members, to educate the public, and to make money.

More often than not, special events reflect in some way the uniqueness of the sponsoring organization, making use of the creative talents of its members. These events are indeed "special," for they create an opportunity for people to come together to have fun, to celebrate, to be moved by others, and to mingle with their peers in a setting made even more inviting and hospitable than their own homes. These events often become treasured memories for their participants.

The creative talents of an organization's membership are indeed valuable commodities. They represent all the inventive qualities that a group has at its disposal, from designing the invitations, to stringing up balloons, to cooking food to be served.

A special event can: (1) involve many new people in the ongoing life of your organization; and (2) serve to reinforce and strengthen the relationships of an organization's existing volunteers and members.

Of all the forms of fundraising, organizations in the United States use special event fundraising more than any other. From the volunteer fire department to the Philharmonic, most groups have, in all likelihood, organized one kind of special event or another to attract constituents and to raise funds. It is no surprise, then, that the array of these events is staggering: garage sales, craft fairs, bowlathons, house tours, concerts, dinners, cocktail parties, wine and cheese receptions, street bazaars, and so on ad infinitum.

Special event fundraising can net anything up to hundreds of thousands of dollars. A major charity ball in a large metropolis might net $250,000, while a garage sale in a suburban community might net $2,000. The inherent appeal, timing, and advance planning of an event determine in good measure its financial success.

WHAT ARE THE ADVANTAGES OF RAISING MONEY THROUGH SPECIAL EVENTS?

If you are methodical in your planning, there can be many advantages in special events.

1. Well-planned special events can assuredly generate revenues. If you are repeating a past event, you are in a better position to know how to reduce your costs as well as predict your net income.

2. A special event provides an opportunity to invite new people and thus broaden your constituency.

3. Special events can be rewarding and fun. No other form of fundraising can bring so much pleasure to both the organizers and the participants.

4. Special events signal to the public at large the numerical strength of your constituency and the resulting leverage that you can bring to bear on any issue your group might decide to tackle.

5. Successful events become traditions in their own right, drawing old and new participants each year.

In short, special events have proven themselves to be reliable and steady sources of income, while also serving to enhance an organization's public image.

WHAT ARE THE DISADVANTAGES OF RAISING MONEY THROUGH SPECIAL EVENTS?

1. Pulling together a good event requires a lot of work. How much work depends on the event's size and scope. Large-scale events such as walkathons, annual dinners, and concerts need many people working for the many hours it takes to plan, implement, and evaluate the project.

Unsuccessful organizers usually sing a sad, familiar refrain: "We didn't raise any money, but everybody had a good time," or "We garnered a lot of favorable publicity which certainly makes up for what we didn't raise in funds."

Sure, a good time for your hard-working volunteers, staff, and board members is important, as is the local publicity, but they are not substitutes for the dollars your organization needs to pay its bills.

The money you raise through a special event is its reason for being. So, when thinking about a new type of special event, first be sure to consider how much staff and volunteer time will be required to make the event successful and decide whether these expenditures are feasible.

2. Like direct mail, some special events require initial investments, necessitating an outlay of funds before realizing any income.

For example, for annual dinners a hotel almost always requires a deposit in advance, just as a movie theater might for a benefit premiere. Small-scale fundraising events, however, require a minimal investment, if any. A raffle requires only the donation of prizes by individuals or businesses, including the printing of the tickets, while items for a tag sale or garage sale can be handmade or second-hand, and all merchandise donated.

3. Some special events can be organized on a shoestring budget with limited lead time (i.e., one month). Many others require more advance planning time, aside from the initial investments just discussed. In fact, the more ambitious your fundraising goals, the more advance time you'll need for planning.

4. Special events can also provide so much fun for volunteers that their efforts may be diverted from the other types of fundraising which are less immediately gratifying and rewarding, such as proposal writing and face-to-face solicitation.

HOW CAN YOUR ORGANIZATION DECIDE WHETHER TO LAUNCH A SPECIAL EVENT?

You're probably already engaging in certain activities or events that are perfect candidates for fundraisers, even though you may not yet have explored the fundraising potential inherent in open houses, tabling efforts, petitioning, annual meetings, and so forth.

Very often fundraising can be "piggybacked" onto, or incorporated into, a programmatic activity without much additional work. If, for example, your organization normally holds an annual meeting to brief members and constituents on the work of the past year, you could easily add to the program of the day an auction or a raffle or a program ad book (individuals and businesses pay "x" dollars to be listed or to advertise their services in the book). Since you'll be doing the publicity for the event, you have already made all the efforts you need to ensure an audience. You are adding only one more activity: a special event.

Churches, clubs, and service organizations often rely on the piggyback method. A church can hold an annual bazaar with booths, food, rides—a perfect opportunity to set up a table and raffle something of value, such as a car, with no additional expense but substantial added income.

Another form of piggyback fundraising is to organize an activity as part of a larger public event, such as a street fair or carnival, where a sponsoring organization assumes the responsibility for promotion and advertising to attract an audience. In these instances, you merely need to decide what products (for example, baked goods, sandwiches, beverages, bumper stickers, buttons, posters) or activities (such as carnival games) would most appeal to the crowds that such public events have attracted in the past. Did you attend the last street fair in your community? What were most of the booths selling? Food? Antiques? Thrift sale items? Just as a small business can hawk its wares on the Fourth of July at the annual town celebration, so can you. (Familiarize yourself with the consumer instincts of your potential customers and when the day arrives, you'll be ready for business.)

Now, our first two piggyback examples are fairly easy to organize: You simply need a winning idea or product and an occasion that already attracts relatively large numbers of people. Make a list of all the events and programs that you normally organize in a given year. Also, enumerate all the major public events in your town or city that attract large crowds each year. Then, review each list to see if any are potential candidates for piggyback fundraising.

Certain occasions seem to warrant organizing a special event. Your group may have a critical need for a small amount of money quickly. You ran out of funds, for example, but are expecting a new grant next month. Or you have a special one-time need, like purchasing a word processor, that you didn't anticipate in your yearly budget. In both instances, a special event can bring in those needed funds without expending a lot of effort.

Triple Jeopardy, a now-defunct grassroots, community-based organization in north Philadelphia concerned with the health of third-world women, had such a need. They were looking for a quick source of money to launch their work. Their need was modest: several hundred dollars to pay for items such as postage and office expenses. They decided to offer a chicken dinner for all their friends, whose orders had been solicited in advance. Their volunteer chauffeurs would then deliver the chicken dinners that night in time for dinner. In this way, Triple Jeopardy earned $300 to pay some of their expenses, with less than a week's efforts.

You may wonder, however, whether to enter into the arena of large-scale special events. If you decide to, move with trepidation, caution, and planning! First of all, answer the following questions, which should provide a useful guide:

1. Do I know my present or anticipated constituency? Would they prefer a benefit night at the local skating rink or the ballet? In short, what activities do they enjoy?

2. What events have already succeeded in my community? What have similar groups organized? Which went well? Which didn't?

3. How large are my present and potential pools of volunteers waiting in the wings to help with the work involved in organizing a special event fundraiser?

See the sample worksheet for more help in planning your special events.

HOW ARE SPECIAL EVENTS ORGANIZED?

Traditionally, special events are organized by volunteers. Volunteers are the planners and the administrators as well as the envelope stuffers, the chauffeurs, the cooks, the leafleteers, and so on. Occasionally, however, salaried staff and even outside fundraising firms may become involved in both the planning and implementation of a fundraising special event.

In contrast to one-to-one solicitations, few volunteers shun the opportunity to work on special event fundraising. Many people are eager to work with others; they enjoy working communally to stage an evening or an event that the audience will find memorable. Moreover, people of any age can join in, from teenagers who organize walkathons in their communities to grandmothers who sell their own homemade pies and cakes at the street fair. Only willingness, not any special talent, is required.

Planning, however, is inherent to the success of any event. Nothing is as depressing as opening the theater on the benefit night to find only fifty stalwart souls, rather than four hundred, in the theater. Planning is the means to see to it that the theater is full that night. In its simplest form, planning is anticipating all the possible questions in advance, such as:

1. How can we fill the theater?

2. Whom should we invite?

3. How can we most effectively reach them?

4. What can they afford to pay for a ticket?

5. What curtain time is most convenient?

The process of defining and answering these questions far enough in advance constitutes planning. Let's illustrate the planning process by taking one common special event, the walkathon.

We can trace the origin of the walkathon to the fall of 1969 in Fargo, North Dakota, where one thousand people, primarily of high school and college age, walked a twenty-five-mile course to raise funds for self-help development projects at home and abroad, and to raise consciousness in their communities about the root causes of poverty and malnutrition.

Each volunteer secured sponsors who were willing to pay from twenty-five cents to five dollars for every mile the volunteer walked, a walk that was called a "Hunger Hike," or a "Walk for Development."

Within four years, committees in more than 1,000 communities, under the auspices of the American Freedom from Hunger Foundation, followed North Fargo's example in organizing such efforts, and raised more than ten million dollars to alleviate human suffering and to foster development around the world.

These walks were the predecessors of the currently popular walkathons, bikeathons, and swimathons that numerous organizations are now using to raise both the visibility of their issues and the funds to support their work.

Organizations such as the Women's Funding Coalition, the Mobilization for Survival, and the Nuclear Freeze all successfully use walkathons to raise funds for their programs and to promote their issues. Even in their early years, Walks for Development mobilized literally hundreds of thousands of participants who managed to raise $100,000 to $250,000 in large urban centers, and all from a one-day activity. These walks were organized by students from local colleges and high schools and even junior high schools.

What was involved in organizing these walks? What made them successful? How can today's organizations replicate these earlier successes? To illustrate how to plan a special event effectively, let's examine the stages involved in organizing these walks.

WALK FOR DEVELOPMENT SAMPLE TIME LINE

3 months before walk date	2 months before walk date	1 month before walk date
Publicity	**Publicity**	**Publicity**
1. Meetings with key media people for programming and articles.	**1.** Schedule of press releases and news conferences covering walk logistics, office address, route maps, walk beneficiary, etc.	**1.** Radio and TV publicity and promo blitz begins.
2. Endorsements of local and state officials.		**2.** Begin button and sticker sales.
3. Brochure planned.		
Recruitment of Walkers	**Recruitment of Walkers**	**Recruitment of Walkers**
1. Invitations to walk.	**1.** School assemblies, meetings with civic leaders and groups, and other speaking engagements.	**1.** Dispersal of walk cards and project information.
2.. Get on agendas and into meetings, school assemblies.		
3. Get on agenda of city councils, school boards.		
Logistics	**Logistics**	**Logistics**
1. Recipient of funds designated.	**1.** Office secured.	**1.** Walk bank acount secured.
2. Checkpoint and starting points approved.	**2.** Accountant secured.	**2.** Final approval of route and check points.
3. Planning of walk-day logistics, including transportation and communication, VIPs and ceremonies.	**3.** Overhead account secured.	
	4. Meeting with police for approval of check points, route, and starting point.	**After Walk**
	5. Walk card layout to printer.	**1.** Process walk cards.

Special Planning Tips

1. *Get it donated.* In organizing a special event, seek to have everything donated. Such costs as space for the event, printing of tickets, posters, brochures, ad books, and refreshments and the like all add up and consume potential profits. Make profits by pursuing all possible routes to obtain these things for free *before* you decide to spend money for them. Another way to cover your overhead costs is to conduct a raffle at the event itself. The proceeds from the raffle can be used to cover the expenses of the event that were not donated, and will add an extra sense of excitement to the event.

2. *Consider honoring individuals at your events.* Nothing helps fill a room more than honoring individuals or even organizations for their contributions. Banquets, parties, luncheons, dinners, and even picnics lend themselves to extending recognition to those who have made contributions to your own organization or to the community at large.

If you do honor someone, don't be shy in asking that party to send out personalized invitations to his or her friends and colleagues, or at least to provide their addresses to you for you to mail out. That's common procedure.

3. *Get volunteers to do it.* Organizing special events, particularly large-scale ones, can be hard work and time consuming, but also very rewarding. That's why it is not only efficient but gratifying for volunteers to provide the people power. They will find pleasure in the work, and provide needed assistance to usually overextended board and staff members.

4. *Pick your date carefully in advance.* Avoid holidays, weekends during the summer, tax season, election day, dates of competing events, and so forth. On a blank year-at-a-glance calendar, cross out all the dates that would be inappropriate due to these and other kinds of conflicts. Now decide which times are the most attractive to your particular constituency.

Once you've set your dates, which preferably you should do a year in advance, ask similar groups in your community to honor your dates by not scheduling their own events too closely to them. Extend them the same courtesy. If negotiation is necessary, it will be worth it. Better negotiate than face a half-full house.

5. *Make your events into annual traditions.* If a special event has been successful, there is no reason why it cannot be successful again in subsequent years. Build on your past success by billing your events 2nd Annual, 5th Annual, 10th Annual, etc. As long as people enjoy themselves, you are extending to them the opportunity for the same pleasure again and again. They will begin to look forward to your annual spring picnic or New Year's Eve dance each year.

6. *Keep your events fun-filled and enjoyable.* Nothing is more deadly than bringing people together, and then making them sit through hours of speeches. Allow people at your programs numerous opportunities to mingle and to meet others. Keep your presentations and programs short and to the point, even at testi-

monial dinners. People invariably would rather talk to each other than sit passively and listen to speeches for long lengths of time.

7. Don't forget about piggybacking. If your staff, board, and volunteer resources are limited for some reason or another at a certain time of the year, don't overlook conducting a piggybacked special event. On these occasions, other groups arrange a street festival, bazaar, arts and crafts fair, concert, or some other event, and take responsibility for all the logistical arrangements and for all the promotion to bring people out. You simply sell your wares—food, T-shirts, buttons, bumper stickers, books, publications, or calendars, etc.—to the throngs that turn out for these events.

Another variation allows other organizations to piggyback on your event to your mutual advantage. For example, if you are organizing a large-scale event like a concert, you could consider selling blocks of tickets to other groups at a discount. They, in turn, will sell those tickets to their own constituents. By doing so, you are more assured of covering all your costs and maximizing your potential profits. Or you may even go a step further and co-host a special event with another organization.

8. Involve your prospective participants as volunteers. One creative way to maximize turnout for a special event is to involve as many people as possible in the planning of the event itself. People can be asked to serve on the sponsor's committee for the program, on any of the volunteer working committees of the event (e.g., decorating, tickets, food), or as hosts or greeters at the event itself. In these ways, you're increasing the investment of more people in the success of the actual event. A secondary advantage is that you have identified a core of people to draw from in recruiting for the event next year.

25th Anniversary Benefit Concert
Coalition for the Homeless

Peter Paul & Mary

BLEECKER TO BROADWAY

The New York Coalition for the Homeless is an advocacy organization dedicated to the proposition that decent shelter, sufficient food and affordable housing are fundamental rights in a civilized society. The Coalition is building a constituency to stop the disgrace of homelessness.

The Coalition fights in Washington, in Albany and in New York to provide relief for the homeless poor of our city. It has won court orders mandating the city of New York to create shelters for the homeless. In addition, it is in the streets seven nights a week feeding hungry, homeless people.

Photograph © Gregory Heisler, 1985
Courtesy Eastman Kodak Company, Professional Photography Division.

Sometimes celebrities lend their talent in support of local nonprofit organizations.

Source: Peter, Paul and Mary 25th Anniversary Concert for New York Coalition for the Homeless, New York, NY. *Artwork:* Milton Glaser. Reprinted with permission.

Creative Special Events

With a little ingenuity and a lot of planning, your special event can be something people will talk about for months afterward, as well as a monetary success. All the better for next year's event too!

Listed below are examples of successful creative special events, most of which were held in the New York City area.

—CARE, the international relief and development agency, holds a No Show banquet. The invitation reads, "You are invited but please don't come." CARE asks people to stay home and contribute in one of four categories: (1) $100: "Count on me. Here's my contribution for the new outfit I don't have to buy for the banquet." (2) $50: "Thank goodness I don't have to eat another chicken dinner." (3) $25: "I won't need a sitter and won't have to pay for parking." (4) Any amount: "Thank you for inviting me. I would be glad not to come so that CARE can provide assistance to those struggling for daily survival."

—The No Elephant Circus, a circus without animals, held a fall benefit treating the guests at the $25-a-plate dinner to their usual sampling of magic, mime, and song. But they were also treated to a juggling act that was entered in the Guinness Book of World Records. Ron Dario, the artistic director of the No Elephant Circus, thought the benefit would be enlivened if a Guinness representative were invited to watch a troupe member juggle seven balls simultaneously. The juggler so impressed his audience, including the Guinness representative, that the Guinness Book of World Records added another category— juggling. The No Elephant Circus is a New York-based, nonprofit group of six actors, mimes, and magicians who clown not in rings but on stages, often for charitable causes.

—The Home and School Association of the Murch Elementary School, in Washington, D.C., had a capital idea for their annual auction. For a pledge of $65.00, they offered an insider's tour of the Capitol building conducted by a member of the House of Representatives, and, for $180.00, lunch at the White House with a member of the White House staff. Among the other donated gifts was "the perfect gift for the person who has everything"—an offer by Washington's mayor, Marion S. Barry, Jr., to exchange a hefty contribution to the school for an official proclamation "establishing a day in your honor" at a personal ceremony in his office. Their auction nets approximately $20,000 each year.

—Each year on Long Island, a mansion that has been placed on the market for sale is chosen as the site for the annual Designers Showcase. And each year a different nonprofit group reaps the benefits of opening the house and grounds to visitors who pay a modest admission price. Besides the grounds and the mansion, visitors are treated to individual rooms, each decorated by a different designer. Local designers donate their services in decorating a room of the mansion, and all proceeds go to the sponsoring group. Last year, fifty thousand visitors paid six dollars each to visit the mansion over a period of four weekends.

—New Dramatists, a national support organization for playwrights, has its own annual tradition—the Celebrity Doodle Sale. Held in 1983 in New York and San Francisco, the group collected thirty "doodles" from such cultural luminaries as Leonard Bernstein, Sir John Gielgud, Sir Laurence Olivier, Colleen Dewhurst, and Jose Ferrer, and auctioned them off at bids starting at $75.00. All told, the two auctions netted $20,000, and planning is underway for next year in the same cities plus Los Angeles. The Celebrity Doodle Sale is sponsored by Alfred Dunhill and Company, manufacturer of tobacco products and clothing. Dunhill underwrites all the expenses of the auctions.

—The Family, a nonprofit repertory theater, staged a play with the inmates of Rikers Island, a correctional facility in New York City, as the stars. The show is about life and death in the ghetto, from the inside looking out. Billed as "An Evening of Theater on Rikers Island," a few hundred contributors paid $50.00 a ticket for the event. The money went to benefit future theater projects at the prison.

—In 1983, the Children's Art Carnival, a nonprofit arts school in Harlem serving about 750 students ranging in age from four to twenty-one, lost $170,000 in federal assistance, according to Betty Blayton-Taylor, the school's director. To bolster its sagging revenues the school sponsored a "noshathon," featuring specialties cooked by 114 men. Billed as "Men Who Cook," the foodfest featured such dishes as insurance executive Patrick Carter's paella, City College program director Ramon Berenguer's empanadas, and CBS News correspondent Stephen Bohannon's cassoulet.

Pitfalls and Lessons (or Special Events Forever)

"Nothing breeds success like success." This maxim applies as much to special events fundraising as to any other activity. So if you organize an event that attracts new constituents, attains its fundraising goal, and enhances your organization's public profile, don't rest on your laurels too long. Build on that success! First, evaluate your event, assess its components, decide which ingredients made it successful. Questions to address: How did people hear of the event? What motivated them to come? What made the event enjoyable? What would have made it more enjoyable? Query some of those who attended, with these same questions.

Remember that a successful special event is the beginning of a new tradition within an organization. It lays the groundwork for an activity that can continue to serve your organization well into the future. And look ahead to the next year as you close the pages on this year's event. Build into this year's planning the foundation for the next time around.

Case Study
THE NO-BENEFIT BENEFIT

For some, it is clearly intriguing NOT to attend a benefit. For the past five years the Fortune Society, one of New York's leading criminal justice organizations, has capitalized on the feeling of many that the hustle and bustle of fundraising parties in any given season can get too overwhelming. Their solution? Like the CARE example recently discussed, to send out a compelling invitation to potential supporters, asking them to stay home. The solicitation letter conjures up the parties that might have been—a dinner at the Waldorf, a disco party at Studio 54—and the reactions that might have been—groans and moans at the thought of attending a party that would start at 1:00 A.M. on a work night. In the end, the Fortune staff tells the reader, they thought better of it all, and offered instead the opportunity to stay at home, curl up with a book, and "help Fortune with all the money you will save by not going out."

The approach is clever, and it clearly works. The No-Benefit Benefit has netted the organization tens of thousands of dollars over the last five years.

Fortune estimates they spent approximately $1,200 in year five for postage and mimeograph paper for invitations, which is about what it had cost in previous years. Close to a thousand people respond each year.

What causes Fortune's constituents to give so generously each year to a nonbenefit for a cause that is surely not one of the most popular around—services to ex-offenders? Staff believes it has something to do with the fact that Fortune takes an approach that reveals a sense of humor. People get a chuckle out of the idea, and the message gets across that Fortune would rather spend its money on services than on extravaganzas—something that obviously touches a chord in donors. The thought that their money will be used frugally, in fact, may encourage people to give more.

There are suggested variations on this theme from other organizations: a No-Baby Baby Shower to raise money for neighboring low-income families; and a No-Banquet Banquet held by a Little League in Hoboken, New Jersey, inviting nonparents to support the local team.

Whatever nonevent you decide to hold, make your opening clever and be sure to include serious information on your program. Fortune includes a several-point list of what specific programs and what specific populations are aided by the money raised.

by Kate Chieco

from
THE FORTUNE SOCIETY

39 West 19th Street, New York, N.Y. 10011
(212) 206-7070

"THE DEGREE OF CIVILIZATION IN A SOCIETY CAN BE JUDGED BY ENTERING ITS PRISONS."

Dostoevski

Dear Fortune Friend:

And you thought that this was to be the winter of discontent.

But it is that time of the year to announce that this is the 6th Annual Fortune Society No-Benefit Benefit. The excitement extends from Alaska to Rio, from Maine to Tucson. You can be part of the Fortune Society's growth. You needn't get gas for the car or purchase new outfits. At this special benefit, there are no supercilious head-waiters or parking problems.

It is our annual middle-of-the-winter extension of love to our supporters. We afford you the opportunity to give without going out. There isn't a disco or hotel which could give you the same pleasure as your own home. So, stay at home! Become better acquainted with your couch, your tv, and the food in the refrigerator.

Then send your check to the Fortune Society. We can continue our work without you spending a cold winter's night slushing through to some dreaded event.

Your support will enable Fortune Society to continue its work with men, women and youth, who have no other door to enter. Our ability, during the last 17 years, to create new opportunities for people who come to us, can affect the quality of life in New York City. It also serves as a role model for similar groups in towns and cities across the nation.

Your support helped us to:

 *Continue our LEARNED STRAIGHT one-to-one tutoring program, which
  last year worked with over 275 different students.
 *More than 2300 ex-offenders came to Fortune during 1983 for one-to-
  one counselling.
 *More than 300 persons were enrolled in vocational training programs or
  found full-time and part-time employment through our Career Development
  Unit.

You also were part of an army of Fortune Society supporters who enabled us to move to our new home without sacrificing our continuity of work.

The Fortune goal is to have less crime and fewer victims. Our approach is not dramatic, but it is surer than the politically expedient. Thanks for your continued support and have a great evening at home!

Cordially,

David Rothenberg
Executive Director

A No-Benefit Benefit has proven to be an effective direct mail solicitation for many organizations.

Source: The Fortune Society, New York, NY. Reprinted with permission.

Case Study
THE ULTIMATE FUNDRAISER

Marty Rogol, executive director of USA for Africa, couldn't keep up with his mail in February of 1985. It came in cartons, full of ideas and requests springing from the astounding success of the rock single, "We Are the World," and its offspring book, video, records, T-shirts, buttons, and posters.

Just sixteen weeks after Harry Belafonte phoned Ken Kragen (agent for such pop stars as Lionel Ritchie and Kenny Rogers) to suggest a fundraising concert for Ethiopian relief, Rogol found himself heading the USA for Africa Foundation. The initial proposed income of $10.8 million promised to total $35 million or more.

What started as an emergency lifeboat operation became a new development organization. Why the great success? What next? And what can local groups learn from this?

It all started when Bob Geldorf, lead singer in the Irish rock group Boomtown Rats, put together a group of British pop stars, called Band Aid, and recorded a single, "Do They Know It's Christmas?" which raised $10 million for victims of the African famine.

Geldorf explained, "We in the music business have made drugs fashionable; we've made wild clothing and hairstyles fashionable; now it is time we made compassion and generosity fashionable."

The idea took hold; groups in France, Canada, and Latin America have followed suit. But the biggest effort so far—the ultimate fundraiser—was by forty-five American pop and rock stars whose "We Are the World" album sold over 4,000,000 within a year.

Disc jockeys from 5,000 radio stations organized a simultaneous spin of "We Are the World" around the planet. Local groups have held singalongs and bake sales to combat hunger both in Africa and at home.

Why the phenomenal success? Is it merely the fact that forty-five superstars assembled for one evening and sang their hearts out to a well-written song (by Michael Jackson and Lionel Ritchie)? Was it the lyrics? The melody? The marketing? The message?

Even Marty Rogol isn't sure. "We may have to wait fifteen years," he asserts, "until a doctoral student does a dissertation." Or does that teenager walking down the street, smiling and humming the tune, already know the answer?

It's worth speculating about the origins of this fabulous outporing of excitement and money (production expenses and artists' fees were all donated), this fundraising story of the century. America's 785,000-plus nonprofit organizations can take some hints about how to move large numbers of people with their own messages:

1. The message is simple. The song title says it in four words: "We are the world." It appeals to an inherent desire for a sense of community, a sense of oneness with others—simple but powerful sentiments.

The words are a rallying call to lofty ideals—not necessarily USA for Africa or any particular organization. Why can't any nonprofit organization develop a slogan that conveys its message in similar terms? A day-care center might say, "Our kids are our future." A senior citizens' center could use "Support our elders. They're your parents, too."

2. Music has always motivated and forged unity among people. That's why each nation chooses a national anthem and colleges, high schools, and summer camps have their own songs.

Why can't a nonprofit ask a local composer to write a song for its use?

3. We all long for that sense of community. When others unite in a worthy cause, the message comes through that we can, too. If forty-five rock stars "can check their egos at the door," as Quincy Jones aptly observed on the night of the recording, why can't neighbors, towns, cities, countries, and the world?

Block clubs, tenant groups, and parent-teacher associations, for example, offer their constituents not only participation but a sense of belonging as well.

4. Compassion is a powerful sensation, perhaps buried and needing nurturing, ready to blossom. You can see it on the artists' faces in "We Are the World." How can one tap that compassion in others?

Direct mail campaigns are much more effective when they show names and faces of real people.

5. "We too can make a difference." Even the superstars are dwarfed in "We Are the World" by the specter of hunger, starvation, and death that flashes on the screen. Yet the sense of hope—and the appeal to do something, anything, to help the situation—is empowering.

Neighbors organizing to save a park from a developer's bulldozer are not only beautifying a corner in their community but demonstrating the power of collective community action.

6. People like to be asked to help. If you provide them with an immediate opportunity to make a modest contribution to a cause they believe in, and they'll respond.

That impulse shows up in high sales of Girl Scout cookies, UNICEF greeting cards, Sierra Club calendars, and so on.

7. Results depend as much on who asks as on what is being asked for. People respond when Kenny Rogers, Tina Turner, Cyndi Lauper, Paul Simon, and Stevie Wonder say "Give what you can."

Every community has its own respected leaders who can be approached to join a board of directors, a standing committee, or a body of advisers. Or, they can be asked to sign direct mail solicitations, chair special events, and speak at testimonial dinners.

These are some of the principles that propelled the phenomenal success of "We Are the World." But it didn't end that night in Los Angeles. It's already spawned hundreds of local efforts:

- community singalongs in schools and community centers from Florence, Alabama, to Greenwich Village, New York, to Vashon, Washington;

- a fundraising concert in St. Louis;

- restaurants in New York and Seattle from where proceeds— from one special night or from certain menu items—went to USA for Africa.

In addition, the "We Are the World" book recommends car washes, bake sales, garage sales, walkathons, bikeathons, and other traditional techniques such as house parties. It also recommends days of fasting—with media coverage—as a way for schools to make a local impact.

Results of the USA for Africa effort are already taking root. Thirty-five percent of its proceeds are earmarked for direct African relief—especially food and medicine. Another 35 percent will buy seeds and agricultural advice and equipment to help those nations become self-supporting. The rest will go for "long-term development projects" aimed at self-sufficiency (20 percent) and to combat hunger in the United States.

Marty Rogol says that none of the group's administrative expenses will come from merchandise sales; salaries of the six staff people will be raised from private sources.

"We Are the World" has clearly earned its niche in the annals of American philanthropy. The final chapter will be written in Africa. And the epilogue will show how nonprofits here have learned from some of the lessons behind this wonderful success story.

by Michael Seltzer
and Steven Silha

Summary Worksheet

for

_____

(name of your organization)

APPROACHING INDIVIDUAL FOR SUPPORT: SPECIAL EVENTS

Building on Special Events to Date

1. Are you already organizing special events to raise funds?

☐ yes   ☐ no

If so, what are they?   What are their net proceeds?
(gross income minus expenses)

a. _____ $_____

b. _____ $_____

c. _____ $_____

d. _____ $_____

e. _____ $_____

2. Which of these events rely more on volunteer energies than on staff energies?

a. _____

b. _____

c. _____

3. Which of those special events are "proven" traditions (i.e., continue to attract more people each year, raise more funds each year, etc.)?

a. _____

b. _____

c. _____

4. Which events should be discarded (due to declining numbers of participants and sagging receipts) or vastly overhauled?

a. _____

b. _____

c. _____

5. How can you enhance the income potential for any of these events (i.e., maximizing use of volunteers, getting more costs donated, etc.)?

Additional Actions Needed

a. _____   _____
                                _____
                                _____

b. _____   _____
                                _____
                                _____

c. _____   _____
                                _____
                                _____

d. _____   _____
                                _____
                                _____

e. _____   _____
                                _____
                                _____

Planning New Special Events

6. What new ideas for special events would you like to explore further? (Note: Convene a brainstorming meeting of your fundraising committee to come up with ideas.)

a. _____

b. _____

c. _____

d. _____

7. Have others tried any of these events in your community? What has been their experience? Have you approached them for advice?

Name of Other Organization

a. _____   _____

b. _____   _____

c. _____   _____

8. What realistic fundraising goals can you set for each of your special events programs, individually and collectively?

Total:

Each Event:

Current   *New*

_____   _____

_____   _____

_____   _____

9. How much people power is needed to organize each event? How much time should be allocated up front to plan each event successfully?

	Advance Planning Time	*People Power Needed*
_____	_____	_____
_____	_____	_____
_____	_____	_____

10. Finding Assistance and Counsel

Name three or more individuals who might be able to advise you on how to more effectively organize special events.

a. _____

b. _____

c. _____

d. _____

e. _____

11. Rating Your Special Events Potential

On the basis of what you have learned, how would you rank your chances of raising funds through special events?

☐ Very Good   ☐ Possible   ☐ Unlikely   ☐ Still Unknown

Special Event Planning Form

1. Where will the event be held?

   _____

2. Can the location be seen as a drawing element?

   ____ yes   ____ no

3. What up-front monetary resources will be needed?

   $_____

4. Is there an interest in this type of event in the community?

   ____ yes   ____ no

5. Will the event draw an audience?

   ____ yes   ____ no

   If yes, what is the reason for them to attend?

   _____

6. What will you be giving to those who attend (i.e., exposure, social time, etc.)?

   _____

7. When will the event be held?

   _____

   Will the event conflict with other events that would interest the same audience?

   ____ yes   ____ no

8. How much planning time does the group need to put the event together?

   _____

9. How will organizational information be introduced?

   _____

10. How will publicity be targeted at the audience? For example, are there related groups with newsletters that would advertise for you?

    _____

11. Who do you know? Who do your friends know? How can you effectively network to attract people to the event?

    _____

    _____

    _____

    _____

12. Does the event lend itself to honoring anyone?

_____ yes   _____ no

13. Is the event attractive enough to be an annual tradition for your organization?

_____ yes   _____ no

14. Are there two people whom you could approach to be co-chairs of the event?

_____ yes   _____ no

If yes, who are they?

a. _____

b. _____

15. Finally, can you anticipate that people will have a good time if they attend?

_____ yes   _____ no

(Adapted from a form used by Amnesty International U.S.A.)

FURTHER READINGS

Ayer Fund-Raising Dinner Guide. Philadelphia: Ayer Press. 1974, 120 pp. $8.90. (Order from: Ayer Press, W. Washington Square, Philadelphia, PA 19106)
   Guide for planning dinners as fundraising events.

Berson, Ginny. *Making a Show of It. A Guide to Concert Production*. Ukiah, CA: Redwood Records. 1980. 102 pp. $5.95. (Order from: Redwood Records, P.O. Box 996, Ukiah, CA 95482)
   Guide to planning a concert, including sample performance contracts, booking checklists, and budgets.

DeSoto, Carole. *For Fun and Funds: Creative Fund-Raising Ideas for Your Organization*. West Nyack, NY: Parker Publishing Co. 1984. 208 pp. $15.95. (Order from: Parker Publishing Co., Englewood Cliffs, NJ 07632)
   Instructions for over 160 money-making activities, both large and small. Covers such topics as advance planning, pricing, procedures, committees, scheduling, and publicity.

Drotning, Philip T. *500 Ways for Small Charities to Raise Money*. Hartsdale, NY: Public Service Materials Center. 1981. 177 pp. $16.00. (Order from: Public Service Materials Center, 111 N. Central Ave., Hartsdale, NY 10530)
   Covers a variety of fundraising strategies including how to organize successful fundraising events.

Flanagan, Joan. *The Grass Roots Fundraising Book: How to Raise Money In Your Community*. Chicago: Contemporary Books, Inc. 1982. 344 pp. $8.95. (Order from: Contemporary Books, 180 North Michigan Ave., Chicago, IL 60601)
   Classic guide for raising money from interested people in ways that also build the organization. Includes how-to information on a variety of special events.

Harrison, Bette Krissell. *The Garage Sale Handbook*. New York: Berkley Publishing Group. 1983. 127 pp. $2.95. (Order from: Berkley Publishing Group, 200 Madison Ave., New York, NY 10016)
   Business approach to the various aspects of garage sales including ads, legal considerations, preparation, pricing and security. Although written for individuals, is also applicable to use of a garage sale as a fundraising event for an organization.

Honig, Lisa. "The Santa Barbara County Run for Justice." *Grassroots Fundraising Journal* (December 1982): 7–9. Single issue $3.50. (Order from: Grassroots Fundraising Journal, 517 Union Ave., Suite 206, Knoxville, TN 37902)
   Information about a fundraising marathon event.

Leibert, Edwin R., and Bernice E. Sheldon. *Handbook of Special Events for Nonprofit Organizations: Tested Ideas for Fund Raising and Public Relations*. Chicago: Association Press/Follett Publishing Co. 1972. 224 pp. $12.95. (Order from: Association Press/Follett Publishing Co., 1010 W. Washington St., Chicago, IL 60607)

Details for planning many big money fundraisers such as charity balls, fashion shows, testimonial dinners and anniversary events. Includes checklists and samples of invitations, programs and records.

Pritchard, J. Harris. *There's Plenty of Money for Nonprofit Groups Willing to Earn Their Share*. Phoenix: Cornucopia Publications, Inc. 1984. 456 pp. $57.00. (Order from: Cornucopia Publications, Inc., 2515 E. Thomas Rd., Phoenix, AZ 85016)

Ideas and plans for many fundraising activities including: marathon and athletic events, decorator tours, telethons, banquets, auctions, theatrical presentations, raffles, and junkets.

Sheerin, Mara. *How to Raise Top Dollars from Special Events*. Hartsdale, NY: Public Service Materials Center. 1984. 123 pp. $24.00. (Order from: Public Service Materials Center, 111 N. Central Ave., Hartsdale, NY 10530)

Guide to planning large-scale special events with samples of letters, invitations, press releases, programs, and budgets.

Stegall, Lael, and Betsy Crone. *Fundraising Events: Making Womanpower Profitable*. Washington, DC: National Women's Political Caucus. 1978. 24 pp. $2.00. (Order from: National Women's Political Caucus, 1411 K St., N.W., Suite 1110, Washington, DC 20005)

Instructions to help any committee plan a special event from beginning to end. Includes sample press release, timeline, response card, tally sheets, mailgram and instructions for workers.

CHAPTER 11

BEYOND THE SIMPLE CASH CONTRIBUTION: PLANNED GIVING

Individuals can make gifts to nonprofit organizations in many forms. Most commonly, Americans make direct gifts of money, either checks or cash, to their favored charitable organizations. But it is not unusual these days for contributors to charge their gifts to their credit cards, or to even make their gift by a "pay by phone" arrangement with their bank. In the case of the latter, the bank pays the contribution, often a set monthly amount, directly to the recipient.

People considering ways to make charitable gifts have several other choices as well. They can make gifts of property (land, securities, equipment, etc.), including their own personal residence; name organizations as beneficiaries of life insurance policies; designate recipients in their wills to receive bequests; and make other various "planned" gifts, either through annuities, trusts, or pooled income funds, whereby they may continue to receive income while the nonprofit recipient also benefits.

The following examples illustrate the range of nonprofit organizations involved in planned giving:

- The United Negro College Fund and The Equitable Life Assurance Society launched in 1986 the "Charitable Gifts of Life" program, whereby individuals purchase Equitable Life insurance policies that name the Fund as owner and beneficiary. This provides the donor with a substantial

The author wishes to thank Judith Bardes and Rochelle Korman, Esq. for their invaluable collaboration on this chapter.

tax-deductible contribution on the premiums and he or she is able to spread the cost of the policy over several years. At the same time, the United Negro College Fund is able to fully use the policies' cash reserves immediately, if they so choose.

● In its brochure, the Harlem School of the Arts suggests ways that individuals can "establish a gift that will perpetuate your memory and help assure that the fruits of the Harlem School of the Arts are carried to future generations." These "special opportunities for giving" include gift annuities and wills.

● In its newsletter, NRDC newsline, the National Resources Defense Council invites its supporters to consider "providing for NRDC" in their wills. "A bequest to NRDC will perpetuate your commitment to natural resources by enabling us to continue our highly effective legal and scientific programs."

● In 1984, the Center for the Study of Women in Society at the University of Oregon received a $3.5 million bequest from Willian Harris and his late wife, Jane Grant. This gift was the largest in the University's history. (See the case study at the end of the chapter for details.)

● Each year, Lambda Legal Defense and Education Fund receives several unsolicited gifts, in the form of bequests or life insurance policies, from committed members.

How do these forms of giving operate? What are the advantages for the donor, as well as for the recipient? How can an organization secure such gifts?

DEFINITION: PLANNED GIVING

Planned giving is the term used to describe those gifts of money, securities, or other property made by a donor for future, or sometimes, present use by the recipient nonprofit organization. Major types of planned gifts include wills, property, life insurance, living trusts, and gift annuities. To be eligible to receive any of the planned gifts described in this chapter, the receiving organization must be nonprofit, and designated as exempt from federal income taxes under section 501(c)(3) of the Internal Revenue Code. The different types of planned gift opportunities are as follows:

Life Insurance

A nonprofit may be named as beneficiary of a new or existing life insurance policy. The nonprofit may be the first ("primary") beneficiary, or a second, third, or later contingent beneficiary for all or part of the policy's proceeds. Individuals may also give life insurance policies to nonprofit organizations and gain income tax deductions. The donor deducts the sum of paid premiums or the cash value of the policy as charitable contributions for income tax purposes.

Individuals occasionally find that the reasons originally motivating their purchase of life insurance policies are no longer as pressing. For example, they may have wanted to make financial provisions for children, who are now grown and self-supporting. In such cases, they may decide to change the beneficiary of their life insurance policy to a favored charity.

Gift Annuities and Trusts

Sometimes individuals want to make a significant gift to a nonprofit organization, but are reluctant to give away property or cash that can produce income for them. They can satisfy both desires with a special type of gift that provides them with income, provides the nonprofit with future assets, and provides immediate income tax deductions. Such gifts are commonly in the form of specialized gift annuities and trusts.

An *annuity* is a form of investment on which a person receives fixed payments for a lifetime or a certain number of years.

A *trust* is a fiduciary arrangement in which property is held and managed by one party for the benefit of another.

Gift annuities and trusts are often referred to as "deferred," since the recipient organization has to wait to use the gift.

In order for the donor to obtain a charitable tax deduction at the time of the gift, whether it is an annuity or a trust, that gift must be irrevocable. Once the gift is made, the donor cannot cancel the arrangement at a later date. For this reason, as well as others, individuals considering such gifts should always be encouraged to consult their legal and financial advisors.

Let's review each major type of gift annuity and trust arrangement:

Bequests

For some of the reasons discussed earlier, individuals may seek to augment the funds they have given away during their own lifetime by gifts given at the time of their death. This is usually done through a will, the legal document that tells how to dispose of what a person owns upon death. The gift itself is a bequest.

A person may give all or part of what he or she owns to a nonprofit organization through a will. He or she may give a specific dollar amount, a percentage of the entire estate, a gift in trust, or specific items, such as paintings or antiques, a book or stamp collection, or 100 shares of X Company. It is also possible to give part ownership in an item, such as 50 percent "partial interest" in real estate or in a painting (in which case, the nonprofit would hold and use the property for six months of the year).

Estate tax deductions can be claimed for charitable bequests. These deductions are beneficial because they reduce the taxable amount of the estate and, therefore, can reduce—or, in some cases, eliminate—estate taxes that would otherwise be payable by heirs.

Gifts of Property (Land, Stock, Equipment, etc.)

Individuals can make gifts of property to nonprofit organizations and claim tax deductions. Individuals can make charitable gifts both during their lifetimes and at the time of death.

Property, here, is interpreted in the broadest sense: land, houses, automobiles, shares of stock, money, clothing, furniture, art collections, gas and oil rights, partnership rights—everything that an individual owns. The amount of income tax deduction is based on a number of variables, such as the current value of the property, the nature of the property, whether the giver owned it for more than six months ("long-term"), and whether the nonprofit can use the gift for its tax-exempt purposes. Depending on such variables, the actual income tax deductions vary as follows:

- zero (for gifts of worthless property);

- cost of materials (for an artist who donates his or her own work);

- acquisition cost (property held "short-term," less than six months);

- full current market value (painting owned "long-term" more than six months, and given to an art museum for its own collection).

Home Real Estate—"Give It But Live In It"

A person can give his or her home to a nonprofit organization and still live there—for one's lifetime or less. In other words, the donor gives the property but keeps the right to live there. This is called a gift of real estate with *retained life estate*.

Your donor can make a substantial gift this way and claim immediate income, estate, and gift tax deductions, which will be based on variables such as age and property values. Some special advantages for the donor apply to this type of gift:

1. A new roof or other capital improvements to the property will count as tax deductions. Since the nonprofit "owns" the property, permanent improvements are considered to benefit the nonprofit organization. The donor may claim the costs of such improvements as charitable gifts.

2. In the future, if the resident chooses to move and decides that he or she no longer wants to keep the right to live in that home, the donor can give up that right and claim another tax deduction, again calculated on the basis of age and property value.

3. The "give it but live in it" strategy can help your donor make a large charitable contribution that otherwise would be unaffordable. He or she can claim tax deductions now and avoid the worry and expense of disposing of the property later.

A word of caution applies: legally, the donor/resident is still responsible for paying real estate and other taxes on the property.

The advantages for the nonprofit organization receiving this type of gift are as follows:

The property, or the earmarked portion thereof, becomes an asset of the nonprofit. Later, when the donor dies, or at the expiration of a designated term of years, the nonprofit recipient has full possession of the property.

A gift of a personal residence, or a portion of that residence, can actually be made quite simply. All that is needed is a properly drawn deed. Additionally there are minimal administrative responsiblities for the nonprofit.

Gift Annuity

Perhaps the "simplest" kind of planned gift is the gift annuity. A donor makes a gift to a nonprofit organization for future use, and receives periodically a fixed amount of lifetime income. That donor receives a current charitable deduction on their federal income taxes for a portion of the gift.

The assets used to purchase a gift annuity may be in the form of cash, securities, real or personal property. In exchange, the charity promises to make fixed payments (called "annuities") to the donor and/or another named person for the duration of their lives. Usually, a portion of the annuity is excluded from gross income, and thus, is tax-free.

The recipient nonprofit is able to use the donated funds after the death of the donor or the last beneficiary. In the meanwhile, it can plan, build, or borrow on the basis of that portion of the gift that will be available to it in the future. If the recipient nonprofit prefers not to assume the obligation of future payments, it can still establish the gift annuity if it reinsures the annuity through a commercial insurance carrier. "Reinsuring" means that the nonprofit sells the annuity to a commerical insurance carrier, which then takes responsibility for the annuity. The legal obligation is thus transferred. When the nonprofit sells the annuity to an insurance company, the nonprofit then receives in cash a portion of the gift annuity that would have ultimately reverted to them, if they had chosen not to sell. That portion, of course, is less than the amount the nonprofit might have ultimately received, if it had chosen not to transfer the annuity to an insurance company. In this manner, the designated nonprofit does get immediate access to the cash proceeds of the gift annuity.

Charitable Remainder Trusts

The donor makes a gift—cash, check, securities or, possibly, real estate—in trust to the charity. The gift entitles the donor and/or another named person to income for life or for a stated period of years, and to a federal income tax deduction in the year the gift is made. At the end of the period, the nonprofit may use what is left in the trust from the gift (the "remainder"). Depending upon investment experience, the remainder may be larger or smaller than the original gift. That is the nonprofit's risk, as are the effects of waiting to use the gift monies.

Two types of charitable remainder trusts are the unitrust and the annuity trust:

Unitrust. Unitrusts provide a fluctuating amount of annual income to the donor or someone else named. The amount is based on annual valuation of the trust and the stated percentage that the trust pays out (at least 5 percent).

Annuity Trust. Annuity trusts provide a fixed amount of yearly income to the donor or someone else named. The amount is determined at the time of the gift; it may be either a stated percentage or a fixed amount (in either case, at least 5 percent of the original gift amount).

Charitable Lead or Charitable Income Trust

The charity may use income from the trust for a stated period of time; what is left after that time goes back to the donor or someone else named. This is the reverse of the charitable remainder trust. There are different kinds of lead trusts that are flexible to meet the varying tax needs of different individuals. In all cases, the remainder of the trust goes to whomever the donor designates.

The three types of lead trusts are as follows:

Grantor. This trust must last less than ten years, after which the donor ("Grantor") gets back what remains in the trust.

Non-Grantor. This trust lasts a specified number of years, after which someone *other than* the donor gets back what remains in the trust.

Testamentary. Taking effect upon the donor's death, this trust lasts a specified number of years, after which a person (or persons) receives what remains in the trust. Charitable remainder trusts can also be "testamentary." The charitable lead trust can be an important tool in estate planning. There are income, gift, and estate tax implications with charitable lead and income trusts.

Pooled Income Fund

Similar to a mutual fund, a pooled income fund provides individuals the opportunity to invest their funds with others. However, through a pooled income fund, the ultimate beneficiary is a designated nonprofit organization. It works as follows: a donor invests money or property in a pooled income fund established by a nonprofit. He or she designates those individuals who will receive regular payments from the interest accrued on the gift. Once all the individual beneficiaries have died, the designated nonprofit receives the principal amount of the fund. The donor, at the time of the gift, receives a charitable tax deduction equal to the calculated present value of what eventually will pass to the nonprofit recipient.

Pooling enables the sponsoring nonprofit organization to allow participation at a relatively modest level. Many major national nonprofits promote their pooled funds, often piggybacking them with their regional and state affiliates.

Income tax deductions for charitable gift annuities and trusts vary, since they are based on actuarial tables as well as the value of the gift. As a result, the donor should determine the tax implications of their anticipated gift with his or her legal or financial advisors in advance of any gift.

Planned gifts also involve responsibilities for administration on the part of the recipient nonprofit, which typically must provide periodic income payments and file annual federal and state tax returns. A separate tax return must be filed for each charitable trust; each person who receives taxable income from a deferred gift (annuity or trust) must receive the appropriate tax form stating the amount to be reported. Due to those responsibilities, small nonprofit organizations typically purchase needed administrative services from banks or, in some cases, from community foundations. It is wise to investigate provisions for administration before embarking on a planned giving program.

Federal law qualifies every nonprofit tax-exempt organization whose activities have been designated as charitable by the Internal Revenue Service under Section 501(c)(3) of the Internal Revenue Code (evidenced by receipt of a "determination" letter of federal tax exemption from the I.R.S.) as potential recipients of any planned gifts. The I.R.S. lists all such organizations in Publication 78, which is available for $35.00 by writing the Superintendent of Documents, U.S. Government Printing Office, Washington, D.C. 20402.

Of course, a donor may make a contribution to an organization or designate it in a will, regardless of tax status. However, unless the group is designated as charitable, the donor may *not* receive all tax advantages possible as a result of the gift.

In 1987, an estimated $5.98 billion was given through bequests alone to nonprofits, according to *Giving USA*. Surprisingly, more people than one would imagine make planned gifts. While historically, some forms of this "advance" giving might have been associated only with the rich, today individuals from varying walks of life choose some of these methods to convey their charitable sentiments. Gifts can range in size from the astronomically large to the very modest. While older and larger nonprofit institutions, such as hospitals and universities, traditionally solicit planned gifts from their donors, today, more and more smaller nonprofits are also engaging in this form of fundraising.

WHAT ARE THE ADVANTAGES OF RAISING MONEY BY PLANNED GIVING?

First and most importantly, you are securing the future of your organization. You are taking steps now to ensure that there will be revenues to support your group's vital work for generations to come. It's a statement of concern for the future.

Second, undertaking a planned giving campaign may begin with modest up-front capital, if your investments are limited to the costs of printed materials, legal counsel and mailings. Of course, you do have the indirect costs of staff and volunteer time and the cost of any materials or seminars that you attend to further your own understanding of this area of charitable giving.

Third, you are demonstrating a laudable degree of seriousness of effort and intent to your public audience. By engaging in any of the planned giving options described, you are signaling to your constituents, new and old, that the leadership of your organization is taking steps today to protect its future tomorrow. You are, in effect, saying, "We know that the social (health, educational, . . .) problems that we are combatting will not totally disappear in the next five or ten years, so we are working now to be sure that our efforts toward world peace (human rights, elimination of hunger, . . .) will continue during future generations as well."

WHAT ARE THE DISADVANTAGES OF RAISING MONEY BY PLANNED GIVING?

You are not raising funds that will pay next month's bills or necessarily even next year's. Planned giving usually provides *deferred* income to an organization. As mentioned earlier, your organization cannot expect to use the gift for its purposes *now*. With wills, life insurance policies, or charitable remainder trusts, the proceeds will be available in the future, when someone dies.

If you are serious in your planning, you must devote time and money to mount a credible planned giving effort. Mere mention of "how to designate your organization as a beneficiary in a will" is not sufficient if you want results.

HOW DOES YOUR ORGANIZATION DECIDE WHETHER PLANNED GIVING WILL BE WORTH THE TIME AND MONEY?

Does your organization plan to be around for the next generation? Do you anticipate that your mission will be as vitally important in the world of the twenty-first century as today? If your leadership thinks about these questions and agrees that there will be ongoing need for your work, then, *yes*, you should engage in some form of planned giving now. It will pave the way for the organization to continue into the future. On the other hand, if you think that your mission will be accomplished within 10 years and that you might go out of business as a result, then, clearly, "planned giving" is not for you.

If you are a college or a hospital, your mission is unending and planned giving has a clear place in your fundraising. If you are a public interest advocacy group seeking to stop construction of a nuclear power plant or seeking to improve the mass transit system in your community, you may well anticipate success within a designated period of time. If so, you will probably choose not to undertake a planned giving campaign.

HOW DO YOU ORGANIZE A PLANNED GIVING EFFORT?

The various types of planned giving arrangements described—bequests, life insurance policies, charitable pooled income funds, gift annuities, and life income trusts, etc.—provide support to an organization *for future use.* You, as fundraiser, are soliciting gifts that cannot be "spent" by the charity now. You will want to think carefully about allocating time and money to planned giving promotions if your organization cannot survive unless immediate cash needs are met. Also, since planned giving can involve large sums of money, substantial personal contributions and lifetime commitments, any nonprofit considering entering this area should approach it carefully and methodically.

The transaction, on the donor side, can be quite simple. In the case of a bequest, the patron simply advises his or her lawyer to write a favored organization into his or her will. For example,

> I hereby give, devise and bequeath the XYZ CHARITY _____
> (identify the property given, such as "the sum of $_____") to further the
> objects and purposes of the XYZ CHARITY.

The lawyer might request a copy of the organization's tax-determination letter from the Internal Revenue Service (proof that it is a nonprofit, tax-exempt organization). Alternatively, a lawyer or prospective donor may first want evidence that the prospective recipient is well-managed, stable, and generally shows the following characteristics of a sound institution:

1. An active and responsible governing body that is publicly acknowledged;

2. An annual financial statement;

3. Some basic written information materials on the organization.

In short, an organization interested in receiving substantial contributions of any sort must be sure that it can demonstrate that it is adequately prepared to handle such contributions. After all, a donor rightfully wants to be sure that the organization will still be functioning after his or her demise. Planned giving campaigns proceed best if the promoting organization takes some simple steps to address the concerns of its prospective donors.

Step 1. *Review your concentric circles.* You need to gauge if you currently have donors who have the financial ability to make such a commitment. Do any individuals in your first two inner circles have the financial ability and the willingness to write a will or purchase a life insurance policy that would benefit your organization? Or to participate in a pooled fund or any other form of deferred giving? If you don't know the answer to this question, some immediate homework awaits you.

Approach several people who are close to you and who might be potential donors of planned gifts. Find out whether they have any initial interest in these ideas. Remember, you are only raising a trial balloon; phrase your questions accordingly, i.e., "We are considering an outreach effort to inform people how they can designate our organization as beneficiary in their wills (or as a beneficiary of a life insurance policy). Since you are close to our work and know us, we were hoping that you could give us some response to this idea."

You will not only obtain some pertinent data, but you will also be setting the groundwork for an actual solicitation further down the road.

Step 2. *Check with related nonprofits* to see if any of them have engaged in this form of fundraising and if their experiences have netted positive results. Ask about the pitfalls as well.

Step 3. *Determine the availability and the cost of professional counsel* (lawyers, accountants, insurance advisers, etc.) to guide you in establishing a planned giving program.

Step 4. *Decide whether this is a good time* in your organization's life to start such a program. Brand-new and recently established groups are not the best candidates for planned giving, since they are just reaching out for the first time to the public for support. Individuals are less likely, on the whole, to respond so generously to a first request. Therefore, older organizations who have already developed a strong network of regular donors are more likely candidates. Certain events also serve as ideal occasions for beginning a planned giving effort, such as a group's tenth or twenty-fifth anniversary, or the purchase and/or renovation of a building. Do you anticipate any such events in the foreseeable future? The following questions will help you to reach a decision.

- Do the finances of your organization convey a sense of stability; i.e., indicate that you will continue to exist?

- Do you or your staff have time and money to devote to planned giving? Can you allot financial resources to training, publications and the like?

- Does your Board of Directors support planned giving, both in concept and in fact?

- Finally, check your mission statement. Will your prospective donors have an interest in seeing your work go on into the future?

Step 5. *Design and launch a planned giving campaign.* You might, for example, begin simply by using your newsletter or annual report to invite individuals to designate your organization in their wills. Or you may decide to proceed on a larger scale by preparing a brochure outlining a number of ways in which individuals can earmark planned or deferred gifts to your organization. Brochures and newsletters that can be personalized with your organization's name or logo are also available from many specialized planned giving consultants. They will readily provide samples. To find the right specialist for your institution, ask for recommendations from fundraisers at institutions similar to yours or check professional magazines, books, or journals to identify planned giving experts. Respond to direct mail invitations to obtain further information about planned giving publications and seminars.

If you choose to prepare your own materials, you should ask the counsel of a tax lawyer and financial adviser, such as an accountant. This caution follows from the fact that you are dealing in legal matters, intricate gifts and large sums of money. Hospitals, colleges, large social service agencies like the Salvation Army and Planned Parenthood, and religious societies often have planned giving materials available upon request. These can serve as guides in the preparation of your own promotional material. In addition, the books listed in the further readings section are good reference works on the subject.

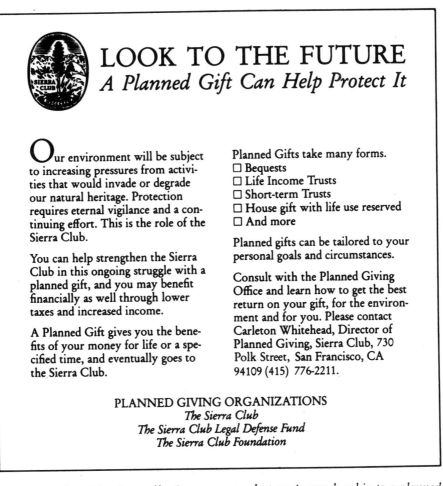

LOOK TO THE FUTURE
A Planned Gift Can Help Protect It

Our environment will be subject to increasing pressures from activities that would invade or degrade our natural heritage. Protection requires eternal vigilance and a continuing effort. This is the role of the Sierra Club.

You can help strengthen the Sierra Club in this ongoing struggle with a planned gift, and you may benefit financially as well through lower taxes and increased income.

A Planned Gift gives you the benefits of your money for life or a specified time, and eventually goes to the Sierra Club.

Planned Gifts take many forms.
☐ Bequests
☐ Life Income Trusts
☐ Short-term Trusts
☐ House gift with life use reserved
☐ And more

Planned gifts can be tailored to your personal goals and circumstances.

Consult with the Planned Giving Office and learn how to get the best return on your gift, for the environment and for you. Please contact Carleton Whitehead, Director of Planned Giving, Sierra Club, 730 Polk Street, San Francisco, CA 94109 (415) 776-2211.

PLANNED GIVING ORGANIZATIONS
The Sierra Club
The Sierra Club Legal Defense Fund
The Sierra Club Foundation

Magazine advertising is an effective means to alert one's membership to a planned giving program.

Source: Sierra Club, San Francisco, CA, *Sierra* Magazine, September/October 1986. Reprinted with permission.

15 Ways you can leave your Legacy to Planned Parenthood

1. Include a simple bequest in your Will to continue the work you have supported during your life. There's no limit to the Federal estate tax deduction for charitable bequests.

2. Designate your bequest to the Endowment Fund to be held and invested perpetually to produce an annual gift for use in Planned Parenthood's work.

3. Establish a living memorial to someone you want to honor — a special fund titled according to your directions.

4. Establish a special fund to carry out a part of Planned Parenthood's work especially important to you.

5. Leave a percentage of your estate or your residual estate to Planned Parenthood instead of a set dollar amount.

6. Consider making a bequest of securities, real estate, personal property.

7. Name Planned Parenthood contingent or final beneficiary of your estate in the event that you outlive all your personal heirs.

8. Purchase life insurance making Planned Parenthood the beneficiary. Or convert an already existing policy when your family responsibilities decrease. If you make Planned Parenthood owner and beneficiary, you can take advantage of certain immediate tax benefits.

9. When you retire, designate Planned Parenthood contingent beneficiary of your pension benefits — a legacy that would come to Planned Parenthood only if everyone you want to provide for predeceases you.

10. Provide a guaranteed life income for a relative or a friend by leaving instructions in your Will to fund a Planned Parenthood gift annuity. The charitable remainder will provide a legacy for Planned Parenthood.

11. Contribute your real estate now but retain the use of it for the rest of your life. Enjoy an immediate tax deduction for the value of the charitable remainder interest.

12. Fund a charitable remainder trust now with a highly appreciated asset — like your real estate or securities. Enjoy income payments for the rest of your life based on the full fair market value without erosion to pay capital gains tax; and enjoy an immediate tax deduction for the value of the charitable remainder interest.

13. Transfer assets to your heirs through a charitable lead trust with income to Planned Parenthood for a period of years. After the stipulated time, the assets go to your heirs with reduced estate or gift taxes.

14. Give now for income later as part of your retirement planning. Fund a deferred payment gift annuity and enjoy an income tax deduction now; start to receive income payments — partially tax free — when your retire.

15. Establish a savings account in trust for Planned Parenthood. You retain complete control during your life and then the savings will go as a legacy to Planned Parenthood.

Your personal situation will determine whether any of these ideas would be advantageous to you. We would be happy to provide more information or talk with you about your own ideas for a legacy. Call or write our Bequests and Deferred Gifts Committee.

Brochures can be developed to inform supporters of planned giving opportunities.

Source: Planned Parenthood Federation of America, Inc. © 1981, Planned Parenthood Federation of America, Inc. Reprinted with permission.

Before implementing your campaign, make a schedule. Decide on an annual basis which specific time of the year you will mention the program in your newsletter, annual reports and other promotional materials. Also, decide when you might actually make targeted approaches to supporters.

Step 6. *Ask someone to make a planned gift.* Once your organization is "ready" for a planned giving effort, you can go ahead and ask for contributions. You may find yourself with some windfall as a result of an unsolicited bequest, but most good things don't come without expending some effort.

Again, you want to impress on your prospective donors your capability as the steward of their contributions. To do so, you might mention the name of your legal counsel or the bank that manages your deferred gifts. You might even establish a Planned Giving Advisory Committee of people who merit respect from those you will approach for gifts.

While the mention in a newsletter or the enclosure of a brochure in a general mailing may spark interest and lay the groundwork, again, personal face-to-face contact is usually vital to persuade donors to sign up. Your promotional materials, at best, may lead people to place a call to your office:

> . . . I've heard about your new effort in encouraging individuals to designate your organization as beneficiary of life insurance policies. I'd like to learn more about it.
> (Your reply?)
> "Thank you for your inquiry. Let me suggest that we sit down in person so I can adequately explain it and answer any questions you might have."
> "That's a good idea! Can you stop by my office next week? . . .

Don't, at these times, confuse your role. Don't present yourself as a donor's legal or financial counsel. You want to present the different options thoroughly. If the donor begins to ask questions like, "Do you think that a contribution of X dollars is more desirable than Y dollars now for tax purposes?" or "Do you think that I should give 100 shares of X Corp. or 150 shares of Y Co.?" suggest that the donor consult his or her lawyer or accountant. Better yet, suggest that you and the donor together talk to his adviser. Be careful to avoid any implication that you are an attorney, accountant or financial planner unless you are certified as such. Always remember that you are merely responsible for presenting the opportunity and the details of how a planned gift to your organization should work.

Step 7. *Acknowledge the gifts received appropriately.* In addition to sending the immediate thank-you note, consider what type of public acknowledgment donors might appreciate for their support. Some donors wish to remain anonymous, but others do not; you cannot make assumptions. Some may be gratified to receive some form of public acknowledgment for their support, such as mention in the annual report, newsletter, or bulletin. Speak to other groups active in planned giving to learn how they handle public acknowledgment.

Step 8. *Develop a relationship with your planned givers.* Be sure that your donors receive regular updates on your programs, so that they are always informed, and that they are treated as specially as your major donors. Even though the benefits of their gifts may not be reaped immediately, their support is significant.

Someone who has designated your organization as the beneficiary of a will or some other planned gift clearly has indicated that he or she supports your work in a substantial way and that your ongoing success is important personally. As a result, you want to keep the door ajar for that donor to support you in other ways as well, unless the donor indicates that his or her support will be limited to a one-time gift.

The more frankly you talk to your donors, the easier you will find it to make an assessment of the possibility of their future gifts. Your donors will probably appreciate your candor and attention too.

PLANNED GIVING FOREVER

Fundraising is not theater; you do not want to appear like a magician, always pulling out more ways to razzle-dazzle your audience with your new ideas, methods and approaches. Your constituents expect a certain regularity and consistency from you. Just as you hope that their donations will become a tradition, they expect that your communication with them will be both predictable and continuous. These considerations apply to planned giving efforts too.

As we have mentioned, planned giving serves donors by providing the opportunity to extend charitable support beyond their lifetimes; for an organization it ensures a future source of income during its own mature years. The benefits can be substantial for both donors and nonprofits—donors receiving plaques or having buildings named in their honor and the recipient organization reaping a substantial gift of income to help secure its future.

Case Study
DOLLARS FOR SCHOLARS

"Go West!"—the refrain of cowpokes and gold prospectors—may become the rallying cry for some feminist scholars. At the end of the long trail to Oregon, they'll find the University of Oregon at Eugene, whose Center for the Study of Women in Society has received unprecedented support.

In June, 1983, the Center received a $3.5 million bequest from stockbroker and journalist William Harris and his late wife, feminist and journalist Jane Grant. The gift has promoted a small, modestly funded research facility into the ranks of the field's superstars. Mariam Chamberlain, president of the National Council for Research on Women, believes that now Oregon, with the Bunting Institute at Radcliffe College "is out in front as far as endowment and continued support" are concerned. She says that the grant, the largest in the university's history, may also be the most sizable gift ever made to an academic center for research on women. William Harris wrote the bequest into his will to honor Grant, who died in 1972. Joan Acker, director of the center, was, of course, delighted. The huge sum will now "make it possible to do things we could only dream about before." Harris died in 1981, but the funds only became available last year.

Most of the $240,000 yearly budget will fund faculty research to encourage "innovative, creative feminist scholarship." Even before the windfall, the center managed to subsidize studies on such topics as development of gender identity, female unemployment, and women in scientific careers. With the legacy, Acker and her colleagues hope to increase the number of studies produced by the center, which, they feel, can help to improve women's position in society.

The center has also been able to afford cosmetic improvements. Its offices on the sixth floor of the Prince Lucien Campbell building have been expanded and refurbished. A previous staff of volunteer faculty will now be paid for their labors, which will be lightened by full-time administrative assistants. They'll even enjoy that most modern of amenities, a computer specialist, who will maintain and manage two brand-new microcomputers.

The center is subsidizing four new fellowships for graduate students. Its visiting scholars program will import such feminist intellectuals as Harriet Holter from Norway and Hélène Cixous from France. The winner of a new competition, open to beginning and established scholars, will study feminist theory for a year at the Eugene campus.

Jane Grant, a pioneeer in her own right, would have been pleased with Acker's desire for innovation. In the early part of the century, she became the *New York Times's* first female general assignment reporter. Later, she founded *The New Yorker* with her first husband, Harold Ross, an accomplishment described in her book *Ross, The New Yorker, and Me.* With Ruth Hale, she also founded the Lucy Stone League, a feminist group devoted to encouraging married women to keep their birth names. Under her presidency, it later became a source of information on women and championed the Equal Rights Amendment.

Grant understood that academics must study women, and determined that she or Harris would give large sums to promote these studies. A 1964 paper, written with a friend, described the great need for such work: "What is unknown about woman is the question most commonly asked. The scholars answer, in effect, 'Practically everything,' that 'there are only mountains of myth.' that 'ignorance of woman and her ways is as prevalent in our times as it has been in the past.'"

Appropriate honors are planned for Jane Grant. Photographs of the serious, dark-haired donor will observe the goings-on at the center's newly prosperous offices, and annual student awards will be known as Jane Grant Fellowships. But despite the size of the bequest, the center will not be named for her. Apparently, Harris felt that their gift was not great enough. "He felt that we needed much more money than he was able to leave us," says Acker, and he feared that a named center might deter future donors.

—Rose Kernochan

Source: Written by Rose Kernochan; published in *Ms.* Magazine, April, 1984. Reprinted with permission of the author.

Summary Worksheet

for

_____

(name of your organization)

APPROACHING INDIVIDUALS FOR SUPPORT: BEQUESTS, LIFE INSURANCE PREMIUMS, AND OTHER FORMS OF PLANNED GIVING

1. Building on Efforts to Date

    a. Have you received any bequests or other planned gifts in the past?

        ☐ yes   ☐ no

    b. If yes, from whom?

    _____

    _____

    _____

    _____

    _____

    c. What characteristics do these individuals share?

Comments:

_____

_____

_____

_____

    d. What is _your_ sense of what they valued in your organization's work?

Comments:

_____

_____

_____

_____

Assessing Your Organization's Planned Giving Readiness

Checklist

	Yes	No
2. Is your organization five years old or more?	☐	☐
3. Is your organization fiscally sound?	☐	☐

4. Do you expect your organization to be in existence and operating in the twenty-first century? ☐ ☐

5. Does your organization have a strong constituency that can be readily identified? ☐ ☐

6. Does that constituency have property or discretionary income? ☐ ☐

7. Will a planned giving effort get committed support from the board of directors of your organization? ☐ ☐

8. Will your organization allot staff and professional time for a planned giving effort? ☐ ☐

9. Will your organization allot the financial resources needed for publications, materials, training, travel, etc.? ☐ ☐

10. Is the staff of your organization committed to planned giving? ☐ ☐

11. **Finding Assistance and Counsel**

Name two or more individuals who might be able to advise you on how to launch a planned giving program effectively:

a. _____

b. _____

c. _____

d. _____

e. _____

12. **Rating Your Planned Giving Potential**

On the basis of what you have learned, how would you rank your chances of securing bequests, life insurance premiums, and other planned gifts?

☐ Very Good   ☐ Possible   ☐ Unlikely   ☐ Still Unknown

FURTHER READINGS

Brown, J. J., Jr. "All About Planned Giving." *Trusts and Estates* vol. 117, no. 12 (1978): 44–52. Single issue $3.50. (Order from: Communication Channels, Inc., 6255 Barfield Rd., Atlanta, GA 30328)

Discusses and gives examples of planned giving in the form of deferred gifts as opposed to outright gifts.

Donaldson, David M., and Carolyn M. Osteen. *The Harvard Manual: Tax Aspects of Charitable Giving.* Sixth Edition. Cambridge, MA: Office of Planned Giving, Harvard University. 1985. 246 pp. $25.00. (Order from: Harvard University, Office of Planned Giving, 943 Holyoke Center, Cambridge, MA 02138)

Outlines, in general terms, the federal tax consequences of various methods of making gifts to Harvard. It is based on the tax law in effect as of September 1, 1985.

Fink, Norman S., and Howard C. Metzler. *The Costs and Benefits of Deferred Giving.* Hartsdale, NY: Public Service Materials Center. 1982. 255 pp. $24.50. (Order from: Public Service Materials Center, 111 N. Central Ave., Hartsdale, NY 10530)

Guide to deferred giving programs including information on how to use them as part of a total fundraising program and how to market and promote such a program. Discussion of what type of plan is best in what circumstances includes clear explanations of the difference between charitable remainder unit trusts, annuity trusts, pooled income funds, and gift annuities. Includes many examples, model forms, and work sheets.

Gift-Giving Guide, The: Methods and Tax Implications of Giving Money. New York: The Funding Exchange. 1981. 61 pp. $6.50. (Order from: The Funding Exchange, 666 Broadway, New York, NY 10003)

Written for individual donors to progressive causes. Gives the "how-to's" for every kind of charitable donation.

Guide to Gifts and Bequests 1984–1986: A Directory of Philanthropically Supported Institutions. New York: The Institutions Press, Inc. 1984. Approx. 200 pp. Free to nonprofits. (Order from: The Institutions Press, Inc., 461 Park Ave. South, New York, NY 10016)

Reference work to provide donors plus their attorneys, accountants, and financial advisors with basic information about the purposes, programs, and people of voluntary institutions. Nonprofit organizations pay to list themselves so they can make themselves known to prospective donors who might be interested in their cause. Because editions are currently available for only New York, California, and Illinois, such listings would only be appropriate for nonprofits that either are located in one of these states or are national in scope.

How to Build a Big Endowment. Third Edition. San Francisco: Public Management Institute. 1985. 604 pp. $95.00. (Order from: Public Management Institute, 358 Brannan St., San Francisco, CA 94107)

Guide to setting up or expanding a planned giving program. Covers the various types of planned gifts plus the staffing and marketing of such a program. Includes forms, tax and income tables, worksheets, and sample agreements and promotions.

King, George V. *Deferred Gifts: How to Get Them*. Ambler, PA: Fundraising Institute, 1982. 198 pp. $43.00. (Order from: Fundraising Institute, Box 365 Ambler, PA 19002)

> Looks at the marketing and management aspects of planned giving programs. Includes advice on identifying and approaching prospective donors.

Knudson, Raymond B. *New Models for Creative Giving*. Second Edition. Wilton, CT: Morehouse-Barlow. 1985. 143 pp. $8.95. (Order from: The Counselor Association, Inc., 31 Langerfield Rd., Hillside, NJ 07642)

> Describes how individuals can make alternative gifts to organizations in the form of property, insurance policies, annuities and charitable remainder trusts, as well as through wills and bequests.

"Planned Giving." *Fund Raising Management*. (December 1986). Single issue $4.00. (Order from: Hoke Communications, 224 Seventh St., Garden City, NY 11530)

> Issue devoted to various aspects of planned giving.

Tax Economics of Charitable Giving. 9th Edition. Chicago: Arthur Anderson and Co., 1985. 215 pp. $9.95. (Order from: Arthur Anderson and Co., 69 West Washington St., Chicago, IL 60602)

> Explains the tax consequences of charitable giving in 1985. Shows through examples how the tax benefits of charitable giving play a vital role in specific charitable giving transactions.

Thorburn, Debra L. *An Introduction to Planned Giving: Fund Raising Through Bequests, Charitable Remainder Trusts, Gift Annuities and Life Insurance*. Cambridge, MA: JLA Publications. 1984. 179 pp. $24.95. (Order from: JLA Publication, 50 Follen St., Suite 507, Cambridge, MA 02138)

> Handbook for a planned giving program which covers program marketing, attracting charitable remainder and annuity trusts, offering gift annuities, establishing income funds, and selling investment objectives to donors. Includes sample forms.

Vecchitto, Daniel W. *An Introduction to Planned Giving: Fund Raising Through Bequests, Charitable Remainder Trusts, Gift Annuities and Life Insurance*. Washington, DC: The Taft Group. 1984. 177 pp. $24.95. (Order from: The Taft Group, 5130 MacArthur Blvd., N.W., Washington, DC 20016)

> Reference on planned giving with information on: starting a planned giving program; the various methods of planned giving; selling investment objectives to donors; and avoiding unnecessary taxes on income, capital gains, and estates.

CHAPTER 12

APPROACHING INDIVIDUALS FOR SUPPORT

EARNED AND VENTURE INCOME

Food products. Greeting cards. Cookbooks. Calendars. Magazines. These are only a few of the consumer products that have become staples for nonprofit organizations in their fundraising efforts. In fact, the array of goods and services that nonprofits have created for sale at the marketplace is endless. Traditional items such as buttons, T-shirts, bumper stickers, and posters have been joined by numerous imaginative and needed goods and services. Consider the following examples.

- The Northwoods Coalition for Battered Women in Bemidji, Minnesota, runs a computer services business to provide financial support for its shelter services and to train battered women in computer-related skills.

- Bronx 2000, a nonprofit development corporation operating in the South Bronx in New York City, operates a recycling center. The center—called R2B2 for Recoverable Resources/Boro Bronx 2000—is putting money into the pockets of the unemployed, the elderly, the homeless, and others.

- The Phillips Collection, an art museum in Washington, D.C., has authorized production of scarves that copy one of the collection's masterpieces, Henri Matisse's "Interior with Egyptian Curtain." The silk reproductions are being produced and sold by Garfinkel's department store for $48.00. Five dollars from each sale goes to the collection.

● Again in the South Bronx, the Bronx Frontier Corporation has built up a composting operation. They have recently added a new product to their line—"Zoodoo"—the outcome of an agreement with the New York Zoological Society, who realized that their animals produced economic assets!

● In Philadelphia, the House of Umoja, a volunteer organization that works with youth gang members, runs a security service that guards shopping centers and all-night grocery stores.

More examples of creative ventures by nonprofits into the consumer marketplace abound in almost every community. This trend is not new, however. After all, the Girl Scouts have been selling cookies for fifty years. The gift shop at New York's Metropolitan Museum of Art was first established in 1908. In fact, some well-known classics in their field, such as the *Fanny Farmer Cookbook*, were originated by nonprofit groups. Fanny Farmer developed her first cookbook to raise funds for the Boston Cooking School in 1896. The War Resisters League, a national organization that promotes Gandhian nonviolence as the method for creating a democratic society free from racism and human exploitation, has designed and sold peace calendars and appointment books for twenty-five years.

Clearly, both new and older nonprofits have learned something about the public: individuals are consumers as well as contributors. Also, both small, community-based groups as well as their larger institutional nonprofit counterparts have learned that they can produce goods and services that are in demand in the marketplace.

We, who are their public and their market, see only the final phase of the entire process, the product itself. We are hardly aware of all the work required to bring these goods to the marketplace.

How do nonprofit groups, unaccustomed to the vagaries of the business world, learn to operate in this environment? How do they decide whether they have something of value to offer that others will be compelled to buy? How can nonprofits develop the necessary business acumen to earn enough from their efforts to cover their direct costs and to add funds to help defray the costs of their core programs? These questions need to be answered before any nonprofit organization can successfully enter the consumer marketplace.

Earned and venture income projects are activities and enterprises that a nonprofit organization undertakes on a regular basis to generate revenues to support its work. These efforts are businesslike in the classic sense, since they involve the exchange of goods or services between two parties.

Earned income is the term used to describe the revenues a nonprofit organization generates through direct program-related activities. Examples include: fees for tuition and classes, ticket sales, book sales, consulting fees, clinic visit fees, and any other fees for services rendered. In the strictest sense, these efforts are usually consonant with the purposes and objectives of the sponsoring organization. These programs, in fact, are launched for mission-related reasons rather than income-generating reasons. That is not to suggest, however, that they do not generate revenues. The YMCA, YWCA, and YM/YWHA are classic examples of nonprofit organizations whose traditional program activities—educational, social, cultural, and athletic programs for adults and children—involve fees and admissions. Nonprofit theater groups are another example, since they usually charge fees for tickets to their performances.

Venture income describes income from projects that are undertaken solely to generate new revenues for an organization. These projects may or may not be consonant with the mission of the sponsoring nonprofit. A museum might operate a gift shop to bring new revenues to its coffers. A school would run a bookstore to do the same. If the museum or the school were motivated for other reasons, such as providing an educational service to their constituents, these efforts would more likely be classified as earned income activities rather than venture income activities. What distinguishes venture income from earned income is the primary intention behind the project. An example of venture income projects are the monasteries in the United States and Europe that produce wine and other alcoholic beverages for sale. The monastery of La Grande Chartreuse in the French Alps has been producing and distributing Chartreuse, an aromatic yellow liqueur, since the eighteenth century. The income generated helps support the Carthusian religious order founded by Saint Bruno in the eleventh century.

Less illustrious examples are the greeting cards and calendars that numerous small and large nonprofits produce each year to raise new funds to support their work. Even parent-teacher associations have joined in: P.S. 41, an elementary school serving Greenwich Village in New York City, designs, produces, markets, and sells a calendar each year featuring the art work of some of its students, contributing to the school's art and music budgets. On a national level, the National Black Development Institute, based in Washington, D.C., produces the *Calendar of Black Children* each year. In 1983, they sold more than 5,000 copies to support their work on behalf of black children in the United States.

Occasionally, economic development projects are categorized as venture or earned income efforts. Such programs are not included in the discussion of nonprofit businesses in this chapter. Economic development projects are organized to better the community and may aim at creating new jobs, building low-income housing, or revitalizing neighborhood businesses. These programs should also generate revenues, but income is secondary to the primary social objective.

How much income can nonprofit organizations generate each year through earned and venture income projects? Hard and fast statistics are not available to answer this question, but according to an article that appeared in the *Wall*

Street Journal on August 7, 1985, over 23,000 nonprofits reported income "not substantially related" to their charitable purposes. Individually, nonprofits have been known to generate from hundreds to millions of dollars in business enterprises.

More nonprofits enter the field as they investigate new ways to raise funds in response to government cutbacks.

What kinds of nonprofit organizations successfully engage in earned and venture income projects? As the examples indicate, both small and large groups have successfully entered the field. What has distinguished those efforts that have succeeded from their less fortunate counterparts?

In most cases, the successful nonprofit has identified a product or service with a ready-made market. That product is related to a tangible asset of the organization, such as its skills, expertise, or knowledge, or even to an intangible asset as long as it can be converted into a product for sale. That product or service has most likely evolved from the group's purpose, since most of its existing resources and assets have resulted from programs related to that purpose. It makes sense then for an organization's first foray into earned income to be related to its purposes.

What motivates individuals and businesses to purchase goods and services from nonprofit organizations? Consumers buy goods and services because they have a need for them. In other words, the product has an inherent value to the purchaser. This holds true even if the product appears to be totally decorative or frivolous in nature.

Of course, some individuals purchase items or services from a favored nonprofit for more altruistic reasons, or because of a sense of obligation. But, these motivations are not as predictable as the former, and they don't automatically translate into a steady source of new revenues.

Many consumers look strictly for the best buy, and this attitude may explain the many thrift shops in most communities that are operated by the Salvation Army, Goodwill Industries, and other charitable groups.

Some people are motivated by a desire to express their personal values by purchasing gifts from organizations that reflect their concerns. This explains, in part, why many nonprofit items enjoy brisk sales around holidays such as Christmas, Hanukkah, Kwanza, etc. The bottom line, however, is that people buy products and services because they need them; thus, the nonprofit needs to identify the goods or services it can provide that really respond to people's needs.

THE INTERNAL REVENUE SERVICE AND NONPROFIT BUSINESS ENTERPRISES

Federal and state laws permit nonprofits to engage in business enterprises within certain guidelines. Usually, the Internal Revenue Service expects income-generating activities to be related to an organization's charitable purposes. A nonprofit can engage in an activity that is not related to its charitable purposes, as long as it is not the group's primary activity and does not account for more than approximately 25 percent of the nonprofit's total expenditures and effort. Additionally, state law allows nonprofits to operate businesses as long as no distribution of income is made to members, directors, or officers.

Some nonprofits that undertake totally unrelated business ventures choose to create new subsidiary for-profit corporations whereby revenues revert to the nonprofit corporation, since the latter is the parent of the offshoot.

Tax law in regard to this form of income is still evolving. Thus, nonprofits would be wise to consult an experienced tax lawyer before starting any enterprises. An experienced accountant will also be needed to advise you on how best to set up your books and the necessary accounting procedures.

WHAT ARE THE ADVANTAGES OF UNDERTAKING EARNED AND VENTURE INCOME VENTURES?

1. Success in earned income efforts increases an organization's independence and self-reliance. Your income is no longer subject to priorities set by outside bodies—government, foundations, corporations. While there are inherent risks in undertaking earned income ventures, there is also the freedom to dispense with the profits in any way you see fit, as long as it is consonant with your legal purposes. You can decide whether your newly found revenues will be used to support your general operating costs or a particular program, new or current, that your board chooses.

2. Your prestige and public image can be enhanced dramatically by your new presence in the marketplace. More people, including potential contributors and consumers of your products, will become aware of your organization, its purposes, and its work. At the same time, you will be reaching new constituencies and spreading educational messages about your work.

Unfortunately, the reverse is true as well. If your project fails, you will inevitably end up with egg on your face, since an earned income enterprise is such a public activity. You should assess in advance how much damage to your reputation might occur if your venture were to fail. This is part of calculating your risk.

3. Your staff will learn, or further develop, skills that will apply to other agency activities, such as public relations, marketing, planning, and budgeting.

4. Morale of staff and board will be enhanced as a new steady source of income evolves.

WHAT ARE THE DISADVANTAGES OF UNDERTAKING EARNED AND VENTURE INCOME VENTURES?

1. Risk. Risk. Risk. As in any small business venture, success is not assured. In fact, the failure rate for small businesses in the United States within the

first two years of operation is staggering. There are no statistics available on the failure rate of nonprofit business ventures. The risk is usually higher for venture income than for earned income activities. Of course, the risk can be reduced with careful advance planning.

2. Ambitious new income-generating ventures can take as long as three to five years to realize a profit and to be fully self-supporting. They are therefore not a likely source of immediate funds. Such enterprises are geared toward future needs.

3. New income-generating enterprises can require hiring new staff and/or re-training existing staff. New employees need supervision as well as support. Sufficient supervison is needed to deal with the new demands on your time.

4. As an income-generating enterprise prospers, an organization can lose sight of its primary charitable purposes in the course of day-to-day operations. Keep in mind that earned income is solely a means to an end, rather than an end in itself. Your objective is strictly to raise funds to support your charitable work. Your attention shouldn't be diverted from building successful programs that reflect your mission. In addition, you want to guard against the temptation to pour all your creative juices into ways of financing your work rather than into the work itself.

5. If your enterprise generates unrelated business income (that is, revenues from projects not consonant with your charitable purposes), your revenues are taxable by local, state, and federal authorities. In fact, your taxes will then be no different from corporate taxes any small business is liable for.

Bear in mind that you can lose your nonprofit tax status as well if the business becomes your primary activity and accounts for more than 25 percent of your total expenditures and effort.

6. Time. Time. Time. Earned income efforts inevitably take more time than you project to be self-supporting and to generate a profit. Regardless of how methodical you may have been in developing your business plan, you will probably find that more time will be needed as the venture proceeds. This may result from factors unseen, or totally beyond your control, or both.

HOW CAN YOU DECIDE WHETHER YOUR ORGANIZATION SHOULD UNDERTAKE AN INCOME-GENERATING VENTURE?

If you need to raise $5,000 in additional funds, organize a special event! Don't start a business. The purpose of income-generating projects is to provide a long-term source of revenues. Review the following list to see whether your organization would be a good candidate to undertake an income-generating endeavor.

1. Are you already involved with potential earned income projects without even realizing it? Are you already providing services for which you could be charging a fee, modest or otherwise?

Animal Kingdom Reports

<u>NO ODOR! NO MESS!</u>

ZooDoo™

Donated by <u>refined</u> Bronx Zoo Animals for healthier plants and prettier flowers.

2 lbs.
(.90718 Kilograms)

Organic
Composted
Manure

bendell

Corn As High As an Elephant's Eye?

The composers of "Oklahoma" didn't know about ZooDoo when they wrote those words. But New York area gardeners may be boasting such crops with the latest organic fertilizer, which hit the market this spring.

ZooDoo is manufactured by Bronx Frontier, a community development corporation in the South Bronx. The major ingredient is manure "donated by refined Bronx Zoo animals." It also contains garbage from Hunts Point Ter-

minal Market, Westchester County municipal leaf collections, and nearby stable manures. Bronx Frontier composts the mixture into an odorless soil additive.

Two-pound bags of ZooDoo are on sale in the zoo Safari Shop and at the New York Botanical Garden. ZooDoo is also available at several local garden centers. Project funds came from the Ford Foundation, the Stewart Mott Foundation, and several corporations.

Earned income ventures such as this unlikely offering from Bronx Frontier often make use of the most unexpected assets.
Source: Animal Kingdom Magazine. © 1984 The New York Zoological Society.
Reprinted with permission.

2. Does your staff possess skills that would be marketable and in demand by the public or by business or by other nonprofits, and can you make these skills available? Fortunately, more and more individuals who have worked in the voluntary sector for a number of years have come to realize that in the process, they have developed specialized expertise that is in demand on the open market. Correspondingly, businesses are appreciating anew some of the abilities that people develop in nonprofit work. Many concepts that originated in the nonprofit sector have become evident and useful in the corporate sector, particularly in such areas as human resource development and employee counseling.

3. Does your mission statement suggest any goods or services that may be feasible projects to develop? Are these "products" already sufficiently available on the open marketplace? Or would you be meeting an existing need?

4. Does your organization have ready or potential access to the types of business skills, such as marketing and advertising, that are inherent in your venture? Do you also have access to the up-front capital needed to mount your earned income venture? In all likelihood, you will need start-up funds to defray your initial expenditures, until such time when revenues will exceed costs.

5. Do you have available staff or skilled, reliable volunteers to devote to all the planning, designing, and implementing stages of the effort?

6. Do your board of directors and your staff support your potential foray into the earned income arena? Undoubtedly, many of their preconceptions about how your organization conducts its affairs will be challenged: they will need, for example, to become accustomed to thinking in terms of profit and loss.

7. Finally, do you and the others most closely associated with your organization have a pioneer spirit and temperament? Are you willing to live with the risks that accompany business ventures?

You are trailblazing as entrepreneurs in the nonprofit sector, an environment unaccustomed to such activity. Failure may result in substantial loss of valuable time, money, and people power for your group—commodities that no nonprofit can afford to part with lightly.

These are some of the important questions that need answers before you undertake an earned income project. By carefully weighing the answers to these questions, you will be able to make a candid assessment of your "nonprofit business" potential.

HOW DOES A NONPROFIT ORGANIZATION DECIDE WHICH GOODS OR SERVICES IT COULD SELL TO THE PUBLIC?

Your first step is to draw up a list of all your tangible and intangible assets. This is an exercise that lends itself to group brainstorming. An inventory of your assets and resources will provide you with an array of products and services to choose from.

Use the following checklist, adapted from *Enterprise in the Nonprofit Sector* by James C. Crimmins and Mary Keil, to develop your list.

Checklist
MAKING AN INVENTORY OF YOUR ASSETS
AND RESOURCES

1. Tangible Assets. What do you own or have the right to use? Real estate? Office, video, or other program-related equipment? Do you have any valuable items (collections, stock, materials)?

a. _____

b. _____

c. _____

d. _____

e. _____

2. People. Make a complete list of people who work for your organization and of all their skills and talents. What kind of skilled and unskilled labor is available on staff and in the community? Do you have, or can you attract, community volunteers? What skills and expertise do members of the board have, and what about the group's active membership?

a. _____

b. _____

c. _____

d. _____

e. _____

3. Traffic. Who comes to your office and who passes by your office? What types of individuals are most likely to be near your office? This exercise helps you to think through the needs of your immediate constituencies.

a. _____

b. _____

c. _____

d. _____

e. _____

4. Facilities: What space do you own or lease? What are its particular advantages—does it have a kitchen, conference facilities, parking lot, warehouse space? What other facilities are available in your community for your use?

a. _____

b. _____

c. _____

d. _____

e. _____

5. Patents, Licenses, and Copyrights. Do you have a product or a program that could be licensed, patented, or published profitably for reproduction and sale?

a. _____

b. _____

c. _____

d. _____

e. _____

6. Time. Think about when your organization's equipment, facilities, and human talent are used and when they aren't used. Is any of your work or usage of equipment or facilities seasonal? Are there times when equipment or people's talents are free to be used for an income-generating project?

a. _____

b. _____

c. _____

d. _____

e. _____

7. Programs. Do you currently charge fees for any of your programs? Do they lend themselves to a fee scale? Can your constituency afford to pay something, or more than they are currently paying, for your program? Are there other constituencies who would pay for the programs you offer?

a. _____

b. _____

c. _____

d. _____

e. _____

8. Reputation: What does your name mean in the community and to whom? What is your area of expertise, and what kinds of products and/or services does this suggest that you could offer?

a. _____

b. _____

c. _____

d. _____

e. _____

Completing this checklist provides an organization with a sense of the range of options it can draw on in choosing an income-generating project. Remember—the process only *begins* with a good idea. What follows is more important. Go over your list, and select the five most promising products and services that you have come up with. Next, determine which of the income-generating activities from the list of prospects you have chosen are feasible. Feasibility can best be assessed by measuring your possible projects by the following factors:

1. Start-up capital required, as well as sufficient funds to cover monthly operating costs and cash flow needs;

2. Special facilities, if any are needed;

3. Professional skills needed, such as pricing, packaging, marketing, etc. Are these skills available among staff, board members, or volunteers, or will they need to be contracted out to consultants or others outside the organization?

4. Demand: Is there a related market or group of consumers that would be interested in purchasing your service or product? How substantial is that market?

5. Competition: Are there other comparable products being offered by other nonprofits or by businesses that would substantially affect your share of the marketplace?

6. "Fit" with the perception of your board, staff, and constituents: Does the contemplated service or product receive support from the individuals who are most closely identified with the organization?

7. Potential profit: How much in gross and net proceeds can your income-generating enterprise accrue?

8. Public image: How does the particular product or service you have chosen affect your public image?

9. Financial risk: To what financial risk does your organization expose itself if you decide to undertake this venture?

Aside from these factors, does your choice of an income-generating project have to be consistent with your purpose or mission as an organization? Some experts would argue that it does. Other consultants have argued that income-generating businesses do not have to be strictly in tune with a nonprofit's purpose. Clearly, the question has stirred up a fair amount of controversy. It's up to you to make the most appropriate decision for your own group.

You may feel ill equipped to arrive at some of these estimations. Don't panic—there are resources to turn to for advice. You can seek out an experienced small business person in your community or contact a local bank or corporation, requesting a volunteer or loaned executive who has expertise in starting up small businesses. Or you might hire a consultant with the particular expertise you need. Also, some graduate business schools have programs that provide counsel to nonprofits through their graduate students or faculty.

As part of your feasibility study, you can also engage in "window shopping" other comparable businesses to have a better sense of your potential market. This is called secondary research.

After completing this initial assessment thoroughly, you will be able to make an educated decision about whether your project is feasible. Don't be embarrassed if you conclude that it isn't. You are better off drawing that conclusion before you commit extensive human and financial resources. If you decide to give the project a green light, what's your next step?

Generally, the more program-related your "product" is the more you will be able to draw from your own expertise. For example, from your past work you should already have some sense of the market for such goods or services. You may not even have to engage in much additional effort if you decide to market existing programs or services for fees. In some of these cases, you may already be charging fees, in which case you merely need to gauge whether your constituency would be willing to pay higher fees, and whether such a charge is consonant with your mission. Are there other constituencies who would be willing to pay for these services or programs?

In most cases, however, you will always benefit from outside advice in areas such as marketing and promotion, unless someone on your staff or board has those skills.

James C. Crimmins and Mary Keil, in their important work, *Enterprise in the Nonprofit Sector*, provide us with the following helpful table and explanation of the spectrum of nonprofit enterprises. On the basis of their research, this chart represents the full array of possible income-generating efforts.

The Spectrum of Nonprofit Enterprise

NEAR/*related to program* ←   → FAR/*from program*

Program	Program Revenues	Convenience		Selling the Name		Downtime	Extensions that are	
		Near	Far	Giving	Royalties		Related	Unrelated
Services specified in the organization's charter	Revenues earned from the program delivery (earned income)	Enterprise activity related to the type of organization — closely related	more distantly related	Marketing the name or prestige of the organization to patrons or supporters (quid pro quo giving); contributions oriented	a wider public (licensing the name)	Income derived from the downtime use of an organization's assets	Offshoot of regular program or necessities of the organization	Business venture totally unrelated to any aspect of the program
EXAMPLES								
Museum: *Contemporary art exhibit*	Admission charge	Sells postcards/prints in shop	Cafeteria open to public after hours	Sells tote bag with name/logo of museum	Sells reproductions of pottery in collection	Rents out exhibit halls for parties	Sponsors tour of European museums	Sells air rights to condominium developer
University: *Under-graduate and graduate degrees*	Tuition	Bookstore; room and board (dorms and cafeterias)	Record department in bookstore	Sells football jerseys, book covers with name of school	Takes patent on drug developed in laboratory—royalties earned; software developed, sold	Sells computer downtime; corporations use dorms and classrooms for conferences	Athletic department runs summer clinics	Leases extra land to farmers; real estate development
Rehabilitation program: *Job training and counseling to handicapped*	Fee for services (client pays and/or government reimburses)	Sells special supplies; provides family counseling	Provides taxi service for handicapped—rides for a fee	Sells T-shirts with name of organization	Sells manual explaining how to replicate its program; consulting	Sells counselor downtime to corporations	Sells product produced by handicapped workers	Invests money in solar energy company
Orchestra: *Symphonic performances*	Ticket sales	Sells programs at performances	Sells drinks during intermission	Sells mugs, paperweights with orchestra name/logo	Produces records of performances; television performances	Rents out hall during downtime	Offers classes or workshops on music; offers music lessons	Runs record store

Source: Reprinted from *Enterprise in the Nonprofit Sector,* by James C. Crimmins and Mary Keil (Washington, DC: Partners for Livable Places, 1983), by permission of the publisher.

The Spectrum of Nonprofit Enterprise

Our survey found that nonprofit enterprise has developed across a wide spectrum, ranging, at the near end, from enterprises *closely related* to the organization's program (ticket sales, tuitions, admissions) to, at the far end business endeavors basically *unrelated* to the organization's program (real estate development, investments in industry).

Based on the data we gathered, we have "filled in" this spectrum with eight different enterprise categories under which, we believe, almost every possible nonprofit enterprise can be placed. The table outlines the categories and illustrates them with examples. It should be noted that none of the four examples represents a real institution—it is rare if not impossible to find any nonprofit that engages in all eight types of enterprise; rather, they are composites of organizations contacted during our study.

The table starts at the far left with those enterprises most closely related to the organization's program or purpose and ends on the far right with those most distantly related to the organization's program or purpose. The categories follow:

☐ *Program* describes what the organization actually does; that is, the services specified in the organization's charter. Examples run the gamut of nonprofits, from ballet companies to zoological societies to halfway houses for runaway teenagers.

☐ *Program revenues* are income earned directly from program activities themselves, such as admissions for performances, tuition for classes, fees for services.

☐ *Convenience* is any enterprise activity related to the purpose or character of the organization that runs it.

Near signifies those convenience-oriented enterprises that are more *closely related* to the character of the organization: a university selling books or renting dorm rooms; a museum renting tape recorders and cassettes for exhibit tours.

Far signifies those enterprises that are more *distantly related* to the purpose of the organization: a college bookstore selling toothpaste; a rehabilitation center providing a taxi service for handicapped clients.

☐ *Selling (e.g., licensing) the name* is marketing the name or prestige of the organization in order to realize a profit.

Giving is contributions oriented and concentrates on the patrons or supporters of the organization. Opera lovers buy the company calendar and tote bag; supporters of an ecological nonprofit buy stationery and T-shirts showing the logo of the organization.

Royalties reach a wider public and involve selling the good name or valuable assets of the nonprofit. A museum can sell reproductions of pieces in its collection; a botanical garden can license the use of its name on packets of flower seeds.

☐ *Downtime* represents income derived from the use of a nonprofit's assets when the organization is not using them. These can be physical assets, such as space that can be rented to other groups (concert halls, offices, conference rooms), or they can be human resources, such as skilled personnel that are "hired out" to other organizations or corporations (computer programmers, counselors).

☐ *Extensions that are related* to the organization take the convenience category one step further. This involves expanding an enterprise activity related to the organization beyond its immediate needs and clientele. Examples include a university opening the student laundry to the public or starting a computer software firm and a nature center expanding its hiking tours of the Alps into a travel service.

☐ *Extensions that are unrelated* to the function of the organization conclude the spectrum. These may evolve out of physical assets that the group can leverage into income or may be strictly business investments that have nothing to do with the organization's purpose. Examples include real estate development of unused land; investments in any type of business, ranging from oil wells to pizza parlors.

Source: Reprinted from *Enterprise in the Nonprofit Sector,* by James C. Crimmins and Mary Keil (Washington, DC: Partners for Livable Places, 1983) by permission of the publisher.

Once an income-generating project idea is selected and its feasibility has been established, how can a nonprofit organization translate that idea into a reality? The next step is to develop a business plan. It will serve as your blueprint for entering the field of nonprofit business ventures. To put it simply, completing a business plan ensures that you have anticipated every major consideration affecting your enterprise *in advance,* and planned accordingly. As William A. Duncan wrote in *Looking At Income-Generating Businesses For Small Non-Profit Organizations,*

> Preparing a full business plan is useful, because it makes you think critically about what you plan to do, describes the business for potential sources of financing, and serves as a management tool once you get started. The larger the undertaking, the larger the planning task will be.

Again, if you feel inexperienced in drawing up a plan, don't hesitate to call on outside resources for advice and guidance. The reading list at the end of this chapter suggests some publications that are available to help you. Also, contact a local management support or technical assistance provider and inquire whether they can refer you to a suitable consultant.

A business plan should include the following:

1. Description of the business or income-generating enterprise and its projected operations.

2. Background on the qualifications of the sponsoring organization and its staff.

3. Details on the potential market of customers for the product offered and the proposed marketing strategy.

4. Assessment of any competition.

5. Information on financing needed to underwrite the costs of the project.

6. Income and expense projections.

Again, the experts in the field cannot overstate the importance of a carefully thought out business plan. Edward Skloot, President of New Ventures, a national consulting firm that specializes in counseling nonprofit organizations on income-generating enterprises, in his article, "Should Not-for-Profits Go Into Business?" (*Harvard Business Review*, January/February, 1983), calls the business plan "the most important financial and planning tool you have." He adds, "Your plan should be comprehensive, literate, and ultimately persuasive. Seek experienced business, legal, and financial advice, as necessary. Be prepared to spend long hours developing and updating it."

LESSONS AND PITFALLS

Entering the marketplace does pose certain ethical questions for a nonprofit organization. For example, should an environmental group print its greeting cards, posters, and calendars on recycled paper? The proposition sounds simple but, unfortunately, it is not; suppose recyclable paper proves to be more expensive, and the additional cost will cut into the product's profit margin. The group may choose to abandon the idea, since it may reduce the resulting sales revenues which are needed to carry on the group's conservation work. Don't be afraid to abandon an idea that conflicts with the organization's values and that is uneconomical.

Consider, for example, the community-based social service agency that has to staff its new thrift shop in the low-income community it serves. Should that agency rely on volunteers from local service organizations, or should it try to provide some jobs at minimum wage to unemployed members of the community?

These two hypothetical situations amply demonstrate how the pursuit of profit can raise basic questions for organizations that are also concerned with factors that don't appear on a profit/loss statement.

It is unrealistic to expect to leave your values outside the door when you undertake income-generating projects. At the same time, you must remember that the purpose of earned and venture income efforts is to produce revenues to support the activities of your group that directly promote the public good.

If you find that your business plan squarely confronts some of your organization's values, address those conflicts head on. You may choose to abandon the project in favor of another potentially less objectionable one.

Similarly, you may want to undertake certain fee-for-service programs that stem from your mission but that will never generate sufficient revenues to pay for any other programs. They may not even cover their own costs. These programs are probably very important to you, and you should continue them without expecting them to be income-generating. They are not, in fact, business ventures; they are merely programs that happen to have certain fees attached to them.

EARNED AND VENTURE INCOME FOREVER

Success in raising funds from business ventures is a heady experience, giving an organization a new sense of accomplishment, confidence, and pride. Alas, failure has the opposite effect. The moral? Explore your prospective projects carefully and wisely before venturing into the world of business.

Case Study
BOSTON WOMEN'S HEALTH BOOK COLLECTIVE

In fifteen years, the Boston Women's Health Book Collective (BWHBC) has raised over $1 million in earned income from the sales of its pioneering work, *Our Bodies, Ourselves (OBOS)*. And its members did it "their way."

The Collective, which is active in women's health issues both in the United States and internationally, began its successful venture into publishing in 1969. In that year, a group of 13 women friends got together to compile a list of "good" ob-gyns; that is, doctors who treated women as partners in health care and who shared information about available treatment options with their women patients. They soon realized how little they know about their own bodies' functioning. Each member of the group then researched a particular health topic, such as menstruation, pregnancy, abortion, and birth control. The results of their labor first appeared as a pamphlet published by the New England Free Press in 1970. By 1974, the book that evolved from this initial effort had sold three million copies worldwide, had been translated into 12 languages, and was providing a continuing funding base for the BWHBC.

Today, the BWHBC operates a center with the most extensive collection of women's health information in the country. It responds to countless inquiries and requests each year. In addition, it undertakes targeted projects to bring health care information to underserved women, such as women in Massachusetts prisons, and advocates changes to improve women's health, such as a tampon project that aims to establish new safety and labeling standards. Its annual operating budget ranges between $150,000 and $250,000.

The Collective's road to success was long and lined with critical management and organizational decisions at each juncture. How did the Collective achieve its financial success? What lessons did its members learn along the way?

Making Decisions. The challenge before the women of the BWHBC was always to maintain a collective decision-making process in which decisions were reached by group discussion and usually consensus. While this process was often time-consuming, the group felt, in the words of BWHBC member Wendy Sanford, "we operated with the most energy, effectiveness, and authenticity when our decisions were based on the shared ideas of every member." It was important for the Collective to pay attention to the personal experiences of members. Individuals' own personal histories were valued as much as any factual information. This was the key principle in *Our Bodies, Ourselves*. Textbook views of "female troubles" were supplanted by women's experiential knowledge, which had previously been considered illegitimate and nonprofessional. The weaving together of information and personal anecdotes played a large role in making the book accessible to a wide spectrum of readers.

Today, the board of directors of BWHBC still makes its decisions by consensus.

Their effective collective process has evolved over many years of practice, and requires a high degree of trust. In turn, the group has been remarkable for its longevity and stability. Of the current 13-member board, eleven have been involved since 1971.

Learning New Skills, "Credentializing" Old Ones.

When *OBOS* first appeared as a pamphlet in 1971, it quickly became a runaway word-of-mouth success. The members of the Collective had pooled $1,300 from their own pockets to make the first printing possible. The pamphlet struck a responsive chord in its readers, who were demanding control over their lives. A huge generation of sexually active young women were looking for ways to deal with a medical establishment that had not yet accepted "what nice unmarried girls do."

As a result of the overwhelming response to its first fledgling effort, BWHBC was approached by Athenaeum, and then by Random House and Simon and Schuster. They were all interested in publishing an expanded edition of its work. As a result, the Collective's members had to quickly learn how to negotiate a contract with a major publishing house. They sought out a feminist lawyer, who was able to secure the terms most desired by the Collective. They included: veto power over cover design and advertising copy; a ceiling on the price of the book; $3,000 towards a Spanish translation of the book; and a special 70 percent discount on book purchases for clinics and health counseling organizations. Simultaneously, the Collective decided to earmark all income from royalties for women's health education projects.

Since everyone in BWHBC wears so many hats, they had to develop many skills. They started out with in-house writers, editors, and a graphic designer, but soon had to learn to be medical researchers, administrators, managers, public speakers, and marketing experts. While Simon and Schuster, the chosen publisher, handled the marketing of *OBOS,* the Collective itself marketed the Spanish edition, mostly by mailing flyers to individuals on mailing lists obtained from other organizations. "We became experts through self-education," Judy Norsigian, a BWHBC co-director, stated. Also, several Collective members strengthened their backgrounds in public health, and thus brought a more sophisticated epidemiological perspective to their work. Norsigian feels that the Collective still needs stronger fiscal management skills in areas such as budgeting, and more systematized office procedures.

Diversifying Income.
Royalties from the sales of *Our Bodies, Ourselves* are still the preeminent source of income for BWHBC, although the percentage of annual revenues derived from book sales varies widely from year to year.

In order to insulate its annual budget from fluctuations in royalties and to secure its financial future, the Collective has taken steps to diversify its funding. Foundations, such as Arco and Helena Rubinstein, have been successfully solicited for particular programs, such as the Spanish-language edition of *OBOS.* The State of Massachusetts provided $60,000 to establish a women's health and learning center in the state prison system.

In addition, BWHBC mails out a fundraising letter to its prime contacts each year. It usually nets a 10 percent return. The last appeal brought in over $22,000. Also, a regular pool of supporters sends in roughly $4,000 each year unsolicited. Finally, BWHBC has been able for two years to invest $50,000 in a stock portfolio, thus producing additional revenues. Today, BWHBC continues to seek out additional ways to broaden its financial base.

The history of the Boston Women's Health Book Collective is a testimony to the ability of a nonprofit organization to generate significant earned income, and a tribute to the women who made *Our Bodies, Ourselves* a classic. In addressing their own personal health concerns, the 13 original Collective members spoke directly to millions of women around the world, and in so doing transformed the relationship of women to the medical profession.

by Ellin Stein and Michael Seltzer

Some organizations' special knowledge can be translated into books with strong consumer potential.

Source: Boston Women's Health Book Collective, Boston, MA

Case Study
UNITED CEREBRAL PALSY OF NASSAU COUNTY

A cookbook is an ideal way to raise money for organizations of all sizes. It's a natural: we all have our favorite recipes and are always looking for new ones. One of the best cookbooks is *Calico Pantry*, prepared by United Cerebral Palsy of Nassau County in New York. It evolved from another fundraiser: informal dinners at the homes of volunteers. The food was prepared by volunteers and brought to the host's home along with the recipes which were collected and saved. After a few years they had accumulated quite a few recipes for delicious, attractive foods that were easy to make. A cookbook was the obvious next step.

Since this form of fundraising does seem to be "easy," many groups have tried it with varying degrees of success. Why, then does *Calico Pantry* stand out? why have the rights to the book been sold to a publisher for over $6,000?

- They had an objective. The recipes they used had to be easy to make with readily available ingredients.

- They had quality control. Each recipe was either personally known by the committee or tested and evaluated. Recipe Evaluation Sheets for each recipe were filled out and returned to the committee.

    Maintaining high standards is most important. The cookbook, as with all items planned for earned income, must equal the quality of "for-profit" products. This being so, what do you do if a recipe submitted by an influential board member just doesn't quite work? One of your skilled testers can most probably determine what's lacking and fix the recipe. Above all, the recipes must work, even for the novice. *Calico Pantry* is used by college students just for that reason.

- They had professional advice. A UCP board member with expertise in publishing served as an adviser. He gave them suggestions on preparing the recipes uniformly and found a printer and binder for them.

    Again, this shows the value of utilizing the expertise of all your members. Although UCP paid for the printing of the cookbook, the finished product is well done.

Without a market, all of this means nothing. They began with their existing mailing lists and word of mouth. There are also order forms printed at the back of the book. In ten years, they've netted $200,000. The book is in its eighth printing, and *Calico Pantry 2* is now out, with 7,000 sold in its first six months. And . . . 90 percent of the work was done by volunteers.

by Phyllis Goodfriend

Summary
Worksheet

for

_____

(name of your organization)

APPROACHING INDIVIDUALS FOR SUPPORT:
EARNED AND VENTURE INCOME

1. Building on Efforts to Date

a. What are the programs, services, and goods that your organization is currently offering?

_____

_____

_____

_____

b. Which of these do you want to continue to provide free or at reduced costs due to the purpose of your organization, the constituencies served, or for some other reason?

_____

_____

_____

_____

c. Which of the items listed in response to question 1a can be potentially converted into income-generating projects?
Definite Ongoing Prospects:

_____

_____

_____

_____

Untested (Further Information Needed):

_____

_____

_____

_____

d. Enumerate which current and potential constituencies would value the programs, services, and goods listed in response to question 1c.

Products, Programs,
and Goods   Constituencies

_____   _____

_____   _____

_____   _____

_____   _____

e. What characteristics do these various constituencies share?
Comments:

_____

_____

_____

f. What is *your* sense of why these individuals value the aforementioned programs, goods, and/or services?
Comments:

_____

_____

_____

_____

2. Identifying New Programs, Goods, and Services That Your Organization Can Use to Generate Income

List the five most promising ideas that you found in completing the worksheet on page 200

a. _____

b. _____

c. _____

d. _____

e. _____

Assessing Your Organization's Earned and Venture Income Readiness
Checklist

	Yes	No
3. Are you already involved with potential earned income projects without even realizing it?	☐	☐
4. Are you already providing some services for which you could be charging a fee, modest or otherwise?	☐	☐
5. Does your staff possess skills that would be "marketable" and in demand by the public or by business or by other nonprofits, and can you make them available?	☐	☐
6. Does your statement of purpose suggest any goods or services that may be feasible projects to develop?	☐	☐

7. If yes, what are they?

_____

_____

_____

	Yes	No
8. Are these "products" already sufficiently available in the marketplace?	☐	☐
9. Would you be meeting a currently unmet need?	☐	☐
10. Does your organization have ready or potential access to the types of business skills, such as marketing and advertising, that are inherent in your venture?	☐	☐
11. Do you have access to the up-front capital needed to mount your earned-income venture?	☐	☐
12. Do your have the available staff or skilled reliable volunteers to plan, design, and implement the project?	☐	☐
13. Do your board of directors, your staff, and your membership support your potential foray into the for-profit arena?	☐	☐
14. Are you and those others most closely associated with your organization willing to live with the risks that accompany business ventures?	☐	☐

15. Finding Assistance and Counsel

Name two or more individuals who might be able to advise you on how to launch an earned or venture income project effectively.

a. _____

b. _____

c. _____

d. _____

e. _____

16. Rating Your Earned or Venture Income Potential

On the basis of what you have learned, how would you rank your chances of generating revenues through the sale of programs, services, and/or goods?

☐ Very Good   ☐ Possible   ☐ Unlikely   ☐ Still Unknown

MAXIMIZING YOUR SUPPORT FROM INDIVIDUALS

The world of money available to nonprofit organizations is vast and so is the variety of ways by which individuals can provide support to your work. Face-to-face solicitation, special events, direct mail, earned income, and planned giving represent some of the major approaches available to you for your consideration.

Which of these interests you most? Which inspire the most interest within your organization? Which particularly lends itself to your use, given your mission and your constituency? You now have a range of methods to choose from to capture the interest and imagination of your prospective individual donors. Think them over, consider them well, use them wherever and however you can!

FURTHER READINGS

Bangs, David H., Jr., and William R. Osgood. *Business Planning Guide*. Ann Arbor, MI: North American Students of Cooperation. 1981. 123 pp. $15.00. (Order from: North American Students of Cooperation, P.O. Box 7715, Ann Arbor, MI 48107)

    Presentation of the how's and why's of business planning, especially as they relate to small retail enterprises.

Breen, George Edward, and A. Blankenship. *Do-It-Yourself Marketing Research*. Second Edition. New York: McGraw-Hill Book Co. 1982. 303 pp. $29.95. (Order from: McGraw-Hill Book Co., 1221 Avenue of the Americas, New York, NY 10020)

    Basic guide to simple, inexpensive marketing research for small or mid-size businesses. Includes many diagrams, forms, and illustrations.

Brown, Deaver. *The Entrepreneurs Guide*. New York: Ballantine Books. 1981. 209 pp. $2.75. (Order from: Ballantine Books, 201 E. 50th St., New York, NY 10022)

    Advice on all aspects of business start-up. Particularly useful chapters on formation and marketing.

Buck Starts Here, The: Enterprise and the Arts. New York: Volunteer Lawyers for the Arts. 1984. 165 pp. $11.95. (Order from: Volunteer Lawyers for the Arts, 1560 Broadway, Suite 711, New York, NY 10036)

    Transcript of a December 1983 conference on business enterprises for arts organizations. Covers such topics as analyzing profit-making potential, legal restrictions on earned income, setting up subsidiary organizations, real estate transactions, financing income-producing projects, merchandising and commercial publishing for nonprofits. Includes a bibliography and resources guide.

Cagnon, Charles. *Business Ventures of Citizen Groups*. Helena, MT: Northern Rockies Action Group. 1982. 50 pp. $7.50 prepaid. (Order from: Northern Rockies Action Group, 9 Placer St., Helena, MT 59601)

    Analysis of business ventures designed for grassroots citizen groups.

Cagnon, Charles. *Successful Business Ventures for Non-Profit Organizations*. Hartsdale, NY: Public Service Materials Center. 1984. 112 pp. $16.75. (Order from: Public Service Materials Center, 111 N. Central Ave., Hartsdale, NY 10530)

    Looks at a variety of business possibilities for a nonprofit agency along with all the considerations which must be taken into account before getting involved in any of them. Includes eleven case histories of successful business ventures undertaken by nonprofit groups.

Community Economic Development Strategies: Creating Successful Businesses. Berkeley, CA: National Economic Development and Law Center. 1983. 375 pp. in 3 volumes. $25.00. (Order from: National Economic Development and Law Center, 1950 Addison St., Berkeley, CA 94704)

Resource for community-based groups interested in developing for-profit ventures. Explains how to build an organizational base for a business venture, how to choose an appropriate opportunity, and how to prepare and assess a business plan. Includes many case study examples.

Crimmins, James C., and Mary Keil. *Enterprise in the Nonprofit Sector*. New York: Publishing Center for Cultural Resources. 1983. 144 pp. $7.00. (Order from: Publishing Center for Cultural Resources, 625 Broadway, New York, NY 10012)

Based on a study, conducted under the auspices of the Center for Policy Research, of eleven nonprofit organizations that have tried business activities. Looks at such topics as competition with private business, possible changes in government laws and regulations, and danger of losing support from other funders. Includes a planning structure for organizations considering such a venture.

Curtin, Richard T. *Running Your Own Show: Mastering the Basics of Small Business*. New York: Mentor Books. 1983. 255 pp. $4.50. (Order from: Mentor Books, 1633 Broadway, New York, NY 10019)

Provides a step-by-step planning process for finding, buying, developing and managing a business. Includes many examples.

Daniells, Lorna M. *Business Information Sources*. Revised Edition. Berkeley, CA: University of California Press. 1985. 673 pp. $19.95. (Order from: University of California Press, 2223 Fulton St., Berkeley, CA 94720)

Reference tool listing numerous sources of information about business-related subjects. Based on the author's experience as the librarian at the Harvard University Graduate School of Business Administration.

Dewan, Bradford N. "Operation of a Business by Non-Profit, Tax-Exempt Organizations." National Economic Development and Law Center Report vol. 18, no. 5 (November/February 1984): 41–44. Single issue $4.00 plus $1.00 postage and handling per order. (Order from: National Economic Development and Law Center, 2150 Shattuck Ave., Suite 300, Berkeley, CA 94704)

Discusses the legal implications of a community-based organization engaging in a trade or business. Such ventures must either be related to the organization's charitable purpose or must constitute only a small portion of the organization's total activities.

Dibhle, Donald M. *Up Your Own Organization*. Revised Edition. Englewood Cliffs, NJ: Reston Publishing Co., Inc. 1986. 423 pp. $24.95; $17.95 paper. (Order from: Prentice-Hall, Inc., Englewood Cliffs, NJ 07632)

Handbook on how to start a business. Sections on the business plan and "forty money sources" are particularly informative. An implementation checklist is included.

Duncan, William. *Looking at Income-Generating Businesses for Small Nonprofit Organizations*. Berea, KY: Mountain Association for Community Economic Development. 1982. 25 pp. $4.00 prepaid. (Order from: Mountain Association for Community Economic Development, 210 Center St., Berea, KY 40403)

Introduction to the risk and responsibilities of starting a business. Includes a list of questions to use in planning. Also provides a useful list of resource publications and organizations.

Fishman, Leo. "Community-Based Development and the Small Business Administration." *Resources for Community-Based Economic Development* vol. 1, no. 9 (October 1983): 1–4. Copy of single article free. (Order from: National Congress for Community Economic Development, 1015 Eye St., N.W., Suite 901, Washington, DC 20006)

Discusses how a community development corporation can take advantage of programs and services of the Small Business Administration.

Fox, Harold W. "Quasi-boards: Useful Small Business Confidants." *Harvard Business Review* vol. 60. no. 1 (January-February 1982): 158–61. Reprints $1.00. (Order from: Harvard Business Review, Graduate School of Business Administration, Harvard University, Boston, MA 02163)

Small businesses can form quasi-boards of directors to assist in decision making. Precisely because they lack official power and are detached from the day-to-day operations of the business, they can have an important influence.

Gould, Sara K. *Struggling Through Tight Times: A Handbook for Women's and Other Nonprofits*. New York: Economic Development Project, Women's Action Alliance, Inc. June 1984. 28 pp. $4.75. (Order from: Women's Action Alliance, Inc., 370 Lexington Ave., New York, NY 10017)

Handbook on increasing a nonprofit organization's self-sufficiency by generating income. Covers diversifying the funding base, improving management, and assessing the potential for undertaking income-generating activities. Presents a method for deciding whether any particular income-generating idea is feasible.

Gumpert, David E. "Entrepreneurship: A New Literature Begins." *Harvard Business Review* vol. 60, no. 2 (March-April 1982): 50–55. Reprints $1.00. (Order from: Harvard Business Review, Graduate School of Business Administration, Harvard University, Boston, MA 02163)

Indentifies and critiques some of the information sources devoted to starting and operating small businesses.

I.N.E. Reports. Quarterly. New York: Institute for Not-for-Profit Entrepreneurship. Free. (Order from: I.N.E. Reports, 100 Trinity Pl., Rm. 421, New York, NY 10006)

News and information about business ventures of nonprofit organizations with emphasis on the activities of its sponsoring organization.

Kamoroff, Bernard. *Small-Time Operator: How to Start Your Own Small Business, Keep Your Books, Pay Your Taxes, and Stay out of Trouble*. Revised Edition. Laytonville, CA: Bell Springs Publishing. 1985. 200 pp. $9.95. (Order from: Bell Springs Publishing, P.O. Box 640, Laytonville, CA 94545)

Kight, Leila K. *The Business Researcher's Handbook*. Washington, DC: Washington Researchers Publishing. 1980. 153 pp. $65.00. (Order from: Washington Researchers Publishing, 2612 P St., N.W., Washington, DC 20007)

Leaver, Robert. *A Toolkit: The Enterpreneur as Artist, Leader and Agent of Change*. Providence, RI: Organizational Futures. 175 pp. $25.00. (Order from: Organizational Futures, One Richmond Square, Providence, RI 02906)
Ideas, exercises, outlines for action, lists of resources and practical information to help those considering starting a business as well as established entrepreneurs wanting to grow or risk a new venture. Includes information on nonprofit enterprise.

Lord, James Gregory. "Marketing Nonprofits." Reprints from *The Grantsmanship Center NEWS*. 8 pp. $3.00 plus $2.00 handling per order. (Order from: The Grantsmanship Center, P.O. Box 6210, 650 S. Spring St., Suite 507, Los Angeles, CA 90014)
Discusses how an agency can use proven techniques to promote its programs.

McClelland, David. *The Achieving Society*. New York: Free Press. 1976. 520 pp. $9.95. (Order from: Free Press, 866 Third Ave., New York, NY 10022)
Presents the conceptual basis for the author's training approach to enhancing entrepreneurial traits in people.

Marshall, Sue, and Neil Mayer. *Neighborhood Organizations and Community Development*. Washington, DC: Urban Institute. 1985. 230 pp. $10.00. (Order from: Urban Institute, 2100 M St., N.W., Washington, DC 20037)
Focuses on examples of successful projects used by groups that participated in HUD's Neighborhood Self-Help Development Program. Offers an inventory of ideas for community groups and funders.

Neighborhood Development Collaborative. *Entrepreneurship in the Non-Profit Sector: 1982*. Crofton, MD: Neighborhood Development Collaborative. 1982. 5 pp. Free. (Order from: Neighborhood Development Collaborative, First Maryland Savings and Loan Building, Suite 200, Crofton, MD 21114)
Examination of how well-prepared nonprofit organizations are to enter the business arena. Found that many groups were interested in profit-making ventures, but most felt that these weren't their first priority.

Newton, Greg, and Camille Buda. *Profit Making for Nonprofit Agencies*. Berkeley, CA: Center for Community Futures. 1986. 170 pp. $75.00. (Order from: Center for Community Futures, P.O. Box 5309, Elmwood Station, Berkeley, CA 94705)
Manual for nonprofit organizations on creating profit-making businesses with chapters on such topics as product ideas, looking at the market, costing and pricing, choosing a structure, financing, legalities and taxes, and creating a business plan. Includes many charts and tables plus examples of profit-making ventures by nonprofit organizations.

Phillips, Michael, and Salli Rasberry. *Honest Business: A Superior Strategy for Starting and Managing Your Own Business*. New York: Random House, Inc. 1981. 209 pp. $10.00; $6.00 paper. (Order from: Random House, Inc., 210 E. 50th St., New York, NY 10022)

Sets out the management approaches which small businesses have used to achieve an honest business environment. Stresses that an open business requires honesty in the marketplace, doesn't require a high degree of capitalization, and can serve society as well as make money.

Robert Morris Associates. *Annual Statement Studies*. Philadelphia, PA: Robert Morris Associates. Annual. Approx. 410 pp. $32.50 (1986). (Order from: Robert Morris Associates, P.O. Box 8500 S-1140, Philadelphia, PA 19178)
Financial and operating ratios for approximately 300 categories of business. Provides a basis for comparing financial projections against the actual experience in a particular industry.

Skloot, Edward. "Enterprise and Commerce in Nonprofit Organizations." In *Handbook of Nonprofit Organizations*, edited by Walter W. Powell. New Haven: Yale University Press. 1986. Price to be determined. (Order from: Yale University Press, 302 Temple St., New Haven, CT 06520)
Background information on business ventures by nonprofit organizations including four case studies. Looks at the varieties of such activities including program-related products and services, staff and client resources, "hard property" (sale, lease, or rental of land and buildings), and "soft property" (copyrights, patents, trademarks, art and artifacts, mailing and membership lists).

Skloot, Edward. "Should Not-for-Profits Go Into Business?" *Harvard Business Review* vol. 61 (January-February 1983): 20-25. Reprints $1.00. (Order from: Harvard Business Review, Graduate School of Business Administration, Harvard University, Boston, MA 02163)
Discusses business ventures as a way for nonprofit organizations to become more financially solvent. Includes a number of examples of successful profit-making ventures. Provides nine steps to help structure the organization's thinking about an earned-income venture.

Stancill, James McNeill. "Realistic Criteria for Judging New Ventures." *Harvard Business Review* vol. 59, no. 6 (November-December 1981): 60–66. Reprints $1.00. (order from: Harvard Business Review, Graduate School of Business Administration, Harvard University, Boston, MA 02163)
Provides a set of objective criteria which can be used in evaluating and assessing the advantages and disadvantages of proposed businesses. Includes criteria in the areas of marketing, new product viability, and projected profitability.

Timmons, Jeffry A., and David E. Gumpert. "Discard Many Old Rules About Getting Venture Capital." *Harvard Business Review* vol. 60, no. 1 (January-February 1982): 152–55. Reprints $1.00 (Order from: Harvard Business Review, Graduate School of Business Administration, Harvard University, Boston, MA 02163)
Based on a survey of 51 venture capital firms, the authors conclude that the chances of getting venture capital to start businesses is better than ever.

Timmons, Jeffry A., Leonard E. Smollen, and Alexander L. M. Dingee, Jr. *New Venture*

Creation, A Guide to Small Business Development. Homewood, IL: Richard D. Irwin, Inc. 1977. 606 pp. $26.95. (Order from: Richard D. Irwin, Inc., 1818 Ridge Rd., Homewood, IL 60430)

Textbook approach to experiences entrepreneurs encounter in conceiving and launching a business. Includes analysis of management skills, business plan development, and financing. Many exercises and a sample venture analysis.

U.S. Internal Revenue Service. *Tax on Unrelated Business Income of Exempt Organizations* (IRS Publication No. 593). Washington, DC: U.S. Internal Revenue Service. May 1985. 18 pp. Free. (Order from: Superintendent of Documents, Washington, DC 20402)

Explains unrelated income tax provisions that apply to most tax-exempt organizations. Generally, tax-exempt organizations with gross income of $1000 or more for the year from unrelated trade or business must file and pay taxes.

U.S. Small Business Administration. *Guides for Profit Planning* (Small Business Management Series No. 25). Washington, DC: Government Printing Office. 1975. 59 pp. $4.50. (Order from: Superintendent of Documents, Washington, DC 20402)

Guides for computing and using the breakeven point, the level of gross profit, and the rate of return on investment. Although intended primarily for small businesses, may provide useful information for nonprofit organizations considering venture income activities.

U.S. Small Business Administration. *Handbook of Small Business Finance* (Small Business Management Series No. 15). Washington, DC: Government Printing Office. 1975. 63 pp. $4.50. (Order from: Superintendent of Documents, Washington, DC 20402)

Indicates the major areas of financial management and describes a few techniques that can help the small business owner. Although intended primarily for small businesses, may provide useful information for nonprofit organizations considering venture income activities.

U.S. Small Business Administration. *Management Aids*. Washington, DC: U.S. Small Business Administration. $0.50 each. (Order from: Small Business Administration, P.O. Box 30, Denver, CO 80201-0030)

Series of small publications intended primarily for small businesses. However, they may provide useful information for nonprofit organizations considering venture income activities.

Accounting Services for Small Service Firms (MA 1.010)
Basic Budgets for Profit Planning (MA 1.004)
Budgeting in a Small Business Firm (MA 1.015)
Business Plan for Small Service Firms (MA 2.022)
Checklist for Going into Business (MA 2.016)
Checklist for Profit Watching (MA 1.018)
Finding a New Product for Your Company (MA 2.006)
Incorporating a Small Business (MA 6.003)
Insurance Checklist for Small Businesses (MA 2.018)

Keeping Records in Small Business (MA 1.017)
Planning and Goal Setting for Small Business (MA 2.010)
Profit Pricing and Costing for Services (MA 1.020)
Selecting the Legal Structure for Your Business (MA 6.004)
Thinking About Going into Business (MA 2.025)
What is the Best Selling Price (MA 1.002)

U.S. Small Business Administration. *Starting and Managing a Small Business of Your Own* (Starting and Managing Series No. 1). Washington, DC: Government Printing Office. 1982. 95 pp. $4.75. (Order from: Superintendent of Documents, Washington, DC 20402)

Designed to help the small entrepreneur "look before leaping" into a business. Although intended primarily for small businesses, may provide useful information for nonprofit organizations considering venture income activities.

Welsh, John A., and Jerry F. White. "A Small Business is Not a Little Business." *Harvard Business Review* vol. 59, no. 4 (July-August 1981): 18–26. Reprints $1.00. (Order from: Harvard Business Review, Graduate School of Business Administration, Harvard University, Boston, MA 02163)

Examines the different principles which must be applied to the financial management of small businesses as opposed to large corporations. These include such financial concepts as cash flow, break-even analysis, return on investment, and debt-equity ratio.

Wiewel, Wim, and Jim Ridker. *Business Spin-Offs: A Manual for Not-for-Profit Organizations*. Chicago: Center for Urban Economic Development. 1982. 105 pp. $12.00. (Order from: Center for Urban Economic Development, University of Illinois at Chicago Circle, Box 4348, Chicago, IL 60680)

Step-by-step guide to setting up a for-profit corporation without endangering nonprofit status. Answers basic legal, tax and management questions. Discusses whether to spin the business off or maintain it in-house.

Williams, Roger M. "Why Don't We Set Up a Profit-Making Subsidiary?" *The Grantsmanship Center NEWS* no. 45 (January/February 1982): 14–23. Single issue $4.75 plus $2.00 handling per order. (Order from: The Grantsmanship Center, P.O. Box 6210, 650 S. Spring St., Suite 507, Los Angeles, CA 90014)

Examination of profit-making efforts by nonprofit organizations with a variety of examples. Includes a list of do's and don'ts from consultants familiar with the problems and processes of profit-making by nonprofits.

Part B
APPROACHING INSTITUTIONS FOR SUPPORT

CHAPTER 13

APPROACHING INSTITUTIONS FOR SUPPORT

APPROACHING FOUNDATIONS

"The rich are different from you and me," wrote F. Scott Fitzgerald at the beginning of *The Great Gatsby*. His simple understatement speaks volumes about the ambivalent feelings we Americans have toward the wealthy among us. We may find ourselves in awe or trying to suppress our envy, but rarely do we find ourselves indifferent. And we are not prepared when we have the occasion to deal face to face, either socially or professionally, with people of means. It is no surprise that our responses to wealth extend to the institutions that involve the wealthy, such as foundations. The word itself conjures the names of Rockefeller, Ford, Carnegie, and Mellon, and images of hushed corridors lined with offices filled with important-looking people hard at work. Power pervades the images.

This picture not only hinders the uninitiated grantseeker, frequently awestruck by the encounter with wealth and power, but plagues the foundation as well, since it does not want to be removed from the world of its grantees. Fortunately, times have changed in the philanthropic world, easing this discomfort by making the grantseeking process less potentially alienating. Increasingly over the last decade, foundations have sought out staff members from the very constituencies from which their grantees are drawn. It is not unusual to discover during a foundation interview that the program officer at the foundation once sat on the other side of the table in a similar encounter. This

welcome change helps remind both parties that they are partners in the charitable process, no matter which side of the grantmaking table they occupy.

Foundations have also taken other steps to lower the barriers between themselves and the public. More and more foundations publish annual reports and
even guidelines for grant application, which are available upon request. The
Minnesota Council on Foundations, an association composed of foundations in
the Minneapolis region, set a new standard for openness in 1977 when it began
inviting the public to its annual meetings. At the 1983 meeting, there was
a record attendance of 800 people. In February 1981, the New York Foundation
invited a cross-section of its grantees to a two-day retreat in a country setting
to discuss its grantmaking policies (NYRAG TIMES, June 1981). Generally,
today's foundations move about in the world of their grantees far more than
their forebears ever did.

Such accessibility, however, is relatively recent and is not uniform across
the board. To date, only 700 of the 24,000 foundations in the United States
publish annual reports. Moreover, foundations unfortunately remain unable to
unlock new sources of dollars when the competition for grants becomes fiercer.
They cannot respond positively to additional requests without dipping into
their capital assets, which they are reluctant to do. At the same time, the
"birth rate" for new foundations has slowed; only 255 new foundations with
assets of at least one million dollars came into existence in the 1970s, compared
with over 1,270 in the 1950s.

These factors add to the difficult task already confronting both the novice
and the veteran grantseeker as they step out to gain a slice of the foundation
grant pie.

This chapter will explain what these foundations are, how they operate,
which organizations receive their largess, and how an organization can share
in this foundation bounty and successfully secure a grant.

Foundations are nonprofit organizations that have been established expressly to support charitable efforts, as defined by the Internal Revenue Service.
In most cases, their support is made through grants to nonprofit organizations.
(The exception is the "operating foundation," which conducts programs consistent with its own purpose and IRS requirements.) A foundation can go by
other names, too, such as *trust, corporation, fund, charity,* etc.

The origins of the foundation go back to the early days of American history.
Foundations usually originate with a benefactor and his or her family, who
decide to leave a specified sum of money for set purposes to be administered
by a designated group of trustees. This is an old tradition in the history of
philanthropy. Benjamin Franklin, Stephen Girard, and Peter Cooper established
such trust funds in the early history of this country. In the nineteenth century,
Andrew Carnegie and John D. Rockefeller created the prototype of the modern
foundation.

Today, *foundation* can describe a variety of charitable institutions. A *family foundation* refers to a trust established by one donor or family. *Community foundations* administer a number of individual charitable trust funds set up by different donors, and usually make most of their grants in a given metropolitan area. Some corporations choose to create *corporate foundations* to allocate their charitable contributions. The majority of these foundations are endowed; in other words, their benefactors' gifts are large enough to make grantmaking possible over an extended number of years. In addition, there are *public charities*, which are also nonprofit organizations; they raise funds each year from individuals and then distribute this money in the form of grants.

HOW DO FOUNDATIONS OPERATE?

In 1987, foundations distributed about $6.38 billion in grants varying in size from several hundred dollars from small family foundations to millions of dollars from some of the country's largest foundations. In total, foundation giving represents approximately 7 percent of the total amount given to non-profit organizations each year.

Most often, foundations make their contributions in the form of grants of money. Grants are given out for a variety of purposes. Considering the diversity of this country's foundations along with their distinctive individual characters, generalizations on the subject are hard to make and can be misleading. But we will attempt to differentiate the major types of grants that foundations make available.

First, grants can be made for *general support purposes*. Here the grantor intends that the grantee use the funds received to support the *general work* and *goals* of the organization, as outlined in the grantee's proposal and the materials it has submitted. For obvious reasons, general support grants are desirable, but foundations are increasingly reluctant to make grants of this nature. They would rather see their funds used for specific purposes, such as program grants or capital grants.

With *program* or *project grants*, the grantor is asked to underwrite a particular endeavor that is of value to its constituency and conforms to the organization's mission; for example, a school might seek support to develop a new math curriculum, or a horticultural society might seek funds to train inner-city youth in urban gardening. In both these instances, the program or project is specific and concrete, and its success can be measured.

Capital grants are grants that are specifically earmarked for "capital" purposes, such as the renovation or purchase of a building or the purchase of necessary equipment, such as computers, typewriters, or other hardware.

In making program grants, foundations might provide *seed money* or *support*, that is, support for new, experimental, or innovative projects· that need initial underwriting to get off the ground, "test their wings," and establish themselves sufficiently to attract money from other sources, such as the government or the public. These projects are sometimes described as *pilot programs* or *demonstration projects*, because they are designed and implemented as models for replication on a larger scale, once they are evaluated.

Another type of grant is the *challenge*, or *matching grant*. Here the funder makes a grant contingent upon the receipt of funds from other sources. If, for example, an arts organization needs $100,000 to secure a building to conduct its classes, the grantor may provide a grant for $50,000 if another $50,000 can be raised from other sources. If the grant is made as a "soft" challenge, the intent of the funder is to encourage the grantee to actively seek out the remaining funds needed, knowing that it will award the initial sum regardless. A "hard" challenge means that the grant will become available only when the additional funds are raised.

In addition to grantmaking, some foundations also engage in *program-related investments*, in which they invest some of their assets or endowment directly in nonprofit enterprises. These investments are made with the intent that the funds will be returned ultimately to the investing foundation. The Ford Foundation has made 125 program-related investments (PRIs) since 1968, totaling approximately $84 million, in such fields as community development, minority enterprise, rural cooperatives, low-income housing, education, and the arts.

Depending on its size and scope, a foundation may or may not employ professional staff to screen potential grantees, assist them through the application process, provide information on the foundation's interests and procedures, and carry out other duties on behalf of the foundation. If the foundation is relatively small, these duties may be carried out by a lawyer who is responsible for the foundation's business, or they may not be carried out at all. Applicants tend to gain a better understanding of a foundation's interests and priorities when professional staff are present.

Grantmaking decisions are usually made by a board of trustees or by a distribution committee whose members are designated by the board. The board of a foundation might meet as frequently as once a month or as rarely as once a year. These governing bodies usually make the final decisions on grant awards, but some foundations empower their staff to make some *discretionary* grants not subject to the approval of a board of trustees or distribution committee. These grants are usually smaller than the average grants the foundation awards. In most cases when the professional staff are present, they make recommendations for action to the governing body. The board also sets general policy on the areas of interest of a foundation.

As discussed earlier, some foundations publish annual reports detailing their past grantees and their specific interest areas, and brochures outlining their application procedures that are mailed out upon request at no charge. But they are not required to do so. All, however, are required to file annual tax returns with the Internal Revenue Service (Form 990PF).

Complete sets of IRS records for all foundations in the country are available for free public use in The Foundation Center's libraries in New York and Washington, D.C. The Center's field offices in San Francisco and Cleveland maintain records for the western and midwestern states, respectively. The Center's cooperating collections, listed in Appendix D, generally have IRS returns for all the foundations in their state.

The IRS also makes copies of foundation information returns available to the public through its district offices. Write to your local district office specifying the returns you wish to review. The district office will notify you when you can visit to inspect the tax returns you have requested, or to make photocopies of them.

Foundations make grants that range in size from $100 to over $1,000,000. Reviewing data on a foundation will reveal its range of grant size. Sometimes foundations provide smaller funds than the grantee has requested. Grantees may then have to secure grants from several foundations or to supplement their grant income with revenues from other sources to raise enough money for a particular program outlined in the grant proposal. In fact, when reviewing a project that requires more monies than they can offer, foundations will look for evidence of plans to raise additional funds.

Some foundations operate with considerable personal contact with prospective grantees, including correspondence, telephone calls, and visits, either in your offices or theirs. Others may decide without any contact at all between the time they receive your proposal and the final funding decision by the grantor's board. The existence of professional staff is one indicator that a foundation desires some personal contact during its decisionmaking process. If the foundation is seriously considering your request, you can usually expect one of its representatives to meet with you to discuss further the outlined project. A foundation staff member will also seek such a meeting to gauge in person the capabilities of your organization and of your staff.

For the applicant who fares less successfully in the grantsmanship process, a personal meeting is less likely. The foundation may reject an application without any personal contact if it considers the organization's activities outside its areas of interest, or if it has insufficient funds to respond positively to all those projects within its areas of interest.

Of course, foundations reject applicants for other reasons as well. Understandably, rejected applicants are frustrated when they are not given the reasons for a foundation declination. If this happens, an applicant can write or phone to request an explanation. The answer will help the grantee whose activity does fall within the foundation's concerns determine whether future prospects will improve.

WHAT MOTIVATES FOUNDATIONS TO GIVE?

Foundations represent the philanthropic interests of their founders and their appointees, who serve as the stewards of the foundation's assets. As foundations outlive their donors, the wishes of the founders might be interpreted, amplified, enlarged, and even changed by the trustees who now stand as guardians. The initial mission of some foundations still serves them well. For example, the founding goal of the Edna McConnell Clark Foundation, as stated by its trustees, was to serve "the least well-served by established institutions." In its present work in reforming the foster care system, schools on behalf of disadvantaged students, the prison system, and the foundation's support of medical research in three tropical diseases, that mission statement is as fitting today as when the foundation's trustees originally adopted it more than a decade ago.

On the less altruistic side, foundations receive distinct tax advantages that influence the extent of their benevolence. In return for these advantages, the federal government has set requirements for the percentage of net investments and assets that foundations must distribute in grants each year; as of 1986, the rate was 5 percent. In fact, most foundations do distribute more than 5 percent each year in grants and contributions.

WHAT ARE THE ADVANTAGES OF RAISING SUPPORT FROM FOUNDATIONS?

1. Foundations can be a good source of startup funds (i.e., seed support) for fledgling programs that might find it difficult to gain support from government or other sources during their initial phases of development.

2. If an organization falls squarely within the interest areas of a particular set of foundations, it has the potential to draw substantial dollar support for its work with less labor than that required to raise comparable amounts of money from other sources.

3. If your organization focuses on improving the performance of government or in advocating on behalf of different constituency groups, you will find that some foundations will be interested in your work to ensure that government is meeting the needs of some of its more vulnerable constituencies, i.e., the homeless, the poor, the elderly, and minorities, or that it is not abrogating the rights of these groups in the course of its actions. In these instances, your efforts will be aligned with those foundations that see their role as supporters of social change.

4. Stature and prestige: foundation grants carry with them a certain prestige that enriches the public image of the grantee.

5. Minimal reporting requirements: foundations usually require a program and a financial report from their grantees within a year of receipt of a grant. The format for such reports is usually not prescribed by the foundations but is left to the design of the grantee. Foundations do not really ask for much in return for their grants.

WHAT ARE THE DISADVANTAGES OF RAISING SUPPORT FROM FOUNDATIONS?

1. Limited size of grants. Needless to say, the size of foundation grants is often determined by conditions external to the needs of the applicant: the total funds available, the competition with other grantees, and the general guidelines for grant size set by the foundation. Applicants may need to look

for grants from a number of foundations before they can raise all the funds required to carry out their entire project.

2. Limited grant renewal. Foundations are less likely than other sources to renew grants for organizations, and grantees cannot easily determine in advance whether a foundation will decide to renew support. It is thus difficult for an organization with a foundation grant to plan its financial health more than a year ahead, particularly if its income depends heavily upon foundation sources.

3. Limited influence on the decisionmaking process. Since foundations are private institutions, outsiders have limited, if any, leverage on their decisionmaking process. Ultimately, a foundation's trustees make their decisions behind closed doors. Those decisions can be changed only by the board of trustees itself. This is dramatically different from government funding, for example, in which the applying organization has a number of avenues of communication to pursue.

4. Timing. Since foundations set their timetables for proposal submission and grant approval as necessary, the timetables may not necessarily conform to your own needs for funds.

5. Time required for up-front research. Foundations do not customarily mail out requests for proposals (RFPs) to potential grantees, urging them to apply for funding. So organizations must devote considerable time to research that will identify potential foundation prospects and make the appropriate targeted approaches.

6. Withstanding rejection. Even the most targeted request may be rejected for reasons already mentioned, external to the merits of the project or its sponsoring organization. As mentioned, a foundation may not even provide the applicant with an explanation of the rejection. Obviously, such refusals may lead to an applicant's sense of frustration and possibly anger, especially considering the amount of time required by the grantsmanship process. Risk is part of grantmanship. Don't be discouraged. Go on.

WHICH ORGANIZATIONS ARE ELIGIBLE TO APPLY AND TO RECEIVE GRANTS FROM FOUNDATIONS?

As discussed earlier, foundation grantmaking is restricted to nonprofit organizations that have been designated as federally tax exempt under Section 501(c)(3) of the Internal Revenue Code. Foundations can also choose to provide support for charitable efforts that are currently tax exempt through their fiscal sponsors (see Chapter 2).

A foundation can also decide to provide support to an organization that is not tax exempt, but would be considered eligible by the Internal Revenue Service if it applied. In these cases the foundation must exercise financial responsibility in allocating a grant. This entails a closer monitoring of the grantee's expenses to be sure that its activities continue to be charitable. This additional requirement discourages many, if not most, foundations from making grants in this fashion.

A small number of foundations also make grants to individuals for the purpose of research, study, fellowships, etc. The Foundation Center's *Foundation Grants to Individuals* provides information on foundations that have an interest in this area.

Finally, foundations have been known to make grants to units of government both in this country and overseas for support of projects that fall within their interest areas.

HOW CAN YOU DECIDE WHETHER YOUR ORGANIZATION SHOULD APPROACH FOUNDATIONS FOR SUPPORT?

In making this decision, you should consider these questions: (1) Are you prepared to do the work outlined in this chapter? (2) Can you set aside the time for writing proposals and undertaking research? If not, can you identify volunteers who would be willing to undertake these tasks?

These are hard but necessary questions. It's tempting to skip certain stages in an attempt to save the time and effort needed to meet the many other demands a typically understaffed and overworked nonprofit organization faces. But, unfortunately, there are few ways to cut corners legitimately. Success in grantsmanship requires careful research, thorough program planning, and conscientious approaches to funders. With experience, you will find that less and less time is required to write solid proposals or to do research to identify prospects. As you work, your own skills will develop and expand. Research will come more easily as your awareness of your prospects grows, as you regularly review foundations' annual reports, or learn of other evidence of their activities through newspaper and magazine articles.

Finally, you may find that you'll need to resist the temptation to approach foundations when you discover that your programs do not fall squarely within their interests or when your minimum budget exceeds the support they can potentially provide. In both these instances, it would be wise to wait for another occasion before approaching foundations for help.

HOW DOES AN ORGANIZATION SUCCESSFULLY SECURE A GRANT FROM A FOUNDATION?

Grantsmanship is the name of the process in which a nonprofit organization attempts to secure a grant. This process has three major components: (1) identifying which programs or projects your organization can present to elicit interest from a potential foundation funder; (2) identifying which foundations might have a potential interest in supporting such a project or projects, or such an organization as a whole; (3) developing a successful match between the grantor and the recipient.

Step 1: Readying Your Organization to Secure Foundation Support

As presented in Section 1, the completion of certain tasks is required to successfully raise funds. These tasks take on added importance when you are approaching foundations for support.

Principally, the prospective grantee must: (1) refine its statement of purpose, or mission; (2) become incorporated and federally tax exempt, or secure the services of a fiscal agent; (3) develop a board of directors; (4) plan its programs for the upcoming year; and (5) establish operating budgets for the organization and for those programs that foundations might support.

While these tasks should precede any fundraising activity, their completion is particularly critical to any subsequent success in foundation grantsmanship. Otherwise, a foundation will be quick to issue a letter declining support of your work. These organizational tasks are thus prerequisites to receiving foundation support.

Step 2: Framing Your Organizational Needs for Prospective Foundation Supporters

Some foundations, particularly unstaffed ones, consider requests for general support. But usually foundations are more likely to designate their grants for particular projects and programs. The applying organization must therefore determine which of its current or projected efforts would be most attractive to prospective foundation supporters.

Grantsmanship encourages groups to plan their various activities coherently in order to accomplish a specific set of objectives that are consistent with their mission. Remember that you need to present a funder with more than an idea, even a good idea. You need to develop a plan of action or implementation that outlines precisely how you intend to carry out that idea. You also need to demonstrate why your organization and particular program are needed. What problems in the society are you addressing? What are the merits of the solutions you are proposing?

In other words, think concretely in terms of programs and outcomes. That will help you to identify the programs you can possibly present to a foundation for consideration. At the same time, in fact, you will also be developing a valuable plan for your organization. The outcome should be a listing of your current and projected programs. Use the following worksheet to list your current and projected activities ready for foundation packaging.

Worksheet

Name of Organization: _____

Date: _____

1. Current Programs and Projects

a. _____

b. _____

c. _____

d. _____

e. _____

f. _____

g. _____

2. Projected programs and projects

a. _____

b. _____

c. _____

d. _____

e. _____

f. _____

g. _____

Step 3: Ranking Your Programs for Possible Submission to Foundation Prospects

The next step is to decide which of your programs are of most interest to funders. You can develop your own list of criteria to help you make this decision, or use the following list. You can, of course, add or delete criteria areas.

1. *Compatibility to Mission.* Is this program consistent with the current stated purpose and mission of your group? Or does it represent an undertaking in a different direction?

2. *Drawn from Acknowledged Expertise.* Does the program flow from the experience and expertise that is popularly associated with your organization? Or does the project require skills or personnel not currently available within the organization?

3. *Achievability.* If you do secure the financial resources that you need to undertake this program, will you be able, within a reasonable period of time, to accomplish the results that you are promising?

4. *Topicality*. Is the problem you are addressing perceived as significant by the public, as evidenced by media coverage within the last year or in speeches by civic leaders or by some other external indices?

5. *Documentation*. Can you adequately demonstrate the seriousness of the problem(s) that your project aims to address?

6. *Competition*. Are there other nonprofit organizations that have also established a reputation in this arena? Are they more, or less visible than your own organization?

7. *Rationale for Foundation Support*. Can you illustrate why foundations, rather than other sources of support, are more logical for this project?

These criteria are some of the major factors that need to be addressed to determine possible programs for submission to foundations. They can help you decide whether your programs are sufficiently prepared for submission or require further consideration. Each of these factors will influence the outcome of your grant request. If the thrust and intention of the project do not flow from your mission, a funder may question your proposal. If the foundation staffers reading your proposal are not aware of the problem you are addressing, they may not view it with the same importance that you do, or they may view other agencies as more appropriate channels for the problem's resolution. You, the grantseeker, must consider these factors carefully in advance and address them directly in your presentations, both written and oral, to your prospective funders.

Step 4: Targeting Potential Foundation Supporters for Your Work

This step can occur simultaneously with Steps 1 through 3.

With the exception of the smallest family foundations, whose interests may appear to be extremely broad, foundations have expressly defined interests in certain fields of endeavor. The accompanying chart provides a list of the categories that The Foundation Center uses to differentiate foundation interests.

Let's look at a hypothetical organization in the light of these topics. Suppose you run a day center for senior citizens in Gunnison, Colorado. Reviewing the COMSEARCH list of topics, you would clearly choose *Aged* and *Community Centers*. Since you serve hot lunches, how about *Food and Nutrition*? You also have cultural programs, so you might also try *Grants for Arts and Cultural Programs* under the Broad Topics. And lastly, you would also pick *Rocky Mountains*. In this way, you can begin to isolate the foundations that have already shown interest in your work.

List of COMSEARCH: SUBJECTS

Order Number/Title

Communications
3. Language, Literature & Journalism
4. Publications

Education
15. Adult & Continuing Education
17. Student & Professional Internships
18. Higher Education—Capital Support
19. Higher Education—Endowments
20. Higher Education—Faculty and Professorships
21. Higher Education—Fellowships
22. Scholarships, Student Aid & Loans
23. Library & Information Services
24. Educational Research
25. Vocational Education, Career Development & Employment
26. International Studies, Education & Exchange
27. Teacher Training

Health
30. Health & Medical Care—Cost Containment
32. Medical Research & Advancement
33. Dentistry
34. Nursing
37. Mental Health
39. Alcohol & Drug Abuse
40. Cancer Care & Research
41. Hospices
42. Abortion, Birth Control & Family Planning
43. Children & Youth—Health Programs
44. Children & Youth—Medical Research

Cultural Activities
46. Humanities Programs
47. Theater
48. Music Schools & Music Education
49. Orchestras & Musical Performances

50. Architecture, Historical Preservation & Historical Societies
51. Dance

Population Groups
64. Boys
65. Blacks
66. Hispanics
67. Blind & Visually Impaired
68. Deaf & Hearing Impaired

Science & Technology
74. Mathematics
75. Biology & Genetics
76. Agriculture & Farming
77. Chemistry
79. Computer Science & Systems
80. Energy
81. Engineering

Social Sciences
85. Business Education
86. Economics
88. Law Schools & Legal Education
89. Psychology & Behavioral Sciences

Welfare
90. Peace Initiatives & Arms Control
91. Legal Services
92. Housing & Transportation
93. Community Funds
95. Child Abuse
97. Community Centers
98. Young Men's & Women's Associations
99. Food & Nutrition
101. Animal Welfare & Wildlife
102. Rural Development
104. Camps & Camperships
105. Parks, Gardens & Zoos
106. Refugee & Relief Services
107. Volunteer Programs
108. Homeless
109. Human Rights

Other
110. Nonprofit Management
111. Philanthropy & Nonprofit Sector Research
112. Governmental Agencies
114. Conferences & Seminars

Learning All You Can About Your Foundation Prospects

Before you apply for a grant, you need to gather as much information as possible about your foundation prospects to determine whether your funding needs match their giving interests, whether they are likely to support organizations in your geographic area, whether they are likely to provide the type and amount of support you need, and how and when to submit your grant request. In using the materials below to complete a Final Prospect Worksheet for each foundation that seems likely to be interested in your proposals, be sure to note the date and source of the information gathered to be sure you have the most current and accurate information available.

STEP 1. FOUNDATION ANNUAL REPORTS are published by over 600 foundations. When available, these are generally the most complete source of information on the foundation's current and future interests, restrictions, and application procedures. Check entries in *Source Book Profiles, The Foundation Directory*, or *The National Data Book* or listings of "Grantmaker Publications" in the *Foundation Grants Index Bimonthly* to find out if a foundation publishes a report.

STEP 2. OTHER FOUNDATION PUBLICATIONS. Over 700 foundations that do not publish annual reports do publish information brochures, application guidelines, or other materials that describe their giving programs. Check entries in *Source Book Profiles, The Foundation Directory*, or listings of "Grantmaker Publications" in the *Foundation Grants Index Bimonthly* to determine if such materials are available.

STEP 3. SOURCE BOOK PROFILES analyzes the 1,000 largest foundations in depth. In the absence of material published by the foundation itself, this is the most complete source of information on the largest foundations.

STEP 4. THE FOUNDATION DIRECTORY provides basic descriptions of foundations with $1 million or more in assets or annual giving of at least $100,000. Also check **THE FOUNDATION DIRECTORY SUPPLEMENT** which updates entries for foundations that have had name, address, personnel, or program changes between editions of the major volume.

STEP 5. FOUNDATION GRANTS INDEX BIMONTHLY includes "Updates on Grantmakers" listing changes in name, address, personnel, or program reported by major foundations in preceding two months.

STEP 6. FOUNDATION INFORMATION RETURNS (IRS FORM 990-PF) are filed annually by all foundations and include complete lists of grants awarded during the tax year covered as well as other information on finances, giving interests and restrictions, and application procedures and deadlines. These are often the only source of information on smaller foundations. Available from the Internal Revenue Service or at Foundation Center libraries.

STEP 7. NEWSPAPER OR MAGAZINE ARTICLES often provide news or insights on personnel or program interests of foundations. Check with your local library for foundation files or indexes to relevant articles.

STEP 8. PEOPLE. Talk to your professional colleagues, board members, volunteers, past and current donors, and others interested in your work for advice on your project proposal and funding prospects.

This is just the first step of the research necessary to the grantsmanship process. The foundations listed within these categories provide a broad universe of prospects. You have to narrow down that list to the most likely prospects. The accompanying chart from *Foundation Fundamentals*, published by The Foundation Center, provides a useful outline of the stages of the research process. Note all the available reference materials that serve as tools in refining this list. The foundation annual report, when it exists, is the most detailed statement of interests to help you estimate a prospect's interest in your work. Reference materials, such as *The Foundation Directory* and *Source Book Profiles*, will also help you isolate a manageable number of prospects that you can then research more fully. If a foundation does not publish an annual report, and the majority do not, you can still secure vital information about them through their tax returns (the "990"). The returns of the five most recent years are available to the public for review at The Foundation Center in New York City at 79 Fifth Avenue, or in one of its affiliated libraries (see Appendix D for addresses).

A copy of a foundation's 990-PF ("PF" stands for "private foundation") can be obtained from the Internal Revenue Service. Annual reports, though, are clearly more useful, since they are written for the public and not for the U. S. Treasury Department.

What you are trying to do is develop a list of prospects whose interests most closely approximate your own. Not long ago grantseekers would mail out blanket requests for general support to any foundation they had heard about— the "shot-in-the-dark" approach," as someone most aptly described it. This method would occasionally net a grant, but most grantseekers obtained nothing for their efforts, discouraging them from any subsequent foundation fundraising.

The limitations of this approach are even more marked when one examines the amount of competition for foundation grants in the 1980s. Since foundations' assets do not increase markedly over the years, increased competition for the limited number of available grants obviously raises the number of rejections that a foundation will issue in a year. The grantseeker ought to target funders more precisely. This is not to suggest that you should tailor your program to a given foundation's interests, contorting it into something other than it is. That effort will not only end up being fruitless, but will, in the long run, reflect poorly on your organization. So, how do you set priorities for using your limited time and resources most productively?

The following worksheet does not provide us with a scientific ranking of the likelihood of a positive response, but it does give an informal ranking of chances, based on such factors as competition with other grantseekers, availability of information, and accessibility to decisionmakers. As you identify those foundations which are good prospects, place them on the worksheet.

Other factors might alter this informal ranking; for example, if you are already familiar with a foundation official of a small national foundation or if your program is strongly compatible with the interests of a particular national corporate foundation, your likelihood of securing grants from these sources would be positively affected.

Now, on the basis of all your information gathering and research, you should be able to assess which of your programs and projects will be of interest to foundations and which foundations those might be.

Worksheet
LOCAL FOUNDATIONS

1. Community Foundations: _____

2. Family Foundations (Staffed; Annual Report Available)

   a. _____

   b. _____

   c. _____

   d. _____

   e. _____

3. Corporate Foundations

   a. _____

   b. _____

   c. _____

4. Unstaffed Foundations

   a. _____

   b. _____

   c. _____

NATIONAL FOUNDATIONS

5. Large National Foundations (i.e., Assets over $100,000,000)

   a. _____

   b. _____

   c. _____

6. Smaller Foundations

   a. _____

   b. _____

   c. _____

Building Your Knowledge about Foundation Prospects through Networking and Information Gathering

1. Subscribe to foundation trade journals, such as *Foundation News* (available from: Foundation News Fulfillment Service, P.O. Box 501, Martinsville, New Jersey 08836; $24/one year) and the newsletter of your local association of grantmakers (see Appendix C for list).

2. Read your major local newspaper regularly for information on foundations.

3. Network with other nonprofits seeking support from foundations to share information.

4. Seek out advice from receptive foundation representatives.

5. Check out pertinent topics discussed at annual meetings of the Council on Foundations through ordering cassette tapes of session topics related to your endeavors. For a list of the topics taped at the last session of its annual meeting and an order form, contact Audio Transcripts, Ltd., 610 Madison St., Alexandria, VA. 22314 (Telephone 703 549-7334).

6. Check out the files at your local Foundation Center collection regularly for new information.

Step 5: Making the Approach to a Prospective Foundation Supporter

Your first tasks in approaching a potential foundation supporter are as follows:

1. *Know thy funder.* Be sure you have reviewed all the materials the foundation has published on its grantmaking policies, such as brochures, annual reports, grant guidelines, etc. In advance of the application, you should be able to state why X foundation should be interested in your project, based on *its* interests.

2. *Know your past history with that funder.* Be sure you have checked your organizational files to see if anyone associated with your group has previously been in touch with the funder in question. You should be aware of any such exchanges.

3. *Check if you have any personal contacts with your foundation prospect.* Do any members of your staff or board know a member of the foundation's staff, or, if the foundation is unstaffed, a member of its board of directors? A pre-existing personal contact *might*, though not necessarily, help your initial overture.

In approaching prospective foundation supporters, you'll want to follow the application procedures that they have outlined in their printed materials. Your goal is clear: to make the most persuasive presentation possible of your project.

Ideally, you'd like to have the opportunity to do that in person. But in all probability, your first contact will be by letter, describing why you are approaching this particular source of funds ("addressing its interests") and outlining the general thrust of your project in relation to its stated interests. The letter should always include a "sign-off," such as, "We would welcome the opportunity to meet with you in person to discuss this project in greater detail, and to answer any questions that you might have."

If the foundation requests a full proposal with your initial inquiry, you would still aim for a meeting in person. Will that come to pass? Will you be able to arrange a meeting with the executive director or program officer of the foundation? Not necessarily, depending on the volume of requests for such meetings the foundation staffers receive. But if you are fortunate, you will have the opportunity to meet in person, and to bring one of your board officers and your project or executive director along to present your case. During that meeting, listen carefully to any concerns or questions the foundation representative may raise. Be sure to address them fully in the proposal you submit, or in a follow-up letter.

A proposal is akin to a passport to a foreign country. It is the document required to get past the door of a foundation to receive a hearing. But submitting a proposal does not automatically lead to a meeting with the foundation representative or to money in hand. For guidelines on proposal preparation, review the Proposal Design Chart and The Major Components of a Proposal. Also, check the reference materials listed at the end of this chapter.

In the heat of writing letters of inquiry and proposals, you can lose track of one important, simple truth: foundations fund people, not paper. The ability to state your ideas clearly and succinctly is vitally important, but ultimately a wise program officer knows that words alone are insufficient. Good, talented people are needed to transform ideas into successful projects. Bear this in mind as you allocate your time to the various phases of grantsmanship.

Proposal Design Chart[1]

Need	Goal	Objective	Procedure	Evaluation
To provide alternative learning opportunities for students who do not benefit from the regular mathematics program.	To assist selected high school students acquire independent study skills in mathematics.	Forty students selected from the tenth grade will be able to demonstrate newly acquired independent study skills by successfully completing a test on a major segment of the mathematics curriculum every two months. Success will be determined by the students achieving a score of 80 percent or more. The test will be devised by an independent consultant.	A mathematics teacher will provide one hour of orientation instruction each week, pointing out the major areas of information to be covered. Supplementary reading material will be distributed following each session. Students will also be given a set of self-tests for each curriculum component. A tutor will be available during the week to answer questions.	A mathematics teacher will administer the test every two months, grade the exams, and report the results to the project director. The director and an independent study consultant will meet with each student to discuss his or her test results and assist in designing additional independent study to remedy any deficiencies.

1. This chart provides only one example in each proposal category. There might, in fact, be several procedures or evaluation strategies for this same objective. A completed chart, including all major items in a proposal, could be several pages long. *Source:* Reprinted from *Developing Skills in Proposal Writing*, by Mary Hall, by permission of the publisher. 1977. Available from Continuing Education Publications, P.O. Box 1491, Portland, Ore. 97207.

The Major Components of a Proposal

Topic	Information to be Provided
Title Page	Title of project, name of applicant and organization, name of agency submitted to, inclusive dates of project, total budget request, signatures of authorized personnel approving submission from the local agency.
Abstract	Summary of the proposal with at least some reference to the major points in the statement of need, objectives, procedures, evaluation, and dissemination components. Should stress the end products. Usually 250 to 500 words.
Problem Statement (or Statement of Need)	Clear and precise statement of the problem to be addressed and the need for its solution. Should establish *significance, relevance, timeliness, generalizability* and *contribution* of the project. *Innovativeness* of proposed methodology may also be substantiated. Usually includes references to previous research or earlier works. Statistical data describing the need is also cited. In research proposals, this component may have a separate section labeled "related research" which includes more lengthy discussion of previous studies.
Objectives	A very specific indication of the proposed outcomes of the project stated as objectives, hypotheses, and/or questions. May also state overall goals of project. Should flow logically from the identified needs/problems.
Procedures	How the objectives will be met or the hypothesis/questions tested. In nonresearch projects this section usually starts with description of the overall approach and then gets into details about methodology, participants, organization and timelines. In a research project, one usually describes design, population and sample, data and instrumentation, analysis, and time schedule. The section should end with clear identification of both short-term and long-term end products expected.
Evaluation*	Details the means by which the local agency and the funding source will know the project has accomplished its purposes. States purpose of evaluation, type of information to be collected, details on instruments, data collection, analysis, and utilization and tells how results will be reported. Evaluative criteria* should be provided for each objective.
Dissemination*	How will products and findings be shared with others? Frequently this section also details reports to be given to the funding source.
Facilities and Equipment	Facilities and equipment required and how these will be provided. This section may also describe any unique equipment or facilities available to the local agency which will facilitate the project.
Personnel	Who are the personnel that will work on the project and what will they do? What are their backgrounds and credentials? If new staff are needed, how many and of what type? How will they be selected? In a research proposal, this section may also include a description of the project's administrative organization. Individuals to serve as consultants should also be identified, their backgrounds described, and use justified.
Budget	Cost of the project. Usually divided into categories such as personnel, supplies and materials, travel, data processing, facilities or equipment, and indirect costs.

*These categories may or may not be included in research proposals, or if required, can be discussed as elements of the procedures component.
SOURCE: Reprinted from *Developing Skills in Proposal Writing*, by Mary Hall, 1977, by permission of the publisher. Available from Continuing Education Publications, P.O. Box 1491, Portland, Ore. 97207.

THE YES

Let's assume that you have carefully targeted your foundation prospects, prepared your written materials conscientiously, and presented your organization skillfully in your face-to-face meeting with the funder's representatives. Your hard work may well be rewarded with a grant! If so, be sure to express your appreciation promptly in a letter and to make note of any reporting requirements that are requested by the funder.

You can now inform other foundations that are considering your request of your good fortune. If your first funder has not underwritten the entire budget of your designated project, your other prospective foundation supporters will be influenced positively by evidence of support from one of their peers. Thus, your first grant will, in fact, help you to "leverage" other foundation support.

THE NO

Foundations often reject requests for support for reasons that are external to the merits of a particular applicant. They may have received more applications than they can possibly respond to, or they may have too many existing commitments. In either case, they do not have sufficient reserves to consider new requests. If the reasons are not evident in their letter, write or call whoever has signed the rejection letter and ask politely for their reasons. You can inquire whether there were any ways in which you could have strengthened your proposal or program design. Ask for advice.

Weigh the advice you receive carefully. You may have the opportunity to reapply in subsequent years, particularly if the reasons for declination were unrelated to your work. If the reasons were directly related to your organization's efforts, you will want to assess whether there will be a future receptive ear to a revised proposal, or whether your mission and the foundations' interests do not converge at all.

PITFALLS AND LESSONS

You should look at the receipt of a grant as the first step in beginning a new relationship. Your foundation supporter will be interested in your progress toward the goals you've presented in your proposal. That foundation now has a stake in your success and in your future. Mail them progress reports (both financial and programmatic), press clippings, invitations to events (open houses, conferences, etc.), and regular mailings, such as newsletters. Don't let them hear from you only when you need funds again.

If they are not in the position to renew their support to you immediately, you may find a new project in the years ahead that might again fall within their interest areas.

Beware of the bounty of too much success in foundation fundraising. Suppose your work was so appealing to foundations that through their munificence, you were able to hire a new staff and considerably expand the efforts of your organization. It does not necessarily follow that you can anticipate the same proportion of foundation funds in the years ahead, when your issues no longer sizzle on the front burner of your funders. Start to plan now for that probability; devote some of your resources to developing other sources of income, so that you will be prepared should you need them. Use some of your hard-earned foundation goodwill to receive a grant that will broaden your fundraising efforts among the public, or from government, or from corporations.

Case Study
THE ASIAN AMERICAN LEGAL DEFENSE AND EDUCATION FUND

Can foundation support be sustained by an organization after ten years of existence? How does the mature nonprofit organization continue to attract foundation grants? Or can it succeed in doing so at all?

These were the questions facing the staff and board of the Asian American Legal Defense and Education Fund on the occasion of its 10th anniversary. The Fund (AALDEF) began in 1974, at a time when foundations were particularly interested in supporting litigation efforts as a civil rights strategy. As a result, AALDEF received start-up grants from a number of small progressive New York-based foundations, who were responsive to the organization's mission: educating Asian American communities about their legal rights, and encouraging them to use the law to protect their rights. The need for such an organization was underlined by the large proportion of Asian Americans unfamiliar with American culture, and with the American legal system in particular.

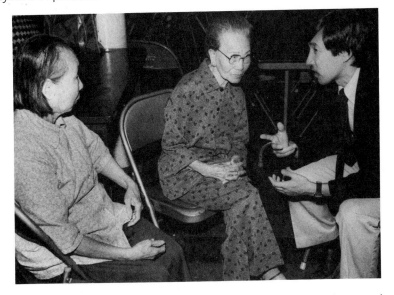

AALDEF provides legal counseling to senior citizens as well as other members of the Asian American community.

Source: Asian-American Legal Defense and Education Fund, New York, NY.

From 1974 to 1980, a relatively large number of local and national foundations made either general support or project-specific grants to AALDEF. While none of these grants were sufficiently large (more than $25,000) to underwrite the total costs of any one program, AALDEF was able to launch a number of programs to serve different communities: informing recent immigrants and non-English speakers of their legal rights; undertaking impact litigation; and recruiting and training Asian law students to be AALDEF interns.

Through foundation support, AALDEF's staff of attorneys was able to devote most of its energies to legal work, while occasionally firing off a proposal to a sympathetic foundation. Over the years, their attorneys earned the organization a solid reputation within the legal civil rights community and respect from their funders. Unfortunately, grant dollars in any given year were never sufficient to ensure any long-term financial security.

Sole grant financing proved to be not only limited, but also more haphazard as AALDEF aged and matured as an institution. In 1982, The Norman Foundation, an early national funder, became concerned that the organization was not raising enough money from other sources besides foundations. The last year that AALDEF could receive funding for general support from Norman was 1983. (The Norman Foundation does not give ongoing support monies more than three years in a row.) Since AALDEF had had many of its initial grants renewed, they had been able to make it into the 80s without a financial crisis. Now, that initial foundation support was severely curtailed, and a severe budget crunch was at hand.

AALDEF had discovered that age was a double-edged asset. "The older you get, the less inclined foundations are to give you general support," says Hildy Simmons, program director of The Norman Foundation. "You end up with in-adequate grants for special projects and no core support for day-to-day operating expenses. In any case, small foundations don't want to be the sole support of any project. Even big foundations like Ford look for partners now." To make matters worse, said Simmons, rejection snowballs—one foundation wonders why the others are pulling out.

As well, small foundations have had to stretch their funding thinner as Federal dollars dwindled in the early 80s. The Norman Foundation, for example, funds 70 out of the 350 proposals it receives annually. One third of these are renewals. But whereas four years ago 25 percent of all proposals received were completely outside the foundation's areas of interest, now only 12 percent fall within that category, an indication of the grant world's heightened competition.

AALDEF knew what the problem was—the question was how to solve it. Staff and board began experimental overtures to other types of funders. After learning from some colleagues about several religious funders, the organization successfully approached the national bodies of the Presbyterian and Methodist Churches for special labor projects. Unfortunately, other church bodies were not as forthcoming with support. On another front, in 1981, the first solicitation for money was made to potentially sympathetic individuals. While the response was positive, the financial return was less than the average past foundation grant. AALDEF had a long road ahead in finding replacement dollars.

However, in 1984, an incentive from The Norman Foundation put the move to expand the base of individual donors into high gear. The Foundation made a challenge grant of $5,000 for general support, to be matched dollar-for-dollar within one month!

In response, AALDEF targeted its past larger ($100 and over) donors, members of the Asian legal community, and community groups, such as the Chinatown Local of the International Ladies' Garment Workers' Union, as well as old friends. AALDEF had been reluctant in making overtures to wealthy individuals in the past because the staff and board members did not have personal contacts. What happened? "We got a tremendous response," Margaret Fung, executive director of AALDEF noted, "and picked up some new supporters." The approach was made through a carefully-crafted direct-mail appeal.

Now, AALDEF is continuing to build a base of individual donors through approaches to particular segments of Asian-American communities, namely, Asian-American partners of law firms and business professionals. A banker and a law firm associate on their board of directors organized a party at the Yale Club, which drew 200 people, most of whom were in finance and banking. Subsequently, many of those in attendance came to a fundraising dinner, and members of such groups as the Asian Financial Society, the National Association of Young Asian Professionals, and the Asian Management and Business Association offered AALDEF their support and assistance. These professional groups have aided AALDEF in building bridges to their members, and perhaps, even to older, more established members of the community.

Pursuing individual supporters, while being clearly productive, is more time-consuming than pursuing foundation grants. As a result, AALDEF has had to change its staffing pattern to free up one of its attorneys to do more fundraising in recognition of the dimensions of the job.

The Asian American Legal Defense and Education Fund learned some hard lessons about foundation support. As Hildy Simmons noted, "foundations should never be perceived as the mainstay, but they are open to approaches where their funds can be used to leverage other sources of support." While individual support has long-term growth potential, it does require a substantial organizational commitment on the part of both board and staff. Individual support, in addition, is more renewable and consistent than foundation support. AALDEF has learned the hard way not to put all its eggs in one basket. Certainly, foundations and other institutional supporters will continue to play a role in the future of the organization, as specific programs matching funders' interests arise. However, AALDEF is on the road to a securer financial future by diversifying and broadening its base of support.

by Ellin Stein and Michael Seltzer

Summary Worksheet

for

_____

(name of your organization)

APPROACHING FOUNDATIONS FOR SUPPORT

1. Building on Past Foundation Support:

a. Have any foundations ever supported your work in the past?

☐ yes   ☐ no

b. If yes, which ones?

_____

_____

_____

_____

c. What characteristics do these funders share? How do their interests correspond to each other?

Comments:

_____

_____

_____

d. What is *your* sense of what they valued in your organization's work?

Comments:

_____

_____

_____

e. Which ones can you reapproach for future support?

Definite Ongoing Prospects:

_____

_____

_____

Untested (Further Information Needed):

_____

_____

_____

Finding New Foundation Supporters: Research and Networking

2. Using The Foundation Center's *COMSEARCH Subject* categories (see chart on page 236), list here the categories within which your work logically falls.

_____   _____

_____   _____

_____   _____

_____

3. List the names of some other organizations similar to yours in mission and in scope, in your own community and in other parts of the country. Which ones have been successful in securing foundation support? Place a check (√) next to those that have.

☐ _____

☐ _____

☐ _____

☐ _____

☐ _____

4. Now, based on your own knowledge or on discussions with representatives of these groups, find out what you can about their funders. List and describe them below.

Name of Foundation	Description (i.e., local, community, national, etc.)	Grant Amount
a. _____	_____	_____
b. _____	_____	_____
c. _____	_____	_____
d. _____	_____	_____
e. _____	_____	_____
f. _____	_____	_____

For What Purpose	To Which Organization
a. _____	_____
b. _____	_____
c. _____	_____
d. _____	_____
e. _____	_____
f. _____	_____

5. Below, list those foundation prospects that you have uncovered from your research and your networking. Limit your listing to the 10 most likely supporters of your organization. In other words, your 10 "Best Bets."

a. Type of Foundation	**b.** Their Stated Areas of Interest that Relate to Your Work	**c.** Appropriate Contact Person, Address, and Telephone #
Family Foundation		
Community Foundation		
Other Local Foundations		
Local Public Charities		
National Foundations		

d. Any Personal Contacts	**e.** Your Program(s) that Correspond to Their Interests	**f.** Grants to Similar Organizations (List)

6. **Making the Match**. For each prospect on the previous list, complete the following worksheet (use your own blank paper).

Foundation Name:

Its Stated Areas of Interest that Pertain to Your Work:
(Draw from their annual reports, reference books, newsclippings, etc.)

Develop one or more sentences relating your work to the interests of the foundation you are approaching. (Or write one or more short sentences demonstrating how the work of your organization reflects the interests of X foundation.)

7. **Finding Assistance and Counsel**. Name 5 or more individuals who might be able to advise you on how to most effectively approach the foundations on your "best bets" list (other organization directors, consultants, members of professional organizations, etc.).

   a. _____

   b. _____

   c. _____

   d. _____

   e. _____

8. **Assessing the Likelihood of Securing Foundation Support**. On the basis of what you have learned, how would you rank your chances of securing support from foundations?

   ☐ Very good   ☐ Possible   ☐ Unlikely   ☐ Still Unknown

FURTHER READINGS

Allen, Herb, ed. *The Bread Game: The Realities of Foundation Fund-raising.* Revised Edition. San Francisco: Regional Young Adult Project. 1981. 192 pp. $9.95. (Order from: Regional Young Adult Project, 944 Market St., # 705, San Francisco, CA 94102)

> Resources for grassroots nonprofit organizations on raising funds from public and private foundations. Includes information on writing proposals, researching foundations, and setting up an accounting system. Sample proposals and forms.

Conrad, Daniel Lynn. *The New Grants Planner: A Systems Approach to Grantsmanship.* San Francisco: Public Management Institute. 1980. 402 pp. $49.00. (Order from: Public Management Institute, 358 Brannan St., San Francisco, CA 94107)

> Shows how to start a Grants Readiness System so that it is possible to respond quickly to grant opportunities. Many forms and worksheets.

Conrad, Daniel Lynn. *The Quick Proposal Workbook.* San Francisco: Public Management Institute. 1980. 120 pp. $19.00. (Order from: Public Management Institute, 358 Brannan St., San Francisco, CA 94107)

> Provides suggestions for step-by-step proposal preparation. Includes a number of useful forms and worksheets.

Council on Foundations Newsletter. Bi-weekly. Washington, DC: Council on Foundations. Free to members; $60.00/yr. for nonmembers. (Order from: Council on Foundations, 1828 L St., N.W., Washington, DC 20036)

> News about foundations and the people involved with them; notice of new publications.

Dermer, Joseph. *How to Write Successful Foundation Proposals.* Hartsdale, NY: Public Service Materials Center. 1980. 80 pp. $11.50. (Order from: Public Service Materials Center, 111 N. Central Ave., Hartsdale, NY 10530)

> How-to manual provides examples of grant-winning presentations with commentary on the thinking that went into them. Includes a section on securing grants for building and/or renovations.

Foundation Center. *Comsearch: Broad Topics.* New York: The Foundation Center. $32.00 each. (Order from: The Foundation Center, 79 Fifth Ave., New York, NY 10003)

> Concise overview of foundation giving in one of 24 broad topic areas (for example, arts and cultural programs, museums, women and girls, community and urban development). For each topic, gives the 15 largest grants reported in the topic area, the total amount of grants reported by each foundation, the total value of grants received by organizations in each state, and the total amount and number of grants awarded by specific types of support.

Foundation Center. *Comsearch: Geographics.* New York: The Foundation Center. $28.00 each. (Order from: The Foundation Center, 79 Fifth Ave., New York, NY 10003)

Listings of grants awarded in specific geographical areas including 2 cities (Washington, DC and New York), 11 states, and 7 broad regions.

Foundation Center. *Comsearch: Subjects.* New York: The Foundation Center. $17.50 each, paper; $6.00 each, microfiche. (Order from: The Foundation Center, 79 Fifth Ave., New York, NY 10003)

Lists actual grants awarded in each of 59 subject categories including specific subdivisions under communications, education, health, cultural activities, population groups, science and technology, social sciences, and welfare.

Foundation Center. *The Foundation Directory.* 10th Edition. New York: The Foundation Center. 1985. 885 pp. $65.00. (Order from: The Foundation Center, 79 Fifth Ave., New York, NY 10003)

Lists over 4,400 foundations with assets of at least $1 million or whose total grants are at least $100,000. Foundations are listed by state and each entry includes purpose and activities, names of administrators, and grants available. Indexed by: subject; foundation name; geographic focus; names of donors, trustees, and officers; and types of support awarded. Charts and tables provide a statistical breakdown of the foundation community.

Foundation Center. *Foundation Grants to Individuals.* Fifth Edition. New York: The Foundation Center. 1986. 284 pp. $18.00. (Order from: The Foundation Center, 79 Fifth Ave., New York, NY 10003)

Full descriptions of the programs of about 950 foundations that provide grants to individuals. Arranged in the categories of: scholarships and loans; fellowships; grants to foreign individuals; general welfare and medical assistance; awards, prizes and grants through nomination; grants restricted to company employees and locations.

Foundation Center. *National Data Book.* 10th Edition. New York: The Foundation Center. 1986. 862 pp. $55.00. (Order from: The Foundation Center, 79 Fifth Ave., New York, NY 10003)

Directory of all of the approximately 24,000 currently active grantmaking foundations in the U.S. Gives such information as name and address, name of principal officer, and fiscal data such as market value of assets, grants paid, and gifts received. Includes a special section on community foundations.

Foundation Center. *Source Book Profiles 1986.* New York: The Foundation Center. 1986. Unpaginated. $275.00 for four cumulative volumes. (Order from: The Foundation Center, 79 Fifth Ave., New York, NY 10003)

Detailed information about the 1000 largest foundations (500 each year), including funding cycles, policies and guidelines, and analysis of the types of grants made. Revised profiles are provided when changes occur in foundations. Indexed by subject, type of support, geographic location, and foundation name.

Foundation Giving Watch/Foundation Updates. Monthly. Washington, DC: The Taft Group. $127.00/yr. (Order from: The Taft Group, 5130 MacArthur Blvd., N.W., Washington, DC 20016)

> News, current trends and opportunities in foundation giving. Information on foundations undergoing change or major development. May also be ordered as part of *The Taft Foundation Information System,* which also includes *The Taft Foundation Reporter* (annual subscription of $367.00 plus $15.00 postage and handling).

Foundation News. Bimonthly. Washington, DC: Council on Foundations, Inc. $24.00/yr. (Order from: Council on Foundations, Inc., 1828 L Street, N.W., Washington, DC 20036)

> Primary focus on grantmakers, grantmaking activities and trends with some information on philanthropy in general.

Hall, Mary. *Developing Skills in Proposal Writing.* Portland, OR: Continuing Education Publications. 1977. 339 pp. $12.50 plus $1.50 shipping and handling. (Order from: Continuing Education Publications, Portland State University, P.O. Box 1491, Portland, OR 97207)

> Thorough discussion of developing ideas, writing proposals, and seeking grants. In addition to covering the actual writing of a proposal, deals with the planning and information collection which is necessary prior to the writing.

Hillman, Howard, and Karin Abarbanel. *The Art of Winning Foundation Grants.* New York: Vanguard Press. 1975. 188 pp. $14.00. (Order from: Public Service Materials Center, 111 N. Central Ave., Hartsdale, NY 10530)

> Basic guide to foundation research: how to identify the appropriate foundation, how to approach them, how to write a proposal. Includes sample proposals, cover letters and tax forms.

Kalish, Susan Ezell, *et al. The Proposal Writer's Swipe File: 15 Winning Fund-Raising Proposals . . . Prototypes of Approaches, Styles, and Structures.* Third Edition. Washington, DC: The Taft Group. 1984. 162 pp. $18.95. (Order from: The Taft Group, 5125 MacArthur Blvd., N.W., Washington, DC 20016)

> Actual proposals in various areas of interest which were awarded substantial grants from a foundation or corporate giving program. Examples of how proposals are organized, styled, and presented.

Kiritz, Norton J. *Program Planning and Proposal Writing.* Los Angeles: The Grantsmanship Center. 1979. 47 pp. $3.25 plus $2.00 handling per order. (Order from: The Grantsmanship Center, P.O. Box 6210, 650 S. Spring St., Suite 507, Los Angeles, CA 90014)

> Step-by-step guide to planning and proposal writing. Includes a summary worksheet, "Proposal Checklist and Evaluation Form," designed to assist in the preparation of a proposal.

Nielsen,Waldemar A. *The Golden Donors: A New Anatomy of the Great Foundations.* New York: E. P. Dutton, Inc. 1985. 448 pp. $25.00. (Order from: E. P. Dutton, Inc., 2 Park Ave., New York, NY 10016)
> Profiles of the country's 36 largest foundations. Inside information on the origins, evolution, power struggles, and gossip of philanthropy.

Public Media Center. *Index of Progressive Funders.* 1985–1986 Edition. 1985. 466 pp. $40.00. (Order from: Public Media Center, 466 Green St., San Francisco, CA 94133)
> Directory of foundations that fund public interest and progressive nonprofit organizations. Includes information on the kinds of projects funded and amounts of the grants plus contact information.

Read, Patricia. *Foundation Fundamentals: A Guide for Grantseekers.* Third Edition. New York: The Foundation Center. 1986. 240 pp. $9.95. (Order from: The Foundation Center, 79 Fifth Ave., New York, NY 10003)
> Basic insights into foundations and how to approach them for funding. Workbook format facilitates learning general information about foundations, who gets foundation grants, how to present an idea to a foundation, etc.

Researching Foundations, Part I. Reprint from *The Grantsmanship Center NEWS.* 24 pp. $3.00 plus $2.00 handling per order. (Order from: The Grantsmanship Center, P.O. Box 6210, 650 S. Spring St., Suite 507, Los Angeles, CA 90014)
> Introduction to the techniques and resources for identifying foundation support. Section on how to use *The Foundation Directory.*

Researching Foundations, Part II. Reprint from *The Grantsmanship Center NEWS.* 24 pp. $3.00 plus $2.00 handling per order. (Order from: The Grantsmanship Center, P.O. Box 6210, 650 S. Spring St., Suite 507, Los Angeles, CA 90014)
> Step-by-step directions for finding information on foundations including details about The Foundation Center Regional Collections and state directories.

Shellow, Jill R., ed. *Grant Seekers Guide: Funding Sourcebook.* Revised Edition. Mt. Kisco, NY: Moyer Bell Limited. 1985. 550 pp. $19.95; $14.95 paper. (Order from: Moyer Bell Limited, Colonial Hill/RFD 1, Mt. Kisco, NY 10549)
> Help in locating sources of funding for cultural, social, and economic justice projects. Particularly useful for nontraditional projects involved in advocacy, organizing, and work with the poor and minorities. Includes chapters on proposal writing, management and organizational accountability, and gaining tax-exempt status.

Smith, Craig W., and Eric W. Skjei. *Getting Grants.* New York: Harper Colophon Books. 1981. 286 pp. $4.95. (Order from: Harper Colophon Books, 10 E. 53rd St., New York, NY 10022)
> Guide to the grants system, including government and private sources. Covers methods for finding funders and writing proposals. Includes many case histories.

Taft Group. *Taft Foundation Reporter.* 17th Edition. Washington, DC: The Taft Group. 1986. 827 pp. $287.00 plus $10.00 postage and handling. (Order from: The Taft Group, 5130 MacArthur Blvd., N.W., Washington, DC 20016)

Information on over 500 of the largest national and regional private foundations. In addition to information about the foundations, includes biographical sketches of the foundation officers and directors. Foundations indexed by field of interest, types of grants, and state; individuals indexed by name, state of birth, and alma mater. May also be ordered as part of *The Taft Foundation Information System,* which also includes *Foundation Giving Watch* and *Foundation Updates* (annual subscription of $367.00 plus $15.00 postage and handling).

White, Virginia. *Grant Proposals That Succeeded.* New York: Plenum Press. 1984. 240 pp. $22.50. (Order from: Plenum Press, 233 Spring St., New York, NY 10013)

Samples of a variety of proposals for grants ranging from $5,500 to $450,000. Gives the step-by-step process that went into securing the grant: initial research, selection of a prospective grantmaker, personal meetings and pre-grant negotiations.

CHAPTER 14

APPROACHING INSTITUTIONS FOR SUPPORT

CORPORATIONS AND BUSINESSES

In the latter part of the nineteenth century, Andrew Carnegie and some of his peers gave credence to the social responsibilities of the wealthy, but those responsibilities were of the individual, not the corporation. As the twentieth century advanced, this outlook began to change. Since the Great Depression, corporations and businesses, large and small alike, have been progressively singing a slightly different tune: "What's good for our community is good for business."

Yet, within corporate circles today, discussions still continue between corporate leaders who view their contributions to the public good solely on the basis of their profit margins and those who believe that their obligations encompass a broad spectrum of civic duties. The latter approach, fortunately, has become the model for corporate leadership. Currently, it is not unusual to find a corporate executive filling the business day with a hectic schedule of board meetings of nonprofit organizations and projects that, at first glance, may not bear directly on the company's profit-and-loss statement.

The full history of small business and its contributions to philanthropy since the country's founding has not yet been written. These contributions may have been modest compared to those of their larger corporate cousins; yet small business has consistently responded generously to the needs of its communities.

Corporate philanthropy is a totally voluntary activity. Tax advantages do provide added inducement; the Internal Revenue Service allows companies to deduct up to 10 percent of their net profits on the basis of their charitable contributions. In Minneapolis, a number of corporate executives even established the "5% Club" to encourage Minnesota's corportions to raise their giving to 5 percent of pretax profits.

Nonetheless, it is still safe to say that the tax advantage is not the initial impetus for corporate philanthropy. Why, then, do corporations willingly give some of their profits to nonprofit organizations? One answer is that:

> By and large, chief executive officers regard corporate philanthropy as a way to help those in need in a manner that is consistent with large corporate objectives. That is, corporate giving is portrayed as a form of enlightened self-interest. . . . CEOs' sense of ethical responsibility coexists with self-interested motives. . . . Corporate giving has a double agenda—the one altruistic and the other self-interested.

This response comes from a study conducted by The Council on Foundations in May 1982, called *Corporate Giving: The Views of Chief Executive Officers of Major American Corporations*. In charge of the study were Arthur H. White and John Bartolomeo; they set out to assess the attitudes of chief executive officers of major American corporations toward corporate philanthropy. The quote above represents the heart of their findings.

The "enlightened self-interest" they mention is exemplified by the following remark, made by a CEO during the course of an interview: "It is in our self-interest to have good health, social welfare, and education institutions in areas in which our employees live and in which our offices and plants are located."

This perspective, apparently, is gaining the upper hand in corporate boardrooms: White and Bartolomeo found that 59 percent of the business leaders interviewed in their survey felt that "business has an ethical responsibility to make contributions to nonprofit organizations." In addition, corporations increasingly are seeing that support of nonprofits is directly beneficial to the public image of a company. As an example, J.P. Morgan and Co., Inc., a bank holding company based in New York City, highlighted its philanthropic activities in its 1984 annual report.

Finally, corporations and the private sector in this country as a whole have been called on by public leaders to increase their activities on behalf of the public good. No less august a body than the President's Task Force on Private Sector Initiatives recommended, on December 8, 1982, that corporations, within four years, *double* the level of cash contributions to nonprofit organizations engaged in public service, with a goal of tax-deductible contributions equaling at least 2 percent of pretax net income.

In short, the 1980s represent a pinnacle in the growing effort of recent decades toward an expanded ethic of corporate social responsibility. How do these businesses express their philanthropic agenda? And, more importantly, how does a nonprofit organization approach them for help? What kind of assistance is it likely to receive?

While corporate philanthropy is most visibly expressed in the form of cash contributions or grants to nonprofit organizations, these transactions really represent only one dimension of corporate support. Corporations, as distinct from foundations, have vast resources available from which to draw in assisting the nonprofit organization, ranging from loaned executives and volunteers to donating printing on their own presses.

In 1987, American companies gave $4.8 billion in gifts of cash, products, and property, according to an annual survey issued by the Conference Board, a nonprofit research organization. The same survey detected a trend whereby companies are giving more noncash gifts, such as computer equipment, pharmaceuticals, and foodstuffs. In the 1985 annual survey on private giving conducted by the American Association of Fund-Raising Counsel, "Giving USA," corporations accounted for 5.4 percent of all private giving (about $4.5 billion). This percentage is dwarfed in comparison to the percentage of support provided by individuals. Comparable statistics are not available in published form on the contributions made by small businesses, the neighborhood mom-and-pop store, or the small-scale local factory.

HOW DO CORPORATIONS AND BUSINESSES EXTEND SUPPORT?

To repeat, cash on the barrel is only one of many ways in which a company can assist the nonprofit. Let's look at the categories of help that businesses may extend to fulfill their philanthropic agendas.

Cash Gifts, Grants, and Contributions

Companies provide financial support in various ways. First, they make direct grants or contributions throughout the year to nonprofit organizations. Second, they usually provide substantial support to the local United Way, which, in turn, makes annual allocations to general health and social welfare agencies. Third, many businesses encourage their employees to make charitable contributions by offering to match their donations. Dollar support can range from a very modest sum—placing an ad in a program book ($25.00)—to funds sufficient to purchase a building.

Material Support

Every business has some goods, products, and/or services that it markets to the public. It is not unusual for companies to make these goods available as gifts to nonprofits. This does not mean that IBM will give away a typewriter or Xerox a duplicating machine to every organization that asks. Material support is often imaginative and sometimes surprising. For example, the Air Products Corporation provides to nonprofit organizations canisters of air to fill balloons for use at street festivals, picnics, etc.

Small businesses are also wonderful sources of donated gifts which may be used in turn as raffle prizes or membership benefits or for special events, such as auctions, bazaars, or garage sales. Restaurants can donate a dinner for two or even the entire facility for a party. The examples are countless, as varied as businesses themselves.

People Power

Businesses employ many talented, highly skilled people whose expertise in areas such as financial management, marketing, personnel, public relations, or planning may well relate to any number of the needs of nonprofits. In addition, many employees are volunteers waiting "in the wings," potential recruits for the willing nonprofit.

As a result, the corporation becomes a fertile hunting ground for new board members, pro bono consultants, and ongoing volunteers. Moreover, many companies encourage their employees to become involved with nonprofit organizations by establishing a variety of related programs, including corporate volunteer programs, loaned executive programs, retired executive programs, and senior consultant programs. In many cities intermediary organizations, such as Volunteer Consulting Group in New York and National Executive Service Corps, nationwide, run board candidate recruitment services and provide professional management consulting, thus serving as a bridge between nonprofits and businesses.

Physical Facilities

Corporations also possess excellent conference rooms, auditoriums, and other meeting facilities that they may make available to organizations for workshops, seminars, annual meetings, special events, and other public functions.

Promotion and Publicity

Corporate sponsorship of a nonprofit or of one of its programs has become more and more mutually beneficial. Through sponsorship, a business is saying that association with a nonprofit endeavor enhances its public image. Accordingly, a business could underwrite such expenses as placing ads in local newspapers, printing promotional flyers and brochures, designing and producing colorful banners, and even lending staff to assist in other promotional tasks. One of the most highly successful examples of such a co-sponsorship is the New York City Marathon, which is organized by the New York Roadrunners Club and has been officially sponsored by Manufacturers Hanover Trust Company, Seiko, Mercedes-Benz, Ellesse, Perrier, the Rudin family, *The Runner* magazine, and Inner City Broadcasting.

Marketing Their Own Wares

Interestingly enough, corporations and businesses may even promote a nonprofit by directly associating a sale of one of its products with that organization. Maximilian, a major furrier in New York City, offered some of its furs to a sale to benefit the work of The Lighthouse, the New York Association for the Blind. Maximilian reduced the selling price of these furs by at least half and then contributed 10 percent of each sale to The Lighthouse.

American Express decided to celebrate the twenty-fifth anniversary of the American Express card throughout the United States by associating itself with the restoration and preservation campaign of the Statue of Liberty and Ellis Island. During 1983, American Express made a one-penny contribution to the Statue of Liberty–Ellis Island Foundation every time an American Express card was used in the United States.

American Express and Maximilian are examples of the same spirit that moves the neighborhood tavern to sponsor the local softball league and to host the winning team's victory party. These different examples show a number of ways that corporations and businesses support nonprofit organizations beyond the cash contribution.

How do corporations and businesses operate their charitable contributions programs and their other community affairs efforts? The answer is simplest when we are referring to the smallest unit of American business, the neighborhood corner store. The store's proprietors make all the decisions, including which charities to support in the community. These proprietors may belong to a local trade association or Chamber of Commerce that will periodically suggest nonprofit organizations worthy of support. This support can range from placing canisters near the cash register, to selling the calendars produced by the PTA of the nearby elementary school, to donating raffle prizes.

The next type of business is the outlet or the branch office of supermarkets, drugstores, banks, fast-food outlets, and so on, that conduct business in the neighborhood. Here the store manager makes the decisions and can choose from a larger variety of charitable options to help your organization. The parent company may sponsor a community-service grants program, through which the branch manager can award grants or refer local organizations to the central office for such grants. Or a bank branch manager may offer the bank's windows or lobby for a display highlighting a nonprofit organization's work, or even offer to mail out literature on your organization's programs, along with its monthly billings. The manager might also be able and inclined to arrange for donated printing of your ad books or raffle tickets.

To continue this tour of local businesses, let's stop next at some ubiquitous citywide establishments: the shopping malls, department stores, utility companies, transit companies, and the like. Now, for the first time, do we encounter the many public relations offices whose staffs work to keep their specific companies before the public eye. These offices are responsible for producing advertisements and placing them in newspapers and on radio and television. They also organize the promotional events that help a store attract shoppers.

And it's precisely these events that offer excellent opportunities for collaboration with nonprofit organizations. Department stores sometimes sponsor "Senior Days" in conjunction with local senior citizen centers, during which time senior citizens are bused in from the surrounding areas for a day of entertainment and shopping at special discount prices, with a luncheon in the store cafeteria or restaurant often thrown in for good measure. Or a store may decide to donate one of its weekly display ads to promote the work of a nonprofit organization.

The marketing or publicity staffs of these metropolitan businesses are usually glad to assist the nonprofit organization in planning and coordinating all the details that such activities require, but the best initial contact remains the chief executive officer of the company or the officer most directly responsible for public relations. His or her approval is necessary for any large-scale promotion or contribution. You should not be deterred, however, from starting simply where you know people, such as a store employee who, once approached, can direct you to the appropriate department for your needs. From there, a sympathetic and knowledgeable employer can show you how to navigate a company's bureaucracy until you find the officer who can best assist you and your purposes.

Finally, we are ready to explore the largest form of business organization in this country—the major corporation—in our search for support. Because of their sheer size, corporations maintain several offices or departments that interest us, described in the following list.

1. *Corporate contributions* (sometimes also known as *community affairs*). Professional staff work in capacities not much different than their counterparts in the foundation world. A corporation's contributions budget is usually set in the fall of every year for the forthcoming year. Some information on areas of funding interest and application guidelines can sometimes be obtained.

2. *Publicity or marketing.* As described earlier, publicity or marketing departments are responsible for the promotional efforts of a corporation, including advertising, media relations, and the like.

3. *Public affairs or governmental relations.* Some corporations maintain departments that oversee all corporate activities relating to the public. Besides those areas already described—charitable contributions and publicity—these offices stay abreast of relationships with government on a local, state, and federal level, and of issues that bear on the well-being of the communities in which the corporation maintains offices or conducts its business or sells its products or services. These departments may consist of one senior executive, or they may be much larger, employing an entire professional staff.

Unless a nonprofit has prior personal contact on the senior level of a company, the nonprofit executive director or board officer usually makes the initial contact with someone in the charitable contributions office. The contributions officer is then in the position to introduce the nonprofit representative to officials of other appropriate offices within the company for assistance.

Decisions on grants and contributions are made directly by the chief executive officer, or by a committee of senior executives designated, perhaps, as the Contributions Committee, or by one senior officer in charge of this area. The larger the grant, the greater likelihood that the final decision will be made by a number of people.

On the other hand, decisions about small requests for money, such as buying ads in the annual program book or purchasing a table at a gala benefit, are made most often by the corporate contributions staff itself.

Unless corporations have chosen to create a foundation to channel their charitable giving, their philanthropy is not subject to exactly the same requirements set by the Internal Revenue Service for foundations. Corporations, for instance, are not required to report their grants in a special annual report (i.e., IRS Form 990). If they are seeking tax deductions for their charitable contributions, however, they report this information in their corporate tax returns which are not available to the general public. Some corporations voluntarily publish annual reports outlining their charitable activity for the year, available free upon request from the charitable contributions office.

Corporations tend to be more general than most professionally staffed foundations in their grantmaking. Their interest areas are defined more broadly: health, education, and welfare. As with foundations, however, it is difficult to generalize, given the scope and diversity of America's corporate community. Some companies do have highly targeted and carefully selected priorities; fortunately, these are usually the same companies that publish annual reports.

Partly because of these broad interests, corporations very often provide general support grants rather than project-specific grants. Corporation grantmaking also differs from foundations' in the range in size of grants. It is not unusual for a company to make a substantial number of small grants to organizations (less than $5,000) while also making substantial grants ($50,000 to $100,000) to a select list of large nonprofit institutions.

Depending on the size of the charitable contributions staff, an applicant may find few or many opportunities to talk directly to a contributions officer or associate. Large visible institutions, such as banks, which have a high public profile in their communities, probably receive a higher volume of requests than more specialized and focused companies. Therefore the applicant may find the latter far more likely to reply to a request with personal contact.

The most important difference between foundation giving and corporate giving lies in the ability of a company to provide more than financial support, as described earlier. Whether or not an applicant is accepted for a grant request, the nonprofit is still free to explore other types of support from that corporation. In fact, the company may welcome the opportunity to place volunteers with your organization or to publicize your work in its company newsletter or magazine.

See the amazing feat with 710 toes.

For dance information, call
Chicago Dance, Inc. at 939-0181.

ChicagOh
The arts put the Oh! in Chicago.

City of Chicago
Jane M. Byrne, Mayor
©1981 Chicago Council on Fine Arts

Advertising agencies often donate their creative services to nonprofit organizations.

Source: Magazine advertisement for the Chicago Council on Fine Arts donated by a major advertising agency. Dennis Maurizi, concept/copy; Bruce Morser, Dave Derby, art direction. © 1981 Chicago Council on Fine Arts. Reprinted with permission.

Reduced federal government spending in meeting human needs and increased competition for foundation support have come to characterize the 1980s. These realities have brought corporate philanthropy in its many forms into the limelight as never before in recent history. Hence, the time is ripe for nonprofits to explore the corporate resource tree actively.

Which organizations are eligible to apply and to receive cash and in-kind contributions from businesses and corporations? To receive credit from the Internal Revenue Service for their contributions, companies and businesses must restrict their financial support to organizations that have been classified as charitable under Section 501(c)(3) of the Internal Revenue Code.

Of course, businesses are free to choose to support other types of non-profit organizations, as long as they do not attempt to claim tax deductions for such support. As a result, a company can choose to support extensive lobbying or electoral activities that might exceed what the IRS allows for 501(c)(3) organizations.

Needless to say, a company has no restrictions in deciding upon the organizations it designates as the recipients of its many in-kind services and contributions, since these services are not deducted on a company's tax return. The exception lies with companies that do deduct for large donations of equipment, such as computers.

WHAT ARE THE ADVANTAGES OF RAISING SUPPORT FROM BUSINESSES AND CORPORATIONS?

1. Once you receive support from a business, you are eligible to receive similar support from that same concern in subsequent years. If you continue to meet the company's charitable goals, you've set the stage for other approaches in the future.

Of course, ongoing support depends upon other factors, as well: (a) the steadiness of the company's profits, enabling it to provide funds for its corporate giving program; (b) your organization's ability to carry out your programs successfully; and (c) the level of competition with other long-standing grantees, especially if a company's charitable resources are shrinking.

2. A dollar gift from a company provides you with sufficient credibility to engage other departments of the company for donated in-kind services.

3. Indication of support for your work by one company in your community will help induce other companies to extend their support as well. Businesses don't regard the presence of their counterparts as competitive, and may even view their absence as negative.

The significant exception, of course, is corporate sponsorship, in which the sponsoring company is seeking substantial publicity and impact on its public image through its association with your program.

4. Corporations, through their in-kind support and services, can enable smaller

groups to tackle larger activities than their own resources usually allow. Loaned executives or volunteers provide a tremendous boost to the human "power potential" of smaller nonprofits.

WHAT ARE THE DISADVANTAGES OF RAISING SUPPORT FROM BUSINESSES AND CORPORATIONS?

1. *Limited size grants.* While corporations certainly make grants in large as well as small amounts, they are apt to make grants of less than $5,000 to small, community-based organizations, especially to those applying for support for the first time. In addition, it is difficult for a corporate grantee to increase the level of support it received from its business benefactors in subsequent years.

Neighborhood businesses, usually a steady source of support for nonprofit organizations in their community, are also limited in the level of support they are able to contribute. Five hundred dollars or $1,000 would be a very large gift from the traditional mom-and-pop store, and may even constitute the average grant from the local bank.

2. *Public association with a business donor.* Since companies and businesses may expect some public recognition or acknowledgment of their contributions, the recipient organization has an obligation, often unstated, to publicize the grant it has received.

This sounds simple enough but it may well not be, for many social issue and advocacy organizations may be attacking certain problems they believe to be fostered or even caused by certain corporations. Those groups may feel that their integrity will be compromised if they accept funds from the companies whose policies they are seeking to change. An environmental group, for example, may decide not to approach a particular utility company for support if the group is actively challenging that company's plans to build a nuclear reactor. Moreover, the company may be eager to extend support to the environmental group simply to demonstrate to the public that it is, in fact, concerned with the quality of the environment, despite charges to the contrary.

3. *Sole public identification.* Similarly, if a company is seeking to enhance its public profile through a grant or actual sponsorship of some event or program of yours, that company may very likely oppose your securing other corporate supporters for the same undertaking. It might well want to be in the limelight alone, with you by its side. Clearly, this depends upon the nature of the project itself, as well as upon the extent of support being provided.

4. *Corporate involvement in the project.* When a company's public image is involved with your particular work, the business may also ask to become involved in some of the promotional tasks that the project entails. This is meant to ensure that the company receives maximum benefits for its support. You might welcome any offer of assistance, but others might find such involvement intrusive.

5. *Corporate and business representatives on your board of directors.* Businesses often look for their own peers and colleagues on the board of a nonprofit as evidence that the group is really interested in the input of business. While some groups might welcome such participation, others may be wary, believing that such business "types" cannot share their view of the world.

HOW CAN YOUR ORGANIZATION DECIDE WHETHER TO APPROACH BUSINESSES AND CORPORATIONS FOR SUPPORT?

In order to make this decision you should consider the following questions.

1. Do local businesses and corporations have resources, in the form of either grants or in-kind services, that your organization could effectively use to carry out your work?

2. Are you prepared to extend recognition to your business supporters? To involve them in some of the decisions relating to your work?

3. Do you have any philosophical or value conflicts that would interfere with your accepting support from certain types of companies?

4. Finally, do you believe that you have the sort of organization or project that would be potentially interesting to a business in your community? Do you have a sufficiently large constituency for that business to see it as part of its market? Do you have other potentially valuable assets for your business backer? Prestige? Visible presence in the community? Wealthy connections?

Or is your work of such direct value to the community in which the business operates that you can demonstrate that its support will have a direct bearing on making the community better, both for business and for its employees?

In essence, what are are you offering to a company in return for its help?

HOW DOES AN ORGANIZATION SUCCESSFULLY SECURE SUPPORT FROM BUSINESSES AND CORPORATIONS?

The road to business support begins the way foundation grantsmanship does. To use the corporate jargon, what are the "products" that you can offer corporations and businesses for their review? Or to put it in nonprofit terms, what programs can you offer for consideration in your search for corporate dollars and resources?

The same criteria that were established to guide you in the search for foundation support serve you equally well in gauging potential business and corporate support. These include: (1) Compatibility with mission; (2) Acknowledged expertise; (3) Achievability; (4) Topicality; and (5) Documentation. (See Chapter 13 for further details on these criteria.) To this list, we can now add the following:

> *Rationale for corporate support.* How does your project or program correspond to the interests of a particular business or corporation? Does it match its stated areas of concern? Or does it conform to a

general corporate interest in the health and welfare of the community in which the business is conducted?

Potential dividends to the corporate supporter. Does the project offer any fringe benefits to the corporate underwriter? Publicity? Exposure? Credibility? Enhanced public image? Increase in product sales?

Competition. Are there other nonprofit organizations within the same geographic scope of a particular business that are more established in your field of activity? Can they "return" more to the business on their charitable "investment," because of the size or scale of their operations? Because of their access to the media?

By weighing your organization's work in relation to these specific considerations, you can ascertain how much potential interest your work will have for businesses and corporations. You will become aware, too, of the issues that need highlighting in your request for assistance. Use the summary worksheet at the end of this chapter to gauge your chances in approaching businesses for help. Are your chances strong? Moderate? Poor?

Now turn to developing a prospect list of businesses and corporations that you might approach for help. Your task is to identify those that have the greatest potential stake in your work. Begin this prospecting process by identifying companies within the following categories:

1. Businesses that your organization and its members and constituents frequent or use regularly, such as corner stores, supermarkets, banks, department stores, etc.

2. Companies for which your members and constituents and their families work.

3. Companies that sell products to your primary constituency.

4. Business concerns whose activities correspond to your programs, for example, pharmaceutical companies to work with health care organizations, computer companies with computer training projects, toy companies with youth programs, etc.

5. Other corporations that have expressed interest in your work through their printed annual reports, grant guidelines, or news reports.

As you find the companies that fit into these categories, place them on the following chart. Then you may begin to rank their accessibility.

Worksheet

1. Businesses and Corporations in Your Immediate Neighborhood

_____   _____

_____   _____

_____   _____

2. Other Businesses in Your Zip Code

_____   _____

_____   _____

_____   _____

3. Metropolitan Area Businesses

_____   _____

_____   _____

_____   _____

4. Corporate Headquarters or Plant Facilities in Your City

_____   _____

_____   _____

_____   _____

5. National or Multinational Corporations Outside Your Community

_____   _____

_____   _____

_____   _____

Corporate prospecting provides you with the opportunity to involve your board, your fundraising committee, local business people, and community supporters in some creative brainstorming to develop a list of businesses for subsequent approaches.

Now you are ready to make the actual approach!

Step 1

Research the interests and activities of the companies listed on your prospect list. Contact them directly, particularly if they are medium-to-large-sized corporations, to request a copy of their grantmaking guidelines, *and* to establish to whom letters requesting support should be addressed. Seek out data that sheds information on their customers, employees, and other constituencies they are interested in. The local mercantile library or chamber of commerce can be of assistance here. "Further Readings" also lists several helpful reference books on corporations.

Step 2

Check within your organization and within your community to see whether you have any existing contacts with the businesses on your prospect list.

Step 3

Decide which of your particular programs would be of the *most* potential interest to your prospects, based on the data you have collected and reviewed.

Step 4

Decide whether your project lends itself to a specialized corporate or business campaign, targeting a number of businesses and corporations, or to an appeal to one company solely.

Step 5

If you decide to undertake a campaign, identify and recruit potential business leaders who can serve as honorary chairs or co-chairs of such an effort, and elicit their help in forming a campaign committee. Also, develop a timetable for the actual campaign, from the kickoff to the finale.

Step 6

Before making any actual contact with a company, ask any inside contacts you have in the company how they might facilitate your request. A letter of support? A friendly informal word? A simple mention on your part in your letter?

Step 7

Place a phone call to the individual contact whom you have previously identified at the corporation or business. If you have not yet identified this person, simply call the central switchboard of the corporation and ask for the name of the staff member in charge of charitable contributions.

Try to engage that person in conversation about your organization. Tell him or her what kind of support you are seeking from X corporation or company and why you are approaching it in particular. Request the opportunity to meet with him or her to talk more about your work. You will be told whether your project falls within the company's interests (which you should have established through your prior research), and whether you should submit a letter and/or a proposal. Some companies might ask you to put your request in writing before they will give you any indication of their interest. In either case, you have already established a personal contact.

Step 8

If they have requested a letter, draft a short one (preferably no longer than two pages) to invite support of your project. The letter should summarize the project and establish the reasons for supporting it. In your letter, mention a mutual contact person if one exists. Close the letter with a request for a meeting to discuss your work in person. Involve your business campaign leader(s) as co-signer(s) of your letter.

Step 9

Prior to any contact, itemize the various types of support, besides a cash contribution, that the business can offer your work. If, for whatever reason, financial support does not appear to be immediately forthcoming, be prepared to discuss other types of assistance. In your contact with a contributions officer following receipt of your letter or phone call, be sure to determine whether there are other members of the company with whom you should be discussing in-kind services, such as the marketing or public relations staff. If so, your first contact can be helpful in arranging further introductions for you.

Step 10

If, after several weeks, you have not had a response to your request for a meeting, make a follow-up phone call. At this time, be prepared to explain succinctly why you have approached X company and what its support would enable you to do.

Bring a board member, business campaign committee member, or community leader with you to the meeting to make your case and to impress your audience with the importance of your work, as others perceive it. Also, invite your prospect to visit your organization.

Step 11

Again, as in a meeting with a foundation representative, listen to the concerns that are raised during the interview and make note of them so that you can answer them fully in your follow-up letter. Your letter should also convey your thanks for the meeting.

The Yes

Victory! The company has indicated that it finds your concerns consonant with its charitable priorities and would like to begin working with your organization.

First, talk to the company representative about the kind of public acknowledgment they would like to receive for their support—a press release, an announcement in your newsletter, a listing in a program bulletin or annual brochure, etc.

Second, as your work proceeds, be sure to fulfill your responsibilities as you have explained them in writing or verbally to your corporate sponsors. If you alter the project substantially, keep your sponsors posted.

Third, involve your corporate sponsors in your program as it progresses. Extend invitations to them to attend appropriate events and send them any press notices, particularly those that mention them. Maintain the degree of personal contact that seems natural for both parties.

The No

If your request has been rejected, contact the corporation by mail or phone to ask: "How could we have made the program stronger or more attractive to you?" or "What factors entered into your decision not to provide support at this time?" While not every business will be forthcoming with this information, some will be—enough to give you some guidance for the next time you approach a company for help.

Take this opportunity once again to explore in-kind services, such as volunteers, donated printing, and the like. Maintain cordial relations; you never know when you may want to return to a specific company for aid.

A FINAL NOTE

Members of a grassroots community organization once went to a corporate office located in their neighborhood to protest that company's inadequate involvement in the community's affairs. A manager, coming out to meet them, greeted them by saying, "We have been waiting for you to come. What can we do for you?"

This story shows how preconceptions may stand in the way of eliciting help from business.

Not every business will respond to your requests for assistance. That does not mean that *all* businesses, small and large, will be equally unresponsive. These are uncharted waters for many nonprofits; the best thing to do is to get out there and explore them.

Case Study
WORKING WOMEN EDUCATION FUND

In 1982, Working Women Education Fund (WWEF), which is affiliated with 9 to 5, the National Association of Working Women, set out to seek financial support for a survey to help working women identify stress in the workplace. The survey's focus was on the causes and effects of psychological stress on health and well-being, and on effective methods to reduce stress and strain.

WWEF had previously established a solid national reputation for its pioneering work in behalf of women in the work force, and it enjoyed considerable foundation support for this work. The stress survey, officially called "The 9 to 5 National Survey on Women and Stress," had qualities that no previous WWEF endeavors had, and staff felt that these qualities might attract the interest of corporate sponsors. Five major national women's magazines—*Ms., Vogue, Essence, Glamour,* and *Working Women*—had agreed not only to print the two-page survey free in their September 1983 issue but also to publish the results free of charge six months later. The donated magazine space had an equivalent value of $136,110 and, more important, the stress test would be seen by more than five million readers. Thus, a corporation putting its name on the test would receive considerable positive exposure.

The stress test project required WWEF to expend a great deal of time developing and designing the test and working out details with the five magazines. The staff also intended to pay a research firm to tabulate the results. All these expenses, therefore, were included in the project budget for which corporate support would be sought.

But which corporations should be approached? Companies that advertised in the magazines that were going to publish the stress test already had an interest in these readers and became the most logical prospects. With that in mind, WWEF staff took an inventory of those corporations simply by reviewing an issue of all five magazines. It could then develop a profile of the types of companies that most frequently advertised—cosmetics, pharmaceuticals, insurance, and so on—as well as a list of the specific corporations that most commonly advertised. Thus a strategy began to emerge.

Then WWEF researched the companies identified through its magazine inventory. The group prepared exploratory letters to these companies, outlining the details of the survey, and mailed out these appeals.

If their research failed to reveal significant information about a corporation, WWEF contacted that corporation directly by telephone to ascertain which office was in charge of charitable contributions and whether any literature was available to the public that detailed its grantmaking interests. In one case, WWEF was actually advised to write directly to the president of the corporation.

What were the results? After four months, WWEF had approached forty corporations and secured support in cash and in in-kind contributions from Avon, American Express, Polaroid Corporation, and Aetna Life and Casualty. In fact, Avon awarded them a challenge grant to encourage other corporations to participate in the survey as sponsors.

All in all, Working Women Education Fund both raised needed funds for one of its programs and established itself as worthy of corporate support for future endeavors. What can we learn from this one experience of a small (albeit national) organization that bears on how other nonprofit organizations might successfully secure corporate support?

First of all, a nonprofit needs to search its memory, and to stretch its thinking to ascertain what it can offer to a business concern that would serve its purposes. Exposure? Visibility? Credibility? Association with a charitable venture? What do corporations stand to gain if they agree to become associated with your work? In the case of the stress test, WWEF was able to offer not only public exposure but an opportunity for corporations concerned about working women to express that concern in a meaningful way.

Second, a nonprofit should conserve its energy and limit its corporate prospects, to those with a clear interest in either its issues or its constituencies.

Another lesson is that inquiries should be directed to the most appropriate offices within a company.

Finally, a nonprofit organization should be prepared to share the limelight with a corporate sponsor or sponsors.

Michael Seltzer

Source: Logo, Working Women Education Fund. Reprinted with permission.

Source: 9 to 5, National Association of Working Women, Cleveland, OH. Reprinted with permission.

Summary Worksheet

for

_____

(name of your organization)

APPROACHING BUSINESSES FOR SUPPORT

1. Building on Past Business and Corporate Support

a. Have any businesses and corporations ever supported your work in the past?

☐ yes   ☐ no

b. If yes, which ones?

_____   _____

_____   _____

_____   _____

_____   _____

c. What characteristics do these businesses share? How do their interests correspond to each other?

Comments:

_____

_____

_____

_____

d. What is *your* sense of what they valued in your organization's work?

Comments:

_____

_____

_____

_____

e. Which ones can you reapproach for future support?

Definite Ongoing Prospects:

_____   _____

_____   _____

_____   _____

Untested (Further Information Needed):

_____   _____

_____   _____

_____   _____

Finding New Business and Corporate Supporters: Research and Networking

2. List those businesses that your members and constituents patronize most frequently:

_____   _____

_____   _____

_____   _____

3. Add to the list businesses that employ your members and constituents:

_____   _____

_____   _____

_____   _____

4. Are there additional businesses and corporations that are marketing their products and services to your particular constituencies?

_____   _____

_____   _____

_____   _____

5. See pages 282 and 283 for this part of the worksheet.

6. Making the Match

For each prospect in the previous list, complete the following worksheet (use your own blank paper).

Name of Business or Corporation:

Its Stated Areas of Interest that Pertain to Your Work (draw from annual reports, reference books, newsclippings, etc.):

Write one or more short sentences demonstrating how the work of your organization reflects the interests of X business.

7. Finding Assistance and Counsel

Name five or more individuals who might be able to advise you on how to most effectively approach the businesses and corporations on your "Best Bets" list:

a. _____

b. _____

c. _____

d. _____

e. _____

8. Addressing the Likelihood of Securing Support

On the basis of what you have learned, how would you rank your chances of securing support from businesses?

☐ Very Good   ☐ Possible   ☐ Unlikely   ☐ Still Unknown

5. List below those business prospects that you have uncovered from your research and your networking. Limit your listing to the ten most likely supporters of your organization—your ten "Best Bets."

a. Type of Business	**b.** Its Stated Areas of Interest that Relate to Your Work	**c.** Appropriate Contact Person, Telephone Number
		d. Personal Contacts
Neighborhood Stores		
Banks, Utility Companies, Department Stores, etc.		
Corporations with Headquarters or Facilities in your Community		
Large National Corporations		

e. Your Program(s) that Correspond to Its Interests	**f.** Level of Potential Financial Support	**g.** Other Types of Support Available

FURTHER READINGS

Banking on Leisure. Chicago: International Events Group. 1985. 150 pp. $52.00 plus $4 shipping and handling. (Order from: International Events Group, 213 W. Institute Place, Suite 303, Chicago, IL 60610)

Proceedings of a seminar on corporate-sponsored special events, such as sports, music and arts festivals and events. Includes information on how corporate marketing executives decide what to sponsor along with the do's and don'ts of successful sponsorship.

Brownrigg, W. Grant. *Effective Corporate Fundraising.* New York: American Council for the Arts. 1982. 161 pp. $14.95. (Order from: American Council for the Arts, 570 Seventh Ave., New York, NY 10018)

Systematic approach to soliciting business contributions. Step-by-step information on appealing to business in terms it understands; writing a case statement, a plan of action and a budget; identifying prospects; using volunteers including the board of directors; and preparing written information and correspondence. Includes many examples of letters, reports, etc.

Conference Board. *The Corporate Contributions Function.* New York: The Conference Board. 1982. 39 pp. $15.00 Associates; $75.00 Non-Associates. (Order from: The Conference Board, 845 Third Ave., New York, NY 10022)

Conference Board. *Corporate Social Programs: Nontraditional Assistance.* New York: The Conference Board. 1983. 11 pp. $10.00 Associates; $50.00 Non-Associates. (Order from: The Conference Board, 845 Third Ave., New York, NY 10022)

Results of a survey of 112 companies with substantial contributions budgets asking them about their nontraditional giving (defined as items *not* deductible as "Contributions" on the U.S. Corporation Federal Income Tax Return). Categories of such giving included grants for basic research, loan of company-paid employees, below-market rate loans/investments, donations of products and property, and provision of services and facilities.

Conference Board. *Giving in America: Toward a Stronger Voluntary Sector.* New York: The Conference Board. 1975. 240 pp. 37 pp. Free for Associates; $2.50 Non-Associates. (Order from: The Conference Board, 845 Third Ave., New York, NY 10022)

Conrad, Daniel Lynn. *How to Get Corporate Grants.* San Francisco: Public Management Institute. 1981. 351 pp. in 3-ring binder. $49.00. (Order from: Public Management Institute, 358 Brannan St., San Francisco, CA 94107)

Manual for identifying corporations most likely to support your organization, reaching the decisionmakers, and presenting your case in a way that meets the corporation's own interests and needs. Includes information on how to use board members, volunteers, and other contacts to ensure funding.

Corporate Fund Raising Directory, The-1985-86. Hartsdale, NY: Public Service Materials Center. 1985. 400 pp. $79.50. (Order from: Public Service Materials Center, 111 N. Central Ave., Hartsdale, NY 10530)

> Directory covering the giving policies of 625 large corporations. Provides information on contact person, application procedure, geographic preference, areas of giving, and total numbers and amounts of grants. Suggests best time to approach each corporation, which corporations expect to increase giving, which issue guidelines, and which contribute executives and materials.

Corporate Giving Watch/Corporate Giving Profiles. Monthly. Washington, DC: The Taft Group. $127.00/yr. (Order from: The Taft Group, 5130 MacArthur Blvd. N.W., Washington, DC 20016)

> *Giving Watch* covers developments in corporate giving, including information about individual companies, their executives and their grant giving. *Giving Profiles* provides profiles on the Fortune 1,000 companies responsible for most of the corporate gifts. May also be ordered as part of *The Taft Corporate Information System* which also includes *The Taft Corporate Giving Directory* (annual subscription of $367.00 plus $15.00 postage and handling).

Corporate Giving Yellow Pages. Washington, DC: The Taft Group. 1986. 101 pp. $57.50. (Order from: The Taft Group, 5130 MacArthur Blvd., N.W., Washington, DC 20016)

> Identifies over 1,300 corporate giving programs, both direct giving and corporate foundations. Includes contact names, addresses, and telephone numbers. Indexed by companies that publish information about their charitable contributions, companies by field of business, and companies by headquarters state.

Corporate 1000, The. Washington, DC: The Washington Monitor, Inc. 1985. 600 pp. $59.95. (Order from: The Washington Monitor, Inc., 1301 Pennsylvania Ave., Suite 1000, Washington, DC 20004)

> Directory of names, addresses and phone numbers of the key executives and board of directors of the top 1000 manufacturing and service companies. Indexed by company name, geography, industry group, and executive name.

Corporate Philanthropy: The Business of Giving. (Special issue of *Foundation News*). Washington, DC: Council on Foundations. 1982. 160 pp. $12.00. (Order from: Council on Foundations, 1828 L St., N.W., Suite 1200, Washington, DC 20036)

> Includes the results of a national study of the attitudes of corporate executive officers of major American corporations toward corporate giving. Discusses the opinions of corporate leaders, foundation directors, journalists and lawyers on corporate giving. Looks at the effects of the new tax laws relating to corporate philanthropy.

Corporate Philanthropy: An Information Service. Bimonthly. Washington, DC: Independent Sector. (Available to members of Independent Sector, 1828 L St., N.W., Washington, DC 20036)

News about corporate giving, particularly as it relates to the publishing organization.

Corporate Philanthropy Report. Monthly. San Francisco: Public Management Institute, $127.00/yr. (Order from: Public Management Institute, 358 Brannan St., San Francisco, CA 94107)

Provides strategies for business/nonprofit partnerships with discussions of how-to, trends and analysis, tips, news and interviews. Looks at cash grants as well as other kinds of support.

Dermer, Joseph and Stephen Wertheimer, eds. *The Complete Guide to Corporate Fund Raising.* Hartsdale, NY: Public Service Materials Center. 1982. 112 pp. $17.75. (Order from: Public Service Materials Center, 111 N. Central Ave., Hartsdale, NY 10530)

Technical manual on winning corporate support with details on how to write a corporate proposal, how to enlist and work with corporate volunteers, how to get appointments with corporate officials, and how to do research on specific corporations. Special sections cover corporate fundraising for universities, hospitals, cultural institutions, advocacy organizations, and social service agencies.

Directory of Corporate Affiliations. Wilmette, IL: National Register Publishing Co. 1986. 1300 pp. $318.00 plus $7.60 postage and handling. (Order from: National Register Publishing Co., 3004 Glenview Rd., Wilmette, IL 60091)

Listings of 44,000 corporate groups including 4,000 parent companies and their 40,000 divisions, subsidiaries and affiliates. Includes indexes for parent company; division, subsidiary, and affiliate; geographic location; and SIC code.

Foundation Center. *Corporate Foundation Profiles.* Fourth Edition. New York: The Foundation Center. 1985. 622 pp. $55.00. (Order from: The Foundation Center, 79 Fifth Ave., New York, NY 10003)

Detailed profiles of 234 of the largest company-sponsored foundations. Brief records for all 725 company-sponsored foundations which have assets of at least $1 million or which grant at least $100,000 annually. Indexed by subject, types of support, and geography.

Fremont-Smith, Marion R. *Philanthropy and the Business Corporation.* New York: Russell Sage Foundation. 1972. 110 pp. $4.50. (Order from: Russell Sage Foundation, 230 Park Ave., New York, NY 10017)

Background information on corporate giving, looking at both an historical perspective and at the present state of the art.

Guide to Corporate Giving 3. New York: American Council for the Arts. 1983.
592 pp. $39.95. (Order from: American Council for the Arts, 570 Seventh Ave.,
New York, NY 10018)

> Current information on the giving policies of over 700 major companies
> in the areas of the arts, health, welfare, education and civic philanthropy.
> Company profiles include the names and addresses of contributions officers,
> application procedures and requirements, and examples of grant recipients.

Harris, James F., and Anne Klepper. *Corporate Philanthropic Public Service Activities.* New York: The Conference Board. 1976. 61 pp. $15.00. (Order from:
The Conference Board, 845 Third Ave., New York, NY 10022)

> Results of a survey of 457 major firms about their corporate giving and
> other forms of corporate philanthropic activity.

Hillman, Howard. *The Art of Winning Corporate Grants.* New York: Vanguard
Press. 1980. 180 pp. $14.95. (Order from: Public Service Materials Center, 111
N. Central Ave., Hartsdale, NY 10530)

> Practical manual on winning business support for organizations. Includes
> details on researching corporate funding opportunities, arranging meetings
> with key corporate officials, writing winning proposals, and retaining the
> good will of a corporation. Also discusses how to work out creative tie-ins
> with corporations.

Knauft, E. B. *Profiles of Effective Corporate Giving Programs.* Washington, DC:
Independent Sector. December 1985. 14 pp. $2.00. (Order from: Independent
Sector, 1828 L St., N.W., Washington, DC 20036)

> Describes a research study of 48 well-established corporate giving programs.
> Data collected included: (1) numerical information about each company and
> its contribution program; and (2) narrative information obtained from in-
> terviews with the contributions managers about such things as how decisions
> are made and by whom, examples of grants recommended by the staff but
> not finally approved, and examples of grants considered to be most creative.

Koch, F. "Fifteen Ways Companies Can Support Non-Profit Groups Without Cash
Contributions." *Management Review* vol. 68, no. 9 (September 1979): 59–62.
Reprints $20.00 (minimum order 20 copies per article). (Order from: American
Management Association, Management Review Reprints, P.O. Box 1026, Sara-
nac Lake, NY 12983)

> Discussion of how corporations can give non-cash support along with 15
> examples of such contributions.

Mittenthal, Stephen. "The Perfect Gift: Examples of Noncash Corporate Philanthropy," *The Grantsmanship Center NEWS* no. 55 (September/October 1983):
50–52. Single issue $4.75 plus $2.00 handling per order. (Order from: The
Grantsmanship Center, P.O. Box 6210, 650 S. Spring St., Suite 507, Los Angeles,
CA 90014)

A listing of a variety of non-cash corporate contributions to low-income communities and to nonprofit organizations. Includes examples of donated products, services and facilities.

National Directory of Corporate Public Affairs, 1985. Washington, DC: Columbia Books, Inc. 1985. 491 pp. $50.00. (Order from: Columbia Books, Inc., 1350 New York Ave., N.W., Suite 207, Washington, DC 20005)

Provides information about the public involvement of 1,500 companies, including their informational, political and philanthropic activities. Lists for each corporation the office and officers responsible for issue identification, advocacy advertising, state and federal lobbying, political action, and corporate contributions activity.

O'Dwyer's Directory of Corporate Communications: 1985 Edition. New York: J. R. O'Dwyer Co., Inc. 1985. 300 pp. $90.00. (Order from: The J. R. O'Dwyer Co., Inc., 271 Madison Ave., New York, NY 10016)

Listings of names, titles, telephone numbers and addresses of the public relations executives of 3,000 major companies and 50 leading trade associations. For companies, also includes such information as amount of sales, type of business, and role of public relations in the company.

Platzer, Linda Cardillo. *Annual Survey of Corporate Contributions.* New York: The Conference Board. Annual, Approximately 37 pp. $15.00 Associates; $75.00 Non-Associates. (Order from: The Conference Board, 845 Third Ave., New York, NY 10022)

Results of an annual survey of the charitable giving activities of U.S. corporations. In addition to cash contributions, non-cash charitable contributions now have an important place in the corporate response to community needs.

Plinio, Alex J., and Joanne B. Scanlan. *Resource Raising: The Role of Non-Cash Assistance in Corporate Philanthropy.* Washington, DC: Independent Sector. 1986. 35 pp. $10.00. (Order from: Independent Sector, 1828 L St., N.W., Washington, DC 20036)

Discusses non-cash corporate gifts of products, human resources, and services. Suggests ways nonprofit organizations can avail themselves of such gifts. Provides examples of organizations that broker contacts between donors of non-cash gifts and potential recipients and gives guidelines on the legal and tax consequences of non-cash assistance.

Public Management Institute. *Corporate 500: The Directory of Corporate Philanthropy.* Fifth Edition. San Francisco: Public Management Institute. 1981. 942 pp. $280.00. (Order from: Public Management Institute, 358 Brannan Street, San Francisco, CA 94107)

Profiles the contribution programs of over 500 of the largest corporations. Entries include: areas of interest, analysis of trends and priorities, geographic areas receiving funds, activities funded, eligible organizations, policy statements, financial profiles, sample grants, and application procedures. Twelve indexes facilitate use.

"Raising Money from Local Businesses." *Conserve Neighborhoods* no. 24 (May-June 1982): 222–24. Single issue $1.00 plus $2.00 postage and handling per order. (Order from: National Trust for Historic Preservation, 1785 Massachusetts Ave., N.W., Washington, DC 20036)

Suggestions for seeking contributions from local businesses of all sizes and types.

Sinclair, James P. *How to Write Successful Corporate Appeals/With Full Examples.* Hartsdale, NY: Public Service Materials Center. 1982. 110 pp. $19.95. (Order from: Public Service Materials Center, 111 N. Central Ave., Hartsdale, NY 10530)

Tips and examples to increase the chances of getting corporate donations. Descriptions and examples for writing letters that get appointments, writing cover letters that sell a proposal, writing general purpose proposals and letters that win grants, and writing proposals for new buildings and renovations.

Special Events Report. Biweekly. Chicago: Special Events Report. $180/yr.; $140/yr. for nonprofits. (Order from: Special Events Report, 213 W. Institute Place, Suite 303. Chicago, IL 60610)

News and information on corporate involvement in special events such as sporting events or music and arts festivals as a means of marketing products and services.

Standard and Poor. *Poor's Register of Corporations, Directors and Executives.* New York: Standard & Poor Corporation. Annual. Approx. 2660 pp. in vol. 1; 1485 pp. in vol. 2; 1110 pp. in vol. 3. $140.00. (Order from: Standard and Poor, 25 Broadway, P.O. Box 992, New York, NY 10275)

Volume 1 alphabetically lists approximately 45,000 corporations with the names, titles, and functions of officers, directors, and other principles. Volume 2 alphabetically lists 72,000 individuals with their business affiliations, titles, business and residential address plus such information as place of birth, college, and memberships. Volume 3 is a series of indexes to the first two volumes including those by geography, family, and industrial classification.

Sternberg, Sam. *National Directory of Corporate Charity.* San Francisco: Regional Young Adult Project. 1984. 500 pp. $80.00. (Order from: The Foundation Center, 79 Fifth Ave., New York, NY 10003)

Directory covers U.S. corporations with gross annual sales of $200 million or more. Entries include company name and address, subsidiaries, the name of the public affairs officer, and data on corporate giving. The comments section of each profile indicates one of four types of contributions programs: direct interest or welfare of its employees; company's direct interest and personal preferences of management; support for traditional nonprofit groups (conservative social interest); and support for some nontraditional recipients (such as the elderly or women's causes).

Taft Group. *Taft Corporate Giving Directory*. 7th Edition. Washington, DC: The Taft Group. 1986. 750 pp. $287.00. (Order from: The Taft Group, 5130 Mac-Arthur Blvd., N.W., Washington, DC 20016)

  Detailed information on over 530 of the largest corporate giving programs. Includes such information as biographical data on corporate officers and trustees; types of grants; giving priorities and budget; typical recipients; contact person; fiscal information; and application procedures. Eight indexes allow a variety of access points. Also available as part of *The Taft Corporate Information System* which also includes *Corporate Giving Watch/Corporate Giving Profiles* (annual subscription of $367.00 plus $15.00 postage and handling.

CHAPTER 15

APPROACHING INSTITUTIONS FOR SUPPORT

GOVERNMENT SUPPORT

Government support is a process by which a unit of government—national, regional, state, county, city, or town—extends its resources to a nonprofit organization. Since the Depression, government has played a central role in supporting nonprofit organizations that provide programs and services to this nation's citizens. The level of support available for specific programs in any given year varies with the national, international, and local climate. Factors that influence appropriations at any level of government include the economy, the political party in office, the popularity of a specific cause, the strength of competing demands, and demography.

According to the Urban Institute's 1982 report, *The Federal Budget and the Nonprofit Sector*, federal support to the nonprofit sector in fiscal year 1980, exclusive of tax and postal subsidies, amounted to more than $40 billion. That report also stated that approximately one-third of the annual revenue of non-profit organizations in 1980 came from government. Yet a 1985 update of the report revealed that nonprofits lost $23 billion in federal support between 1982 and 1986, or an average of $4.6 billion each year. These drastic cutbacks promise to be even more severe as a result of the passage of the Gramm-Rudman-Hollings Act in 1986. In addition, the Reagan Administration's budget projections for fiscal years 1987 to 1989 forecast further significant cuts. The nonprofit sector is thus facing a daunting outlook for the coming years.

The author wishes to thank Dr. Winifred deLoazya for her invaluable collaboration on this chapter.

Concurrently, since 1980 there has been a substantial shift from the federal government as the direct source of funds to state and local government as providers of public support. The federal government's use of large block grants to the states has been a means of giving individual states greater administrative responsibility for program priorities and allocations. However, state and local governments are being forced to do more with less.

State and local governments also appropriate money for their own programs, which may operate independently or in complicated interrelationships with federal programs. In New York State, for example, agencies such as the Division for Youth, the Department of Social Service, Office of Mental Retardation, the State Education Department, Office of Mental Health, the Division of Alcohol and Alcohol Abuse, Department of Health, Office of the Aging, Division of Substance Abuse Services Administration, among others, administer both federal funds coming to New York State and programs generated by the New York State legislature. Frequently these monies are passed through the state bureaucratic structure and administered by counties; sometimes by city or village governments.

The permutations and combinations of funding programs emanating from federal, state, and local government are endlessly complex and fluid. To illustrate what could happen, a nonprofit agency may be the recipient of:

- A federal grant administered by a federal program officer.

- Program funds granted and administered by a state agency, but funded by a block grant from the federal government.

- A contract for services with a state agency, mandated by state legislation and funded by state tax funds.

- County tax funds granted through a county agency as a match to state and federal funds.

Nonprofit organizations, sensitive to ever-changing opportunities, may be in a good position to use their expertise, resources, local political support, and reasonable expenditures as a means of attracting government funds for their work.

Understanding the relationship between government and nonprofit sector goes beyond the fact that government is a major source of support. Historically nonprofit organizations have tended to precede government as originators of programs and services and as a testing ground for new solutions to social problems. In recent years nonprofit groups have consolidated their interests and organized nationally into a distinct, separate sector of the economy, referred to as the third sector, the voluntary sector, or the independent sector. As this sector's relationships with all levels of government assume greater definition, fostered by increased research, publication, and education, the public/private partnerships operating for the public good become stronger and more numerous.

Government funding is extended either as direct or indirect support. *Direct support* is provided in two ways: grants and purchase-of-service contracts. *Grants* are awards to organizations for a negotiated amount of funds to carry out a project or program for a specific period of time. *Purchase-of-service contracts* are mechanisms by which a government agency enters into a legal agreement with an organization to deliver specific services to eligible clients.

Indirect support consists of:

1. *Tax exemptions.* Nonprofits are granted federal, state, and local exemptions from corporate income tax. Some municipalities also exempt nonprofits from real estate and sales taxes.

2. *Reduced mail rates.* Nonprofits are entitled to certain privileged mailing rates through the U.S. Postal Service.

3. *Public employee charitable solicitations.* Public agencies cooperate with local fundraising campaigns for nonprofit organizations by providing release time to staff for solicitation purposes and by allowing payroll deductions.

4. *Support for revenue-generating programs.* Some states permit charitable organizations to raise tax-free money through bingo, casino gambling, and canvassing.

5. *Access to public forums for debate.* Legislative and commission hearings are open to nonprofits for the purpose of speaking out on issues that concern them.

Government is motivated to fund nonprofit organizations because it needs them. They include thousands of educational, social service, health service, research, religious, and cultural institutions, as well as civic, social, fraternal, and advocacy groups that make up the very fabric of our society. Nonprofits can do some things better, more quickly, or more cost effectively than a public agency. In many instances nonprofits already have the experience it would take a public agency years to develop. Nonprofits may be less constrained by legal and bureaucratic requirements. Over more than two centuries such organizations have proved to be effective testing grounds for creative ideas and new solutions—and they are in a good position to take risks.

HOW DO GOVERNMENT PROGRAMS
THAT BENEFIT NONPROFITS OPERATE?

Seeking public funds requires an understanding of budgetary process and the ways information about the availability of funds is made public at the federal, state, and local levels. Each budget process is unique in its detail and timing, but there are commonalities across levels of government that are important for the grantseeker or contractseeker to know. In every budget process there are points at which the leadership of a nonprofit organization or coalition of nonprofit agencies can influence the characteristics of a program and the amount of money available to fund that program.

The beginning of any budget cycle is usually closed to outsiders. Agency staff, budget divisions, and executive staff establish agency priorities for program funding, prepare budgets, hold internal hearings, and negotiate budget proposals. To influence the process at this key stage would require an outsider to have influence with the agency at a sufficiently high level for the ideas to be given credence on the executive agenda. Internal conversations, presentations, and/or research papers may be used to move a program idea into a budget proposal. Eventually, the executive budget is moved to Congress or to a state or local legislative body for action.

It is in the legislative body that the public has its best opportunity to influence the budget. The committees that deal with the budget all hold hearings at which nonprofits can express their views regarding the executive budget. These hearings are seasonal. For example, in New York State these important hearings take place in September, October, and November; in California they occur from February to May. Once the executive budget is passed and appropriations are made, the executive branch usually regains control of the administration of the funds. The executive branch distributes the money using contracts or grants, including block grants.

Grants and contracts are allocated through a request for proposal process (RFP). Executive staff prepare a request for proposal that defines the type of program that is desired to fulfill legislative intent. At the federal level, preliminary guidelines are published in the *Federal Register*. This central resource is available daily at what are called depository libraries. These are public or university libraries in all areas of the country that have been designated to receive copies of government publications for public use.

These guidelines are open to public comment. Frequently, professionals interested in influencing the design of programs make comments in writing to the administration. Sometimes they visit the staff of agencies to discuss the guidelines and follow up their visit with written commentary. Once a request for proposal is formalized, it is reissued in the *Federal Register*. Announcements for federal agencies seeking bids on contracts can be found in the *Business Commerce Daily*.

At the state and local level, the proposal process is not so straightforward. There is no publication similar to the *Federal Register* or the *Commerce Daily* within the states or counties. Even large state agencies such as departments of education do not have a central publication that announces the requests for proposals. In some states, including New York and Illinois, RFPs are often published in the notice section of major newspapers in the state. Each agency, division, or bureau that administers programs for which a request for proposal process is used writes and distributes its own requests for proposals. In New York, each of these divisions or bureaus has its own lists of potential organizations from which it seeks proposals.

In other states, the lists are maintained at the department level. In Illinois, for example, the Department of Public Aid maintains central lists for all the subdivisions within that department. The grant- or contractseeker needs to identify the individual in each bureau or division who is a potential source of funds and to get placed on the list of potential contract agencies.

It is not unusual for a legislative body to appropriate more money than the administration spends. For example, several million dollars may be appropriated by Congress for a program, but the administration might spend only a fraction of that. One way to accomplish this saving is through delaying the RFP process. Naturally, program people are anxious for all the appropriations to be used. Legislators who are interested in the program often exert pressure on the executive body to expend allocated funds through conducting oversight hearings.

When you know that funds have been allocated but no request for proposals has been forthcoming, you can consider requesting to participate in such oversight hearings. Sometimes the state or county legislature does not grant total administrative power to the agencies but reserves some decision-making approval for itself. In these cases, support for your program from the legislature is vitally important.

The executive budget process is not the only channel open for nonprofit organizations. For example, in New York State and California, individual legislators can propose bills to support programs for a single nonprofit organization in their home districts. It is not unusual for a powerful legislator to sponsor a bill allocating money to be channeled through some state agency to a single organization in his or her home district. In these instances, the contract or grants management process is assigned to a state agency. In New York State, the time to influence this process is in January, February and March.

Another way of obtaining public funds that is open to some nonprofits is by making sure your agency is licensed, certified, and approved to provide certain mandated services such as foster care, Medicare or Medicaid, or foster care prevention services. Institutionalized, ongoing funding streams of this kind offer a very secure funding source to nonprofit agencies.

At the local level, many of the same processes and points of influence work. Local governments frequently engage in comprehensive planning. Planning committees determine priorities and agendas for local spending. Becoming involved in these processes and understanding the legislative process at the local level may be your first step in getting and keeping public funding.

Competition for funds varies at each level of government. As currently designed, the most competitive market for public funds is federal. The inexperienced, unknown agency is best linked with a university, major research firm, or state agency in seeking federal dollars. Agencies with the capacity to raise funds from private sources to match their government grants are also good partners. Seeking federal funds is a highly professional skill that requires large investments of time and money with small odds for an adequate return on investment for the grassroots agency.

The process of seeking state funds or local funds is somewhat less competitive. Fewer organizations receive the request for proposals and there is some commitment to distributing funds aimed at programmatic needs according to population density, geographic location, and ethnic and racial representation.

Some excellent resources for nonprofit organizations seeking funding from government are:

• *The Catalog of Federal Domestic Assistance.* This federal document lists all programs administered by every federal department.

• The State Budget. This document describes in detail the various programs funded by a state government and the dollar amounts allocated to them.

• State Plans. These documents project the programmatic plans of a state agency for a specific period of time.

• The County/City Budget. This document describes in detail the various programs funded by a locality.

Which organizations are eligible to apply for and to receive grants and contracts from government agencies? Governments give funds to projects conducted by businesses, unions, trade associations, and all kinds of nonprofit organizations. Governments sometimes fund individuals to produce a service on a contractual basis; however, the amount of money awarded to individuals is small (usually under $5,000).

WHAT ARE THE ADVANTAGES OF RAISING SUPPORT FROM GOVERNMENT?

There are a variety of advantages to gaining government support for a program.

1. Ongoing support. Compared with foundation and corporate giving, government funding has more continuity. The most secure funds are those provided through legislated mandates such as services to neglected, abused, or foster care children, Medicare, and Medicaid. Other government programs are more short-lived. Most programs can expect a minimum of one year of support from a federal or state program.These grants are considered "seed money" or demonstration projects. The possibility of refunding is enhanced if the program shows demonstrable results in a timely fashion and builds a positive working relationship with the funding agency. Alliances with local political figures also help promote ongoing support. Frequently, such individuals have influence on which local programs receive funding.

2. Substantial support. Government grants and contracts are frequently larger than those awarded by foundations or corporations. Sometimes a government grant or contract is sufficiently large to finance an entire program. Indeed, some government programs prefer that contract agencies receive no additional funds. This policy ensures programmatic control and accountability to the funding source.

3. Credibility. Support from one governmental agency or department will enhance credibility with other public funding sources, and it shows a proven track record in managing public tax dollars as well. A previous government contract provides evidence that a nonprofit can meet both the fiscal and programmatic expectations of government officials.

4. Meeting expectations of other funding sources, such as foundations and corporations. Some foundations and corporations view their funds as seed support for projects that will ultimately be underwritten by government. This policy reflects the reality of difference between the level of resources available through government funding and private philanthropy. For example, a demonstration social services program that is clearly within the realm of governmental priorities might be funded initially by private sources. A nonprofit's ability to get public funds to replicate or institutionalize a demonstration program will encourage private investment in its new ventures. Its success gives credence to its ability to become independent of private donors in the future.

5. Easier access to decisionmakers and the decisionmaking process. Once a nonprofit has government support, it becomes known to the agency staff from which it receives support. An entire network of contacts can be built over the years that can help the fundseeker identify potential sources of funds and craft proposals and programs that are likely to gain support. Eventually, a nonprofit becomes able to influence the decisionmaking process regarding the priorities and allocation of funds since its experience and knowledge will be respected. The longer it is around and the longer it serves its community well, the more likely it is to be successful at building public support.

In sum, the staff of nonprofits can utilize a number of different avenues and strategies to present its case to governmental officials. The applicant will usually find that there are individuals behind every governmental program who can be potential allies. These public employees can help you understand the details of their grantmaking procedure, e.g., What was the intent of the legislation authorizing their program? What would be included in a strong proposal? Who would be involved with the actual decisionmaking process? They can help you in your search for support.

An applicant can also enlist the aid of elected officials, who can write letters of support or even make phone calls to prospective public funders in regard to your proposal. City council members, town selectmen, mayors, governors, state and county legislators, congressional representatives, state and U.S. senators, state and local commissioners are just some of the elected officials who could support your program. While their involvement does not necessarily guarantee forthcoming support, their endorsement will strengthen your competitive position. The agencies from whom you are seeking a grant or contract are interested in maintaining the goodwill of these officials. And don't forget to ask for the support of nonelected community leaders who favor your program.

WHAT ARE THE DISADVANTAGES OF RAISING SUPPORT FROM GOVERNMENT?

There are a number of potential disadvantages to raising government support that need to be carefully weighed against the advantages.

1. Time limitations. Many government grants are time limited and support a declining proportion of program expenses. For example, you may get a three-year award with the first year funded at 100 percent, the second year at 75 percent, and the third year at 50 percent.

2. Unanticipated or uncovered additional expenses. A government grant or contract does not necessarily cover all expenses that you might incur. According to *Managing Government Funded Programs in Voluntary Agencies,* a publication of the Greater New York Fund/United Way, voluntary agencies spend approximately $20,000 over and above every $100,000 obtained from government contracts to implement and conduct the prescribed program. That additional money must be raised from other sources.

3. Paperwork. The wise use of public funds is a primary value for government employees. Governments are accountable to the taxpayer. Extensive record-keeping is an attempt to ensure that the taxpayers' money is used wisely. Both financial and programmatic data are reported on a regular basis. These requirements are inherent in the use of public dollars.

The paperwork associated with a federal contract or grant will force you to expand the responsibilities and possibly the work hours of your management and clerical staff. Your program staff will have to adapt to keeping records on services delivered in a more exhaustive manner than they are accustomed to. This may mean some additional training of your financial and program staff. If you have not already engaged the services of an accountant to review your books and to conduct an annual audit, you will now certainly have to do so. Of course, all of these additional steps have built-in advantages as well, such as better fiscal management control and enhanced public image. Auditor's reports also increase your credibility with a public funding source.

4. Legal responsibility. The use of public funds incurs both moral and legal obligations. Government grants and contracts are tightly monitored, and misuse of funds can result in legal action. Government grants and contracts require compliance with regulations that are specific to the program and with other standard regulations on fiscal management and affirmative action. The worst case scenario is that the Internal Revenue Service could revoke an organization's tax-exemption. Repayment of the misused funds might also be required.

5. Potential negative impact on your public image. "They don't need my charitable dollar. They are receiving money from the government," or "They are already receiving my tax dollars." While most organizations that receive public support are wisely also receiving revenues from charitable sources (or continue to need other revenues for reasons already mentioned, or for other programs), they need to make their case for such support clear to the giving public. In other words, the responsibility is on the receiving organization to be forthright in explaining to potential donors why charitable support is also needed. This would be particularly true for those institutions that the public knows as public institutions, such as land grant colleges and universities, public elementary and secondary schools, and actual departments of government that directly solicit the public for support.

6. Potential adverse effect on the agency's internal organization. Due to the many requirements and regulations set by public funders, an agency receiving public money has less flexibility in how it chooses to structure its delivery of services or programs. Also, public monies may result in a certain level of bureaucratization in your organization. This may be altogether desirable; however, the impulse behind such changes are externally induced—by a governmental body, rather than by a mandate of your board of directors or by the executive director. Such changes may affect the morale of your staff and volunteers, who may have shaped the previous mode of operation. It is also harder to predict how all of these changes will impact on your organization and to plan for their consequences.

HOW CAN YOUR ORGANIZATION DECIDE WHETHER TO APPROACH GOVERNMENT FOR SUPPORT?

How does a new or existing nonprofit organization determine whether its current or prospective programs could warrant governmental revenues, in the form of grants or contracts? The answer is not necessarily automatic or simple. You must engage in some research to answer this question. Begin by making inquiries with other local organizations and agencies that are active in your field of interest. You will then begin not only to develop a sense of who is doing what but also to explore who is funding what. Contact these providers and ask where each of these programs obtains revenues to conduct its programs. This is a perfect project for a capable volunteer or intern. The local United Way or health and welfare planning body or arts coordinating council can be of invaluable assistance in gathering this information.

As you analyze the information amassed, ask yourself these questions: Can you address any gaps in the current service delivery system? Can you see any ways to maximize the impact of the funding sources now pouring in? Are the funds appropriately targeted for the needs of the client population?

In the search for public funds for your program, you can also check with local and governmental offices, elected officials, and community leaders in your field of interest to assess whether there are funds available for your work. You can write or call public agencies directly and ask them for information. Request that your organization be added to any mailing list they maintain to send program announcements to potential applicants.

One other possible route is to identify and to contact organizations similar to yours in other parts of the country and to obtain their knowledge of the subject at hand. This approach will also help you identify national foundations and corporations that are prospects for support. Librarians at your main local library can assist you in identifying these other kindred groups by using standard reference materials (see "Further Readings" list at the end of this chapter). There may also be one or more national associations representing the interests of such organizations, who can provide you with the information you seek. For example, the Center for Community Change, based in Washington, D.C., provides community-based and neighborhood organizations with pertinent information on federal programs. Additionallly, there are some reference books on federal funding that are listed also in the "Further Readings" list for this chapter.

Up to this point, we have presumed that there are *existing* government programs that correspond to the work of your organization, and that the only task is to identify them. What if you are really involved with an issue that is so new or pioneering that it has not yet captured the interest of government? This is often the case, since nonprofits are the cutting edge of many social issues.

In deciding whether to approach government for support in these instances, consider the following questions:

- Does the problem that my organization is addressing affect a substantial number of individuals, or a specific segment of the population?

- Can I document or demonstrate the need for the programs that my organization is suggesting?

- Will these programs, if supported, result in positive changes in regard to the problem that I have set out to address?

- Can I mobilize sufficient local support among (1) those who are affected by the problem, (2) elected governmental representatives, and (3) recognized community leaders, such as civic and religious figures?

Be assured that this road is not an easy one. If the government has not yet acknowledged the critical nature of the problems your organization is addressing, you would probably be more successful approaching other funding sources for initial support, such as foundations or individuals. Government could be more forthcoming later, after the need for your program has been established. In fact, government is not a particularly solid source of support for the kinds of controversial and evolving issues that frequently prompt individuals or groups to establish new nonprofit organizations.

HOW DOES AN ORGANIZATION SUCCESSFULLY SECURE SUPPORT FROM GOVERNMENT?

Now that you have located the appropriate source(s) for public funds, you need to secure that support for your program. To succeed in this venture, you need to engage in the following tasks:

Step 1 Design a Program That Conforms to the Interests of the Funding Agency

You may find that you have an existing project or program that falls within the interests stated by a governmental agency or department. Their interests are usually stated in the legislation that brought their programs into existence, and in the ensuing regulations that the department issued governing the disbursement of grants or contracts.

But you might discover instead that although your organization is active in the general field, you do not have a current project that corresponds to the specific interests set forth by a particular government source. If this is the case, you should not hesitate to design a program for your organization that does correspond to these interests.

The same criteria that we established to guide us in our matching projects with foundation and corporate interests also serve us in building a stronger case for government support:

1. Compatibility with Mission

2. Acknowledged Expertise

3. Achievability

4. Topicality

5. Documentation

The ability to accomplish a specific set of objectives (criterion 3) and the capacity to demonstrate the extent of the seriousness of a problem (criterion 4) are factors quite important to government funders, who wish to see a measurable return on the funds they allocate. That proof may rest with your eventual documentation (in your reports subsequent to the approval of a grant or contract) of a reduction in the incidence of the problem you set out to tackle, or in an increase in the number of individuals to whom you have been able to provide mandated services.

Step 2. Enlisting Local Counsel and Support for Your Work

You may have a wonderful idea, but you will in all likelihood not succeed in eliciting government support unless you can obtain critical support on a local level. Governmental agencies, institutes, and departments want to see evidence of popular support among the constituencies you are planning to serve and in your community at large. This demonstrates to them that they can fund you with the assurance that your efforts will, in fact, make an impact.

This kind of support to strengthen your request for funds can be provided by elected officials (such as city council representatives, town selectmen, mayors, state legislators, or congressional representatives); civic and community leaders (such as United Way officials, religious leaders, or chamber of commerce officers); and board officers and/or executive directors of related organizations that may be prominent in your field. These individuals can most effectively express their support by mailing a letter on their organizational letterhead that states why they believe your project is worthwhile and why they believe your organization is qualified to implement it. But you should leave the method of contact to the discretion of the individuals you are asking. They may know the particular official of the agency to which you are applying, or may even know a member of the advisory body that makes all final funding decisions. Your contacts may prefer to place a phone call, or to mention their support at an upcoming meeting or gathering with the official in question. They may be in the best position to gauge what type of contact would be most appropriate.

Step 3. Seek out a Preapplication Meeting with the Public Officials in Charge of the Governmental Program to Which You Are Applying

Presuming that you have identified which government departments are likely prospects for support, your next step is to contact them directly. You want to request any information that they make available to prospective applicants, including the application form, instruction booklet, and a copy of the bill or act that authorized or established the program to which you are applying. In addition, you should identify which particular public official will be in charge of handling all applications. That is the person with whom you want to request a preapplication meeting. That request is best made by a letter, followed by a phone call scheduling the appointment.

The purpose of this meeting is to discuss what the government official's agency is really looking for in proposals or applications. In other words, are there any particular types of projects it is on the lookout for? Has it already delegated certain types of programs to the low-priority heap? This information-gathering visit can help you in designing the program you will submit for consideration and also in completing the required application or proposal. Don't hesitate to ask questions about completing the application. The government official does not expect you to be totally knowledgeable in government grantsmanship. This same official will be your ongoing contact throughout the application process, and in future years as well. Thus, you should endeavor to strike a positive tone for your meeting, since you want to maintain good relations. You should even send a letter simply thanking the civil servant for his or her time and counsel.

Step 4. Complete and Submit the Required Application in a Timely and Thorough Fashion

Most government funding bodies make available application forms or formats for proposals. Others request a proposal addressing a problem or set of tasks that they have identified. In either case, the proposal or the application is a very important document, for it is your opportunity to demonstrate who you are, what you hope to accomplish, and how you are particularly qualified to work toward the objectives that you have set forth. Again, if you have any questions that arise while you are preparing your written materials, don't hesitate to recontact the official with whom you have already met.

Typically, the application requires a well-documented statement of the problem, which is usually generated from one of two processes: problem analysis or needs assessment. A *problem analysis* strategy involves ascertaining the causes of problems and is usually used to define problems that will be addressed by programs designed as demonstrations of innovative new approaches to a problem. The *needs assessment* approach is used to apply for funds for a program to serve a recognized population in need. The needs assessment uses statistics and social indicator data to document the extent and seriousness of a recognized problem in a geographic location.

Whatever the nature of the problem statement, the argument presented should logically lead to programmatic goals. A programmatic goal states in broad strokes what the program seeks to achieve. This goal is made more specific by using objectives. Program objectives are statements of the results that can be expected from the project.

Program objectives are followed by an approach to the problem. In this section you will describe what you intend to do to achieve the objectives. This description should reflect a logical connection to both the statement of the problem and the objectives. You should show how your approach to the problem will deal with the causes of the problem or will specifically address the needs laid out in the problem statement.

The approach to the problem is followed by a description of the tasks you will undertake in order to achieve your objectives. Each of these tasks should be described in some detail. These tasks are the blueprint on which the budget is built. The list and description of tasks is followed by a timeline that indicates the sequence in which tasks will be accomplished.

The proposal should always include an evaluation section, briefly outlining how you intend to show that the intended results were achieved and that achievement was the result of the program and not of chance.

The budget section reflects the cost of the project in detail. It should be justified in relationship to the tasks. Job descriptions of all staff are presented in this section along with a description of the organizational structure.

The budget section is followed by a section called the capability of the contractor. This section documents the reasons your agency is in a strong position to conduct this program. Your past history, resources, and letters of support should be included with this section.

Frequently, government grant proposals are lengthier than foundation and corporation proposals, often because of the detail required. Rich detail in clear prose, free of jargon, is appreciated. Rather than overcrowding the main text, you might want to use appendices. A section should be included that addresses your plans for future funding.

THE YES

You have been awarded a grant or a contract! Congratulations! You can now get down to business. Make sure you understand all the financial reporting requirements that accompany your award. Remember that you will be receiving public tax dollars, which carry greater fiscal responsibility than you may have previously been accustomed to. Be sure that you and your bookkeeping staff understand all the financial forms you will be required to file on a regular basis. If you have any questions, pick up the phone and make an appointment with a fiscal officer at the agency that has awarded you the grant or contract. You may also wish to clarify when you will actually receive the funds that have been earmarked for your organization. Given the red tape that is inherent in any bureaucracy, you may have to wait a number of months before you actually receive your first installment. Because of the problems produced by delays in receiving government funds, a number of foundations around the country have established cash-flow loan programs through which nonprofits can apply for interest-free or modest interest loans against their aproved governmental allocations.

THE NO

Don't despair totally. Inquire why your proposal was rejected. You are entitled to an explanation. Find out what were the strengths of your proposal and what were its weaknesses. Ask how you can submit an application the next time around that addresses the issues that have been raised during this first review process. You can always apply again. Persistence will be your best ally as long as any subsequent application demonstrates that you have dealt with the concerns that prompted the first rejection.

Be sure you have been added to the mailing list of the targeted agency to receive future requests for proposals and any other information that they periodically make available for prospective applicants. Thank the officials with whom you have been in touch for their time and consideration. Keep a friendly door open for the next time around.

LESSONS FOR THE FUTURE

Federal support as we knew it in the late 1960s and the 1970s has changed dramatically. The Reagan administration attempted to turn back the clock on the notion that the government has first and foremost the overriding responsibility for protecting and promoting the welfare of the country's citizenry. That effort will no doubt falter as social problems demonstrate their pernicious nature and their resistance to change. To overcome these problems, a serious commitment needs to be made and adequate resources allocated. That response can be successfully mounted only by government. As Vernon Jordan in his speech, "We Cannot Live for Ourselves Alone," said: "Because government has immense resources, legal powers of persuasion and is politically accountable it must hold a central position in marshalling our society's efforts toward political, social and economic equality."

Meanwhile, nonprofits still have to be prepared to operate in this current period of government retrenchment and reorganization. The federal government will be seeking to transfer more responsibilities to the states. Local governments—cities, towns, and counties—will be demanding greater voice in state capitals, where much of the decisionmaking process will now be taking place. While some government dollars will certainly continue to flow directly to nonprofit organizations from Washington D.C., the political arena of the 1980s will be more and more the state capitals. Fortunately, the distance to the state capital is shorter than the road to Washington, D.C. Many nonprofits will have to learn, or relearn, how the political processes of their own state governments work. State elected officials can expect more visitors on their doorsteps.

One result of the changes on the federal level will be that state and local governments will be experimenting more with new ways to allocate resources, as they weigh which programs formerly supported by federal dollars deserve their support. Some nonprofits will benefit from this transfer of fiscal resources to the local level, but others will not.

State and local governments will also be experimenting with new forms of taxation and revenue generation, such as lotteries and gambling, to finance some of these programs. For example:

● The Commonwealth of Massachusetts has provided millions in revenues each year to its nonprofit arts organizations through its state lottery.

● The state of Kentucky recently raised the cost of a marriage license to raise funds to support nonprofit shelters for battered women throughout the state.

● In New York State, a proposal similar to the one in Kentucky has been made to raise funds for day-care centers.

Other ideas will continue to arise as both nonprofits and government seek ways to raise needed dollars. Lotteries have actually become the fastest-growing source of state revenues nationwide. Gross revenues from state-run lotteries have risen almost tenfold in ten years, to more than four billion dollars in 1983.

   If nonprofits can organize themselves effectively, they can become a powerful force in helping direct these newfound revenues. Certainly, the future does provide numerous opportunities for nonprofits who are creative, resourceful, in touch with today's realities, and focused on tomorrow's possibilities.

Case Study
LEGAL ACTION CENTER

The Legal Action Center (LAC) is a nonprofit organization that focuses on the legal rights of substance abusers and ex-offenders. These constituencies suffer from discrimination in employment and in other aspects of their lives due to existing prejudices. Much of LAC's work centers around issues of confidentiality of treatment records. Since its inception in 1973, it has provided legal consultation not only to individuals but also to substance abuse treatment programs.

Starting in 1976, the Legal Action Center received funds from a federal agency, the National Institute on Drug Abuse, a division of the Department of Health and Human Services. This funding, which supported litigation, counseling, training, and a newsletter, continued for eight years, and by 1983 made up over two-thirds of LAC's total budget. The remaining one-third came from foundations.

When NIDA's budget was slashed dramatically in President Reagan's first term, LAC's federal funding dried up. "It was obvious the only possibility of continuing the Center's existence was to get support on the state level," said Paul Samuels, Executive Vice-President of LAC. The Center's work is national in scope, but its staff had done a lot of work in New York State, its home base. Although the Center had never approached the state for funding before, within two years two divisions of New York's Office of Alcoholism and Substance Abuse—the Division of Substance Abuse Services and the Division of Alcoholism and Alcohol Abuse—had replaced much of the vanished federal monies.

"Getting state money is no different from getting other kinds of funding," Samuels declared. "You have to know where to send the application, what the terms are, who the key people are, and where support to demonstrate you have something of value can come from." LAC was in an unusually favorable position because its staff had worked in the past with people in the offices they approached for funding. "We were known to and knew people in the state divisions," Samuels said. "Without those kinds of contacts you have to look to legislators who can apply political influence." In addition to contacts, LAC had a track record, experienced staff, and support from people throughout its field who helped convince the funding agencies that LAC's services were considered essential in combating drug abuse. "You've got to stay in touch with your constituency," Samuels said. "They can help you make a case that what you're doing is important."

Having obtained state funding for two years running, LAC does not rest on its laurels but keeps developing an evolving relationship with the two state divisions. "We keep our funding source continually apprised of what we're doing," Samuels noted. "Besides filing the required reports, that means maintaining phone contact with the people in the agencies, making them feel they can call us, and sending them publications."

One publication the Center sends is its newsletter, which itself has become a source of earned income since the federal cutbacks. Formerly supported by federal money and distributed gratis, the newsletter, which keeps administrators and program staff in the substance abuse field abreast of legal issues relevant to their clients, is currently sent out by paid subscription. Although they now put out six issues instead of four, LAC has been able to cover costs and make the newsletter self-supporting.

Another way LAC is able to enhance a sense of partnership with the state is by pointing out that many of its activities help other publicly supported agencies, so that state money already given to existing agencies goes further because of LAC.

Samuels emphasizes that state-level support from a state other than its home is unlikely. "We did a lot of training for the New Jersey State drug agency and so were able to get some support from New Jersey, but on the whole it's very difficult for a state to justify funding an out-of-state agency," he said. New York State money has to be spent on programs within New York, so without national funding it has become more difficult for LAC to maintain its national focus. That it can do so at all is because of foundation support, which still constitutes one-third of its total funding. But, Samuels warns, it is unrealistic to expect foundations to pick up the federal slack. Not only do foundations have a fraction of the resources available from the government but "it's very difficult to get a foundation besides the original funder to pick up an ongoing program—they want to support new programs. The public sector, on the other hand, wants to support something that's been shown to work."

Finally, an organization has to be fortunate enough to be located in a sympathetic state. "We are extremely grateful, and also lucky, that the current administration in New York is progressive at a time when the administration in Washington is not," Samuels said. One moral of LAC's story is that it's wise not to wait until the boom is lowered to identify which state agencies might fund your organization, but to start getting to know them better now.

by Ellin Stein

Summary Worksheet

for

_____

(name of your organization)

APPROACHING GOVERNMENT FOR SUPPORT

1. Building on Past Government Support

a. Have any units of government ever supported your work in the past?

☐ yes   ☐ no

b. If yes, which ones?

_____

_____

_____

_____

c. What characteristics do these funders share? How do their interests correspond to each other?

Comments:

_____

_____

_____

_____

d. What is *your* sense of what they valued in your organization's work?

Comments:

_____

_____

_____

_____

e. Which ones can you reapproach for future support?

Definite Ongoing Projects:

_____

_____

_____

_____

Untested (Further Information Needed):

_____

_____

_____

_____

Finding New Government Supporters:
Research and Networking

2. List the categories of government interest that your work falls within (i.e., housing, employment, education, criminal justice, social services, etc.):

_____   _____

_____   _____

_____   _____

_____   _____

_____   _____

3. List the units of the local, state, and federal governments that have responsibility for these program areas (i.e., departments, agencies, bureaus, commissions, etc.):

Local

_____

_____

_____

_____

State

_____

_____

_____

_____

Federal

_____

_____

_____

_____

4.

a. List the names of other organizations similar to yours in mission and in scope in your own community, and in other parts of the country.

_____

_____

_____

_____

_____

_____

b. Which ones have been successful in securing support from units of government? Place a check (√) next to those that have. Now, based on your own knowledge or on discussions with representatives of these groups, find out what you can about their funders. List and describe them below:

Unit of Government	Description (i.e., local, state, federal)
_____	
_____	_____
_____	
_____	_____
_____	
_____	_____
_____	
_____	_____
_____	
_____	_____

5. See pages 312 and 313 for this part of the worksheet.

6. For each prospect on the previous list, complete the following worksheet (use your own blank paper).

Name of Government Program:

Its Areas of Interest That Pertain to Your Work

Develop one or more sentences relating your work to the interests of the unit of government that you are approaching. (Or write one or more short sentences demonstrating how the work of your organization reflects the interests of X unit of government.)

5. List below the government programs that you have uncovered from your research and your networking. Limit your listing to the most likely supporters of your organization (your "best bets").

a. Unit of Government	**b.** Its Stated Areas of Interest that Relate To Your Work	**c.** Appropriate Contact Person, Address, and Telephone Number
Local		
State		
Federal		

d. Personal Contacts	**e.** Your Program(s) That Correspond to Their Interests	

7. Finding Assistance and Counsel

Name 5 or more individuals who might be able to advise you on how to most effectively approach the government programs on your prospect list:

a. _____

b. _____

c. _____

d. _____

e. _____

8. Assessing the Likelihood of Securing Government Support

On the basis of what you have learned, how would you rank your chances of securing support from government?

☐ Very Good ☐ Possible ☐ Unlikely ☐ Still Unknown

FURTHER READINGS

Alston, Frank M., *et al. Contracting with the Federal Government.* New York: John Wiley and Sons, Inc. 1984. 525 pp. $55.00. (Order from: John Wiley and Sons, Inc., 605 Third Ave., New York, NY 10158)

> Discusses various aspects of contracting with the federal government, including cost accounting standards for government contractors. Includes forms, case histories, interpretations of some regulations, and sample contract clauses.

Bauer, David G. *The "How To" Grants Manual.* NY: American Council on Education/ Macmillan Publishing Co. 1984. 225 pp. $19.95. (Order from: Macmillan Publishing Co., 866 Third Ave., New York, NY 10022)

> Step-by-step system for preparing successful grants. Chapters on government funding describe how to use reference tools to research the government marketplace, how to contact government funding sources, and how to submit proposals. Includes discussion of the characteristics of government grants plus a project planner and checklist.

Catalog of Federal Domestic Assistance. Washington, DC: Government Printing Office. Annual with supplementary updates. Looseleaf in 3-ring binder. $32.00. (Order from: Superintendent of Documents, Washington, DC 20402)

> The government's most complete listing of the federal programs and activities which provide assistance or benefits to state and local governments, nonprofit organizations, etc. Extensive descriptions of each program include eligibility requirements, application procedures, and amounts of grants. Indexed by agency program, function, popular name, applicant eligibility and subject.

Civitex. New York: Citizens Forum on Self-Government. Database. (Order from: Citizens Forum on Self-Government, National Municipal League, Inc., 55 W. 44th St., New York, NY 10036)

> Database of profiles on various community projects and initiatives throughout the country which can be used by individuals and organizations to look for information about how other groups are solving similar problems.

Commerce Business Daily. Daily 5 times a week. Washington, DC: U.S. Government Printing Office. $160.00/yr. (Order from: Superintendent of Documents, Washington, DC 20402)

> Announcements about government contracts for which bids are being accepted. Also includes information on sales of surplus government property.

Congressional Directory. Washington, DC: U.S. Government Printing Office. Biannual with annual supplements. Approximately 1200 pp. $16.00, $12.00 paper. (Order from: Superintendent of Documents, Washington, DC 20402)

> Reference source issued for each Congress with a supplement for the second session. Biographical information on members of Congress plus committees,

staff personnel, aides and secretaries. Less detailed information on the Executive and Judicial branches. Personal name index.

Congressional Yellow Book. Washington, DC: The Washington Monitor, Inc. Annual with quarterly updates. Unpaginated in looseleaf notebook. $95.00. (Order from: The Washington Monitor, Inc., 1301 Pennsylvania Ave., N.W., Washington, DC 20004)

Directory giving address and phone number, key staff aides, and committee assignments for all members of Congress. Also gives the jurisdiction, membership roster and staff of each committee and subcommittee.

Derfner, Carol. *City Hall: An Important Resource for Your Organization.* Los Angeles: The Grantsmanship Center. 1975. 8 pp. Reprint $3.00 plus $2.00 handling per order. (Order from: The Grantsmanship Center, P.O. Box 6210, 650 S. Spring St., Suite 570, Los Angeles, CA 90014)

Case history of approaching a city government for an arts project with tips for working with city hall.

DesMarais, Philip. *How to Get Government Grants.* Hartsdale, NY: Public Service Materials Center. 1975. 160 pp. $15.50. (Order from: Public Service Materials Center, 111 N. Central Ave., Hartsdale, NY 10530)

Details on carrying out a program for obtaining government grants. Includes what to do before attempting to secure a federal grant, what reference books to consult, how to write a proposal, and how to prepare a budget. Gives many case histories.

Dumouchel, J. Robert. *Government Assistance Almanac 1985–86: The Guide to All Federal Programs Available to the American Public.* Washington, DC: Foggy Bottom Publications. 1985. 591 pp. $19.95 plus $3.50 shipping and handling. (Order from: Foggy Bottom Publications, Box 57150 West End Station, Washington, DC 20037)

Information on 1,013 domestic assistance programs with types of assistance, eligibility, range of funding, and contacts. Provides a funding summary for four fiscal years. Includes an introductory section on how to obtain federal assistance.

Federal Assistance Program Retrieval System (FAPRS). Washington, DC: U.S. Office of Management and Budget. Database. (Order from: Federal Program Information Branch, Budget Review Division, Office of Management and Budget, 6001 New Executive Office Bldg., Washington, DC 10503)

Database listing more than 1,100 federal grant programs, planning and technical assistance. Furnishes information on whether a locality is eligible for a particular project. All states have FAPRS services available through state, county and local agencies as well as through the federal extension services.

Federal Funding Guide. Arlington, VA: Government Information Services. Annual with quarterly supplements. Approximately 560 pp. $122.95 plus $6.50 postage and handling. (Order from: Government Information Services, 1611 N. Kent St., Suite 568, Arlington, VA 22209)

Details on federal funding programs including 79 major sources for non-profit organizations. Information provided includes program description, contacts, eligibility, deadlines, and tips for success.

Federal Grants and Contracts Weekly. Weekly. Arlington, VA: Capitol Publications, Inc. $191.00/yr. (Order from: Capitol Publications, Inc., 1300 N. 17th St., Arlington, VA 22209)

Weekly reports on the latest contracting opportunities and upcoming grants. Regular features include Grants Alert, RFPs Available, Grants and RFPs calendars, profiles of particular agencies, and information about contracts awarded.

Federal Information Sources and Systems. Washington, DC: U.S. Government Printing Office. 1984. 1,178 pp. $18.00. (Order from: Information Handling and Support Facility, General Accounting Office. Box 6015, Gaithersburg, MD 20877)

Descriptions and contact information about 800 federal publications and facilities and about 1700 federal information systems. Lists such information sources as document centers, clearinghouses, research centers and libraries.

Federal Register. 5 times a week. Washington, DC: U.S. Government Printing Office. $75.00/yr. (Order from: Superintendent of Documents, Washington, DC 20402)

Official news publication for the federal government which includes official announcements of granting programs, regulations and deadlines.

Federal Register Digest. Bimonthly. Old Saybrook, CT: Institute for Management. $96.00/yr. (Order from: Institute for Management, IFM Building, Old Saybrook, CT 06475)

Provides summaries of changes in regulations and funding opportunities which have appeared in the *Federal Register.*

Federal Yellow Book. Washington, DC: The Washington Monitor, Inc. Annual with bimonthly updates. Approximately 600 pp. in looseleaf binder. $130.00. (Order from: The Washington Monitor, 1301 Pennsylvania Ave., N.W., Washington, DC 20004)

Directory information on the Executive Branch including the White House, Executive Office of the President, and the approximately 29,000 personnel in all departments and agencies.

Government Information Services. *Federal Funding Guide.* Arlington, VA: Government Information Services. Annual. Approximately 560 pp. $122.95. (Order from: Government Information Services, 1611 N. Kent St., Suite 508, Arlington, VA 22209)

Describes about 130 federal funding programs to aid state and local government, about two thirds of which are also open to nonprofit organizations. Covers most categories of programs other than education. Includes application guidelines.

The Grantseeker. Biweekly. Washington, DC: The Grantseeker. $108.00/yr. (Order from: The Grantseeker, 2120 L St., N.W., Suite 210, Washington, DC 20037)
Newsletter for state and local government officials to alert them to the federal grant program opportunities and changes.

Guide to State and Federal Resources for Economic Development. Washington, DC: Northeast/Midwest Institute. Expected publication 1986. Approximately 175 pp. Anticipated price $15.00 prepaid. (Order from: Center for Regional Policy, Northeast/Midwest Institute, 218 D St., S.E., Washington, DC 20003)
Information on federal and state government departments and agencies with economic development programs, tax incentive programs, etc. Includes eligibility requirements, funding cycles, and examples of past recipients. Arranged by department or unit level and indexed by type of need; type of assistance; and department, agency, or program title.

Hartogs, Nelly, and Joseph Weber. *Managing Government Funded Programs in Voluntary Agencies.* New York: Greater New York Fund/United Way. 1979. 26 pp. $1.50. (Order from: Greater New York Fund/United Way, 99 Park Ave., New York, NY 10016)
Covers in an outline format the factors for voluntary agencies to consider in deciding whether to apply for government funding. Also discusses the impact of such funds. Looks at the subsequent requirements if an agency does decide to apply.

Health Grants and Contracts Weekly. Weekly. Arlington, VA: Capitol Publications. Inc. $152.00/yr. (Order from: Capitol Publications, Inc., 1300 N. 17th St., Arlington, VA 20009)
Provides information on health and medical projects and research opportunities.

Hillman, Howard. *The Art of Winning Government Grants.* New York: Vanguard Press, Inc. 1977. 246 pp. $10.95. (Order from: Vanguard Press, Inc., 424 Madison Ave., New York, NY 10017)
Information on the major funding agencies along with details on how to research, prepare, and submit proposals for government grants.

Lesko, Matthew. *Getting Yours: The Complete Guide to Government Money.* New York: Viking-Penguin, Inc. 1982. 324 pp. $16.95. (Order from: Viking-Penguin, Inc., 40 W. 23rd St., New York, NY 10010)
Information about federal funding programs condensed from the *Catalog of Federal Domestic Assistance.* Includes short anecdotes about people and organizations that have received federal loans and grants for a variety of projects.

Lesko, Matthew. *Information U.S.A.* New York: Viking-Penguin, Inc. 1983. 1024 pp. $52.00; $19.95 paper. (Order from: Viking-Penguin, Inc., 40 W. 23rd St., New York, NY 10017)

Guide to sources of free information available through the federal government.

Monitor. 6 times a year. Washington, DC: Center for Community Change. $5.00/yr., nonprofit organizations and individuals with limited budgets; $10.00/yr., nonprofit organizations and individuals; $25.00/yr., government agencies, institutions. (Order from: Publications Department, Center for Community Change, 1000 Wisconsin Ave., N.W., Washington, DC 20007)

Provides analysis of federal legislation and policy from the perspective of community organizations. Information on activities of local organizations.

Palmer, John L., and Isabel V. Sawhill, eds. *The Reagan Experiment: An Examination of Economic and Social Policies Under the Reagan Administration.* Washington, DC: The Urban Institute. 1982. 530 pp. $29.95; $12.95 paper. (Order from: The Urban Institute Press, P.O. Box 19958, Hampden Station, Baltimore, MD 21211)

Collection of essays analyzing the economic and social policies of the first 18 months of the Reagan Administration. In addition to putting the policies in perspective, looks at their preliminary impact on people and localities.

Parker, Richard, and Tamsin Taylor. *Strategic Investment: An Alternative for Public Funds.* Washington, DC: Conference on Alternative State and Local Policies. 1980. 35 pp. $5.95; $9.95 institutions. (Order from: Conference Publications, 2000 Florida Ave., N.W., Washington, DC 20009)

Salaman, Lester M., series editor. *The Nonprofit Sector Project Reports.* Washington, DC: The Urban Institute. 1984–1985. $12.95 plus $2.00 postage and handling. (Order from: The Urban Institute Press, P.O. Box 19958, Hampden Station, Baltimore, MD 21211)

Reports of a three-year project to examine the scope and operations of the nonprofit sector in the U.S. and to assess the impact of changes in public policy on these organizations and those they serve. Reports are available on the following local sites.

Rhode Island
Chicago/Cook County
Atlanta/Fulton County
Pittsburgh
San Francisco
Minneapolis/St. Paul
Flint/Genesee County and Tuscola County, Michigan
Boise/Ada County
Jackson/Hinds County and Vicksburg/Warren County, Mississippi
In most cases, Executive Summaries are available free.

Salaman, Lester M., and Alan J. Abramson. *The Federal Budget and the Non-profit Sector*. Washington, DC: The Urban Institute. 1982. 116 pp. $11.50. (Order from: The Urban Institute, P.O. Box 19958, Hampden Station, Baltimore, MD 21211)

> Analysis of the scope and structure of nonprofit organizations and their capacity to fill the gap in services left by the cuts in federal programs and services. Concludes that the cuts in public programs also threaten the financial well-being of the nonprofit sector.

States and Communities: The Challenge for Economic Development. Washington, DC: National Congress for Community Economic Development. 1983. 150 pp. $7.50 members; $15.00 non-members. (Order from: National Congress for Community Economic Development, 2025 I St., N.W., Suite 901, Washington, DC 20006)

> Analytical information and guidance to help community-based economic development groups and state government officials make better use of available resources.

Sugarman, Jule M. *A Citizen's Guide to Changes in Human Service Programs*. Washington, DC: Human Services Information Center. 1981. 111 pp. $7.00. (Order from: Human Services Information Center, 1408 N. Fillmore St., Suite 7, Arlington, VA 22201)

> Summary of the budget and legislative changes affecting human service programs enacted by Congress in 1981 in response to the Reagan Administration's proposals. Encourages thinking on the actions which might be necessary at the state and local level to respond to these changes.

Sugarman, Jule M., and Nancy Amidei. *A Citizen's Guide to Gramm-Rudman-Hollings*. Washington, DC: OMB Watch. 1986. 51 pp. $5.00. (Order from OMB Watch, 2001 O St., N.W., Washington, DC 20036)

> Provides information to help citizens understand Gramm-Rudman-Hollings, officially known as the Balanced Budget and Emergency Deficit Control Act. Answers such questions as which programs are vulnerable to cuts, how this act alters the budget process, and how it will affect revenue sharing.

United States Government Manual. Washington, DC: U.S. Government Printing Office. Annual. Approximately 900 pp. $10.00. (Order from: Superintendent of Documents, Washington, DC 20402)

> Official handbook of the U.S. government describes and lists the principal personnel of agencies and other bodies of all branches of government (although the Executive Branch is covered in the greatest depth). Arrangement is by department or agency but the text is concerned with programs and activities rather than administrative structure.

Washington Information Directory, 1985–86. Washington, DC: Congressional Quarterly, Inc. 1985. 900 pp. $39.95 plus $2.50 postage and handling. (Order from: Congressional Quarterly, Inc., 1414 22nd St., N.W., Washington, DC 20037)

Listings of 5000 government agencies, Congressional committees, and non-government associations considered competent sources of specialized information. Includes name, address, phone, contact name, and annotation of function or activity. Arrangement is by broad classification areas such as ecomonics and business or housing and urban affairs with index for subject, agency, and organization.

Ways & Means. Quarterly. Washington, DC: Conference on Alternative State and Local Policies. $12.00/yr.; $24.00/yr., institutions (Order from: Conference on Alternative State and Local Policies. 2000 Florida Ave., N.W., Washington, DC 20009)

News on innovative state and local policies. Includes information on emerging public policy issues, new legislation, resources, and Conference activities.

CHAPTER 16

APPROACHING INSTITUTIONS FOR SUPPORT

RELIGIOUS INSTITUTIONS

Philanthropy and charity—supporting those in need—are precepts whose origins can be traced back to the great religions of the world. Throughout history, religious bodies and their institutions have been in the forefront of providing assistance to the poor, oppressed, downtrodden, and disdadvantaged. In Western civilization, religious communities organized the first philanthropic institutions.

The tradition of individual giving is very much in evidence in both the Old and the New Testaments and in the very fabric of Judeo-Christian life. In the Torah, prophets and lawmakers alike stress God's command: "You shall open wide your hand to your brother, to the needy and to the poor in the land" (Deuteronomy 15:11). Different passages of both testaments suggest that honor to God is demonstrated by acts to assist the needy and the downtrodden. Jesus proclaimed salvation to a house where a rich tax collector gave half of his goods to the poor (Luke 19:1–11).

In the Judaic tradition, charity is equated with justice and ethical conduct. In fact, the Hebrew word *tsedakah* encompasses both "justice" and "charity." One gave out of a sense of righteousness. Generosity was, in essence, a commandment.

It is thus not surprising that organized religion has been a driving force throughout history for social, political, and economic betterment. Most recently in this country, religious leaders have been in the forefront of the civil rights movement of the 1950s and 1960s and the antiwar movement of the 1960s and 1970s. That concern has also been translated into dollars. In 1987, the largest share of all philanthropic giving in this country went to religious bodies and their affiliates, which received about $43.61 billion.

These gifts were given not only at the church or synagogue but through the mail, at the workplace, and at the banquet table. Since one of the essential characteristics of organized religion today is charity, the highest percentage of those dollars go directly to support the charitable activities that religious bodies conduct directly. On the local, national, and international levels, religious bodies are actively channeling resources to the vulnerable and less enfranchised populations at home and abroad. This assistance is sometimes in the form of direct services such as food, shelter, and health care. Assistance is also provided for self-help efforts that empower local communities to create better lives for their inhabitants.

These latter efforts reflect a growing tendency in religious circles to supplant traditional works of charity with more modern interpretations of philanthropy. The new emphasis on self-help reflects a philosophy that is most vividly expressed in a widely used proverb: "If you give a man a fish, he can eat for a day. If you teach a man how to fish, he can eat for a lifetime."

Even though religious institutions most frequently use charitable contributions for their own denomination's activities, some provide various types of support to different nonprofit organizations whose work reflects the ideals of their faith.

Which religious institutions provide support to nonsectarian nonprofit organizations? What kinds of support do they provide? How can an organization identify those appropriate religious structures and secure assistance from them?

Religious funding sources include units of religious organization ranging from the local parish or church to the national denominational structure. They provide varying kinds of support to nonprofit efforts. Some of these sources exist solely as grantmaking institutions, such as the Campaign for Human Development of the United States Catholic Conference. Others are concerned individual churches and synagogues that make contributions to community-based efforts as part of their community service.

In America, these religious sources can be found within every major religion. For all of these faiths the most common meeting ground is the local place of worship, which bears different names depending on the particular religion—church, synagogue, temple, meeting, congregation, mosque, etc. These local faith communities usually belong to local, regional, and national structures of the same faith that represent their interests and missions to the public and to other members of the same faith. The regional/metropolitan bodies are usually referred to as *judicatories*; they may be called diocese, synod, presbytery, meeting, conference, or association. The judicatories in turn normally belong to a national body.

Additionally, local faith communities may belong to various metropolitan or regional ecumenical bodies, such as a council of churches or an interfaith council, through which they regularly communicate with their counterparts in other religions and act in concert on issues of mutual concern. Protestant denominations may also belong to national ecumenical bodies, such as the National Council of Churches.

On the regional or metropolitan level, religious bodies have created organizations such as Catholic Charities and Jewish Federations which serve as umbrella bodies for all denominationally related health, social service, and welfare agencies within their respective communities. For example, Jewish Federations exist first and foremost to coordinate and fund the activities of constituent agencies, which maintain a communal relationship with the Federation.

HOW DO RELIGIOUS SOURCES EXTEND SUPPORT TO NONPROFIT ORGANIZATIONS?

Support from religious institutions comes in all shapes and forms. The following table outlines the types of support offered to nonprofits by religious institutions. As indicated earlier, grants and contributions of money are available from some religious structures on the local, regional, and national levels. The average church or synagogue is not a funder per se. But circumstances do vary from one parish to the next.

Religious institutions are involved in providing a wide spectrum of nonmonetary support to nonprofits, particularly those that are community-based. Probably the greatest asset they can make available for outside use is physical space for offices, programs, meetings, conferences, rallies, etc. *Initiatives for Community Self-Help: Efforts to Increase Recognition and Support*, a report issued by the New World Foundation in May 1980, enumerates some other valuable forms of help: "Access to office machines and materials, telephones, staff service, and the expertise of professional clergy with the skills they bring in terms of writing, speaking, proposal development, administration." Religious leaders can also aid local nonprofit initiatives by serving as advocates, representatives, and brokers on behalf of their interests vis-à-vis elected officials, funders, civic leaders, and others who control local resources. As the New World Foundation report states, "Church identification with self-help groups provides crucial legitimization in the early stages of a group's development, both within its own community and with the community at large." Because religious leaders couple their community involvement with their deeply held religious beliefs and values, support from religious institutions is often the most dependable and reliable assistance a nonprofit can receive from any quarter. It is important for nonprofit organizations to recognize this source of valuable support and seek to communicate with local clergy.

Support from Religious Institutions for Nonprofit Organizations

	Individual Faith Communities (churches, temples, etc.)	Metropolitan or Regional Jurisdictions (diocese, meeting)	Metropolitan or Regional Council of Churches (or other local ecumenical bodies)	Religious Federated Campaigns	National Denominational Bodies	National Ecumenical Bodies	National Religiously Affiliated Social Service/Human Welfare/Peace and Justice/Relief and Development Agencies
1. Grants and Contributions	some	many	few	all	some	few	few
2. Space for Offices	many	few	few	some	few	few	few
3. Space for Meetings	most	most	some	some	many	many	many
4. Space for Social Services	some	few	none	some	none	none	none
5. Advocacy Support	all	all	all	all	all	all	all
6. Access to Office Machines	some	few	few	some	some	few	few
7. Professional Counsel in Fundraising and Other Matters	most	most	most	all	all	all	all
8. Volunteers	all	some	some	some	few	few	few

Patterns of support and resources available from various religious bodies and institutions are extremely varied. Therefore it is difficult to make generalizations about average size of grant or application procedures. Additionally, the structure of organized religion in this country varies a great deal among and within the different major religions.

HOW DO RELIGIOUS STRUCTURES OPERATE FUNDING PROGRAMS? HOW DO THEY PROVIDE NONMONETARY SUPPORT?

Religious financial sources can be divided into two categories: *primary grantmakers* and *secondary supporters*. Primary grantmakers are those that, by conscious design, operate as grantmakers. They include many funds associated with national and regional religious bodies, such as the Campaign for Human Development of the United States Catholic Conference; The Minority Group Self-Development Fund of the Commission on Religion and Race, sponsored by the United Methodist Church; and the Coalition for Human Needs of the Episcopal Church.

Religious primary grantmakers are in one sense similar to other grantmaking institutions such as foundations and corporations. They usually publish guidelines and application procedures but not necessarily an annual report. In accordance with their status under the law as religious institutions, they are not subject to many of the legal requirements set for foundations. For a variety of other reasons, they tend to be less publicly known as grantmakers in their immediate communities.

There are also religiously motivated grantmakers that are not formally affiliated with a religious body. For example, the Jewish Fund for Justice has recently been founded to provide grants to organizations addressing the root causes of poverty and disenfranchisement in the United States, focusing on Jewish and non-Jewish organizations that need start-up funds. Wealthy individuals of different faiths have also established family foundations that express their religious beliefs in their grantmaking.

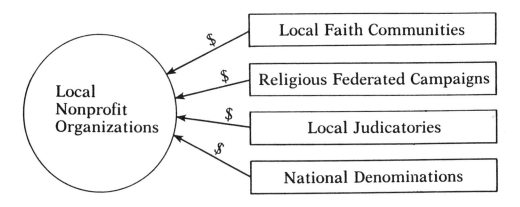

On the local level, a number of socially-conscious congregations around the country have established specific grantmaking mechanisms. In New York City, for instance, both Riverside Church and Trinity Church operate local grantmaking programs. These churches are unusual, however, since most local faith communities do not have the resources to set up such programs.

Cities and other communities where significant numbers of Catholics and Jews reside may have religiously affiliated federations, such as a Jewish Federation or a Catholic Charities, which identify community needs, coordinate the programmatic response from appropriate social welfare and health agencies, and conduct annual fundraising campaigns to finance these efforts. Their relationship with their beneficiary agencies is communal, involving technical assistance as well as funding. A beneficiary agency is expected to forego certain types of independent fundraising in exchange for the support it receives from the federated campaign.

Admittance to these federations is a very formal procedure that may be time-consuming. While member agencies are not usually sectarian in their delivery of services, they are viewed as an extension of the broad responsibilities to a community of a particular religious group. Since these local federations are autonomous, the grantseeker is best advised to become acquainted with their criteria for agency membership. Additionally, some of these federations also have endowments, trust funds, or donor-advised funds which have separate allocation procedures and may, in fact, give support to nonmember, nonprofit agencies. Federations also often act in concert with other nonprofits on issues of mutual concern through cosponsorship of conferences, coalition efforts, and other forms of advocacy.

Secondary supporters exist to conduct their own programs or to provide principally a place of worship. Any philanthropic or charitable activities on their part are therefore incidental or, at best, secondary to their prime purposes. This category includes most local congregations and faith communities, their regional judicatories, local and national ecumenical structures, and national religious bodies.

Religious secondary supporters (religious institutions that carry out their own programs) range from the average congregation that conducts a canned food drive for the poor in its community to the national religious body that has established domestic and overseas programs to further its faith's beliefs and mission. These groups are more likely to make available nonmonetary support rather than actual cash contributions, except to programs of nonprofit organizations whose missions coincide with theirs. For example, when the problems of homeless individuals hit crisis proportions in the United States in the early 1980s, religious leaders of all persuasions helped create and support new nonprofit organizations to provide food, shelter, and social services to homeless people. At the same time, many churches and temples opened their facilities as shelters and soup kitchens not only for the homeless but for the poor and unemployed as well. This represented an active role by religious officials, both laity and clergy, to initiate programs that would respond to their own concerns. Often, a local council of churches or interfaith council acts as a broker for local nonprofits whose activities reflect their concerns. As broker, it might aid them in obtaining financial support from other sources and in gaining access to critical decisionmakers within the community. There are not the same set of formal guidelines that might accompany an institution whose primary purpose is grantmaking.

To complete this list of religious philanthropic sources, it is important to add individuals who are members of various faith communities. Many individuals give not only through their own religious bodies but also directly to numerous nonprofit organizations. Some may even be motivated to set up family foundations or trust funds at a local community foundation or at religious federations.

Religious beliefs and traditions foster charitable giving.
Source: Logo, Jewish Fund for Justice, Washington, DC. Reprinted with permission.

WHICH NONPROFITS ARE MOST LIKELY TO RECEIVE SUPPORT FROM RELIGIOUS ORGANIZATIONS?

A religious institution is most likely to support nonprofit organizations in which the members are involved, either as staff, volunteers, trustees, or constituents—and/or nonprofits that are active—in the fields of interest that most closely correspond to its faith. In general, issues of interest to religious communities include: social welfare and human needs; food, hunger, and nutrition; civil rights and social justice; peace and disarmament; international relief, reconstruction, and development work; immigration and resettlement of refugees; human rights and antidiscrimination work; community development and empowerment; prison reform; domestic violence; child care; women's issues; and unemployment, job retraining, and worker-owned businesses. This list is extensive yet it is by no means complete—religious organizations, in fact, address the entire array of social and economic issues that face low-income, minority, and vulnerable populations in the Americas and throughout the world, as well as issues such as disarmament and peace that face each and every individual.

Within these issue areas, there are some religious structures and organizations that are concerned more with "binding up the wounds of poverty" by supporting efforts like soup kitchens and shelters for the homeless. Others will take the lead in supporting efforts that "prevent the wounds in the first place" through social activist programs, such as advocacy efforts to prevent further unemployment in a community and the encouragement of new industrial economic investment in a poor community. Quite often the same religious organizations, or different faith communities within a particular denomination, are active in both relief and advocacy programs.

What perhaps distinguishes today's organized religions from their predecessors is a greater ability and mission to serve a broad variety of those in need as well as to work toward social change, instead of focusing only on nurturing their immediate members. Many are, in fact, nonsectarian in their service and their advocacy efforts.

This is a fairly recent development. In earlier times, organized religious traditions had often to devote resources primarily to members of their own faith who were suffering discrimination and oppression. For example, America's first Jewish settlers encountered anti-Semitism even before they disembarked on New Amsterdam's shores (later Manhattan) in the mid-1600s. The Governor of the Dutch colony, Peter Stuyvesant, turned a deaf ear to their needs and even attempted to curtail their emigration to the New World entirely. Their Jewish traditions served them well, as the emigrants immediately began to take steps to care for the less fortunate among them. This story, recounted by Milton Goldin in his landmark book, *Why They Give: American Jews and Their Philanthropies*, illustrates how early Jewish charity took root in this country by focusing on the immediate needs of members of its faith.

As discrimination against members of minority religious faiths lessened, charitable agencies established by religious bodies began to extend their resources to other disadvantaged groups at home and abroad. Now, the philanthropic agenda of the religious sector of our society clearly covers most of the social problems reported in the daily newspapers. In the 1980s religious leaders have spoken out against the growing threat of nuclear war. In 1984, individual religious leaders, as well as some national religious bodies, boldly called for an end to U.S. government intervention in the internal affairs of Central American nations. In these instances religious institutions and their representatives looked to the scriptures and to their own beliefs as guides for response to contemporary issues.

WHICH ORGANIZATIONS SHOULD APPROACH RELIGIOUS INSTITUTIONS FOR SUPPORT?

Many nonprofits can approach religious groups for support in either outright cash contributions, grants, meeting and office space, or volunteers, especially since the interests and concerns of religious bodies are diverse.

However, some fields of interest are of less interest to religious sources than others. For example, religious institutions are less likely to provide financial support to arts groups, unless a particular expression of art reflects the social concerns of that religious body. Yet, at the same time, it is in fact common in some communities for churches and temples to provide performance space for a range of nonprofit theater, dance, jazz, and other cultural groups. There are no hard-and-fast rules about which nonprofits would or would not fall within the interest areas of some religious institutions.

Certain current social issues, such as gay and lesbian rights and reproductive rights for women, however, clearly create conflict in some religious communities. Certain religions have lent support to these efforts; others oppose them.

Suffice it to say that your chances of receiving support are much greater if your work is in the immediate community of a particular religious organization or if it directly addresses some of its stated concerns.

WHAT ARE THE ADVANTAGES OF RAISING SUPPORT FROM RELIGIOUS INSTITUTIONS?

1. *Occasional speedy assistance.* If you do fit squarely into the interests of a religious source, you will likely receive some kind of assistance. That help can consist of a small grant, useful advice, or meeting space. This is particularly important for resource-poor organizations that are just getting off the ground.

2. *Credibility.* To the public and to funders, in particular, who look for signs of community participation and support as factors to be considered in their grantmaking process, religious support in any form is a sign of endorsement. Religious backing is a very definite "credential" in this regard.

3. *Good advice.* Ministers and rabbis are often asked to serve on the boards of nonprofits because of their experience in the community, their expertise in working with disparate political forces and their experience as board members. An organization can directly approach religious leaders to serve on its board of directors or advisory group, or simply draw on them for counsel at critical junctures.

4. *Ready sources of people power.* Congregations are ready-made gatherings of individuals who share some common concerns and values, including a commitment to help others. As a result, they are a wonderful source of people power for appropriate nonprofit groups. Congregations can provide volunteers for a board, committees, fundraising projects, canvassing, tabling, and any number of volunteer projects that a group might sponsor. Very often, they will be the most reliable and hard-working volunteers. A congregation also comprises a host of potential financial contributors. It may choose to make a gift on behalf of its entire membership by conducting a special offering among all of its parishioners, by asking in the newsletter for contributions, or by hosting a special fundraising event among its membership.

WHAT ARE THE DISADVANTAGES OF RAISING SUPPORT FROM RELIGIOUS INSTITUTIONS?

1. *Limited financial assistance.* Most religious institutions are not able to extend

substantial financial support to nonprofit organizations. Grants and contributions from those that can provide such help usually average between $100 and $5,000. There are, however, significant exceptions.

Additionally, some religious sources regard their financial support primarily as "seed money" to launch new efforts, not as ongoing financial support. They are, therefore, likely to withdraw their annual contributions once a group achieves wider support from foundations, corporations, and government. (This is not unlike many foundations, however.) Nonprofit agencies that are sectarian in their governance, although not in their programs, may receive steady annual support from religious federations.

2. *Limited available information on sources.* There is little information on religious funding sources, such as annual reports or general directories. There are few written reference tools to help guide the prospective grantseeker, who must rely instead on obtaining information through personal contacts with people who are more intimately involved with religious life. The "Further Readings" section for this chapter lists some of the major materials on organized religions.

3. *Need to demonstrate religious involvement.* Some religious sources expect an organization to involve members of their faith as board members or staff, or they suggest such a step in return for their help. There are probably as many exceptions to this premise as there are examples, but you should be aware of this possibility with any support received and be willing to accommodate such interests. Given the range of skills that talented religious leaders can bring to an organization, it's worth doing so.

HOW CAN YOUR ORGANIZATION DECIDE WHETHER TO APPROACH RELIGIOUS INSTITUTIONS FOR SUPPORT?

Does your organization benefit from the direct involvement of members of any particular faith, as either staff, volunteers, board members, or constituents? Does your work correspond to areas of interest to the religious community as enumerated on page 329? Does your work provide direct benefits to a community or neighborhood where a church, temple, or synagogue is located, or where there is a high proportion of members of a certain faith?

If your organization can answer yes to any of these questions, you should certainly explore religious sources as potential supporters and sources of assistance.

If your primary need is for large sums of money (more than several thousand dollars), you would be advised to look to sources other than religious ones for substantial support, *unless* you squarely fit within the priorities and guidelines of national or local religious grantmaking bodies. If you don't qualify, you would spend your time more wisely by researching foundations, corporations, or government as prospective supporters.

If your financial needs are modest, religious structures can be a fairly easy source of support. Churches, synagogues, and temples can also be a quick source of small amounts of money for emergency needs, such as purchase of food for soup kitchens, or rental of buses for demonstrations on pressing social issues.

To view religious bodies solely as financial supporters, rather than also as sources of advice, people power, physical space, and advocacy help, however, is to diminish their significance to nonprofit work.

HOW DOES AN ORGANIZATION SUCCESSFULLY SECURE SUPPORT FROM RELIGIOUS INSTITUTIONS?

When approaching religious sources for assistance, you would be advised to start locally, just as you would when approaching foundations, businesses, or government. Develop an inventory of the religious organizations, ranging from the actual churches and synagogues to the local religious federations, that have a physical presence in your community. They are the most logical groups to contact first.

Now, categorize the individual faith communities to see which would be the most logical to approach. Your criteria for making these choices could be as follows: personal membership in a congregation; prior personal contact; its reputation for community involvement; and involvement of your organization's members in a particular faith's community affairs.

As discussed, organized religion is composed of complex levels of organization that are not easy to understand initially. You will probably need the assistance of a sympathetic minister or clergy member or a well-versed parishioner to serve as your guide through the maze of structures that exist within each religious tradition. Your most logical and accessible ally in this process is often a local parish clergyperson.

Now you are ready to make the actual approach.

Step 1

Identify individuals within your organization who have active ties to local faith communities, regardless of the particular religion. Your task could be made even easier by circulating throughout your group a list of all the churches, synagogues, and temples within your area. Draw up a list with the names of the particular congregations and their religious leaders (i.e., minister, rabbi, priest, deacon, etc.).

Step 2

Simultaneously, list the needs you have that a religious body might be able to fill. Draw from the items enumerated earlier, such as financial support; volunteers; expert counsel in certain areas; advocacy support; physical space for offices, meetings, and special events; and use of equipment, such as mimeograph or duplicating machines, telephones, and chairs.

Step 3

Prepare a brief statement on how your organization has provided assistance, or plans to do so, to the immediate community you share with the congregation. The purpose of this exercise is to aid you in thinking through why a community-minded religious institution should be interested in your work. At the same time, the resulting statement will also be useful for drafting the initial letter of inquiry.

Step 4

Make the initial approach to the targeted congregations. The approach should be made to the clergy member who is responsible for the parish's affairs. If a member of your group knows that religious leader, let that individual make the first contact to request a meeting.

If no one in your group knows any of your prospects personally, it is best to make the initial approach by letter requesting a meeting. The letter outlines what your plans are, drawing from your previous working statement, and requests the opportunity to meet to elicit the minister's or rabbi's advice and assistance.

Step 5

Bring to the meeting one or two other people, preferably members of that congregation. Speak from your heart about why you are involved with the particular issue your organization is working on. Be forthright in stating your needs. You are exploring whether there is sufficient mutuality of interest for the congregation to become involved with your work.

If some mutual interest is established, inquire whether there are any ways in which the local congregation can help your efforts. Find out whether there is a committee within the church or synagogue handling social concerns, social justice, social action, or peace and justice, and whether it would be appropriate for you to discuss your needs with the committee. You can also offer your organization's assistance to the congregation.

Be prepared to enumerate the needs of your group. Don't suggest that money is your sole or your most important need, unless it really is. Also, don't ask for everything at your first meeting. Remember that you are establishing a relationship that should serve your organization over a long period of time. You will have plenty of subsequent opportunities to ask for specific assistance once a positive initial meeting has taken place.

If your clergyperson has been responsive to your queries, you can also use the occasion to ask about other local, similarly inclined, ministers or rabbis whom you should contact, and anyone in the citywide office of that particular denomination or religion whom you should approach for advice and assistance. If you are fortunate, you will have found a navigator to help steer you through the local maze of religious organizations.

Step 6

If you have been offered any assistance, be sure to act quickly in following up the offer. If the clerical leader has been especially helpful and supportive, you might consider how you might more actively involve him or her in the life of your group, for example, as a board member or a formal adviser or sponsor.

Step 7

Your next steps are to follow the leads provided in Step 5. At the judicatory level, you will probably meet with a minister who has been especially assigned to community issues, social concerns, social action, urban ministry, or some similar area. This new guide can tell you which denominations on a citywide basis have discretionary or program-related funding mechanisms that you might take advantage of. You can also seek guidance to the next level of religious organization—the national religious headquarters or policymaking body. You can also ask about appropriate ecumenical organizations and metropolitan religiously affiliated federations. Refer back to the table showing the types of assistance that you can draw from the different levels of religious organizations.

Step 8

If it appears that you fit within the guidelines of some of the religious grantmaking programs in your city or nationally, request from the appropriate bodies copies of their guidelines and application procedures, including deadlines for application. Also request an annual report describing their previous grant recipients. Review these materials to make sure that your work does fall within their interest areas.

Step 9

For those who are definite prospects, make telephone contact and follow up with a personal visit when possible before making formal application. Preferably, invite the person to visit your program. This preapplication interview, provides you with the opportunity to get a more detailed idea of the funder's priorities and may answer some of your own questions about how best to draft a proposal or application for assistance. Very often religious grantmakers, unlike their foundation counterparts, make available actual application forms. Otherwise, you should engage in the same process as you would if you were preparing a proposal for submission to a foundation. Be sure to present the support of the local congregation and judicatory when approaching the national body. Depending on the mores of a particular religion, evidence of such support and involvement is sometimes crucial to receiving support from the national body. Solicit letters of support toward that end.

RELIGIOUS SUPPORT FOREVER

The majority of nonprofit organizations that are able to secure financial support from religious bodies use that funding as an incidental source during a critical period of their development, such as their formation, or in an emergency. A small minority of nonprofits, whose activities match the stated interests of religious bodies closely, may be able to gain admittance to a religious federated fundraising campaign which will assure them of steady, ongoing support.

There is usually no time limit on the nonmonetary support that a religious institution provides to nonprofits that reflect its beliefs and interests. Due to the mutuality of concerns that can bind nonprofit endeavors and religious institutions together, many nonprofits can expect ongoing assistance of one form or another. Financial support, however, may be short-lived or sporadic, depending on the peculiarities of the particular religious supporters.

Case Study
NORTHERN PLAINS RESOURCE COUNCIL

Access to large national funding sources is not easy for many organizations working in the rural West and South. In Montana, Northern Plains Resource Council (NPRC) is a fourteen-year-old statewide organizing group that focuses on natural resource and agricultural issues. Their members are involved in saving family farms and monitoring and shaping state policy on coal and mineral development. Supported by a strong membership base that includes over 2,000 families, NPRC has an annual budget of $225,000. Other sources of income include a canvass, major donor program, special events and foundation grants.

In 1976, the staff and board started to research the possibilities of obtaining funding from religious institutions. In many of the Montana communities where NPRC members live, churches are important, influential institutions where local people gather. Some clergy have been involved in NPRC affiliate outreach and organizing. Church meeting space has been used for training sessions and special events. Churches have also been a source of volunteers and even staff members.

One local NPRC board member was a United Church of Christ (UCC) minister. This minister worked with staff and members to develop a proposal that was submitted to the UCC's United Church Board of Homeland Ministries (BHM). The UCC has an annual "Neighbors in Need Offering Fund." One area of concern for disbursement of these program funds was farming and the effects of energy development on people and the land.

After an on-site visit by the Board of Homeland Ministries staff, a grant of $5,000 was approved for general operating funds. This initial grant application process took several months. However, with careful followup, including regular program and financial reports, funder visits to Montana, and NPRC staff and board member visits to the BHM offices in New York, NPRC and its regional association have been recipients of annual grants since 1976. The grants have ranged from $5,000 to $20,000. At times these grants have been for specific projects, at other times for general operating expenses. The BHM staff have also offered valuable technical assistance on organizing strategy and development. NPRC has also gotten funding from other religiously affiliated organizations, including the Campaign for Human Development and the Presbyterian Church.

Thus, with a demonstrated history of both membership support and participation, and the creative involvement of local religious leaders, NPRC has been able to gain access to major national religious funders. NPRC has taken the interest and legitimacy of local religious leaders and lay people and further developed their organization. With a carefully chosen approach and project that fit the funders guidelines and interest, NPRC has been able to sustain and build an important source of funds. With religious backing NPRC has been able to reach new constituencies and further build its political and organizing coalition. Reaching new people has in turn resulted in increased membership dollars.

by Tim Sweeney

Summary Worksheet

for

_____

(name of your organization)

APPROACHING RELIGIOUS INSTITUTIONS FOR SUPPORT

1. Building on Past Support

a. Have any religious institutions ever supported your work in the past?

☐ yes   ☐ no

b. If yes, which ones?

_____   _____

_____   _____

_____   _____

c. What characteristics do these institutions share? How do their interests correspond to each other?

Comments:

_____

_____

_____

d. What is _your_ sense of what they valued in your organization's work?

Comments:

_____

_____

_____

e. Which ones can you reapproach for future support?

Definite Ongoing Projects: Untested
                                        (Further Information Needed)

_____   _____

_____   _____

_____   _____

Finding New Religious Supporters:

2. Are there individuals within your own organization with active ties to local churches, temples, or other faith communities? If yes, who are they and what are their ties?

☐ yes ☐ no

_____   _____
_____   _____
_____   _____
_____   _____

3. What are the particular religious congregations that have a physical presence in your community or have expressed an interest in your targeted constituency?

_____   _____
_____   _____
_____   _____

4. Which religious bodies have publicly expressed an interest in the issues that comprise your organization's work?

_____   _____
_____   _____
_____   _____

5. See pages 340 and 341 for this part of the worksheet.

6. Making the Match

For each prospect on the previous list, complete the following exercise (use your own blank paper).

Name of Religious Institution:

Its Stated Areas of Interest That Pertain to your Work:

Develop one or more sentences relating your work to the interests of the religious institution that you are approaching (or write one or more short sentences demonstrating how the work of your organization reflects the interests of X religious institution).

7. Finding Assistance and Counsel

Name 5 or more individuals who might be able to advise you on how to most effectively approach the religious institutions on your "Best Bets" list:

a. _____
b. _____
c. _____
d. _____
e. _____

5. List below the religious instutitions you have uncovered from your research and your networking. Limit your listing to the ten most likely supporters of your organization—your ten "Best Bets."

a. Type of Religious Institution	**b.** Its Stated Areas of Interest that Relate to Your Work	**c.** Appropriate Contact Person, Address, and Telephone Number
Individual churches, temples, and other faith communities		
Metropolitan or Regional Jurisdictions		
Metropolitan or Regional Ecumenical Bodies		
Religious Federations		
National Religious Bodies		

d. Personal Contacts

e. Your Program(s) that Correspond to Its Interests

8. Assessing the Likelihood of Securing Support from Religious Institutions

On the basis of what you have learned, how would you rank your chances of securing support from religious institutions?

☐ Very Good   ☐ Possible   ☐ Unlikely   ☐ Still Unknown

FURTHER READINGS

American Jewish Committee. *American Jewish Year Book, The.* New York: American Jewish Committee, Annual. Approx. 450 pp. $25.95. (Order from: Institute of Human Relations, 165 E. 56 St., New York, NY 10022)

Directory of 1000 national Jewish organizations; Jewish periodicals; Jewish federations and welfare funds. Includes such information as name, address, officers, and aims or purpose.

Center for Third World Organizing. *Directory of Church Funding Sources.* Revised Edition. Oakland, CA: Center for Third World Organizing. Expected publication 1986. Approximately 10 pp. $4.00. (Order from: Center for Third World Organizing, 3861 Martin Luther King, Jr. Way, Oakland, CA 94609)

Lists sources of funding from religious denominations on both a local and national level. Includes such information as contacts, application deadlines, grant sizes, and restrictions.

Council on Foundations. *The Philanthropy of Organized Religion.* Washington, DC: Council on Foundations. 1985. 112 pp. $10 members; $15.00 nonmembers plus $2.00 postage and handling. (Order from: Council on Foundations, 1828 L St., N.W., Washington, DC 20036)

Report of a study on the philanthropic activities of organized religion shows giving patterns of various denominations to outside causes. Includes many figures and tables.

Delgado, Gary. "Raising Money from Churches." *Grassroots Fundraising Journal* vol. 5, no. 1 (February 1986): 5–11. Single issue $3.50. (Order from: Grassroots Fundraising Journal, P.O. Box 14754, San Francisco, CA 94114)

Systematic approach to seeking funds from churches on both the local and national level. Includes chart of denominational structures of major protestant churches.

Funding for Justice Project. *Church Funds for Social Justice.* Minneapolis: Funding for Justice Project. 1984. 94 leaves. $8.00 plus postage. (Order from: 122 W. Franklin Ave., Room 218, Minneapolis, MN 55404)

Directory of church funding sources at the local, regional, and national levels for social change organizations.

National Council of Churches. *Yearbook of American and Canadian Churches.* New York: National Council of Churches. Annual. Approx. 300 pp. $17.95 plus $1.25 postage. (Order from: National Council of Churches, Office of Research, Evaluation and Planning, Room 876, 475 Riverside Dr., New York, NY 10115)

Directory of over 500 established religious groups with brief summary of history and beliefs, address of general headquarters, and names and addresses of principal officers. Also includes information on church councils, theological seminaries, church-related colleges and universities, and religious periodicals.

Newsbriefs, Monthly. Washington, DC: Lutheran Resources Commission. $50.00/ yr. (Order from: Lutheran Resources Commission, 1346 Connecticut Ave., N.W., Washington, DC)

Information on diverse fundraising and grants information from the Lutheran Resources Commission which is a grants consultation agency to many national religious bodies.

Official Catholic Directory, The. Wilmette, IL: P. J. Kenedy. Annual. Approx. 1600 pp. $74.70 plus $2.50 postage. (Order from: P. J. Kenedy, 3004 Glenview Rd., Wilmette, IL 60091)

Directory of officials and governing bodies of the Church in the Vatican and in the United States. Also includes information on Catholic schools, camps, and religious communities.

"Philanthropy of Organized Religion." *Foundation News* vol. 25, no. 5 (September/October 1984). Single issue $5.00 plus $2.00 postage and handling. (Order from: Council on Foundations, 1828 L St., N.W., Washington, DC 20036)

Whole issue on the philanthropic activities of organized religions including historic information, trends, and other background details.

Shellow, Jill R. ed. *Grant Seekers Guide: Funding Sourcebook*, Revised Edition. Mt. Kisco, NY: Moyer Bell Limited. 1985. 550 pp. $19.95 hardcover; $14.95 paper. (Order from: Moyer Bell Limited, Colonial Hill/RFD 1, Mt. Kisco, NY 10549)

Includes excellent directory of national religious funding sources.

CHAPTER 17

APPROACHING INSTITUTIONS FOR SUPPORT

FEDERATED FUNDRAISING ORGANIZATIONS

In 1829, a Philadelphia publisher named Matthew Cary started the first foray into federated fundraising in the United States. He solicited other Philadelphians for single donations earmarked for the city's (then) thirty-three charities. The next attempt at federation, The Charity Organization Society, was initiated by a priest, a rabbi, and two ministers in Denver in 1887. They conducted a single fundraising campaign to benefit ten local agencies, raising $21,700 and distributing $18,000 to their beneficiaries. It would be years until federated drives would be firmly established, but the concept of the single fundraising effort in behalf of a number of charitable organizations did eventually take root and flourish.

In 1913, Cleveland established the first modern umbrella group that took the initiative to raise funds from the public and to allocate them to local agencies. Over the next fourteen years, over three hundred other communities followed Cleveland's lead, establishing what was then referred to as *community chests*. By 1931, these groups had passed the $100 million mark in funds raised. By 1948, more than 1,000 community chests were in existence. Today, what is now known as the United Way of America includes over 2,200 affiliated federations that raise and distribute funds each year. In 1988, United Way received $2.78 billion in pledges and grants, and supported some 37,000 health and human care groups.

The author wishes to thank Kate McQueen for her invaluable collaboration on this chapter.

The motivation behind the evolution of these federated drives was not entirely altruistic. While funds were certainly needed by the country's growing number of nonprofits, employers and some labor union leaders were concerned about the loss in employee productivity resulting from the use of the workplace for charitable solicitation by numerous groups. In the late 1940s, the Detroit auto industry, under the leadership of Henry Ford II, established the first "United Fund" citywide appeal. He was motivated partially by a concern over the cost of the plethora of individual charities desiring access to his factories. The Ford Motor Company had calculated that each charitable solicitation drive at its factories translated to a $40,000 loss in employee labor.

The hallmark of the federated campaigns became easy access to the nation's workplaces for charitable solicitations, and centralized allocation to recipient beneficiaries by one organization in each city. The United Ways were the first federated fundraising efforts to really benefit from payroll deduction programs. What made the worksite a particularly lucrative source of contributions was the system of payroll deductions: employees would designate a fixed sum of dollars from their weekly paycheck, which the employer automatically deducts and distributes to the earmarked beneficiary.

By the 1960s, newer nonprofit organizations that had not benefited from United Way support began to organize to gain access to what was clearly established as a lucrative fundraising environment—the workplace. No longer was it presumed that charity began and ended at home. The slogan, "I gave at the office," greeted many charitable solicitors as they knocked on the doors of their neighbors.

The federal government led the change in the 1960s by allowing other national nonprofit organizations, such as international relief and health groups, to solicit their employees in a combined campaign, whereby the United Way and all other charities vied for these workplace dollars at the same time. Soon other large national charities also gained access to public employees. As of July 1985, thirty state and numerous local governments, including New York City, Philadelphia, and St. Paul, followed the federal government's lead by allowing non–United Way organizations to solicit contributions from their employees.

State Governments That Allow Employees to Designate Charitable Contributions to Non–United Way Charities:

Alabama	Minnesota
Alaska	Nebraska
Arizona	Nevada
California	New Jersey
Connecticut	New Mexico
Florida	New York
Georgia	North Carolina
Idaho	Pennsylvania
Illinois	Rhode Island
Indiana	South Carolina
Iowa	Utah
Maine	Vermont
Maryland	Washington
Massachusetts	West Virginia
Michigan	Wisconsin

Source: National Committee for Responsive Philanthropy.

Nineteen sixty-eight marked the arrival of alternative fund federated drives on the scene—Walter Bremond founded the Brotherhood Crusade of Los Angeles, the precursor of today's local Black United Funds that exist in fifteen different cities. By the early 1980s, more than fifty additional alternative funds had joined the ranks of the early Black United Funds, including women's funds, the Environmental Federation of California, an emerging Native American Fund in New Mexico, social action funds, and United Arts funds. In 1983, these alternative funds raised $13.7 million from payroll deductions through workplace solicitations. In the majority of these cases, the impetus for organizing these funds originated with the recipients themselves, who wanted their share of the workplace charitable pie. More recently, individual nonprofits, particularly those with strong support among workers, such as Philadelphia Area Project on Occupational Safety and Health (PHILAPOSH), would also engage directly in workplace solicitation through semi-affiliation with the local United Way through a donor option program, or totally autonomously.

What implication does this history hold for today's nonprofits seeking new sources of support? Can they tap into their local United Ways for support? How can they approach the workplaces of their community directly, either as members of alternative funds or directly on their own? The purpose of this chapter is to aid you in answering these questions.

Federated fundraising organizations are nonprofit organizations usually organized along geographic lines for the primary purpose of raising charitable contributions and distributing them to designated nonprofit groups. Their beneficiaries usually reflect the values and beliefs of the organization's governing bodies. The most common federations are: United Ways, religiously affiliated federations, and alternative funds.

United Ways are fundraising and allocating organizations that support a variety of social service agencies on the local level. Additionally, United Ways may undertake other activities that aid the well-being of their nonprofit member agencies and their own communities, such as management assistance programs, long-term planning, and information and referral services.

While each United Way is locally autonomous, the majority are members of the national United Way of America. Local United Ways range in size from predominantly volunteer bodies to large, professionally staffed enterprises in major metropolitan areas.

Local United Ways are also characterized by their methods of fundraising and their sources of revenue. By and large, they receive the bulk of their support from company employees, who have been solicited at the workplace, and from major companies through grants.

Religiously affiliated federations are generally established by religious and/ or lay leadership to raise money from individuals in the churches and synagogues to provide financial support to organizations that represent the social welfare and health interests of a particular religious faith. Examples include local Catholic Charities and Jewish Federations (these federations are discussed in Chapter 16).

Alternative funds are public charities established to raise and distribute funds to organizations that share a particular constituency or set of common concerns.

In their article, *Fund-Raising at the Workplace* (*Social Policy* magazine, Spring 1984), Stanley Wenocur, Richard V. Cook, and Nancy L. Steketee distinguish an alternative fund in the following manner:

> Its alternative nature stems from two sources. It is not a United Way fund and therefore represents an alternative system of fund collection and distribution. Also, in many instances, it distributes funds to newer, non-traditional, more change-oriented organizations customarily excluded from United Way.

Examples of non–United Way funds are United Arts Funds and Combined Health Agency funds. Examples of social-change–oriented funds are Women's Funds and Black United Funds. Other examples are the Bread and Roses Community Fund in Philadelphia, which raises funds to support grassroots advocacy efforts promoting social change, and Cooperating Fund Drive in Minneapolis–St. Paul, which raises funds for twenty-eight neighborhood centers, women's groups, and other organizations outside the cultural mainstream. These "activist" funds, as they are occasionally dubbed, each raise and distribute anywhere from $25,000 to $1,000,000 a year in the case of the Los Angeles Brotherhood Crusade (a black United Fund affiliate).

HOW MUCH DO FEDERATED AND ALTERNATIVE FUNDS RAISE EACH YEAR?

Local United Ways reported pledges and foundation/corporation grants of $2.78 billion in 1988. Results of other federated campaigns are as follows:

- In 1987, fifty local United Arts Fund organizations raised a total of $2.9 million in payroll deductions.

- The Cooperating Fund Drive of Minneapolis–St. Paul raised a total of $620,500 for support to community-based, self-help organizations, including advocacy as well as service groups.

- In 1987, Womens Way, a federation of Philadelphia women's organizations, raised $1,011,841 to support the work of its members, which included Women Organized Against Rape, Elizabeth Blackwell Health Center for Women, CHOICE, Women's Law Project, and others.

- In 1987, Black United Funds, through its ten local affiliates in nine states, raised nearly $2.3 million by means of the payroll deduction plan; these funds supported programs in black and minority communities that emphasize self-help, mutual aid, and self-determination.

As statistics demonstrate, the gross revenues from federated campaigns range dramatically from small to large.

Since each United Way and alternative fund is unique and independent, it is difficult to make generalizations about the level of financial support that federated campaigns provide to recipient groups. A United Way may fund less than 5 percent or more than 50 percent of an organization's budget. Since most alternative funds are still evolving, they usually provide modest support to their beneficiaries. Some of the older ones however, can provide a more substantial level of support to their recipient organizations. Clearly, United Ways remain the dominant fundraising organizations in their communities by virtue of their history, resources, and unrestricted access to numerous company worksites. They still distribute much larger sums than any existing alternative funds.

HOW DO FEDERATED FUNDS DISTRIBUTE FUNDS TO NONPROFITS?

Federated funds provide financial support to nonprofits in three different ways:

1. Bestowing *member agency* status on a nonprofit, which qualifies it for ongoing annual allocations.

2. Providing grants through various *discretionary* programs, sometimes known as venture or community development grants.

3. Sponsoring *donor option* programs, which allow individual employees to make on-the-job gifts during a United Way campaign to non–United Way member agencies, or alternative funds.

Membership. Many federated funds traditionally confer the title of "membership" on their beneficiaries. This suggests in principle and in fact a close communal relationship between the federation funder and its "grantees." United Ways bestow membership status on agencies receiving ongoing support. Some alternative funds, such as The Women's Funding Coalition in New York City and Community Works in Boston, were established as fundraising umbrellas for certain member organizations. Other funds, for example, The Fund for Southern Communities in Atlanta, consider all grantees (new and old) as member organizations.

In return for financial support, beneficiaries may be asked to agree to certain restrictions on their own fundraising activity. Usually, these restrictions reflect an interest on the part of the federation to maintain an exclusive relationship with current and prospective contributors. Membership also brings certain benefits, in addition to funding, such as access to technical and management assistance resources and publicity during the course of the annual fundraising drive.

Generally, the board of directors, either directly or upon recommendations of a standing allocations or selection committee, chooses its member or recipient agencies for the year. Most federated funds require their beneficiaries to go through some form of annual review process. However, it's rare for any to terminate membership status for an agency (unless it has engaged in serious legal or financial misconduct or failed to meet ongoing requirements for membership). This is particularly true of United Ways. A federation may choose, however, to reduce the level of support that an organization may receive in any given year. That sum is determined not only by the gross revenues that a federation raises each year but also by sometimes elaborate allocation formulas.

The composition of federation governing boards varies considerably. Most United Ways are governed by a mix of business leaders, with an interspersing of civic, union, and member agency representatives. Their allocation committees, who make recommendations to a central board, enjoy larger representation from the nonprofit community itself, particularly United Way member agencies.

Alternative funds vary more dramatically in the composition of their governing bodies and their allocation committees. Since many of them were started as coalitions of groups who were not receiving United Way assistance and were seeking a slice of the charitable pie, their boards may be composed exclusively of representatives of recipient organizations. Others may have a broader representation of community and nonprofit interests on their boards and committees. In the case of the Bread and Roses Community Fund in Philadelphia, established initially as the People's Fund in 1970, each and every contributor who attends the annual convention elects members of the board of directors and Community Funding Board for the upcoming year.

Discretionary Grants. In addition, some United Ways and alternative funds have discretionary funds set aside each year that are available to nonprofits on a competitive basis. Grants from these funds do not convey any membership status within a federation. Currently, a number of United Ways across the country have such special or *venture* grants programs for less established nonprofit service organizations. Guidelines for these funds vary for every federation.

Since most federations raise the bulk of their funds each year from annual campaigns (usually conducted in the fall, but occasionally conducted year-round), they also award grants only once a year, after their fundraising efforts have been completed. This may lead to a long period from initial application to actual receipt of funding.

Donor Option Programs. In recent years, a number of United Ways around the country have provided individuals with an option to designate a particular nonprofit, federally tax-exempt health or human service organization as the recipient of their contribution. This is called a *donor option* plan. The local United Way board of directors decides whether it will provide this option to contributors. A recent UWA fact sheet explains how these programs operate:

> No two donor option programs are identical. There is no one ideal mode. However, several characteristics are fairly common to all. An employee donor wishing to participate completes a payroll authorization card and a donor option form. The donor may designate any 501(c)(3) health and human service organization that meets general eligibility requirements, which sometimes include geographic limitations. In many cases, a minimum gift may be required. An administration fee is determined, announced, and deducted from each designation prior to the payment of the designated agency. Cash gifts are sent to the designated agency as soon as possible. All other gifts are generally paid on a monthly or quarterly basis.

The donor option program provides the initial opportunity for many non–United Way agencies to benefit from charitable solicitation at the workplace.

Many alternative funds, as well as individual nonprofits, have sought to take advantage of these donor option plans, often against great odds. They have applied to the local United Way for inclusion in the list of "accredited" nonprofits that is sometimes distributed to those interested in earmarking their contribution, and have attempted to make their case directly to workers themselves. Where donor option is available to workers, the necessary donor option cards must be requested. The road to substantial workplace support for non–United Way member agencies through donor option programs is a long haul. A study conducted by the Neighborhoods Institute in Baltimore for the National Committee for Responsive Philanthropy disclosed the following results.

> A low percentage of workplace gifts went to non–United Way charities—6.3 percent in Philadelphia, 4.3 percent in San Francisco, and 2 percent in Sacramento.

While many agencies receive donor option gifts (780 in Philadelphia and 700 in San Francisco), most get only a tiny amount of money. In Philadelphia, for example, the vast majority of groups received less than $100 each.

However, since the donor option program is still relatively new in most locales, there is reason to hope that as more nonprofits persuade local United Ways to incorporate donor option programs into their campaigns a greater slice of the charitable work solicitation pie will accrue to nonprofits.

Womens Way and Donor Option

In July 1979, Womens Way, a fundraising coalition of women's groups in Philadelphia, applied for membership in the United Way of Southeastern Pennsylvania. Six months later, the organization received notification that the application for membership had been rejected, apparently because several of Womens Way's member agencies provided contraceptive and abortion-related services. United Way had an unpublicized agreement with the Archdiocese of Philadelphia to refuse funding to any program or service that the Archdiocese considered to be in opposition to the moral teachings and principles of the Catholic church. The rejection letter stated that "Womens Way's insistence on including agencies and services that would contravene United Way's agreement with the Catholic Archdiocese made it unacceptable for United Way funding." In order to quell the community outrage over its hidden membership and allocations criteria, United Way of Southeastern Pennsylvania instituted a new donor option plan and revamped its guidelines for admitting new member agencies. Womens Way launched an aggressive public relations campaign in the fall of 1980 to alert the public that contributions could be made to Womens Way through this donor option program and received more than $100,000 in donor option pledges that first year.

Kate McQueen

Alternative funds and some individual nonprofits have been able to obtain support from employees through workplace solicitation either by utilizing an existing United Way donor option program or by obtaining direct access from a company to its workplace for the purposes of charitable solicitation. Such diverse companies as Cummins Engine, TRW, and Crocker National Bank allow employees to make charitable contributions through payroll deductions to a wide array of nonprofit organizations that are not members of local United Ways. Others, like International Business Machines Corporation and Bell Laboratories, have included Black United Funds in the literature packets dispersed to their employees during the charitable solicitation campaign.

Many government employees on the city, state, and federal levels have been able to make workplace gifts to certain non–United Way charities for a number of years. Nonprofits wishing to be beneficiaries of state employees' charitable largesse must register with the appropriate department of their state government. In most cases, the appropriate governmental authority assembles a master list of the agencies deemed appropriate. On the federal level, the solicitation drive is known as the Combined Federal Campaign (CFC), and the master list is prepared by the Office of Personnel Management and the federal officials who run the more than 500 local campaigns. The CFC netted over $138,500,000 in 1986 in charitable donations for national and local nonprofits. Of that total, $71.9 million was shared by charitable organizations other than United Ways. Since the Reagan administration attempted to exclude a number of nonprofits from the prior approved official list, especially those doing advocacy work, the CFC has been embroiled in political controversy. In 1986, Congress instructed the Office of Personnel Management to include those targeted nonprofits in the Combined Federal Campaign.

WHICH ORGANIZATIONS ARE ELIGIBLE TO APPLY AND TO RECEIVE SUPPORT FROM FEDERATED FUNDRAISING ORGANIZATIONS?

As illustrated, federated fundraising has expanded to include a variety of organizations in addition to the traditional United Way campaigns. As a result, the range of beneficiaries has also undergone some dramatic changes.

Each nonprofit organization can assess whether it qualifies for support from its local United Way or from an existing alternative fund. It can even choose to establish a new alternative fund in conjunction with other similar groups on the local level. Let's review who receives support from the existing federated funds.

United Ways generally support the delivery of traditional health and social services. These services may include:

Adoption	Information and Referral
Advocacy	Hotlines
Adult Education	Job Training
Alcoholism Services	Legal Aid
Camping	Mental Health Education
Community Health Clinics	Rape Crisis Relief
Consumer Protection	Recreation
Crime Prevention	Rehabilitation Services
Day Care	Services for Disabled
Drug Abuse Services	Individuals
Emergency Food and Shelter	Services for Elderly
Family Counseling	Individuals
First Aid	Services for Women
Food Banks	Social Adjustment, Development,
Foster Care	Functioning
Health Research	Special Transportation
Home and Mobile Meals	Suicide Prevention
Individual and Family Counseling	Voluntarism

Source: Fact Sheet, *Basic Facts About United Ways*, United Way of America

According to "Activists' Guide for Organizing an Alternative Fund," by Richard Cook, the word *alternative* in the term *alternative fund* refers to the fact that "many of the organizations and agencies supported by the fund have represented alternative and newer approaches to solving the society's problems than have been the tradition of social agencies." This "alternative" approach to solving society's problems is best captured by the campaign slogan of the Bread and Roses Community Fund of Philadelphia; "Support Change, Not Charity." These alternative funds support organizations involved in advocacy and community organizing programs around such issues as tenants' rights, disarmament, occupational health and safety, reproductive rights, consumer rights, and America's intervention in Central America. They may also be organized to support particular constituencies such as organizations that serve blacks, hispanics, women, gay men and lesbians, and Native Americans as their beneficiaries. In most cases, recipients of alternative funds represent a cross-section of the thousands of social action, grassroots organizations that came into existence in America in the 1970s and continue to do so.

Some alternative funds came into existence instead to create a broader lobby for certain sets of social issues, such as conserving the environment or community economic development.

WHAT ARE THE ADVANTAGES OF SECURING SUPPORT FROM FEDERATED FUNDS?

1. *Reliable source of steady income.* If you are fortunate enough to gain admittance to a federated fund as a member or beneficiary agency, you are generally assured of its ongoing support for as long as you continue to meet its qualifications for membership. Of course, the extent of that support varies considerably from one community to the next and from one type of federated fund to the next.

Allocations formulas vary from one United Way to another. In determining what each member agency receives each year, the United Ways review the entire operating budget of the recipient. The percentage of budgets underwritten by the United Way varies from agency to agency.

On the other hand, alternative funds are still experimenting with their allocation procedures, and they have a wide range of formulas. Some funds allocate equal shares to all beneficiaries, while others take into consideration the size of the budget and the amount of time donated to the operation of the alternative fund.

2. *Savings in your own fundraising time and budget.* One of the ostensible purposes of a federated fundraising campaign is to raise funds more efficiently than the separate fundraising efforts of its affiliated organizations. In other words, the collective effort should generate more funds than could the individual agencies working on their own, and should minimize staff outlay, volunteer time, and resources needed to raise a comparable amount of funds on their own.

Workplace fundraising is the least expensive type of fundraising a fund or

Federated fundraising organizations depend on public support to raise revenues.
Source: Fund for Community Progress, Providence, RI. Reprinted with permission.

federation can undertake because a large number of people are solicited in a short period of time. And it is generally accepted that people donate three times more through payroll deductions than through a one-time gift to charity. In addition, workplace fundraising costs 5¢ to 10¢ for every dollar raised, whereas other fundraising mechanisms, such as special events or direct mail solicitation, cost much more per dollar.

3. *Heightened public profile.* By participating in a federated fundraising campaign, your organization should become better known to the public and to the media, owing to the publicity that a federated campaign usually engenders about its beneficiary agencies.

Because the United Way campaign gets press coverage in most locales, being a member agency guarantees some publicity, if only in the local United Way's printed material. Often during the campaign, individuals are asked to make presentations at various workplaces about their organizations as part of United Way; hence, a "captive audience" will learn about your organization's specific issues or services.

Of course, your public image will be intertwined with the federated fund you are affiliated with.

With some of the newer alternative funds that are gaining (or attempting to gain) access to the workplace, media coverage may come as a result of conflicts or disagreements with the local United Way (see the "Womens Way and Donor Option" sidebar). In a number of cities, United Way has argued that the newer funds not be allowed into various state, city, or private sector campaigns because this would be a duplication of services. In these cases, the alternative funds have been able, through the media, to capitalize on the fact that United Way was not meeting the needs of the organizations or issues or constituency represented by their funds.

4. *Enhanced reputation.* By association with a federated effort, you usually can receive a boost in your own reputation. After all, a well-organized solid federation has extensive ties throughout a community. Those contacts can, on occasion, be of value to your work.

It is wise to review the members of the board of directors and other standing committees of your federation. They can serve as potential resources to you in your work. For example, if you hope to approach a local company for in-kind contributions and you are a United Way grantee, you might start with the representative of that company who sits on the United Way's board of directors. In your letter of inquiry, you can acknowledge your mutual participation in the United Way as one way to open the door.

In the case of funds that have had publicized conflicts with United Way, your organization (through its affiliation with that fund) may enhance its reputation within the community for "taking on" the United Way's monopoly on workplace solicitation; the themes of the freedom of employees to donate to charities of their choosing and equal access to the workplace are seen as just demands.

5. *Networking and technical assistance.* By participating in a fundraising federation, you usually find yourself in more regular contact with similar organizations. You get to know their staff and trustees, and thus broaden your own base of organization-building knowledge as well as expand your universe of potentially helpful contacts.

You also benefit from some of the technical and management assistance programs that local funds operate to enhance the skills of the staff and trustees of its member organizations. For example, Aid to Wisconsin Organizations (AWO), a federation of community groups in Milwaukee, regularly offers workshops for the community on such topics as grassroots fundraising, time management, grantwriting, and organizational development. The Women's Funding Alliance in Seattle has seminars on Women Managing Inherited Wealth, as well as antiracism and antihomophobia workshops for its member organizations and other nonprofits.

Many United Ways run management assistance programs (MAPS) which conduct training sessions, consultations, seminars, and technical assistance for the staff of their member agencies. They often recruit corporate executives to lend their expertise to nonprofits. Inquire with your local United Way to find out whether it has such a program, and whether nonmember agencies are eligible for assistance.

WHAT ARE THE DISADVANTAGES OF SECURING SUPPORT FROM FEDERATED FUNDS?

1. *Restrictions on your own fundraising.* Admittance to large established federations, such as United Way, usually involves an agreement on the part of the beneficiary to refrain from certain fundraising activities, generally those that are perceived contrary to the best interests of a large federation. The federation, not the beneficiary, makes that assessment. This may involve restrictions during the course of the annual fall-to-winter campaigns or throughout the entire year. It may also govern individual approaches to corporations for gifts or access to individual employees at the workplace, or both.

Alternative funds tend not to have as many comparable restrictions except when they decide that a unified approach to a funding prospect, such as a corporation, will be strategically more effective. Again, given the autonomy of all local federated efforts, the extent of any restrictions will vary from one community to the next, and from one fund to another.

2. *Long waiting period prior to admission (or rejection).* Due to the annual allocations and fundraising procedures inherent in many federations and the bureaucracies of larger federations such as United Way, nonprofit organizations often have to wait a considerable period of time before a decision is reached on their application for membership status. A year could lapse for an approved new agency between the submission of the initial application and the receipt of the first check. This can also apply to acceptance into donor option programs and to approval for discretionary nonmember grants.

The essence of workplace solicitation is that the funds come from payroll deductions in periodic (usually monthly or quarterly) amounts after having been deducted from the workers' paychecks.

There have been reports that some alternative funds have had to wait inordinately long periods of time to receive funds from United Way's donor option program.

3. *Fluctuating levels of support.* Membership status is fairly secure over a period of time, as long as your group is living up to its stated purpose and its programs continue to produce concrete results, but your level of annual budget allocation (grant size) from a federation can fluctuate. This would be particularly true for newer, less-established member agencies. For example, United Ways review the entire operating budgets of their beneficiary agencies each year before deciding what level of support an agency will receive in the forthcoming fiscal year; the level of funding from United Way changes very little from one year to the next, however. Since most alternative funds are still fairly young and growing, the size of their grants is governed more by the total sum of monies raised in a given year's campaign than by any internal allocation formulas.

4. *Contributions of time and labor to actual fundraising campaigns.* All federated fundraising requires a lot of volunteer effort. Member agencies of United Way are usually called on to provide volunteers for various fundraising and public speaking tasks, especially during the campaign. Minimally, they may be asked to solicit their own employees for contributions to the federated drive to which they belong. Where a local United Way encourages the management of a member agency to obtain 100 percent participation of workers in a United Way campaign, workplace charitable solicitation within that agency can fall prey to coercion and other abuses—although United Way of America does officially discourage such practices.

Most, if not all, alternative funds require member groups to be active during the workplace campaign. They also require that groups participate in activities such as presentations about their work throughout the year. For newer funds, volunteer and staff hours are critical to the life of the fund and the success of the campaign.

5. *Subtle pressure toward conformity.* While a federation cannot ostensibly tell a member agency what to do, it can potentially exert subtle pressures. For example, if United Way announces that it is particularly interested in funding certain types of projects in the upcoming year, the member agency and staff know that a program addressing these concerns might be viewed more favorably than others and might ultimately affect their budget allocation. Membership status in both United Ways and alternative funds usually involves pressure to conform to the philosophy and policies set by the federation. When the beneficiaries play a role within the decisionmaking structure of the federation, as they do with most alternative funds, they are usually more comfortable with any policies that might be established. However, when they don't have that

opportunity, as with United Way, they can rightfully feel disenfranchised in the setting of policies.

HOW CAN YOUR ORGANIZATION DECIDE WHETHER TO APPROACH A FEDERATED FUND FOR SUPPORT?

Are your activities and programs service-oriented or advocacy- and organizing-oriented? Does your organization conform to the profile of other United Way member agencies in your community? Does your work enjoy broad-based popular support in your community, or are you viewed as controversial by the local power structure? The answers to these questions will help you gauge whether you should approach the local United Way for support, or whether you would fare better by approaching the local alternative fund or even by establishing one with other kindred groups. Finally, you might also become involved in the donor option program of the local United Way, if one exists, or work to gain direct access to public and private workplaces for the purposes of charitable solicitation.

These decisions are usually weighed very carefully by an organization. My Sister's Place, a battered women's shelter in Washington, D.C., was rejected by United Way in the early 1980s; the shelter has since been approached for membership by the local United Way, after having received more than $80,000 from the CFC and becoming a member of the Women's Fund of Greater Washington, D.C. My Sister's Place remains with the Women's Fund.

The nonprofit unfamiliar with the local United Way needs to decide whether it would qualify for United Way support as a member agency or as a recipient of a discretionary grant. Both determinations will depend not only on United Way's guidelines for membership or discretionary grants but also on the nonprofit's focus or politics; if it is social-change–oriented, the organization may be too controversial for United Way even to consider, or it may not want to affiliate with United Way's mainstream image. Also, if an alternative fund does exist in your community, check its membership or allocations guidelines to find out whether it accepts new members.

You will also want to review carefully in advance of any application whatever restrictions might govern your fundraising activities if you were to be admitted as a member agency to a local United Way. For example, if you already enjoy substantial support from local corporations, how will United Way member agency status affect that support? Will you be restrained from approaching these companies directly again for grants? Inquire, again in advance, how much funding you might expect to receive from the United Way, so you can measure the relative merits of its support versus the grants that you might continue to receive from corporations, if you were to remain independent.

HOW DOES AN ORGANIZATION SUCCESSFULLY SECURE SUPPORT FROM FEDERATED FUNDS?

A goal of any organization interested in support from a federation is access to the lucrative area of charitable workplace solicitation. Some fundraisers see this arena as a critical source of new funds for many newer nonprofits in the decade ahead. If that is the case, the forward-looking nonprofit would be advised to start staking out that field now. As mentioned, a nonprofit can work toward this goal in a variety of ways:

1. Join the local United Way as a member agency.

2. Apply to the United Way for a discretionary or a venture grant.

3. Seek participation in an existing United Way donor option program.

4. Join another federation, such as an alternative fund.

5. Form a new federation with other similar organizations in your community.

Each of these routes poses different advantages and disadvantages for the uninitiated organization. You need to investigate the pros and cons of each thoroughly before you decide which is most appropriate to your needs.

Step 1

Contact your local United Way, and find out whether it has any discretionary grant programs for nonmember agencies. Ask for details on how to apply for membership status. Ask for the most recent materials on these programs, including application forms and guidelines, and the most recent list of past grantees and members. If you have organizational letterhead, make the request in writing. Be advised, however, that very few new organizations are admitted to a given United Way each year. At the same time, check to see whether there are any other federated funds in your community. The National Committee for Responsive Philanthropy (NCRP) (2001 S Street, N.W., Suite 620, Washington, D.C., 20009, telephone 202 387–9177) can tell you whether any exist locally. Make similar inquiries with any such funds.

Step 2

Find out from your local municipal and/or state government whether they conduct a charitable contributions drive among their employees each year, and whether non–United Way member agencies can participate. Usually, the personnel office of your local government will be able to provide this information, since it usually administers payroll deductions for all purposes, including charitable contributions. Also, find out whether the United Way has a donor option program for nonmember agencies.

If you are a national organization or a local organization in a city with a large number of federal employees, you would be advised to make a similar inquiry with the federal government about the Combined Federal Campaign.

The NCRP can advise groups here as well. Check with your local municipal and state governments. Consult the earlier list of state governments that currently allow their employees to make charitable contributions through payroll deductions to non–United Way agencies.

Step 3

Contact some existing recipient organizations of local federations (both United Way and alternative funds) and ask about their experiences. How would they assess the pros and cons of that support? How did they obtain it? Did they find an individual within the local United Way or the local alternative fund who was particularly helpful to them during the application process?

You now have completed all the information gathering that you need to do. You might also want to obtain further materials from the National Committee for Responsive Philanthropy, which maintains an excellent publications program. United Way of America can also provide you with some general materials on United Ways (701 North Fairfax Street, Alexandria, Virginia 22314–2045, telephone 703-836-7100).

Step 4

Weigh the relative advantages and disadvantages for your organization of the various options available to you, and decide which would be best for you. You may decide to apply for a discretionary grant from the United Way before any formal application for membership, or you may decide to pursue workplace solicitation directly through a donor option program. Remember that one course of action does not necessarily preclude another.

Step 5

Regardless of which action you decide to take, you will more than likely have to complete a formal application and submit a set of pertinent materials. This will undoubtedly be required with any requests for grants, membership, or participation in a donor option program. Be sure to submit these required forms in a timely fashion.

Step 6

You can solicit letters of support from community and civic leaders who can attest to the importance of your work.

Don't hesitate to demonstrate your credentials during the preapplication period. You do not have to stay idle once you have submitted your application. Any letters of support submitted will be added to your file and considered at the appropriate time. This is an opportunity for you to organize your supporters toward a specific goal. Several excellent articles on how United Ways operate and what influences their decisionmaking procedures have appeared in *The Grantsmanship Center News* (see the "Further Readings" list for this chapter).

The following excerpts illustrate how one United Way (Ventura County, California—as of 1982) and one alternative fund (Bread and Roses Community Fund, Philadelphia—as of 1985) make their allocation decisions.

Step 7

If you have chosen to participate in a United Way donor option program or directly engage in a workplace solicitation program of your own, your work is truly cut out for you. While workplace fundraising usually costs less (5¢ to 10¢ on the dollar) and reaches more people than other methods, it is still left to the nonprofit to organize a campaign whereby the public learns about its organization and teams of "askers" are mobilized at targeted worksites. But because each United Way donor option program is different, if you go this route, be sure to investigate the stipulations United Way puts on your organization's publicity campaign; in some cases, publicity by an individual organization outside of United Way's presentations is prohibited. And if you are not going to participate in a donor option plan, gaining access to workplaces in order to solicit employees is a very strenuous process. Because of the work involved, many of the groups that do workplace fundraising strongly suggest that an organization join or form a federation before attempting to gain access. Groups in Baltimore, Pittsburgh, and Philadelphia formed fundraising coalitions even to get access to donor option programs.

If you decide to go it alone, you are advised to start with a modest number of workplaces. You can choose those where you have the most existing contacts, where your work is the most well known and/or relevant, and where the management is amenable to your presence. This approach is more effective initially than a massive-scale campaign, unless, for whatever reasons, your work has engendered a lot of positive publicity.

Step 8

If you decide to apply to a local federated fund for support and membership and your application is approved, you will undoubtedly be asked to become active in the fund. You might participate in its governance, in some of its fundraising activities, or both, depending on the nature of the specific fund.

Ventura County California United Way

If you have never applied to a United Way for funding, you may want to do so for the experience as well as for the possibility that you will be funded.

The following is a description of how the Ventura County United Way allocations process worked in 1982 (the process can vary from year to year in certain respects, but on the whole the steps are the same). Keep in mind that each United Way is autonomous and has its own policies, procedures, internal politics, funding priorities, fund limitations, and human quirks; therefore, the way Ventura allocates funds is not necessarily the way Peoria does so.

Beginning in January, applications were sent to member agencies, and announcements were made in the local newspapers that United Way was accepting applications for membership.

All agencies were given a certain period of time to complete the applications and turn them in to the United Way office, where they were reviewed for accuracy and completeness. These applications were then returned to the agencies for correction, and the final copies were turned in some 10 days later.

At the same time, members were recruited for the Allocations Committee by the chairman and vice chairman of the committee—both officers of the United Way board. This committee is made up of volunteers who make the decisions regarding which agencies to fund and how much funding to provide. Volunteers were solicited from the previous year's committee, from among prominent people in the community, from other United Way volunteer committees, and from the community at large. The Allocations Committee initially included 170 people but had dropped to about 150 participants by the end of the process.

Participants were divided into 12 panels, and each panel was given the responsibility of reviewing three to four agencies. A chairman and a vice chairman were selected for each panel, and these members, together with the chairman and the vice chairman of the parent Allocations Committee, made up the Allocations Executive Committee.

A special Audit Committee composed of auditors, CPAs, and financial experts was also chosen. Its job was to review agency applications, especially budget materials, and to generate questions for the allocations panels on the basis of whatever inconsistencies or problem areas were revealed. Each agency's budget was reviewed by an auditor.

The Allocations Executive Committee established some general guidelines for the process and for increases to member agencies. Generally, agencies could expect to receive a seven to eight percent increase in their allocations unless they had new programs that justified additional funding or unless problems in an agency justified a smaller increase or none at all. These guidelines were given to the panels at the time members were being trained by the chairmen and vice chairmen.

Trainers of the allocations volunteers stressed that each agency should be evaluated on the basis of the need and cost-effectiveness of its services, the impact of its programs on its client group, the qualifications of the agency's staff to provide its services, the agency's relationship to other agencies in the community, the way in which volunteers were used and the strength of the agency's board of directors, the manner in which United Way funds would be used, and the reason for the increase in the agency's request from United Way.

Members of the three panels that were considering the admission of new agencies were told that these agencies had to (1) be nonprofit, tax-exempt corporations; (2) operate in the health, welfare, recreation, or character-building field; (3) serve the people of Ventura County; (4) have been in existence at least two years prior to application; (5) have a sizable and active board and membership; (6) offer services that do not duplicate those of other agencies; and (7) show evidence of broad community support in both funding and leadership.

Both member and nonmember agencies were also eligible to seek grants aside from or instead of an allocation. These were given to member agencies to start up new programs on a pilot basis as well as to new agencies that did not qualify as members but did qualify for some support.

All allocations panels were instructed not to fund an agency for more than 50 percent of its entire budget, as this was felt not to be in the best interest of either the agency or United Way.

After training, panel members paid a two-hour visit to each agency that they were assigned to review. During these visits, they toured the agencies' facilities and asked questions regarding the material in the applications.

A second meeting between each agency and the panel took place in May. At this time, the panel resolved any questions that had arisen. Following this meeting, the panel developed a recommended funding level for each agency as well as some comments that were forwarded back to the agency.

After each panel had had a final meeting with the agencies and had made its recommendations, the Allocations Executive Committee met to go over all the recommendations. They then finalized the recommendations and forwarded them to the United Way board of directors.

The chairman and vice chairman of the Allocations Committee presented the recommendations to the board's Executive Committee and finally to the full board. They were approved at the June meeting and formed the basis for the fall campaign.

—J. Dawn Hodson

Bread and Roses Community Fund of Philadelphia

The Funding Process. Groups wishing to apply for a Bread and Roses grant are required to fill out a written application and submit current literature and background materials. Once the staff has ascertained that the application falls under the funding guidelines and is complete, it is distributed to members of the 12-person Community Funding Board (CFB) which may choose to interview the group or arrange an on-site visit. Following careful review and discussion, they recommend approval or rejection and determine the grant size. Rejected groups may submit a written appeal requesting reconsideration. Final approval of funding recommendations is made by the Bread and Roses Board of Directors.

Community Funding Board. The most unique aspect of Bread and Roses is the degree of community control built into the grantmaking process. The Fund believes that people should have control over the institutions that affect their lives and that real knowledge of community needs is found among community people themselves. CFB members are selected from people active in local social change work who support the philosophy and funding guidelines of Bread and Roses and are willing to make a two-year commitment. To ensure adequate representation from groups traditionally excluded from decision making, the Board has a quota system. Therefore the membership must include at least six national minority representatives, including two Hispanics; five women; and one gay man and woman.

Although not in favor of donor control, Bread and Roses feels that donors bring an important and unique perspective to the funding process and encourages donor involvement through representation on the Board.

Improvements in the Funding Process: Bread and Roses Shifts to Two Funding Cycles. Starting in 1985, Bread and Roses will be making general fund grants semi-annually. The Fall/Winter funding cycle was recently completed and applications for the Spring cycle were due in mid-February. Grants will be distributed in March and June, accordingly.

In moving to two funding cycles, Bread and Roses was faced with a number of questions. The issue wasn't why—we knew that doing this would help us to broaden and better serve our grantee community—the issue was how. How do we take what was traditionally a six-month process and make it a less arduous, less concentrated three- or four-month process? Relying on the experience of our fellow fund in New York, North Star, we looked at new ways to achieve our goals.

The procedure which follows was designed to replace what was, in the past, far too many meetings and an inordinately lengthy process. While we were generally pleased with the outcome, this process took its toll on staff, Community Funding Board Members, and applicant groups alike.

Funding cycles now start with a Screening Meeting at which all applications are briefly reviewed and discussed by the Community Funding Board. Those which fall outside of Bread and Roses' guidelines of funding capacity are screened out. Interviewing teams (composed of two Board members and one staff person) are then set up to interview all remaining applicants. The interviewing process provides an opportunity to learn more about the applicant organizations, meet some of their principal characters, and frequently get a firsthand look at their office and operation. The interviewing team prepares a written report which summarizes their findings and recommends to fund or not to fund and a suggested grant or range. These reports are compiled and forwarded to the entire Community Funding Board, which then holds its Decision and Allocations Meeting for the cycle. A third and final meeting for Evaluation and Reconsideration then occurs to review any requests for reconsideration and to evaluate the process and decisions of the cycle. What was once over a dozen meetings has been condensed into three focused sessions, and it works!

Source: Bread and Roses Community Fund Annual Report

THE FUTURE OF FEDERATED FUNDRAISING

Clearly the 1980s marked the continuing growth of local United Ways as well as the ongoing emergence of new alternative funds. These parallel developments demonstrate the ever-expanding generosity of Americans when given the opportunity. Also, they are signs that some of the country's nonprofits are becoming more aggressive and sophisticated in their fundraising techniques.

Due to the pressures exerted by these newer, less traditional members of the nonprofit community, United Ways themselves may also undertake changes in their efforts to be more responsive. The slogan, "I gave at the office," will take on meaning for a larger proportion of the country's nonprofit community.

NEIGHBORHOOD FUND
INVEST IN NEIGHBORHOODS INC.

Case Study
NEIGHBORHOOD FUND
INVEST IN NEIGHBORHOODS INC.

The last time you went to a meeting of your neighborhood association, did anyone suggest raising a one-million-dollar endowment fund to support neighborhood projects? Probably not, but that is what is happening in Cincinnati, Ohio, with the creation of Invest in Neighborhoods.

Starting in 1978, all of Cincinnati's 47 community councils were receiving grants of a few thousand dollars each from a program of the Charles Stewart Mott Foundation called Project SNAP (Stimulating the Neighborhood Action Process). The funds were used for over 700 innovative projects ranging from membership campaigns to community clean-ups. One council conducted a housing inventory that was used to win a $50,000 housing rehabilitation grant.

By 1980, a group of neighborhood leaders realized that the good projects going throughout the city were based on funds from a five-year project that would end in 1982. The neighborhood councils, with the help of the city government, began studying the idea of a neighborhood endowment of trust. It took over two years of research, planning and coalition building to establish Invest in Neighborhoods, Inc. Its board of directors is elected by the community councils and is responsible for raising a one-million-dollar endowment fund. The money is being raised by both the councils themselves through grassroots efforts and from corporate and small business contributions. The interest from the endowment fund dollars will be an ongoing source of funds for neighborhood projects.

There were many difficulties in creating Invest. Sherry Marshall, one of the original organizers, saw three major hurdles in organizing the neighborhoods. One was to get neighborhoods thinking in long range terms, rather than just concentrating on the immediate projects. The second hurdle was getting low-income neighborhoods convinced that an endowment fund made sense, since it was a new concept in how to use money. The third difficulty was deciding what rules would be used to guide the distribution of funds: competitive proposals or uniform allotments.

Another money issue was for the Invest organizers to negotiate with the Greater Cincinnati Foundation, the city's community foundation. The endowment fund is held by the foundation, but the neighborhoods wanted to control what projects got funded rather than the foundation. The result was that the Invest board made final decisions about funding projects, as long as they do not jeopardize the foundation's tax-exempt status. Invest also controls how its money is invested, and guidelines include a prohibition against investing in companies that operate in South Africa.

The last two years have been devoted to fundraising for Invest. To date, 45 out of 47 councils are paying members, which includes both dollars and volunteer time. Over $500,000 has been raised, half from the neighborhood councils and the other half in donations from the business community. Changing the corporations' view of neighborhood organizations was very difficult. Business people tended to see community councils as small special interest groups that often bickered with each other. It has been a major accomplishment to demonstrate that neighborhood groups can work together for the good of the whole community.

Although the board and members of Invest are still working to raise the other half of the one million dollars, they decided to distribute $25,000 for meritorious neighborhood awards plus give each member council $300–$500 worth of interest. As current Invest president James J. Crowe says, "We have to show what we can accomplish in order to raise more money."

One of the awards went to the Linwood Community Council, which is starting a community computer lab in conjunction with a local elementary school. In the morning, school children will use the computers; in the afternoon, an adult employment retraining program will use the lab; in the evening, school teachers will hold classes for community residents. Another award went to the Carthage Civic League, which is purchasing a storefront property. Part of the property will be made into low-income housing apartments, while the storefront will be used to set up a tool lending library.

Invest has also sponsored a neighborhood festival to raise money for community councils. The "A Day In Eden" festival at a local park has been a great success and has started a new tradition of celebrating Cincinnati's neighborhoods.

The yearly festival is only one of many signs that Invest is more than an innovative fundraising technique. As Sherry Marshall noted, "Invest in Neighborhoods has established a real neighborhood coalition. Invest in Neighborhoods is to neighborhoods what the Chamber of Commerce is to business." The community councils have become members of Invest and are together promoting and demonstrating to the city as a whole the importance and value of strong neighborhoods.

For more information about Invest in Neighborhoods, contact James J. Crowe, 1 Eastwood Drive, Cincinnati, OH 45227; 513/527-7501.

by Rob Baird

Source: Rain Magazine, May/June 1985, Portland, OR.
Source: Logo, Neighborhood Fund—Invest in Neighborhoods Inc., Cincinnati, OH. Reprinted with permission.

Summary Worksheet

for

_____

(name of your organization)

APPROACHING FEDERATED FUNDRAISING ORGANIZATIONS

1. Identifying Federated Fundraising Organizations in your Community.

List the federated fundraising organizations (i.e., United Way, Alternative Fund, etc.) that operate in your community.

_____

_____

_____

_____

2. Now enumerate the ways that each of those listed provide financial support to nonprofit organizations.

Name of Federated Fundraising Organization	Membership Organization (yes/no)	Operating Grants Available (yes/no)	Discretionary Grants Available (yes/no)	Donor Option Programs Available (yes/no)
a.				
b.				
c.				
d.				

3. Gauging Community Support for Your Efforts

Are any of the federated fundraising organizations in your community supporting organizations similar to yours? If yes, what are they?

_____

_____

_____

_____

4. On the basis of its printed guidelines, does your organization reflect the interest areas or priorities of your community's federated fundraising organizations? Which ones?

_____

_____

_____

_____

5. Does your local United Way have a donor option program? If yes, is your organization eligible to participate?

☐ yes ☐ no

6. See pages 370 and 371 for this part of the worksheet.

7. Making the Match

For each prospect on the previous list, complete the following worksheet (use your own blank paper).

Name of Federated Fundraising Organization:

Its Stated Areas of Interest That Pertain to Your Work: (Draw from their annual report).

Write one or more short sentences demonstrating how the work of your organization reflects the interests of X organization.

8. Finding Assistance and Counsel

Name those individuals who might be able to advise you on how to most effectively approach the federated fundraising organization(s) on your list:

a. _____

b. _____

c. _____

d. _____

e. _____

9. Assessing the Likelihood of Securing Support from Federated Fundraising Organizations

On the basis of what you have learned, how would you rank your chances of securing support from federated fundraising organizations?

☐ Very Good ☐ Possible ☐ Unlikely ☐ Still Unknown

6. List below the federated fundraising organization(s) that might provide support for your work. Limit your listing to the most likely supporters of your organization.

a. Name of Federated Fundraising Organizations	**b.** Its Stated Areas of Interest that Relate to Your Work	**c.** Appropriate Contact Person, and Telephone Number

d. Personal Contacts	**e.** Your Program(s) that Correspond to Its Interest	**f.** Level of Potential Financial Support

FURTHER READINGS

Bothwell, Robert O. *Fundraising at the Workplace: The New Options for Nonprofit Groups Not Members of United Ways.* Washington, DC: National Committee for Responsive Philanthropy. May 1979. 56 pp. $20.00. (Order from: National Committee for Responsive Philanthropy, 2001 S St., N.W., Suite 620, Washington, DC 20009)

    Report, prepared for a national meeting held in 1979, explores ways nonprofit organizations which are not a part of United Ways can take advantage of fundraising opportunities in the workplace. Includes recommendations for action to open this area to a wider range of nonprofit organizations.

Bothwell, Robert O., and Timothy Saasta. "Donor Option: There's Less To It Than Meets the Eye." *The Grantsmanship Center NEWS* no. 49 (September/October 1982): 56–57. Single issue $4.75 plus $2.00 handling per order. (Order from: The Grantsmanship Center, P.O. Box 6210, 650 S. Spring St., Suite 507, Los Angeles, CA 90014)

    Discussion of United Way of America's 1982 recommendation that local United Ways develop "donor option" programs.

Cook, Richard. *Activist's Guide for Organizing an Alternative Fund.* Washington, DC: National Committee for Responsive Philanthropy. $20.00. (Order from: National Committee for Responsive Philanthropy, 2001 S St., N.W., Suite 620, Washington, DC 20009)

    Discussion of the mechanics of organizing an alternative fund, based on the experiences of those who have organized such funds. Includes an analysis of the issues confronting funds.

Hodson, J. Dawn. "United Way: Have You Considered Joining?" *Grantsmanship Center NEWS* no. 49 (September/October 1982): 40–46. Single issue $4.75 plus $2.00 handling per order. (Order from: The Grantsmanship Center, P.O. Box 6210, 650 S. Spring St., Suite 507, Los Angeles, CA 90014)

    Insights into the pros and cons of applying for United Way membership from a former local United Way official.

National Committee for Responsive Philanthropy. *Charity Begins at Work: Alternatives to United Way Dramatically Change the Billion Dollar World of Workplace Fund Raising.* 1986. 64 pp. $20.00. (Order from: National Committee for Responsive Philanthropy, 2001 S St., N.W., Suite 620, Washington, DC 20009)

    Collection of articles on the ways nonprofit organizations are raising funds through payroll deduction outside of United Ways. Looks at efforts by all levels of government, businesses, and unions to establish such fundraising mechanisms. Includes sections on black united funds, social action funds, women's funds, combined health appeals, international service agencies, and united arts funds.

Paprocki, Steven L. *Introduction to Payroll Deduction Solicitation.* St. Paul: Co-operative Fund Drive. 1980. 23 pp. $4.00. (Order from: Cooperative Fund Drive, Liberty Bank Building, #215 Snelling and Selby Ave., St. Paul, MN 55104)

> Explains how to start a payroll deduction plan for workers in a community. Includes the problems and possibilities of such a plan.

Porter, Robert, ed. *United Arts Fundraising: 1981.* New York: American Council for the Arts. 1981. 64 pp. $15.00 plus shipping and handling. (Order from: American Council for the Arts, Department 230, 570 Seventh Ave., New York, NY 10018)

> Analysis of 49 federated arts campaigns in 1981 with information on solicitation procedures, dollars received, allocation of funds and costs.

Responsive Philanthropy. Quarterly. Washington, DC: National Committee for Responsive Philanthropy. Free. (Order from: National Committee for Responsive Philanthropy, 2001 S. St., N.W., Washington, DC 20009)

> News and information about philanthropic activities of interest to organizations working to achieve social justice, equal opportunity and fair representation for disenfranchised people.

United Way of America. *United Way of America, Annual Report.* Alexandria, VA: United Way of America. Annual. Approx. 32 pp. Free to approved groups. (Order from: United Way of America, 701 N. Fairfax St., Alexandria, VA 22314–2045)

> Report of the yearly activities of the national organization.

United Way of America Fact Sheets. Alexandria, VA: United Way of America. Free upon request. (Order from: United Way of America, 701 N. Fairfax St., Alexandria, VA 22314-2045)

> Series explains various aspects of United Way's history and activities. Titles include "Basic Facts About United Ways," "United Way and Services for New Agencies, Minorities and Women," and "Information and Referral Services" among others.

Weiss, Nancy. "The United Way" *NPO Resource Review* vol. II, no. 6 (July/August 1984): 1, 3, 7–8. (Order from: NPO Resource Review, Caller Box A-6, Cathedral Station, New York, NY 10025)

> Explains how The United Way operates and how it might benefit a nonprofit organization.

Wenocur, Stanley. "The Structure and Politics of Local United Way Organizations." *The Grantsmanship Center NEWS* no. 26 (September/December 1978). Single issue $4.75 plus $2.00 handling per order. (Order from: The Grantsmanship Center, P.O. Box 6210, 650 S. Spring St., Suite 507, Los Angeles, CA 90014)

ASSOCIATIONS OF INDIVIDUALS

Banding together with others for a common purpose is a familiar aspect of our lives. Most individuals belong to one form of association or another. It may be a block club or a parents' group or a reading club or a food co-op, or a civic association. Your neighbor may belong to Alcoholics Anonymous or a service organization such as the Lions or the Soroptomists, or a sports team. There is no limit to the array of associations that individuals, especially Americans, establish.

The most renowned traveler to our shores, Alexis de Tocqueville, commented on this phenomenon in his work *Democracy in America*, in 1835:

> Americans of all ages, all conditions, and all dispositions constantly form associations. They have not only commercial and manufacturing companies, in which all take part, but associations of a thousand other kinds, religious, moral, serious, futile, general or restricted, enormous or diminutive. The Americans make associations to give entertainments, to found seminaries, to build inns, to construct churches, to diffuse books, to send missionaries to the antipodes; in this manner they found hospitals, prisons and schools. If it is proposed to inculcate some truth or to foster some feeling by the encouragement of a great example, they form a society. Wherever at the head of some new undertaking you see the government in France, or a man of rank in England, in the United States you will be sure to find an association.

More than 150 years have passed since de Tocqueville made this observation. Yet, what he described is even more evident today. The plethora of self-help organizations is even more remarkable when contrasted with the popular Horatio Alger image in our society, which projects the notion of a country filled with self-reliant and self-made individuals. That notion is belied by the countless examples of individuals working together for personal and collective benefit.

Self-help is clearly a basic element of many voluntary associations. For example, consider this partial list of groups that have formed because of parental concerns:

- Parent-Teacher Associations
- Parents of Lesbians and Gays
- Parents' League of American Students of Medicine Abroad
- Parents of Murdered Children

- Mothers Against Drunk Driving
- Parents Anonymous
- Parents for Toy Safety
- Parents of Premature and High-Risk Infants
- Parents Without Partners

A theme for many of these groups is clear, heartfelt concern for others. Very often, individuals who have experienced loss, discrimination, or illness unite to help others who find themselves in similar situations. That concern may extend to one's immediate community, the country, and even the world itself.

Other associations can trace their origins to philanthropic concerns. For example, the first Junior League in America was established in 1901 in New York City by Mary Harriman and a group of eighty-five young women to promote volunteer service in the settlement houses of the city, according to the

Members of Rockettes Alumnae Association, which annually raises funds to support charitable endeavors, perform one of their routines at Radio City Music Hall.

Source: Vic deLucia/New York Times Pictures. Reprinted with permission.

reference work *NTPA '84: National Trade and Professional Associations of the United States.* From work in settlement houses, early Junior Leagues rapidly expanded their activities to founding well-baby clinics, conducting classes in home nursing, establishing orphanages, and organizing garment factories to employ needy women. Today, there are over 148,000 women active in 252 leagues across the nation.

Associations that benefit charitable and nonprofit organizations as part of their work continue to form every year. In 1955, the Rockette Alumni Association was founded to provide its members opportunities to come together socially and to unite for philanthropic causes. Currently, it has over 335 members, all former members of the Radio City Music Hall dance troupe, the Rockettes. Each year, they hold an annual charity ball to raise funds for different nonprofit efforts. In a similar vein, singles' groups in many cities have joined to provide a new social outlet to their members, combined with get-together parties that benefit different causes and organizations.

Admittedly, many associations flirt with the ridiculous, for example, the International Flat Earth Research Society, whose 1,400 members contend that the world is flat, and the Procrastination Club of America, whose 3,500 members finally protested the War of 1812 in 1966.

Can any of these associations or others assist you in your efforts to find new revenue sources for your organization? How do you proceed to identify them and to approach them for assistance?

The Flat Earth Society is one of the more unusual associations of individuals.

Source: *Express* Magazine, February, 1983. Illustration by Ed Renfro, New York, NY. Reprinted with permission.

An *association* is a group of individuals who voluntarily come together to work toward a common objective, based on some common beliefs, values, or experiences. They may choose to organize for sheer social reasons, or for professional enrichment purposes, philanthropic purposes, or any other variety of reasons. Often, they are joined by individuals who come together to solve, through concerted action, a problem that they could not solve alone.

In the United States, a number of associations have evolved to represent the concerns of professions and trades. According to Alyse Reckson, an advertising sales representative for *The New York Times* and author of the article, "Non-Profit Organizations Offer Profitable Work," "an association is a not-for-profit organization whose sole purpose is to work for the benefit of its membership—a membership that is joined to exchange ideas and work for a common goal and mutual interests." She goes on to add, "[trade] associations represent almost every conceivable interest group; their functions include keeping members informed of industry trends; acting as a spokesman for member causes; playing an integral role in determining industry standards; performing research and development; playing a major role in relations with government, and lobbying for favorable legislation."

As defined, associations can range in size from the smallest neighborhood-based block club to huge professional societies, such as the American Medical Association, which has more than 235,000 members and professional staff as well. As Will Rogers once remarked, any two Americans meeting on the street for the first time would almost certainly form some sort of organization right there on the spot.

HOW DO ASSOCIATIONS EXTEND SUPPORT TO NONPROFITS? WHAT ISSUES CONCERN THEM?

Unfortunately, statistics are not easily available on the aggregate dollar total of contributions made by associations to nonprofits each year. The range of charitable distributions made by associations is quite diverse. A local chapter of a national service organization might make a contribution of a hundred dollars in response to a speaker at its monthly meeting; or it could make a much more substantial contribution as the result of an annual charity ball.

Associations in their broadest sense probably provide more assistance as a ready source of volunteers than as a source of funds. They can provide help in tasks from envelope stuffing to job counseling. For example, in 1984 Delta Sigma Theta Sorority, Inc., the largest organization of black women in the United States, proclaimed *Summit Two, A Call to Action in Support of Black Single Mothers* as a national campaign for its membership of 125,000 women in 712 colleges and alumni chapters. In response to this mandate, local chapters implemented a variety of programs. In Houston, 125 Delta members joined a sister-to-sister program in which each woman helped and encouraged a single mother. In Columbia, South Carolina, chapter members in concert with representatives from 20 other local organizations and businesses decided to give single mothers financial assistance. In Montgomery County, Maryland, 200 women are working to enforce existing laws on alimony and child support.

Other groups, such as the 140,000-member National Federation of Business and Professional Women's Clubs, Inc., (BPW/USA) include grantmaking as part of their program agenda. Their purpose as stated by their founders in 1919 is to serve the career advancement needs of business and professional women. Toward this goal, the Federation established the Business and Professional Women's Foundation in 1956 to extend services and support to all working women. The Foundation is both an operating and a grantmaking body, and its efforts include research, information and referral, and a diverse program of educational financial aid. The 1982–83 program included making grants to nine women scholars to explore the impact of occupational segregation on minority and immigrant women and public policy implications for the work and family lives of women. They also awarded $180,000 in scholarships and loans to women returning to school in order to enter, reenter, or advance in the work force.

These examples illustrate how only two of the country's more than 16,000 national associations respond to different social problems through the use of their resources.

HOW DO ASSOCIATIONS OPERATE?

A local association can be an informally structured, grassroots group or a formally organized chapter of a national association. They conduct their affairs in many different ways.

For the most part, associations are membership organizations in which members vote on most critical decisions directly or through their elected representatives. A local civic association might, at its monthly meeting, poll members on an important issue such as support or opposition to a redevelopment project slated for their neighborhood. On the other hand, local chapters of large national associations such as the League of Women Voters and the National Organization for Women (NOW) would be more likely to vote on various issues (such as ratification of the Equal Rights Amendment) at state and national conventions, where representatives from all chapters attend and vote. Chapters would thus ordinarily make decisions on major policy within the confines set by the voting membership from across the country.

When it comes to supporting other nonprofit organizations with funds or volunteers, the decision usually rests with the local chapter. If there is a national grantmaking program within the association, it would most likely be aware of it and refer you to it. Some chapters may also belong to a city- or state-wide body of their association that may, on occasion, make contributions. However, the majority of requests are usually first received by the local chapter.

Some associations see their role as supporting the charitable work of other existing organizations, while others are interested in becoming directly involved in projects as volunteer workers. Some associations are willing to do both. Of course, many associations do exist exclusively to carry out projects within their own stated interests, which may not correspond to those of other nonprofits.

Larger associations may have staff on a local and a national level. Usually, chapters would not have staff unless perhaps they covered a major metropolitan area. An association may have officers, such as president or chair or co-chairs, vice president, treasurer, and secretary, who represent the association between the regularly scheduled meetings of its members.

Associations usually derive their income from a system in which members pay annual dues. If there is a national body, each member's dues are usually shared between the local and national chapters. For example, a dues allocation of 75¢ per member raises over $100,000 each year from members of the National Federation of Business and Professional Women to support the work of their foundation. They also organize special events, such as house tours and benefit concerts, to raise special funds for philanthropic purposes.

Membership in associations is generally open to anyone who has an interest in joining, although some associations do set requirements for membership, such as references from existing members, professional experience, etc.

Associations can also provide benefits that are consistent with its purposes. For example, the Association of Independent Video and Filmmakers, the national trade association of independent producers and individuals involved in independent video and film, provides a broad range of educational and professional services to its members, including group medical and life insurance, group equipment insurance, workshops and seminars, free publications, subscriptions to the monthly magazine *The Independent,* and more. All of these programs enable their members to practice their craft more effectively.

WHICH ORGANIZATIONS ARE MOST LIKELY TO RECEIVE SUPPORT FROM ASSOCIATIONS?

More than 40,000 associations exist in the United States, counting national organizations, their local chapters, and independent local and regional groups. This *excludes* thousands of grassroots associations, such as block clubs, co-operatives, tenants' groups, and community organizations. There are more associations than foundations (24,000+). Consequently, it is even harder to generalize about the interest areas of associations than it is about foundations.

For the nonprofit moneyseeker, the task is complicated since even highly sympathetic associations that are supportive of your work may choose to become involved in your field of endeavor personally, rather than providing you with funds to do so. You then gain an important ally and perhaps a source of volunteers, but not necessarily any funds.

The myriad of associations on the local and national levels makes it likely that there are some associations that would be willing to extend support to numerous nonprofit efforts in one form or another, such as making contributions, providing volunteers, and serving as allies in advocacy efforts.

WHAT ARE THE ADVANTAGES OF RAISING SUPPORT FROM ASSOCIATIONS?

1. *Quick source of small amounts of money.* Suppose you need to raise several hundred dollars, or even a thousand, quickly. Where can you turn? Local associations are one source. You can contact those that you have selected on the basis of some mutuality of interests. The association might respond to your request by inviting you to address its members at a monthly meeting and paying you a speaker's honorarium or passing the hat among those in attendance. Some groups may even have a contributions fund specifically established for philanthropic purposes. While the financial capacity of associations varies considerably, an organization can raise hundreds of dollars by appealing to a number of them for support during a relatively short period of time.

2. *Source of volunteers.* Associations usually attract civic-minded individuals who are interested in the well-being of their communities. Very often these individuals are also organization-minded in the sense that they understand how groups function best, based on their own personal past experiences as workers and board members in an association. That background makes them good prospects for a board of directors or standing committee of nonprofits seeking out new sources of people power. Additionally, they may possess some of the skills that you currently lack on your board, and they may be prepared to work as skilled volunteers in some of your programs.

3. *Source of useful contacts.* Have you ever knocked your head against a bureaucracy's door seeking some form of assistance, only to discover that the door swings wide open when you have a prior personal relationship with somebody on the other side?

Nonprofits are usually always in need of new contacts within government agencies, corporations, and larger nonprofit institutions. Often, individuals from these groups belong to local service associations where they seek out collegial interaction. By approaching an association for assistance, or even becoming personally involved yourself, you broaden your own network of people to turn to in times of need.

4. *Partner in advocacy efforts.* If you are building popular support for a bill pending before the state legislature that affects your constituency, or are working to galvanize popular opinion around a broad public issue, associations are excellent channels to reach out to other circles within your own community.

Associations are useful allies, since many are familiar with electoral and legislative processes and know how they can be used to advance issues. The skills of such groups as the League of Women Voters and the American Association of University Women are well known. In any coalition-building efforts, therefore, be advised to include some associations on your list.

This is why the President of the United States and other candidates running for office during an election year address the delegates to the national conventions of so many associations.

5. *Evidence of community support.* There is no better way to illustrate popular support for your organization and the issues you address than by highlighting the assistance that associations provide to you. That support can be useful when approaching government or corporations for their support. The backing of associations helps show the depth of popular following that your organization enjoys among the public.

WHAT ARE THE DISADVANTAGES OF RAISING SUPPORT FROM ASSOCIATIONS?

1. *Limited financial support.* Associations, with some major exceptions, are not sources of substantial financial support for nonprofit organizations. While some can raise generous sums of money at charitable balls or other special events to benefit designated nonprofits, the majority are more likely to extend financial assistance in smaller amounts (that is, hundreds rather than thousands of dollars). For many programs and emergency needs, however, several hundred dollars can make a solid difference.

2. *Time involved.* You can't secure help from most associations simply by dropping a letter in the mail. Social, civic, fraternal, ethnic, and professional groups transact their affairs through personal contacts. To elicit their assistance, you must be prepared to meet with one of their officers initially and then to address a membership meeting. You may prefer such direct personal contact yourself, but such meetings do take time from an already crowded schedule. Moreover, you may have to wait, as many groups meet only once a month and schedule their meeting speakers far in advance.

3. *Potential disappointment.* Have you ever been a luncheon speaker for a group in which your comments stirred no more interest than the rubbery chicken your listeners dined on? And yet they invited you to speak!

Associations are occasionally eager to find a new speaker for monthly get-togethers. Often the chair of their program committee has run out of new ideas and turned to you out of desperation.

Unfortunately, you may discover that your audience has no interest in or even sympathy for your views, and their response can range from indifference to hostility. Your inviter has wasted your time and left you with an unpleasant memory or a challenge to your mettle or both.

The lesson here is to choose your potential audiences carefully.

HOW CAN YOUR ORGANIZATION DECIDE WHETHER TO APPROACH ASSOCIATIONS FOR SUPPORT?

How well do you know the associations in your community? Is there a mutuality of interests between your endeavors and those of some of the associations that do exist in your town or city? Are there potential allies among them who would be willing and forthcoming supporters of your work if you were to approach them?

Some alliances are logical and self-evident. Peace groups naturally seek out each other's support. Across the country, local chapters of Women's International League for Peace and Freedom, Women's Strike for Peace, SANE and others work side by side against militarism and the nuclear arms race.

Other alliances are less obvious. For example, the Foundation for the Peoples of the South Pacific, a New York-based development agency organized to foster self-help efforts among South Pacific peoples, found a receptive audience in the Veterans of Foreign Wars. VFW members were a logical charitable constituency to turn to for assistance, since many from their ranks served in the armed forces in the South Pacific during World War II. During their overseas experiences, many of them developed an appreciation of the culture and lives of the South Pacific peoples and were thus positively inclined to the appeals for funds made by the Foundation forty years later.

Your potential association supporters may be clearly evident or not immediately apparent. The challenge for every nonprofit organization is to search among its nonprofit neighbors for likely candidates.

If your work involves coalition building and advocacy, your time will be well spent in developing relationships with associations in your community. If you ever have an occasional need for small sums of money or for volunteers, these alliances will serve you well.

HOW DOES AN ORGANIZATION SUCCESSFULLY SECURE SUPPORT FROM ASSOCIATIONS?

Step 1. Identifying Potentially Supportive Associations In Your Community

Your first step is to inventory the associations within your community that would most likely support your work. You are developing a prospect list, just as you would with foundations. Look for logical allies as well as less apparent ones. The yellow pages of your local phone book list local associations under Service Organizations. Review the results of your circles exercise from Chapter 7. What kinds of organizations might some of your prime constituencies belong to? Which professional bodies? Religiously oriented groups? Civic associations? Women's organizations? Labor unions? Social welfare societies?

By thinking through who your individual supporters are and what their professional and personal interests are, you'll begin to have a sense of which associations will support your work.

Also, assess your organization's immediate clients, constituents, and recipients of services. What kinds of clubs, groups, or associations do they belong to? For example, starting in the mid-1970s many committees for occupational safety and health ("COSHs") formed around the country to educate industrial workers and others about health and safety hazards in the workplace and to advocate more stringent governmental protection measures. Since their most immediate constituents were workers themselves, they logically turned to labor unions for support, advice, encouragement, and even funding.

The work of groups such as New York Committee on Occupational Safety and Health (NYCOSH) and Philadelphia Area Project on Occupational Safety and Health (PHILAPOSH) proved to be of immediate and long-standing interest to concerned unions in their respective cities.

• Your elected officials are in a good position to know which associations in their districts might be responsive to your issue. After all, their staff spends much of its time doing constituent work, responding to inquiries, requests, and positions put forth by a wide array of local groups. You could benefit in your prospecting by speaking to staff members in the district offices of your city, state, and federally elected officials.

Several excellent reference works on nationally oriented associations also exist to guide the uninitiated. See the "Further Readings" section for this chapter and look for the works listed in your public library.

After brainstorming with your staff, board, or organizing committee, speaking to staff of friendly elected officials, and checking some of the available reference materials, you should be able to develop a fairly solid prospect list of five to fifteen local associations worthy of exploration.

Step 2. Making the Actual Approach

Associations are generally less formal in conducting their affairs than are other institutions. You can approach them initially by placing a phone call to a member of an association whom you already know or to an officer.

Introduce yourself and explain that you are seeking the opportunity to address the members of the _____ Association to elicit support for your organization's work. Suggest that you would be most willing to meet to discuss your work with officers of the association so that they will be able to gauge whether their members would be interested in learning more about the problems that your organization tackles. Don't hesitate to bring one or two others to the initial exploratory meeting. Also, bring some organizational literature with you, such as pamphlets, brochures, and newsletters.

Step 3. Conducting the Meeting

Your goal is to get the members of an association involved through their understanding of the particular problems your organization works on. By virtue of your work, you are an authoritative source of information on certain issues. You will need to articulate why any civic-minded group would have an interest in those problems and their resolution. You are building a case on the basis of mutually understood concerns. Your role is to educate your listeners about the extent of the problem, the needed resolution, and the work of your organization.

If your listener has been receptive to your story, you can then seek out a wider audience with the association's membership. Inquire how you can best proceed to let others within the local association learn about your work. Are there regular meetings that you can address? If the association is a chapter of a statewide or a national body, are there conferences or conventions that other chapters also attend? Seek out the advice of the officers whom you are visiting on how best to proceed. Be clear about the types of assistance your organization would benefit from. With luck, you will have won over the audience of your first presentation to the degree that it will be willing to help you approach its organization for assistance.

Step 4. Addressing the Association's Membership

You've secured an opportunity to make your case to the membership of an association at its regular meeting. Congratulations! How can you make the most effective presentation?

Nothing better enhances the quality of a speech than visual aids. Do you have any slide shows, charts, or photographs you can use to illustrate your comments? If by chance you are an excellent artist, you might even illustrate your comments on a blackboard or flip-chart paper as you proceed. You could also recruit the services of a graphic artist to prepare some visuals to accompany your remarks. If you are anticipating making a number of presentations in the course of a year, such an investment will serve you many times over.

In your prepared comments, be ready to tell your audience how, as members of the association and as individuals, it can assist your work. In essence, a presentation has three components:

1. Vivid description of a problem and how it bears on the lives of your constituents and your listeners as well, if that is appropriate.

2. Illustration of how your organization is tackling this particular problem.

3. Statement of how your audience can help you reduce the incidence of or lessen the consequences of that particular problem (i.e., providing you with funds or volunteers, adding its voice to a lobbying effort you might be engaged in, etc.).

Leave your listeners with the opportunity to pose questions, and thank them for the opportunity to address their group. If your audience has been receptive to your remarks, offer to return the following year to give them an update on your progress.

Step. 5. Follow-Up

An association may thank you for your speech by awarding you a speaker's honorarium. You, of course, can also use the opportunity to solicit membership and contributions. Be sure to bring appropriate literature to distribute.

You should thank your host in a follow-up letter that acknowledges the support and states how the contributions will be put to use. The association's potential further involvement in your work will be enhanced if you demonstrate to what specific end you have put their monies. You might earmark the contribution for a program that seemed to capture its interests the most during the course of your presentation. Generally, this course of action is wiser in the long run than is designating the contributions for general use.

If you have not been offered any financial stipend for your presentation, you can request a contribution in your follow-up letter. Also, if the experience has proven fruitful, you can inquire about other chapters or associations that your hosts might suggest you approach. If the association has an active local philanthropic program or belongs to a national body that does, you can also inquire how you might qualify for further support.

Be sure to add your official host and the association itself to your mailing list, so they will receive newsletters, ongoing membership appeals, and invitations to any special events or open houses you might sponsor in the future. As is the case with religious leaders, you are initiating a relationship that you hope will serve your organization for a long time to come.

SUMMARY

Reaching out to associations deepens your support base in your own community, as well as providing you with concrete assistance. You have enlarged your reservoir of potential allies to turn to when the occasion calls for a show of support. Addressing their membership meetings also provides you with the opportunity to sharpen your public speaking skills and those of your board and staff members. While the financial rewards might be limited, the returns in enhanced people power and in strong political clout are incalculable.

Case Study
THE STRONG CHILDREN'S MEDICAL CENTER: BUILDING STRENGTH FOR STRONG CHILDREN

Strong Pediatrics, the children's division of the University of Rochester Medical Center, received permission from the University of Rochester's Board of Trustees in late 1983 to raise funds independently. We hoped this decision would assure the continuance of quality health care for the children and families from Rochester and the Finger Lakes region of New York State who came to this tertiary care center for medical treatment.

In January 1984, we decided to participate in a national telethon that raised funds for children's hospitals and medical centers across the nation. The Children's Miracle Network Telethon was unique because all of the funds that would be raised locally would remain local, benefitting Strong Pediatrics. [As of January 1, 1985, Strong Pediatrics, the chidren's division of the University of Rochester, has changed its name to the Strong Children's Medical Center.]

With less than four months lead time, a small but grateful patient-donor corps, and a mandate from the University that said we could not approach past corporate and individual University donors, we needed to develop a fundraising vehicle to create awareness, enlarge our donor base, and assure the Telethon's success.

With assistance from our newly created Advisory Board, composed of health professionals and community leaders, we approached the Rochester Home Builders' Association (RHBA). This prosperous organization of builders and suppliers was celebrating its 50th anniversary in our community. Although it appeared to have had little past involvement with local charities, we felt that they might be interested in the publicity we could generate for them.

We proposed that they construct a home at their annual "Homearama" home show, installing safety features for "kids of all ages." It was our hope that, in addition to focusing on the importance and ease of safety installations, the RHBA would consider donating a portion of the proceeds from the sale of the home to the Strong Children's Miracle Telethon.

In mid-May, two weeks before the Telethon (June 1 and 2, 1984), we were informed that the RHBA membership had accepted our proposal and had committed to making a contribution of at least $30,000 to us, dependent on the sale of the home that they had yet to construct.

They resolved that they would construct and display a model house at their Homearama show in September, which would be known as "Sandy's House" (named for the poster child of Strong Pediatrics). They offered to contribute the net proceeds from the sale of the home to Strong Pediatrics.

FUNDRAISING GOAL

The Rochester Home Builders' Association felt that they could solicit donations of labor and materials from their membership in order to keep the costs of the actual construction down. The home that they decided to build would sell in the $150,000 range.

The RHBA took on the following tasks in its role in our fundraising project:

- Purchase a lot for the construction of the home.

- Obtain a building loan up to the sum of $100,000 for the acquisition, construction, and furnishings.

- Enter into all necessary contracts to construct and furnish Sandy's House.

- Arrange for the sale of such a house and carry out the foregoing resolution.

We at Strong Pediatrics would do the following:

- Develop a logo for this project using the cartoon poster child, Sandy Strong.

- Highlight the donation from the RHBA during the local segment of the national Telethon.

- Send representatives from the RHBA to the national Telethon in Utah in order to publicize this creative fundraising project on the national Telethon.

- Staff the display home with volunteers during the three-week exhibit.

The groundbreaking for Sandy's House took place on May 24, 1984. A press conference was held, and one week later, during the Telethon, the $30,000 pledge assured the Telethon's success. Dr. Ruth Lawrence, an associate professor of pediatrics at the University of Rochester Medical Center and a nationally recognized authority on child safety, worked with the architects from the RHBA to ensure the installation of appropriate safety features. The RHBA appealed to its membership for contributors and was overwhelmed with the response.

Homearama opened on September 7, 1985. Faculty, staff, and volunteers from Strong Pediatrics attended the opening and assumed responsibility for "housesitting" throughout the three-week exhibit. During this period, more than 30,000 individuals visited Sandy's House. Each received a special edition newsletter discussing the safety features, the generous contributors, and Strong Pediatrics. Visitors' names were collected by holding a drawing for a television set and a trip, both donated by local businesses. These names formed the basis for our prospect list. (We collected 10,000 names for mailing; these individuals have recently received a direct-mail piece, encouraging them to become new donors to the Strong Children's Medical Center.)

Sandy's House sold for $149,000. Because of the response from builders and suppliers, the Rochester Home Builders' Association was able to present the Strong Children's Fund with a gift of $50,000, $20,000 over their pledged amount.

RESULTS

The RHBA helped turn the dreams of Strong Pediatrics into reality. The project was successful because we enlisted the help of our Advisory Board members, who played a strategic role in involving the RHBA; because we found an organization that could benefit from positive exposure; and because the RHBA ultimately felt good about making an investment in their community's future.

Thus, "Building Strength for Strong Children" succeeded in a more positive fashion than we ever envisioned and developed a prototype fundraiser that builders across the nation could utilize to benefit their favorite local charity.

by Brenda Babitz

Source: This article appeared in the May/June 1985 issue of *The Grantsmanship Center News.* Copyright © 1985 The Grantsmanship Center, Los Angeles, CA. Reprinted with permission.
Source: Logo, The Strong Children's Medical Center, University of Rochester, Rochester, NY. Reprinted with permission.

Summary Worksheet

for

_____

(name of your organization)

APPROACHING ASSOCIATIONS OF INDIVIDUALS FOR SUPPORT

1. Building on Past Association Support

a. Have any associations ever supported your work in the past?

☐ yes   ☐ no

b. If yes, which ones? How?

_____   _____

_____   _____

_____   _____

_____   _____

c. What characteristics do these associations share? How do their interests correspond to each other?

Comments:

_____

_____

_____

_____

d. What is _your_ sense of what they valued in your organization's work?

Comments:

_____

_____

_____

_____

e. Which ones can you reapproach for future support?

| | Untested |
| Definite Ongoing Projects: | (Further Information Needed) |

_____   _____

_____   _____

_____   _____

2. Finding New Association Supporters:
Research and Networking

Using reference materials at your local library, such as the ones listed in the Further Readings for this chapter, list some associations that could be prospective supporters of your work.

_____   _____

_____   _____

_____   _____

3. What are some of the reasons that would attract such associations to your work?

_____

_____

_____

_____

4. See pages 392 and 393 for this part of the worksheet.

5. Making the Match

For each prospect on the previous list, complete the following worksheet (use your own blank paper).

Name of Association:

Its Stated Areas of Interest that Pertain to your Work
(draw from printed literature, informal conversations, news clippings, etc.):

Write one or more short sentences demonstrating how the work of your organization reflects the interests of X association.

6. Finding Assistance and Counsel

Name 5 or more individuals who might be able to advise you on how to most effectively approach the associations on your "best bets" list:

a. _____

b. _____

c. _____

d. _____

e. _____

7. Addressing the Likelihood of Securing Support from Associations

On the basis of what you have learned, how would you rank your chances of securing support from associations?

☐ Very Good   ☐ Possible   ☐ Unlikely   ☐ Still Unknown

4. List below the association prospects you have uncovered from your research and your networking. Limit your listing to the most likely supporters of your organization.

a. Type of Association	**b.** Its Stated Areas of Interest that Relate to Your Work	**c.** Appropriate Contact Person, Address, and Telephone Number
Neighborhood or Community-Based		
Citywide		
National		

d. Personal Contacts	**e.** Your Program(s) that Correspond to Its Interest	**f.** Type and Amount of Support Available

FURTHER READINGS

Close, Arthur C., and Judy Curtis, eds. *Washington Representatives <Year>*. Washington, DC: Columbia Books, Inc. Annual. Approximately 650 pp. $45.00. (Order from: Columbia Books, 777 14th St., N.W., No. 236, Washington, DC 20005)

> Directory of over 9000 individuals and law or public relations firms registered as lobbyists or foreign agents who are representatives in Washington for companies, associations, labor unions, or special interest groups. For individuals, includes name, title, address and phone. For organizations, lists name, headquarters, and names of representatives.

Encyclopedia of Associations. Detroit, MI: Gale Research Co. Biennial. Approx. 1935 pp. 4 volumes. $170.00. (Order from: Gale Research Co., Book Tower, Detroit, MI 48226)

> Directory of institutional and professional associations. Volume 1 provides detailed information on over 19,000 nonprofit member organizations of the U.S. divided by such broad categories as trade, business, and commercial; legal and governmental; educational; and cultural. It is indexed by name and key word. Volume 2 includes geographic and executive indexes. Volume 3 is issued between editions and lists new associations and projects. Volume 4 covers international organizations.

Felmley, Jenrose. *Directory of National Women's Organizations*. Chicago: Allstate Insurance Co. and Sears, Roebuck and Co. 1985. 30 pp. $19.95. (Order from: American Association of University Women, 2401 Virginia Ave., N.W., Washington, DC 20037)

> Listing of nearly 300 women's organizations including those involved in career planning, civil rights, employment, and philanthropy. Indexed by organization name, geography, and subject.

Guide to Black Organizations, A. New York: Philip Morris U.S.A. 1984. 98 pp. Free. (Order from: Philip Morris U.S.A., Public Affairs Department, 120 Park Ave., New York, NY 10017)

> Alphabetical list of approximately 140 Black organizations including organization name, address, phone number, names of officers, purpose, activities, and publications.

Guide to Hispanic Organizations. New York: Philip Morris U.S.A. 1985. Free. (Order from: Philip Morris U.S.A., Public Affairs Department, 120 Park Ave,. New York, NY 10017)

> Lists 131 nonprofit national, regional and local Hispanic organizations which conduct programs ranging from career counseling to adult education to voter registration drives.

National Avocational Organizations Directory. Washington, DC: Columbia Books, Inc. Annual. Approx. 136 pp. $30.00. (Order from: Columbia Books, Inc., 1350 New York Ave., N.W., Washington, DC 20006)

Directory of cultural, ethnic, fraternal, and civic organizations. Information includes address and phone number, staff, budget, publications, convention plans, and descriptive historic note.

National Trade and Professional Associations of the United States. Washington, DC: Columbia Books, Inc. Annual. Approximately 425 pp. $45.00. (Order from: Columbia Books, Inc., 777 14th St., N.W., No. 236, Washington, DC 20005)
Listings for 6000 associations including name, year established, chief executive, address, phone, number of members, budget, annual meeting, publications, and historical data.

Washington <Year>. Washington, DC: Columbia Books, Inc. Annual. Approximately 500 pp. $40.00. (Order from: Columbia Books, 777 14th St., N.W., No. 236, Washington, DC 20005)
Lists over 300 federal and district government offices, business associations, publications, etc. in the Washington, DC area. Arrangement is by subject or government agency.

DEVELOPING YOUR OVERALL FUNDRAISING PLAN

CHAPTER 19

CHOOSING YOUR FUNDING MIX AND THE STRATEGIES TO SECURE IT

Section 1 outlined the tasks that must be completed before you can successfully embark on your fundraising. To summarize, completion of tasks such as program planning and budgeting ensures both to the organization and to others that the nonprofit undertaking has put its house in order before appealing to others for support. Your prospective supporters need to see evidence of your capabilities. Blind faith, at best, elicits short-term support. On the other hand, demonstrated capability engenders lasting confidence.

Sections 1 and 2 prepared you to venture into the world of philanthropy. As outlined, you will immediately be faced with a variety of financial sources to choose from and key questions to answer such as: Which of the many institutional sources described in Section 2 are most appropriate for your organization? Should you put your energies into pursuing government grants and contracts, for example? Or toward obtaining a grant from the local community foundation? Or both? How can you best proceed to develop an individual membership base? Which approaches to individuals will net the greatest return (face-to-face solicitation, direct mail, special events)?

As has been stressed, you are looking for the most likely *mix* of appropriate sources. You are looking not for one source of revenue but rather for a number of prospects most interested in your work.

Envision your funding as a multilegged stool. If one leg is removed, the stool will continue to stand. In the same sense, that's how the funding base for your organization should work, each of its legs supplying a different major source of revenue for your organization. If, for whatever reasons, one source ceases to exist, your organization will become slightly handicapped but will nonetheless be able to persevere on the basis of income from other sources. The stool will continue to stand.

Thus, an organization totally dependent on federal grants and contracts for its revenues is extremely vulnerable, while another group that receives support also from foundations, a fundraising federation, and a pool of individuals, in addition to the federal government, is clearly stronger and more secure.

Section 2 provided an introduction to the world of money available to nonprofits. It showed how to secure support most effectively from any of the sources enumerated, and how to decide which are most appropriate to your own situation.

You still need to answer the following questions: How can you choose your own mix to build a strong multilegged financial base for your own organization? How can you best develop a fundraising strategy that will succeed? What is the best way to plan your fundraising work?

Section 3 provides you with a blueprint for planning and implementing efforts to secure financial support. The ten phases of this process are summarized below and then discussed in detail.

Phase 1. *Taking Stock of Your Strengths and Assets.* What can you bring to the funders' table? What do you have to offer in exchange for the dollars you wish to receive?

Fundraising, in its finest sense, is a collaboration among different parties that are moved to act on the same set of concerns.

Phase 1 enables the leaders of both old and new efforts to take an inventory of their assets and strengths, thereby increasing their awareness of the assets they bring to a collaboration.

Phase 2. *Choosing Funding Partners.* As Section 2 showed, there are numerous potential stakeholders out there to choose from. The task before you is to select from among these stakeholders those who will become your most committed partners.

Phase 2 provides you with the opportunity to gather all the answers to the questionnaires at the end of Chapters 8 through 18 and to select the most appropriate list of partners for your organization.

Phase 3. *Setting Fundraising Goals.* How can you present your financial needs to your supporters? How much should you ask your prospective partners for?

Phase 3 builds on program planning and budgeting work (see Chapters 4 and 5) to help you effectively set fundraising goals that will elicit positive responses from your prospective supporters.

Phase 4. *Developing a Strategy to Secure Support from Individuals.* It is a truism that individuals always serve as the most consistent supporters of nonprofit organizations. Their dollars are both reliable and renewable.

Chapters 8 through 12 presented some popular methods for gaining support from individuals. Phase 4 shows you how to identify your most likely individual backers and how to proceed to secure their ongoing support.

Phase 5. *Developing a Strategy to Secure Support from Institutions.* The world of institutional support is vast and potentially intimidating. Institutions represent the corporate interests of their boards of directors, their members, and their constituents. These interests comprise separate cultures, each with their own rules and regulations.

Chapters 13 through 18 showed how these various prospective stakeholders operate and how you can match up your own efforts with their priorities.

Phase 5 outlines a procedure for identifying the institutions most likely to support your work and explains how to successfully elicit their support.

Phase 6. *Making the Case.* A script can often aid you in asking others for support. The writing exercises presented in Phase 6 will enable you to organize your information coherently and will help you in making oral presentations. Your work on this phase will be eased by the amount of time you spent in developing a statement of purpose (Chapter 1) and the depth of analysis you achieved during Phase 1 ("Taking Stock of Your Strengths and Assets"). When you have completed Phases 4 and 5, you will have determined also the audiences for your fully developed materials.

Phase 7. *Preparing the Final Fundraising Plan and Calendar.* The research and preparation stages of your fundraising are now drawing to a close. You will have chosen your most likely sources of support and developed the materials you need to approach them.

It is now time to organize the tasks and activities before you. Place them on a work calendar to provide yourself a blueprint of action for the upcoming year.

Phase 8. *Making the Approach.* The style of your presentation influences the outcome of your appeal for support. Although your program may be well thought out and you may have chosen your prospects with careful discrimination, your fundraising efforts may nonetheless falter with the wrong approach.

Phase 6, "Making the Case," will have provided solicitors with the necessary background to representing your organization's work. Chapters 8 through 18 offer detailed suggestions for approaching particular individual and institutional supporters. Phase 8 guides you through the asking process.

Phase 9. *Building the Relationship with Your Supporters.* Securing funding from any particular source, individual or institution, can be the first stage of a long-term collegial and professional relationship. You can choose to nurture that incipient relationship, or, unwisely, to ignore it. This phase discusses how you can sustain and strengthen your supporters' interest and involvement in your work.

Phase 10. *Monitoring and Evaluating Your Fundraising Efforts: Laying the Groundwork for Next Year.* Your efforts to secure funds will benefit immensely from ongoing monitoring and evaluation. After all, your own experiences provide the best data about what does and does not work.

Phase 10 offers guidance on monitoring and evaluating your fundraising activities to ensure your overall success.

The planning process outlined in these ten phases is cyclical and ongoing. Different events and outcomes (e.g., a rejection letter or unforeseen revenues) may cause you to return to a previous phase.

PHASE 1: TAKING STOCK OF YOUR STRENGTHS AND ASSETS

The purpose of Phase 1 is to take stock of your organizational assets and strengths. By doing so, you put yourself in the best position to build a strong case for support to prospective funders.

Why should taking stock of your strengths and assets be so important? Simply because we are often so busy doing the work of our organization that we fail to pay sufficient attention to what makes us unique. Yet, it is those very attributes that frequently lead to new support from individuals and institutions who were previously unfamiliar with our work.

Where do you look for your assets and strengths? Every existing organization has a history and a reputation. Its past probably reveals successes, accomplishments, and some false starts as well. An organization's history is a treasure trove of assets that may readily be converted into credentials—and credentials are important. It is not enough simply to state the problem and your group's plan to deal with it. Such statements, while they may elicit some support, are abstract; you need, in addition, to demonstrate precisely how your organization is qualified both to address this problem and to make genuine headway toward solving it.

Don't despair, however, if your organization is new. You still have the personal histories of all the people involved with your beginning effort, and part of those histories will surely illustrate past ability to create beneficial change. Your core group members have earned a reputation on their own or by working for other organizations or both. Thus, you should begin by searching their professional and personal histories for evidence of the qualifications you need to show others to establish credibility.

In short, you are pinpointing your organization's capabilities. You can then illustrate your effectiveness to the outside world and give both new and old prospective funders good reason to believe in you.

To sum up, both young and old organizations need to take a careful inventory of their past histories to retrieve and select the qualities that can build a persuasive case for support. These qualities will provide the information necessary for foundation proposals, direct mail appeals, and any other approach for funding that you may consider.

What are these qualities? Any tangible evidence, past or present, that illustrates both your individual and organizational competency as it relates to the problems and responding programs that define the purpose of your work.

The following worksheet is designed to help you take stock.

Worksheet
TAKING STOCK OF YOUR
STRENGTHS AND WEAKNESSES
Program History

1. What projects or programs has your organization successfully implemented?

A. _____ _____ (year)

B. _____ _____ (year)

C. _____ _____ (year)

D. _____ _____ (year)

2. Explain why these efforts succeeded. What changes did they effect?

A. _____ Results: _____

_____ _____

_____ _____

B. _____ Results: _____

_____ _____

_____ _____

C. _____ Results: _____

_____ _____

_____ _____

D. _____ Results: _____

_____ _____

_____ _____

3. What skills and abilities enabled you to succeed in these efforts (personal or organizational or both)?

_____

_____

_____

_____

_____

_____

4. In what ways can you show external evidence of success in your past work?

A. Statistics: _____

_____

_____

B. Letters of appreciation: _____

_____

_____

C. Assessments by outside bodies: (i. e. funders, government agencies, professional associations, etc.): _____

_____

_____

D. Media Coverage:
(i.e. articles in local and national newspapers and magazines, television and radio coverage, etc.) _____

_____

_____

E. Miscellaneous: _____

_____

_____

Board and Staff History

5. What are the qualifications of your past and current board members and staff?

Board   *Staff*

_____   _____

_____   _____

_____   _____

6. What commendations have they received in recognition of their talents and contributions?

Board   *Staff*

_____   _____

_____   _____

_____   _____

7. How would you describe their most unique abilities?

Board   *Staff*

_____   _____

_____   _____

_____   _____

Organizational History

8. How long has your organization been in existence?

_____ Brand New _____ Years Old

9. What distinguishes your past work from other similar organizations? In which explicit ways are you unique?

_____

_____

_____

_____

10. What recognition has your organization as a whole received since its inception? (i.e. invitations to speak at conferences, workshops, public rallies, legislative hearings, etc.; certificates of commendation; quotations in scholarly or popular journals and magazines, etc.; letters of appreciation; etc.)

_____

_____

_____

_____

Funding History

11. What kinds of institutions have supported your work in the past? Who are they?

A. Foundations:

_____

B. Corporations:

_____

C. Religious sources:

_____

D. Associations of individuals:

_____

F. Other:

_____

12. How many individuals pay dues, make contributions, or do both to support your work? What percentage renew their support to you each year?

_____

13. How diversified is your financial base (i.e. how many different sources extend support to you? And what percentages of your total income do they comprise?

14. What reports do you file annually with your State government to satisfy their requirements for nonprofit organizations.?

_____

You are welcome to add your own questions to this list. It is only one means to help you collect the specific information to best illustrate how and why you are qualified to undertake your program.

Please note: When demonstrating support from third parties, it's important to distinguish between *endorsements* and *observations*. Endorsements are "rhetorical salutes," which are not necessarily the best substantiation of your expertise. Thoughtful observations, on the other hand, provide useful commentaries on your work.

A nonprofit organization should always maintain a specific *credibility file* for gathering this information on a steady basis. Staff and board members should do the same for their own use, as well as for the organization's. Such files simplify fundraising tasks—from making a personal solicitation of a donor to interesting a local business in extending support to your work. Moreover, this information is also excellent for use in promotional materials, such as brochures, annual reports, and press releases.

PHASE 2. CHOOSING FUNDING PARTNERS

Fundraising, in its best sense, represents collaboration between a nonprofit organization and a group of financial backers. Just as a bank underwrites a business, so do individuals, foundations, government, corporations, and the other sources presented in Section 2 underwrite the expenses of a nonprofit. The bank looks for a strict financial return on its investment; financial partners seek a different type of return. They want to see the concrete changes in the world, as projected by the nonprofit's mission, objectives, and program plans. Selecting these financial partners can be a time-consuming pursuit unless you are methodical.

Let's amass the results of the worksheets that accompanied each chapter in Section 2. Use the following worksheet to gather the pertinent information you developed from your review of those chapters.

In cases where you can be more specific in enumerating your prospects, go ahead and do so. If you know, for example, that your local community foundation is a solid prospect but that other foundations are not, place that particular foundation in the "very good" column. Be as specific as your information permits.

Worksheet
SELECTING PROSPECTIVE FUNDING PARTNERS IN YOUR NONPROFIT ENDEAVOR

Sources	Assessing Chances of Support			
	Very Good	Possible	Unlikely	Still Unknown

1. Individuals via:

a. Face-to-face Solicitation

b. Direct Mail

c. Special Events

d. Planned Giving

e. Earned or Venture Income Projects

f. Other:

2. Foundations

a. Family Foundations

b. Community Foundations

c. Other Local Foundations

d. Local Public Charities

e. National Foundations

3. Business and Corporations

a. Neighborhood Stores

b. Banks, Utility Companies, Department Stores, etc.

c. Corporations with Headquarters or Facilities in your Community

d. Large National Corporations

WORKSHEET
SELECTING PROSPECTIVE FUNDING PARTNERS IN YOUR NONPROFIT ENDEAVOR

Sources	Assessing Chances of Support			
	Very Good	Possible	Unilkely	Still Unknown

4. Government
  (grants and contracts)

a. Local Government
  Units:

b. State Government
  Units:

c. Federal Government
  Units:

5. Religious Institutions

a. Individual Churches,
  Temples, and other
  Faith Communities

b. Metropolitan and Regional
  Religious Bodies

c. Metropolitan and Regional
  Ecumenical Bodies

d. Religious Federated
  Organizations

e. National Religious Bodies

**6. Federated Fundraising
  Organizations**

a. United Way

b. Other Community Chests

c. Alternative Funds

**7. Associations of
  Individuals**

a. Neighborhood or
  Community-based
  Associations

b. Citywide Associations

c. National Associations

Completing this worksheet will help you identify your strongest potential supporters, those who are capable of and willing to support your work at some level.

Historically, many nonprofit leaders have engaged in "stop-and-go" fundraising, in which one particular type of funding, such as foundation or government, is obtained and used exclusively until it is exhausted. At that point, the search for a replacement source begins anew. What is being suggested here is that you pinpoint *in advance* your entire array of partners before you charge off in pursuit of just one on your prospect list.

The following procedure will help you visualize your specific range of supporters by transposing your responses onto the archery target below. Place your *best* prospects in the bull's-eye, your remaining *possible* sources in the second circle of the target, and your *unlikely* possibilities in the outer circle. Finally, place the funding sources whose ability and willingness to support your work has yet to be ascertained outside the target on your list of *unknowns*.

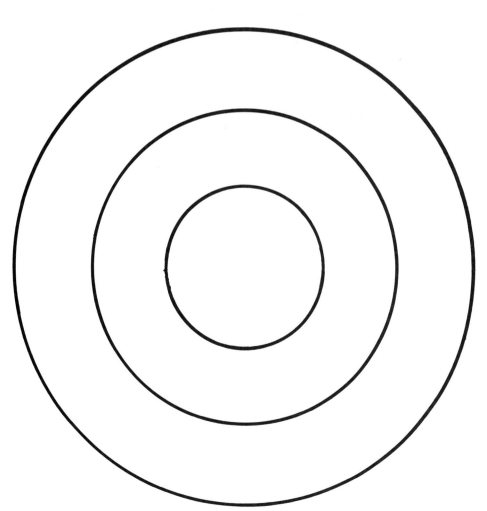

Remember that as you complete your information-gathering steps, through research and networking, you will be able to move sources from your unknown list into the target. Don't try to limit your choices at this stage by the actual amount of funds that a source can potentially provide. You are more interested here in isolating the particular mix of funding sources, those who, in principle, are your most likely partners.

You have "ranked" your prospective funders through the exercises outlined in this phase. In lieu of "stop and go" fundraising, you can now begin to look comprehensively at your best bets list (those in the bull's-eye). From all your information gathering, you should now answer some questions about these prospects.

- What is the level of potential support they can provide?

- How good is your access to individuals in a decision-making capacity?

- Which sources appear to have the potential for significant long-term support?

- How much time and up-front expenditure of human and financial capital is need to tap into these particular sources?

By answering these often hard questions, you are making your forthcoming fundraising activity more targeted and potentially more successful. Use the earlier worksheet to gather your responses. Certain patterns will emerge as a result of analyzing the information put forth on this worksheet.

For example, neighborhood and grassroots groups will probably find that individual residents of their own communities are their easiest target. Arts organizations will find that their initial universe is broader, since they have programs that likely transcend any one community. Citywide advocacy and public interest nonprofits may find more institutional prospects on their list of top prospects. Be sure to trust your own experience and knowledge, for each and every nonprofit organization is trailblazing its own path when its leadership sets out in search of support.

Keep in mind that your future is best secured by tapping into a mix of sources now, so let's turn our attention to matching our prospects with our specific fundraising needs.

PHASE 3. SETTING FUNDRAISING GOALS

Any fundraising effort must be directed toward a set of clearly stated financial goals. You need to set in advance the total amount of money you want to raise within a given timeframe. Your program planning and budgeting work (see Chapters 4 and 5) enables you to "cost out" your work, so you can develop fundraising goals.

How can you translate these dollar amounts into the fundraising goals that are essential for every fundraising activity? You should be able to tell your prospects exactly what they are contributing toward, just as you need to include a budget in a foundation proposal that outlines the ways in which you plan to spend the requested funds.

Your budgeting exercises provide the raw data for ascribing a dollar value either to the entire work of your organization or to its specific projects. On the strength of your projected specific expenses, then, you can set the sum you need to raise. That sum becomes your overall goal.

Setting fundraising goals is important for two reasons: (1) It motivates individuals to give. Just as program objectives encourage people to work harder to achieve success, a fundraising goal inspires your constituents to give and to keep giving until you have pushed your organization over the top—that is, reached your destination: the projected amount required for carrying out your programs for a year or for undertaking a special effort. (2) Internally, setting fundraising objectives enables you to estimate how much money you must raise to support your activities and, subsequently, to compare that amount to what in fact is available from your prospective funders.

In this sense, budgeting and fundraising go hand in hand. Without a comprehensive sense of how much money an organization plans to expend, it cannot possibly project realistic fundraising goals. At the same time, unless an organization raises all the money it considers necessary to support its year's activities, the budget has to be reduced accordingly. One informs the other.

Your organization can set fundraising goals in three ways:

1. Set the total sum of monies you need to raise in a given year in order to carry out the programs you hope to implement, as well as to cover the administrative costs implicit in those programs.

2. Set the total sum of monies you need in order to implement a particular project, such as constructing a new building or purchasing a computer.

3. Ascribe a dollar amount to a service or program (i.e., a "unit of service") your organization performs.

You can draw on one or all of these methods to assist you in your fundraising work. Let's examine each of these methods to determine how it can best serve your organization.

Setting Your Annual Fundraising Goal

By completing the budgeting process outlined in Chapter 5, you will be able to determine your total anticipated expenditures for personnel and non-personnel items for the upcoming year. The total of that organizational budget (sample worksheet, page 68) is the total amount you need to raise to underwrite your projected activities. With that in mind, you can embark on a community-wide drive to elicit contributions that will equal that desired sum, or you can design a strategy by which a mix of funding sources will provide that total.

For example, a neighborhood day care center projects its total annual costs at $50,000, to cover the salary of its staff, rent, utilities, and other ancillary expenses. Since it receives close to $30,000 in fees from parents who utilize the center, the organization may decide to set a fundraising goal of $20,000 for the year.

Chart A

Total Anticipated Expenses for the Year	$ _____
Minus	
Anticipated Income from Program Fees	$ _____
Equals	
Annual Fundraising Campaign Total	$ _____

Setting Program Fundraising Goals

Just as you have budgeted all the expenditures included in your organization's entire operating costs, so can you assess those expenses inherent in any particular project or program (see sample worksheet on page 70). For example, if a group wishes to create an information and referral program for the public on consumer issues, it can cost out the equipment (computer and accompanying software) as well as the salaries of the necessary personnel needed to implement this public information program.

Chart B

Total Projected Expenses for X Project	$ _____
Minus	
Donated, or In-kind Services	$ _____
Equals	
Program Fundraising Goal	$ _____

Setting Unit of Service Fundraising Goals

Review your programs to determine whether you provide any services that might have inherent interest to prospective donors that you could quantify. Likely candidates include direct-service programs and capital expenditures (such as purchase of buildings, vehicles, and computers). Less attractive are programs that affect only one's administrative capacities, such as upgrading filing systems, renovating offices, increasing salaries, or purchasing a new duplicating machine.

For example, a rape crisis center counselor can report assisting ten individuals every week to regain a sense of well-being and dignity after an assault. Since there are five counselors who work full-time, seeing an average of ten victims each week, the center can report that it assists 2,600 individuals each year (5 counselors × 10 clients × 52 weeks = 2,600 cases).

By dividing the organization's entire annual budget by the number of client interventions, you can ascertain the cost of assistance to one individual.

Continuing with the example of the rape crisis center, let's presume that its annual operating budget is $100,000. Its cost for assistance to one individual (unit of service cost) is approximately $38.50 ($100,000 ÷ 2,600 clients = $38.46).

This example presumes, of course, that rape crisis counseling is the only program activity of the center. If, however, there are other programs, such as training hospital emergency-room personnel to work effectively with rape victims or training police officials to counsel women immediately on the scene, the formula for determining the unit of service cost changes.

In such instances you would determine the total direct costs of the counseling program and add a percentage of the indirect administrative expenses that correspond to the ratio of that program to the entire programmatic budget of the center. In other words, if the counseling program costs $50,000 and the training program costs a total of $25,000, the percentage of administrative costs attached to the counseling program would be two times more than the costs attached to the training program. If the administrative costs total $25,000, then two-thirds of that cost can be associated with the counseling program ($16,666.67) and one-third with the training program ($8,333,33).

Using Your Fundraising Goals

As previously mentioned, a nonprofit may use any or all of the three different fundraising goals to serve its purposes. Depending on the audience and the occasion, simply choose the type of goalsetting that best suits your needs.

For example, if you are looking for a goal for a special event, you might choose a program goal. If you are looking for a goal for your entire year's fundraising efforts to put in your campaign literature, you would choose your annual fundraising goal. If you are looking for a goal for a direct mail appeal, you could easily select a unit-of-service fundraising goal.

During the course of a year's fundraising activities, you will no doubt use all three goals. Let's examine how the hypothetical rape crisis center uses these goals in its efforts to generate funds and support.

In September, the rape crisis center announces its annual campaign to raise $100,000 to provide desperately needed services during the upcoming year. As one of its first outreach efforts, the center sends out a direct mail appeal to its past supporters, asking for contributions of $38.50. The appeal says, "One gift of $38.50 will enable one rape victim to receive valuable assistance this year," or "a contribution of $38.50 will enable us to assist one individual regain a sense of well-being."

The center may go one step further and confer on those who respond to the appeal a special title of membership, such as "angels," "supporters," "patrons," "benefactors," or "sponsors." (The exact word chosen to bestow on your supporters, by the way, need not come from this conventional list. You are free to use terms that may convey more of the personal flavor of your work or of your values.)

The rape crisis center has prepared a special appeal that will go to contributors who have given them more than $100 in the past. In this direct mail appeal, the center decides to use some variation of the unit-of-service approach to encourage their larger donors to make gifts at certain levels. For example, the appeal might read as follows:

Membership can take many forms.

We are conducting our annual effort to provide rape crisis services to the thousands who are sexually assaulted in our city each year. You can help by making a contribution to our annual drive.

- If you make a gift of $100, we will be able to assist three individuals this year;
- If you pledge $38.50 each month (a total of $462.00 for the year), we will be able to assist one person each month, and a total of twelve during the year!!
- If you can make an outright gift of $1,000, we will be able this year to help 25 people who turn to us out of desperation and fear for sensitive help and support.

In its approaches to foundations and corporations, the center makes greater use of its program-related fundraising goals as part of its proposals to these prospects. For example, it may decide to approach the local community foundation for a grant of $17,000 to set up a pilot counseling program directly on-site in the emergency room of the major municipal hospital. It may also decide to approach a local corporation for a grant of $12,000 to underwrite the costs of a subway and bus poster campaign announcing the crisis center's hotline number and some of the services it provides.

In each of these examples, the staff and fundraising volunteers and board members of the rape crisis center have targeted their prospective audience of funders with requests tailored to their respective abilities to give.

Your audience of supporters is not homogeneous. It includes individuals and institutions, all with varying abilities to support your work. You are responsible for setting their sights on the amount to give. Putting it bluntly, people usually give what they are asked. So you should make your requests for specific amounts. Through all of these methods—annual goals, program goals, unit-of-service goals—you are defining for your potential supporters the levels of assistance that you need and the *total* amount required for maintaining your operations for a given year.

Challenge and Matching Grants

Another variation of "customized" fundraising involves the challenge or matching gift or grant. It is not unusual for a foundation or a corporation or a government agency or even an individual, on occasion, to make a gift contingent on a corresponding match from another funder or funders, on either a one-to-one or a two-to-one basis. In such cases, the initial funder makes a contribution of, for example, $5,000, which is contingent on a match from other sources of $5,000 (one-to-one) or of $10,000 (two-to-one). In total, the organization makes either $10,000 or $15,000 from the initial gift of $5,000. The donors who respond to these challenges are gratified that their dollars are producing additional dollars of support beyond their own gift, and the initial donor receives that same sense of gratification.

For foundations and corporations that may be wary of an organization's ability to raise all the funds needed to implement a program, the challenge or matching grant ensures that the organization will not draw on its funds until it has raised all the funds needed to implement the entire project.

PHASE 4: DEVELOPING A STRATEGY TO SECURE SUPPORT FROM INDIVIDUALS

Individuals should form the core support for practically any kind of nonprofit endeavor. That support is important for a number of reasons. Individuals are, beyond a doubt, the most reliable, ongoing, and consistent source of income for nonprofit organizations in America. Their investment in your work will not waiver as long as you continue to fulfill your mission adequately and acknowledge the individual supporters for their aid. Individuals form very personal relationships with the charitable organizations they support. As long as you encourage, recognize, and nurture that relationship, you can anticipate retaining the majority of your individual donors year in and out. They serve as your life insurance policy for the future, for they will be around even if institutional supporters such as government, foundations, and corporations withdraw their support.

Nevertheless, some organizations scoff at the idea of reaching out to individuals for support, believing that the public is apathetic to their issues or that their immediate constituency is too poor or hard-pressed to provide any significant help. Other groups simply don't know how to petition the public effectively for financial support and find themselves bewildered by the variety of methods and techniques available to elicit contributions from individuals.

But the nonprofits that overcome these obstacles will be gratified in the long run by finding a growing core of individual sustainers who outlast practically every other form of support and who may be even more responsive than institutional sources to pleas for certain types of programs that otherwise would languish. The most modest start at support from individuals may soon prove to be worthwhile and ultimately substantial.

Membership is the most common method that groups use to encourage

What's Magical, Practical, And Fun?

MEMBERSHIP IN THE NEW YORK ZOOLOGICAL SOCIETY

Join the New York Zoological Society and see a world of wildlife. Membership opens the gates to the New Bronx Zoo and the New York Aquarium. Membership means free admission, free rides, free parking and a free subscription to ANIMAL KINGDOM magazine. Membership admits you to exciting events, exhibits and previews. Membership makes you our special guest at the Society's spring garden party and stimulating annual meeting.

Become an Individual Member for just $25.00 and enjoy all of the following advantages:

- Unlimited free admission to the Zoo and the Aquarium.
- Free subscription to ANIMAL KINGDOM, the Society's fascinating bi-monthly magazine.
- 5 free parking tickets.
- 10 tickets for free admission to animal rides, Safari Tour Train, Skyfari and Bengali Express rides, and the world-famous Children's Zoo.
- 2 free tickets to the annual meeting.
- Invitations to all Zoo and Aquarium events.
- 2 free tickets to the Society's garden party, held exclusively for members.
- Use of the Zoo's Staff Dining Room on weekends and holidays by reservation.
- Travel privileges on Society sponsored and conducted tours.
- Special member's rate on education courses offered by the Society.

Become a Family Member for just $35.00 and enjoy all of the following advantages: All of the privileges of Individual Membership plus...

- Unlimited free admission for the Family Member's spouse and children to the age of 16.
- 5 additional free parking tickets.
- 10 extra tickets for rides and the Children's Zoo.
- An extra ticket to the annual meeting and the garden party.

- -

I wish to become a member of the New York Zoological Society. | | $25 Individual | | $35 Family

Name _____ Address _____ City, State, Zip _____

Charge my | | Mastercard
            | | Visa
            | | American Express

My check for $_____ is enclosed. Please make checks payable to the New York Zoological Society and mail with your application to: the Membership Department, Bronx Zoo, Bronx, New York 10460.

_____
My account number   Expiration date

_____
Signature

Or, call (212) 220-5090 and charge your membership by phone.

Organizations potentially can have a broad array of membership benefits to offer.

Source: The New York Zoological Society. Reprinted with permission.

individual support. Membership sometimes carries certain rights within an organization, such as voting for officers and board members. In most cases, however, membership does not confer voting privileges but rather suggests a sense of belonging to an organization. An individual might also receive certain tangible benefits by joining as a member.

Channel 13, New York City's public television station, actively conducts a membership campaign each year which is similar to the drives conducted by PBS stations throughout the country. In the New York metropolitan area, over 300,000 people were members of Channel 13 in 1984. Willoughby Newton, Director of Institutional Development at Channel 13, explains why it is preferable to become a member rather than simply to make contributions:

> Persons who make donations do not seem to feel that their gifts establish a mutually understood commitment nor does this form of giving provide an obvious incentive to repeat the gift on a later occasion. Gifts may indeed be repeated, but there is no reason to expect that they will be, unless there is a repeated solicitation.
>
> However, persons who become members of an organization *tend to accept the fact that they have become involved and have made a commitment.*

Other advantages also accrue to the organization that encourages individuals to become members. Again, according to Newton:

> A membership is generally perceived by both the donor and the institution to be renewable. This permits the donors to project their annual membership as a regular part of their yearly pattern, and it permits the institution to project a specific amount of income from Membership support, allowing for some attrition, of course.
>
> Donors can be encouraged to become Members at a level commensurate with their interest and concern *and* means.
>
> A pattern of graduated perquisites can give donors the incentive to increase their generosity, and thus they can be upgraded from one category of Membership to another.

Some groups strive to make their membership invitations more attractive by offering concrete benefits to individuals who join. The accompanying illustration describes the benefits that accompany membership in the New York Zoological Society. A zoo has many resources at its fingertips to offer as benefits, but small groups nonetheless can offer such "perks" as T-shirts, buttons, discounted admissions to special events and educational programs, and invitations to members' parties. Actually, your imagination and knowledge of your own constituency can help you design a membership package of benefits to suit almost any organization.

Don't lose sight of the fact, however, that while tangible membership benefits serve as an incentive to individuals to give and to give more, they rarely serve as the primary stimulus. Individuals join as members and make contributions for a variety of usually intangible reasons (see Chapter 7). You can best decide if you need to sweeten your membership program with distinct benefits, for you know your constituents best.

FOR THE FIRST TIME IN HISTORY, GORILLAS ARE TALKING TO US.

We've learned, for example, that Koko and Michael, two lively lowland gorillas, are highly sophisticated animals capable of humor, modesty and affection. Using American Sign Language, the conversations have been lively and complex. We've had them cuss us out, we've caught them lying, and we've seen them create names for objects and concepts that were new to them. ☐ The research is adding to our understanding of the great apes–particularly the seriously endangered gorilla–which will further our goal of encouraging the protection, preservation and propagation of anthropoid apes. The benefits for humans are in the teaching methodologies we use that can be applied to helping autistic children, the severely retarded, and other handicapped individuals with whom communication is difficult. ☐ The demands of the research create substantial ongoing financial needs that can be met only through contributions and memberships in the Gorilla Foundation which includes a subscription to our Journal. Michael and Koko would be pleased to welcome you into membership in their organization. All memberships, which start at $15, are tax deductible and may be sent to:

THE GORILLA
FOUNDATION
17820 Skyline Boulevard
Woodside
California 94062

For more information
on the work of the
Gorilla Foundation, see:
NATIONAL GEOGRAPHIC
October, 1978,
"Conversations with a
Gorilla."

THE EDUCATION OF KOKO
By Francine Patterson
and Eugene Linden
Holt, Rinehard and Winston, 1981
Available for $15 through the
Gorilla Foundation

WHAT WE'RE LEARNING FROM THEM STAGGERS THE IMAGINATION.

Gorillas need human friends, too.

Source: Material reprinted courtesy of The Gorilla Foundation, Woodside, CA.

If they feel a strong sense of kinship with your organization, your constituents will inevitably respond well to requests for funds, whether received through the mail or at their doorstep. When your donors are already quite loyal, you may not need to sweeten your membership offer to elicit the desired response. However, you can still consider providing unique opportunities to your supporters to *increase* their level of support by offering specific benefits tied to different giving levels. For example, you can offer a silkscreen poster signed by the artist to all contributors who give, for example, $100 or more. If your organization's claim on the conscience and wallets of your public is less strong, then benefits can serve as a greater incentive to prompt individuals to respond to your requests.

The first step in tapping individuals for membership is to identify the particular constituencies most likely to be committed to your work, who can then be approached for money and membership. Turn first to your internal constituency—your board, your volunteers, and even your staff members. This may sound like heresy to some individuals who already give generously of their time to a group and feel that this sufficiently demonstrates their commitment. And in part that's true. Still, there is nothing like a commitment of money to signify to everyone else the importance they ascribe to their organization. Also, since all of your board, staff, and volunteers should, at one point or another, ask others to give to your organization, they will be able to say to a prospective member, "I joined because I felt that what we are doing is critically important. Won't you join, too?"

Now you are ready to go outside your own organization for further support. Your task becomes one of identifying and targeting which individuals are most likely to extend support to your work. Undoubtedly, you will be able to develop some sense of how to identify these individuals and to decide what constituencies they might belong to. Brainstorm with other members of your organizing committee, board of directors, or fundraising committee. The circles exercise in Chapter 7 will help.

If your organization already receives support from individuals through a variety of ways, start out by analyzing those supporters. List them by their common denominators: are they teachers, social workers, lawyers, parents, activists, doctors, women, gays, liberals, progressives? What distinguishes them from one another? You are not trying to stereotype your supporters but to differentiate them so that you know how you may most effectively reach them. For example, if you decided to undertake a direct mail campaign, you would need to select lists of names to mail to. *The more you know about your current members, the more readily you will be able to identify other kindred souls.* For example, which magazines do most of your members subscribe to? What newspapers do they read? This information will help you target your publicity efforts.

As an exercise, make your own list of the five most frequent types of contributors to your organization.

1. _____
2. _____
3. _____
4. _____
5. _____

Think through what you know about these constituencies. Would they prefer to go to a movie or a ballet party or an educational seminar? Do they enjoy opportunities to socialize with their peers? Would they prefer a picnic or a testimonial dinner? Do any other groups of concerned individuals come to mind that you currently do not have among your present membership? If so, name them:

1. _____
2. _____
3. _____

The sharper your sense of your current and prospective donors, the easier it will be to choose among the various approaches to donors that are available to you. And ultimately, you will be more successful in attracting others to your cause.

Let's examine "Tenants United for Fair Housing" (TUFH) as a hypothetical example to illustrate the process. Their core group, at its monthly meeting, came up with the following list of potential individual supporters:

1. Core group members.

2. Their families and friends.

3. Others tenants in their neighborhood.

4. Local business people.

5. Local clergy.

The second step in securing support from individuals is to brainstorm a variety of ways to approach them for assistance.

Now, TUFH's task was to list the possible ways each of these groups of prospective supporters could give money, or how to best ask them for support *on a regular basis*.

Let's see what TUFH came up with:

Constituencies

1. Core group members   • Pass the hat at regular meetings

                                            • Pay monthly membership dues

	• Purchase raffle tickets, buttons, bumper stickers, etc.
	• Attend special events
2. Their families and friends	• Purchase raffle tickets
	• Attend special events
	• Make contributions
3. Other tenants in the neighborhood	• Pay monthly membership dues
	• Attend special events
	• Buy raffle tickets, buttons, bumper stickers, etc.
	• Make contributions and/or pledges in response to direct mail/newsletter appeal
	• Purchase subscriptions to newsletter
4. Local business people	• Make contributions after direct personal solicitation
	• Place canisters near cash registers
	• Donate items for raffles and special events
	• Purchase ads in newsletter
5. Local clergy	• Make personal contributions
	• Appeal for funds through their own newsletters
	• Host a special event

Let's take another hypothetical example to illustrate once more how an organization can identify its key individual supporters. Members of the core group of Artists Against Apartheid asked themselves the following question: Which individuals are the most likely supporters of our work to help bring about an end to apartheid in South Africa?

As a result of brainstorming together, Artists Against Apartheid found that they had many constituencies, due to the overwhelming community of concern about apartheid. These included:

1. Core group members.

2. Their families and friends.

3. Other politically aware (socially concerned) artists.

4. Socially concerned members of the arts-oriented public in their community.

5. Human rights organization leaders.

6. Black community leaders.

7. Religious leaders.

8. Union officials.

9. Exiled South Africans in their communities.

10. Sympathetic journalists.

Clearly, Artists Against Apartheid has many potential constituencies to turn to for support. Let's list the possible ways each of these groups of prospective supporters can give support, or how to best ask them for support *on a regular basis:*

Constituencies:

1. Core group members	• Sell tickets to special events
	• Ask friends and other artists to donate individual pieces of art to an annual art auction
	• Design special art postcards to be sold to raise funds
2. Their friends and families	• Buy tickets to special events and purchase postcards
	• Join Artists Against Apartheid as members
	• Host art shows of donated art in their homes to sell to other friends
3. Other politically aware artists	• Donate works of art for sale
	• Attend special events
4. Socially concerned members of the arts-oriented public	• Attend special events and art auction
	• Purchase individual works of art and other items put up for sale
5. Human rights organization leaders	• Advertise events in their group newsletters and post flyers in their offices
6. Black community leaders	• Enclose a notice on events in mailings to their own members
7. Religious leaders	• Speak at the events
8. Union officials	• Provide mailing lists for a direct mail solicitation
9. Exiled South Africans in their communities	• Join as members
	• Participate in programs as speakers and resource people
10. Sympathetic journalists	• Aid in publicizing programs and events
	• Join as members

As the hypothetical cases of Tenants United for Fair Housing and Artists Against Apartheid illustrate, there are many ways individuals can choose to support a particular nonprofit undertaking. Both of these groups, just like your own, can expand their lists by sharing them with others.

What approaches did your core group identify?

Constituencies	*Approaches*
1. _____	_____
_____	_____
_____	_____
_____	_____
2. _____	_____
_____	_____
_____	_____
3. _____	_____
_____	_____
_____	_____
4. _____	_____
_____	_____
_____	_____
5. _____	_____
_____	_____
_____	_____

The third step is to choose from these brainstorming lists those approaches or methods your core group wants to pursue. Ask your planning committee, which is responsible for your fundraising efforts, which of the possible approaches you should use.

Let's select three to start with. Which of the previously listed ways of asking individuals for money does the committee want to pursue?

It is important that outreach to individuals be predicated on the basis of an ongoing relationship, for you want to reach out to your donors in ways that they will respond to positively not only once but repeatedly in the future. Your goal is to instill in your donors special feelings of affinity and community toward your organization, with the hope that your supporters will ultimately feel a sense of ownership of your organization akin to your own. If your building burns down, if you are faced with a dramatic setback, they will be ready to rally around the organization. That sense of "ownership" of your work needs continuous nurturing. People don't automatically gain it.

Your aim is to encourage your supporters to participate and to become involved in the life of your organization and, as a result, to develop a sense of belonging and responsibility toward your efforts.

Finally, you want to make sure that you extend recognition to your supporters for their contributions. Support can be acknowledged both privately and publicly. Private acknowledgment begins with a thank-you note for a contribution. Further acknowledgment can take the form of mailing newsletters, "insiders' memos," annual reports, and other publications to your donors to keep them posted about the work that they have made possible. Let them know consistently that your flourishing, ongoing work would be impossible without their help.

Public acknowledgment can be as simple as listing your new members in a newsletter on an ongoing basis, if their number is manageable. If you are offering different categories of membership to your constituents, you can list your supporters by the category they have chosen. This is the same principle underlying the lists of benefactors that you often see in the playbills of nonprofit theater groups or on the walls of buildings of nonprofit facilities. Just as a university gives recognition to major donors by naming buildings after them, a smaller nonprofit institution can convey the same appreciation to its supporters through some form of public listing.

In light of these considerations, let's return to the task before Tenants United for Fair Housing and Artists Against Apartheid—choosing the best possible approaches to their prime constituents.

TUFH's committee decided to focus on: a membership dues program; passing the hat at monthly meetings; two special events; and two "free" holiday open houses (in December and July). They chose these four approaches because they provided TUFH with the means to ask their constituents regularly for support. The benefits and open houses also provide TUFH with opportunities to strengthen personal relationships with their supporters. In addition, they decided to list in their monthly newsletter the names of their members as they joined or renewed their memberships.

The core group of Artists Against Apartheid decided to focus on: a campaign to sell specially designed art postcards to the memberships of other sympathetic organizations through direct mail; asking famous socially concerned artists known to them to donate works of art for an annual auction; organizing a tour of artists' studios for the public.

You will note that these approaches include a mix of face-to-face solicitation (Chapter 8), direct mail (Chapter 9), special events (Chapter 10), and earned income (Chapter 12).

Artists Against Apartheid chose this particular mix of approaches to individuals for several reasons. As artists, they realized that they had access to something of value to others—their work and the works of other artists. They also knew that there was much competition in soliciting contributions from their targeted constituencies, since other, more established organizations were already tapping the same people regularly. As a result, they decided to raise money by selling art postcards in lieu of simple solicitation for support.

They were also capitalizing on the knowledge and skills of their core group. Some of their members had personal relationships with famous artists, and one member had experience in designing and marketing postcards for sale.

After discussing their plans with more resource people outside their immediate circles, including the local art auction house and several gallery owners, they were able to make reasonable estimates of projected income from these activities. They decided to drop the tour of artists' studios, for others did not find the concept very appealing. They discovered that their artists' friends were not members of any existing human rights organizations, so they decided to institute a membership program. Since their friends included both struggling and successful artists, they decided to offer a two-tiered membership program to enable both groups to give according to their means.

The final step before the actual fundraising gets under way is to make some conservative estimates on how much each of the chosen efforts can net in a year. Artists Against Apartheid came up with the following summary:

Individual Supporters:	
A. 250 dues-paying members @ $10/year	= $ 2,500
B. 100 dues-paying patrons @ $50/year	= 5,000
C. 500 packets of 10 postcards each sold @ $5/packet	= 2,500
D. 1 annual art auction of donated works	= 7,500
TOTAL RAISED FROM INDIVIDUALS	= $17,500

They decided to list all the artists who joined as members and patrons, or who contributed their own work, in a full-page ad in the local arts newspaper each year to thank them publicly for their support.

The TUFH committee has to ask itself the following questions: How much can we ask each person to donate at a monthly meeting? How many people will be able to contribute that amount at each meeting? How much can we expect people to pay in membership dues? How many members can we sign up in a year? What kinds of special events should we plan? How much can we expect to net from each one? And so on . . .

By answering questions as specific as these, the committee can then reasonably estimate how much it can raise from individuals in a given year. TUFH came up with this summary:

Individual Supporters:
A. 1,000 dues-paying membrs @ $10/year   = $10,000
B. 12 monthly collections × 20 people × $2 each   =   480
C. 2 special events (spring tag sale and bazaar @ $2,000 each)   =   4,000
TOTAL RAISED FROM INDIVIDUALS   = $14,480

TUFH and Artists Against Apartheid were aware of the methods available to them to secure memberships and contributions. You may not be. Chapters 8 to 12 outline many of the major methods an organization can use to approach individuals for support, such as face-to-face solicitation, direct mail, special events, deferred giving, and others. Refer to them for a fuller explanation of the pros and cons of each of these methods. Just as TUFH and Artists Against Apartheid chose a mix of these approaches, you can now do the same.

Remember, in choosing your approaches to individuals, you are looking for ways in which to ask them for money regularly, to provide them with opportunities for personal involvement in your work, and to recognize their support.

Which approaches are your final choices? Make your own conservative estimates of what these strategies to secure individual support will net.

Individual Supporters:

A.	= $
B.	=
C.	=
TOTAL RAISED FROM INDIVIDUALS	= $

To build up your individual support base, you should keep the following guidelines in mind:

1. *Always talk up membership.* Wherever your members go, they should always seek out new members for your organization. It's the first way for others to become involved in your work. Don't neglect any personal opportunity to ask someone to become a member. Nothing can be as effective as making a personal approach.

2. *Be on the lookout for prospective new constituencies.* Be alert to other like-minded groups with whom you may be in touch. Are there other organizations that you belong to? Or magazines or periodicals that you subscribe to? Their membership or subscription lists could prove to be good prospects for your own effort. In the words of the direct mail consultant, "keep on prospecting."

3. *Make your membership clearly annual.* People are usually asked to become members for one year. Thus, the onus is on the organization to ask for that membership to be renewed at the appropriate time. You would be advised even to label your membership dues by year; for example, "We

are writing you to ask you to renew your membership for 1989, or for '89–'90." This makes it easier for both you and your donors to keep track of their dues, and to become accustomed to the renewal process. It is preferable, too, to send out a renewal notice about eleven months after receipt of a membership check, rather than to mail them all out at the same time of the year. Don't hesitate to send out a second or even a third reminder notice to encourage renewals.

4. *Seek to "upgrade" your givers each year.* Don't overlook the opportunity to ask your members to increase the size of their gift and, thus, their class of membership. The increase may be as modest as 10 percent more than the previous year's b ic membership dues, or much more substantial, if the donor has the means. You can promote your classes of membership each year so you can ask each and every member to consider renewing at the next highest category. You can also sweeten the request by giving each category of membership its own distinct benefits. There is no law that says you cannot ask your loyal supporters to increase their level of support each year; yet, you would be surprised to learn how few organizations actually do.

5. *Send out a thank-you note promptly.* There is nothing so important as a personalized note acknowledging receipt of a check and a membership application. Your efforts will be repaid ten times over if you send a personalized thank-you note as often as possible. The note can be short and simple. You can even use a postcard. The spirit of a gift is somehow violated if the recipient fails to acknowledge it. Use yourself as the test— if you sent in a membership check, what would you ordinarily expect in return? Take special care, too, that you don't rely excessively upon the word processor. Nothing can take the place of the personal note, in and of itself, or added as a postscript to a standard letter. The more personally you treat your donors, the more likely they are to be generous in return.

6. *Amass data on your supporters, especially your large donors.* Don't view your individual donors solely as sources of funds. Get to know them as individuals with varying and particular interests. Appreciate those interests and take them into account when you select special events or membership benefits. Try to find out what especially interests them in your organization.

7. *You can treat different kinds of members differently, and you should.* Obviously, the contribution from a $100 supporter is more valuable than that of a $25 donor, and that of a $500 sustainer more important to your work than that of the $100 supporter. The rule of thumb is that the greater the amount of the gift, the more personal the contact should be. If you can visit only X number of donors, it logically follows that you should visit those who have given the most dollars *or* have the potential to do so.

8. *Keep current and accurate records.* In order to nurture your members' interests, you need to be aware of what those interests are. Develop individual files on your large donors, just as you would on a foundation. Keep your records clearly enough to easily review the "giving history" of each of your members. Computerization of membership records is desirable for this reason alone.

9. *Don't contact your members only when you need money.* Let your members hear from you throughout the year, and not only when you are asking for funds. That is why a membership newsletter, or some other form of regular communication, is valuable.

10. *You can ask for contributions more than once a year.* Membership does not preclude an individual from making other contributions to an organization during the course of the year. If you can make a good case for needing financial help, you should certainly not hesitate to make an appeal to your membership mailing list. There is no magic rule about how many times a year you can ask the same people to give. You can mail out as many appeals as will net consistent positive responses and cover more than their printing and mailing costs. Again, use your own judgment: How many solicitations would *you* be willing to receive? If each appeal had merit on its own, you would probably feel differently than if each appeal sounded exactly like the one preceding it. Beware of "crying wolf" more than once! You can go to your membership once and *perhaps* raise funds in response to a crisis or emergency within an organization, but success the second time around is unlikely.

PHASE 5: DEVELOPING A STRATEGY TO SECURE SUPPORT FROM INSTITUTIONS

Some nonprofit organizations have supported their work totally through individual contributions. Undoubtedly, these are membership organizations that constantly reach out to new donors. Others have used their revenues from individuals to underwrite the general operating expenses of their group, while reaching out to institutional sources for support of particular programs and projects. Either of these routes can achieve desirable goals for nonprofits. To reiterate, individual support remains the most reliable, renewable, and consistent source of support. So, in the best of worlds, institutional support should be only incidental to your financial base. Some, however, would argue that government should be the foremost funder of nonprofit activity, since both the public and the nonprofit sector share responsibiilty for the public good. In fact, it is quite common for units of local government to contract out responsibility for certain social services to nonprofits. The Human Resources Administration of the City of New York, for instance, contracts out close to $1 billion each year to various nonprofit social service agencies to deliver services to New Yorkers that are mandated by legislation.

But most nonprofit groups do not enjoy total support from either individuals or government. These groups are more apt to draw on a mix of both individual and institutional sources to finance their work. It is their job to pursue aggressively that mix of individual and institutional prospects that are the most likely to extend support.

Your next set of tasks is to identify your universe of prospective institutional supporters. Then, you should proceed to identify your "best bets" from your prospect list. Once done, you are ready to make actual approaches to these funders.

As Chapters 13 to 18 illustrate, the world of institutional support is truly a vast one. It includes:

- *Government.*
Town, county, village, city, state, region, and federal.

- *Foundations.*
Family, private, company-sponsored, community, local and national, grantmaking public charities.

- *Businesses and Corporations.*
Neighborhood corner stores, chain stores, bank branches, utility companies, department stores, specialty shops, restaurants, companies, local and national corporations.

- *Religious Institutions.*
Churches, temples, synagogues, and other faith communities; local and regional religious decisionmaking bodies; local and national ecumenical structures; and national religious bodies.

- *Fundraising Federations.*
United Way, Community Chest, Catholic Charities, United Jewish Appeal, alternative funds, such as Women's Way in Philadelphia and Women's Funding Coalition in New York City.

- *Associations of Individuals.*
Service clubs such as Rotarians, Lions, Soroptomists, Junior League, Hadassah, American Association of University Women; local and national labor unions; professional, business, and trade associations, such as the local Bar Association and Chamber of Commerce.

These chapters outline in detail how each of these institutional sources extends support to nonprofits, how much they make available in grants and in-kind (non-cash) contributions, the advantages and disadvantages of raising support from them, what motivates them to provide philanthropic assistance, and how to proceed successfully to obtain their assistance. At the end of each of these chapters is a worksheet that will aid you in deciding whether to explore this particular type of support for your own organization.

Your fundraising strategy should encompass a mix of these institutional sources. This will further strengthen your funding base.

We now turn back to the task before us: identifying those particular institutional sources that are the most likely to extend their support. Remember that you are looking *to identify a manageable number of prospects that can be pursued with some fair measure of success.* It is best to narrow down your list of prospects as much as possible, so that you will be free to give adequate personal attention to each of them. Successful institutional fundraising requires careful personal approaches to your prospects. Therefore, the fewer prospects you target, the more likely you will be able to devote the appropriate time and attention to making the best approach and subsequent follow-up.

Your first prospect list will be broader and more inclusive than your final one. Now your research, networking, and other information-gathering pursuits begin.

Research involves reviewing the printed materials and informed gossip that are publicly available on foundations, corporations, government, religious sources, fundraising federations, and associations of individuals. There are standard reference materials available at your local library or the local regional collection of The Foundation Center (see Appendix D to locate your nearest collection). Specific reference sources are also enumerated in some of the previous chapters. In addition, some institutional sources—a number of foundations, corporations, most government agencies, most federated campaigns, and some religious sources—make available free upon request application guidelines, lists of past grantees, and annual reports. You are looking for:

1. Funders that are similar to those from whom you already receive support.

2. Funders that have an interest in your work based on your locale.

3. Funders that have an interest in your work based on the subject of your program.

4. Funders that can provide the level of financial support you are seeking.

First, explore funders similar to those from whom you are already receiving support. If you are receiving grants from national foundations on the basis of your groundbreaking work in an issue of national import, research other national foundations to ascertain whether there are others that share an interest in this area. In the same way, if you have elicited positive responses from certain kinds of corporations in the past, you might explore other corporations in the same industry for potential support. Success in securing a grant from a foundation or corporation does not automatically lead to success with their counterparts. It does, however, suggest a possibility worth exploring. Most funding sources are influenced in their decisionmaking by the evidence of their colleagues' involvement, for that translates into credibility.

Second, you are now ready to explore other sectors of support apart from the ones you are currently tapping. In exploring these new sources, start at the most local level. In other words, approach your local parish before going to the metropolitan religious body or to its national headquarters. For one thing, you are more likely to have some personal contacts at this level of organization already; for another, you face less competition from other similar organizations at the most local level. Competition tends to increase as you reach out to sources with a wider geographic scope. The closer to your locale your sources are, the greater investment they have in the political success of your effort.

There are exceptions to the theory that you will potentially gain more support from those sources closer to home than those farther away. Some national sources, including religious bodies, government, corporations, and foundations, might well be attracted to your work for a variety of factors, such as: high correlation to their particular interests; unique characteristics of your efforts; potential of your work to serve as a model or demonstration project for other communities; or the vanguard nature of your work.

For example, in the early years of the women's movement, a number of progressive-minded national foundations made grants to local women's organizations before their local foundation counterparts did. In these cases, national foundations laid the groundwork for local foundations to build on. By the mid-1980s, a similar scenario was in evidence in funding disarmament projects.

Nor would it be unusual for a national foundation to fund a local organization that is perceived by the local funding community as too controversial because of its area of interest or its form of advocacy.

For these reasons, some organizations should engage in subject-related research, as well as geographic-based research into prospective funding sources.

A secondary method for gaining information is networking, a concept that has fortunately gained popular support. Networking is no more than cooperation among individuals and organizations with similar needs (and goals) to aid each other in accomplishing their goals.

Each and every nonprofit has counterpart organizations locally and around the country whose experiences can save them valuable time so that they don't have to reinvent the wheel. Those counterparts share a similar field of activity, or a similar constituency, or the same geographic locale.

The first step in networking is to brainstorm a list of your most likely counterpart organizations. Think in terms of issues, geography and constituency.

Find out what they have learned from their own fundraising efforts. Other groups can share with you valuable information that may not necessarily be printed in any materials, such as: which funders are the most likely to give pre-application meetings? What is of most interest to staff in a funding proposal? How much work is involved in making an appropriate application?

You can also network with development (fundraising) professionals at nearby large nonprofit institutions, such as hospitals, colleges and universities, museums, etc., to elicit their suggestions. Finally, conferences, seminars and meetings provide splendid opportunities to network not only with other nonprofits, but with funders as well. Some cities even have support organizations composed of nonprofits themselves that supply meeting grounds for various nonprofits. Examples of these latter groups include Washington Council of Agencies in Washington, D.C., The Non-Profit Coordinating Committee of New York, and the Center for Non-Profit Organizations in New Jersey.

Fill in the following worksheet with the results of your research and networking. It will thus provide you with a handy list of the universe of your funding prospects. To make your prospect list even more helpful, add information on potential grant size and existing contacts or door openers.

Network until you feel that you have a comprehensive understanding of your prospects. Don't hesitate to eliminate any from your list because of such factors as small size of grants, lack of personal contacts, or inappropriate subject area, to cite just a few examples.

You would spend your time best by making thorough approaches to a small number of select funders than by trying to cover the waterfront. You will not be able to pursue all the prospective sources of support that you have uncovered with the same degree of vigor. You need to reduce your list to a manageable number. Look for reasons to eliminate prospects rather than reasons to keep them. In other words, choose the prospects that really are your "best bets." You might aim for a final prospect list of no more than ten institutional sources as candidates of support.

To build up your institutional support base, you should keep the following guidelines in mind:

1. *Do your homework well.* The days of successful "shotgun" grantsmanship are over, if they ever really existed at all. Mailing out a large number of proposals to a group of undifferentiated institutional sources is the least effective way to achieve fundraising goals.

The key word in today's competitive climate is *targeting.* In other words, you should spend your limited time and resources researching those prospective supporters that are most *appropriate* and *sympathetic* to your work. Immerse yourself in their published literature (annual reports, newsletters, guidelines for applicants) and gather further information through networking with others who are familiar with their work. Armed with the fruits of careful preparation and thought, you will be in the best position to select a group of funders.

In your letter of inquiry or the cover letter accompanying your proposal, you will be able to demonstrate *why* you are approaching this particular institutional source. You will have made a "targeted" approach.

Your research and information gathering will force you to abandon some prospects, since your activities will fall outside their interest areas. That's fine. Remember, you are honing down your prospect list to your ten "best bets."

2. *Establish personal contact as early as possible in the application process.* Establishing personal contact can be the most difficult step in the application process. As foundations and corporations are increasingly deluged with requests for support in the wake of federal cutbacks, their staffs have less time available to respond to the volume of worthy inquiries they regularly receive.

Yet, people still respond most readily to personal appeals. Paper does not sell programs, people themselves do. You, therefore, want to take steps such as suggesting a meeting in your letter of inquiry or in the cover letter accompanying your proposal. Use that meeting to provide the human dimension that complements your plans on paper.

If the institutional source being approached does not respond to your suggestion, you may still have opportunity to meet later on. Don't give up! In the future, be attentive to program occasions, such as open houses, conferences, forums, or seminars, when you can extend personal invitations to targeted funders. Think carefully about what activities would be of interest to them. In other words, keep your eye on their interests, and on developing a long-term relationship. (More suggestions on nurturing such a relationship can be found in Phase 9.)

3. *Keep your eyes on the long-term relationship.* Disappointment is only natural when you receive a rejection letter from a prospective institutional supporter. Their decision not to back your efforts, whose value you believe in strongly, strikes deep. But remember, rejection of your proposal may have been the result of factors that have no connection to your work, such as a volume of deserving requests for funding that far surpasses a funder's resources, or the desire to distribute available funds evenly over a given geographic area.

Once you have determined that you were not rejected because your work fell outside the scope of your prospect's interests, keep the door open for the future by keeping them posted on your ongoing work. The opportunity to reapply may arise in the future.

4. *Organizational leadership is integral to success in grantsmanship.* Although grants are made to organizations, funders know that individuals are the key ingredients to organizational success. After all is said and done, it's people who make projects flourish and succeed.

Funders will seek evidence of the strength and quality of your organization's leadership from the start of your relationship. So, in your initial letter of inquiry, you can best give evidence of the capabilities of your leadership by stating your case clearly and completely. Don't hesitate to refer to one of your past successes if it is pertinent. Later on, when you submit your full proposal, include concise résumés of the staff members who will be directly involved in the work outlined in the proposal.

It is important that the acknowledged leaders of your organization be present at the first meeting with a prospective institutional supporter. In most cases, this means the executive director and the board chair or president. De-

Worksheet
SUMMARIZING THE INFORMATION GATHERED
ON YOUR INSTITUTIONAL PROJECTS

Institutional Prospects for Support

Existing or Past Funders	New Funders Similar to Past Ones	Funders Interested on the Basis of Locale

Funders Interested on the Basis of Program Activity	Level of Potential Financial Support Available	Your Degree of Access to Decisionmakers (Existing Contacts)

pending on the agenda of the meeting, you may choose to include one or two other individuals, such as program staff, other board members, constituents, or key community supporters, if they can make a concrete contribution to the meeting that no one else can make. Choose the attendees carefully to ensure that the strongest and most well rounded case for your organization or program will be presented.

5. *Anticipate the questions your prospects are likely to pose, and answer them.* The best way to prepare yourself for the application process is to list the questions a particular prospect is likely to pose. Take the time to ask the hard questions and to play devil's advocate—the tougher you are now, the stronger your final proposal will be.

Once you have completed your list, answer all the questions one by one in writing. Then incorporate your responses, to the extent possible, into your initial letter and proposal. Do *not* wait until you are face to face with prospective supporters to address their concerns. Seize the opportunity in advance and answer them head-on in your first communication. They will realize quickly that you are thoroughly familiar with the problem you propose to address and that your thoughtful and well-planned strategy merits a closer look.

6. *Know your niche.* Many nonprofits operate in a field of endeavor in which other organizations are also at work. Each group has its own particular strengths and makes a unique contribution.

More often than not, institutional supporters are aware of the matrix of groups on an issue of mutual concern. They will be the first to ask such questions as: How is your work different from that of other existing organizations? It is the responsibility of the grantseeker to delineate what special resources they bring to their work that distinguish them from the other actors. Your uniqueness, whether it is in your philosophy, your constituency, or your approach to a problem, will be a major factor in winning institutional backing.

Grantseekers often try to be all things to all people. This obfuscates your own strengths and blurs your mission. The materials you send to institutional funders should clearly state how your approach to a mutual concern sets you apart from other groups active in the same field.

7. *Be prepared to discuss nonmonetary needs with a prospective institutional supporter.* Remember, it is better to walk away with something than with nothing at all.

If you have done your homework well, your prospects will be in a position to aid you in a number of ways. Money may be at the top of your list, but don't overlook other forms of support. After all, an institution's financial resources may be limited or fully committed when you make your request.

Prepare a list of other types of support that your prospect might provide and keep it handy. Such assistance may be advice or in-kind services, such as donated printing or products. Since competition for non-cash assistance is less fierce, you may be able to leave a meeting with an important piece of information or the promise of an in-kind contribution. You will have also established the basis for an ongoing relationship and eventual financial support.

8. *Be alert to opportunities to provide something of value to funders.* Relations with funders should not be a one-way street. While some corporate backers may be quick to point out ways grantees can be of assistance to them, other funders may be less forthcoming.

You can strengthen your relationships with funders by anticipating the occasions on which you can be of help to them. That assistance might take the form of information on a subject of interest, or public recognition of their support. In the growing climate of partnership between the nonprofit sector and the private and public sectors, more opportunities for collaboration are emerging whereby nonprofits can contribute to funders' initiatives.

9. *Prepare your written materials conscientiously.* Personal communication is always important, but your written communications form the permanent record of your relationship with a funder.

The proposal is the most important piece of documentation. Funders may summarize it or circulate it in its entirety to a board of trustees or to others who have a say in their decisionmaking process. The proposal represents your work to individuals to whom you may not have the opportunity to present your case in person.

Writing the proposal provides you with the chance to organize all of the pertinent data relating to your work in order to build a strong case for support. You should be sure that you have included your strongest arguments in the proposal or the accompanying cover letter. Also incorporate any information that reinforces your organization's credentials and its ability to succeed in its work. This may be done through reference to past successes, a letter of support from a recognized authority in your field, or a mention of recognition your organization has received in the press.

10. *Explore possible personal contacts before making a "cold approach."* This guideline is probably the most controversial of any in this list. Many funders' staff members decry the process whereby the executive director of a nonprofit makes an initial overture to a member of the funder's board of directors, who in turn makes a recommendation to the staff member. After all, it is the staffer's job to screen and recommend to the board potential projects for support, not the other way around. Make these contacts carefully, since you will be circumventing established procedure and possibly risking the loss of a staff member's support.

On the other hand, grantsmanship is a competitive process, and the personal factor certainly does affect the outcome of an appeal. The lesson here is to tread lightly, but do tread nonetheless. If any of your institutional prospects are totally new to you, compose a list of the contact people and others involved in the decisionmaking process. Circulate that list among your own active constituents (staff, board, key volunteers, etc.) to find out whether any of your own people know anybody on your list personally. When a connection is made, ask your own contact if he or she knows an appropriate way to approach that funder. Trust intuition and experience: let him or her decide whether placing an inquiry with the friend would be a wise approach. Your contact can also pose a question, such as "X organization, on whose board of directors I serve, is considering making an approach to your foundation for support. Could I take a moment of your time to tell you why I think our work is worthy of your support?" If the response is encouraging, ask him or her to suggest how to present your work effectively to the institution.

If any foundations are on your targeted list, check Chapter 13, Approaching Foundations, on how to proceed in tapping foundations. The same holds true for other institutional "best bets" as well. In each case, check the appropriate chapter for specific guidance on how to proceed in your quest for institutional support.

As in projecting individual support, you should now endeavor to make some conservative estimates of how much can be raised in funds by approaching your institutional prospects. Conservative estimates are made on the basis of what you can assuredly expect rather than what you hope to receive. If you have received support from institutions in the past year, gauge which of them are really likely to renew their grants, contracts, or contributions in the upcoming year, and project a realistic financial estimate of their support.

Now, turn to your "best bets" lists on pp. 434–435. Ascribe an average grant size to each of them. You can garner this information through either your research or your networking. Review the list: Are there sources from whom you are confident of receiving support? Who are they? What level of support can you assuredly predict, if any? Where you are *not* confident or are unsure, err on the conservative side and don't count any "questionables" in your final estimate figure. In that way, you will be pleasantly surprised if you exceed your goal rather than disappointed if you fall below.

If this is your first foray into seeking financial support from government, foundations, or corporations, you may find it difficult to gauge what your chances at success will be. Don't panic. Most nonprofits starting out are in a similar position. If you are still in the dark after all your information gathering, you can decide to make no projections for anticipated level of institutional support. That does not mean that you don't pursue your "best bets." You will simply not count on their support until you have sufficient evidence to draw that conclusion.

Another route would be to take three prospects from your "best bets" list that are most closely matched to your specific programs and purposes. Then, base your total estimates on their average grant size for organizations similar to yours in size, budget, program thrust, and so on.

Computing estimates on likely institutional support enables you to set a realizable fundraising objective from these sources.

PHASE 6: MAKING THE CASE

What role does writing play in nonprofit fundraising? Won't a face-to-face presentation always accomplish more than any written materials?

Generating support for nonprofit endeavors inevitably involves writing. Regardless of which funding sources you finally target, you will undoubtedly need written materials as part of your presentation. Those might include brochures, proposals, direct mail appeals, newsletters, annual reports, and letters of inquiry.

One way to avoid the perennial writer's anxiety and to save time as well is to do exactly what most veteran professional fundraisers and development officers at hospitals, museums, universities, and other large nonprofit institutions do—write one document in advance of a fundraising campaign that will satisfy fundraising needs before they develop. That document has the rather lofty-sounding title of a *case statement*.

A case statement is simply a written document that states the most important facts about an organization. It can range in length from a wallet-sized card to twenty pages. The most common case statement for the small to medium-sized nonprofit probably ranges between five and ten pages. Preparing such a statement provides you with the opportunity to amass data that will best illustrate the competence and effectiveness of your work. Your objective is to present sufficient information to your potential investors to elicit a positive response. In many ways, the case statement is not unlike the general support proposal that you might prepare for submission to a foundation. Both provide the reader with answers to the following questions in an organized fashion:

1. Why does your organization exist? What are the problems in society that you plan to address? Demonstrate the severity and seriousness of those problems in a concrete way.

   Your objective here is to assure the reader that your work is a response to proven and defensible needs.

2. What do you plan to do to alleviate these problems? What can you realistically hope to accomplish?

   Your objective here is to state succinctly your organizational purpose or mission and your specific program objectives.

3. What qualifies your staff and board to tackle these problems with any expectation of success?

   Your objective here is to attest to the skills, qualifications, and experiences of your staff, board, and volunteers, whose efforts will have impact on the stated problem.

4. How much in revenues is needed to enable you to go forward in your efforts?

   Your objective here is to illustrate the costs of your efforts through budgeting.

5. How do you anticipate raising all the revenues you will need?

Your objective here is to delineate all your fundraising and income-generating plans to illustrate that you can, with some degree of certainty, raise all the funds you need.

Your work in Section 1 of this book should provide you with much of the information you need to answer these questions thoroughly. Furthermore, the data from your completed exercises in Phases 1 and 3 will also be useful. Draw also from your credibility file.

Remember, in preparing a case statement, to present the most compelling, rational arguments you have at your disposal to convince potential supporters of the worthiness of your organization.

Once you have finished writing your overall document to service your later fundraising needs, you'll need to type or print it in a clear and presentable manner. Minimally, type up a crisp and clean-looking copy and duplicate it on quality paper. You can get fancier if you feel it would be appropriate for any of the particular prospective supporters you will be targeting. Be aware also that graphics can enhance the visual appearance and appeal of your written materials, so you would be wise to pay attention to the design elements of case statements, direct mail appeals, newsletters, proposals, and brochures. Your materials do not have to be fancy; they should be appropriate to who you are and to whom you are addressing. Minimally, they should be attractive enough to interest the intended audience to read the contents of the material.

To summarize, writing a clear and concise case statement or general support proposal (or whatever you choose to name this working document) will serve you in a number of invaluable ways. It will give you a way to engage others early on in the fundraising process. You can circulate your draft for comments and suggestions to those you are counting on to help you when the time for fundraising actually arrives. By doing so, you foster their investment in your efforts and improve the chances that they will devote time and energy to your fundraising when you need them later on.

You now have a document from which you will be able to draw sentences, paragraphs, pages, and even sections for all the written materials you are required to prepare as your fundraising efforts continue. You will have saved yourself precious time. When you have to write that proposal or direct mail appeal, you will not have to start from scratch. You may even choose to use your case statement as your primary fundraising document with individual large donors and foundations.

Additionally, you'll have in your hands a versatile set of materials that you can put in the hands of others associated with your group to serve a number of other purposes. It will be useful, for example, to those who have to make speeches, conduct workshops, or write articles for publication. Also, it will be invaluable to those in your organization who will be called on to make personal solicitations of potential donors and investors. It serves as their briefing papers.

You can also use your case statement as a tool for recruiting new board members. Since you have put your best foot forward in the body of this statement, it should serve you well in correspondence and in meetings with prospective board candidates.

Finally, you can also circulate a draft to some close financial supporters whom you intend to target as part of your campaign. In soliciting their feedback and suggestions, you are recognizing their vital importance to the success of your fundraising efforts. You are engaging their intellects before you ask them to dip into their wallets and pocketbooks. Inevitably, they will be more motivated to give later, when formally approached.

For all of these reasons, your fundraising efforts will ultimately be strengthened when you take the time to prepare in advance a written set of materials to serve your subsequent needs. Save yourself from later anxiety and frustration. Start your writing now. You will reap the rewards many times over later on!

Writer's Block—A Nonprofit's Monkey Wrench

If you are like the average person active in nonprofit pursuits, you will do your utmost to postpone any writing tasks, whether case statement or holiday appeal, until you are left with no other choice. Deadline pressures, simple procrastination, and lack of confidence in writing skills can have serious adverse effects on the best of projects.

Reluctance to write is altogether common. Just look at what some prolific and noted writers have said about the writing process:

> I play patience, or draw marvelously intricate patterns on backs of old newspapers while I am solving the crossword. Then I feel ashamed and try to get back to work, but the phone rings or Edith calls me to tea, so I put it off for a later day.
>
> —J. R. R. Tolkien

> I'll write letters, answer mail, get things off my mind before I start writing for the day.
>
> —Irving Wallace

> Let's face it, writing is hell.
>
> —William Styron

If you have such a reluctance, as you see, you are not alone. If, however, you are among those chosen few who warm to every writing task with the greatest ease, cherish your gift. The rest of us can either find someone to help us in our writing endeavors or learn to overcome writing blocks. Obviously, taking the latter road will serve you best in the long run.

If You Need Help

Fortunately, a number of resources do exist to aid frustrated writers to gain confidence in their abilities. You will find a bookshelf of how-to titles at your local library or major bookstore ready for your use. Recommended are:

1. *The Elements of Style*, by William Strunk and E. B. White (New York: Macmillan, 1979); 92 pages; $3.50.

2. *Writing Without Teachers*, by Peter Elbow (London: Oxford University Press, 1975); 196 pages; $4.95.

3. *Overcoming Writing Blocks*, by Karin Mack, Ph.D. and Eric Skjei, Ph.D. (Boston: Tarcher/Houghton Mifflin, 1979); 240 pages; $6.95.

Other services exist, too, to help the "challenged" writer. For example, twenty colleges and universities across the country have established *grammar hotlines*. Callers receive free advice from college faculty members on correct grammatical usage. A listing of these hotlines is in Appendix E.

PHASE 7: PREPARING THE FUNDRAISING PLAN AND CALENDAR

You've established your fundraising goal for the year (Phase 3), targeted your potential individual and institutional backers, set conservative estimates on their potential level of support (Phases 4 and 5), and prepared the documents necessary to develop a variety of fundraising materials. This information provides you with the framework for your own particular fundraising strategy. Summarize your results on the following worksheet:

Worksheet
SUMMARY OF FUNDRAISING STRATEGY

Fill in the results from your exercises in Phases 4 and 5:

1. Individual Supporters:

A. _____ Memberships @ $ _____/each   = $ _____

B. _____ Special events @ _____/each   = $ _____

C. _____ Large contributions @ _____/each   = $ _____

D. _____ Other forms of individual support: = $ _____

            _____

            _____

            _____

            _____

                      Subtotal   = $ _____

2. Institutional Supporters:

A. Federations   = $ _____

B. Corporations   = $ _____

C. Government   = $ _____

D. Religious institutions   = $ _____

E. Federated drives   = $ _____

F. Associations of individuals   = $ _____

                      Subtotal   = $ _____

                      TOTAL   = $ _____

You now have a realistic sense of the funding you can anticipate in the forthcoming year. Does this match your fundraising goals as set in Phase 3? If so, you're in good shape. If not, you need to go back and see whether you can reduce your operating budget or reasonably increase your fundraising projections. Don't implement programs against revenues that aren't assured.

Next, to implement this strategy, sketch out the next twelve months of the year on some poster paper on a wall or on a large year-at-a-glance calendar. At the top of each monthly column, fill in the dollar amount that you need for monthly operating expenses. You are now ready to plot out your efforts (see the "Fundraising Calendar" worksheet).

1. Mark on the calendar your "proven traditions" for securing individual support, such as past membership appeals, special events, raffles, etc., and projected income from each for this year.

2. Fill in those grants and contributions from past institutional supporters that you can safely anticipate receiving again.

3. Add to the calendar the tasks you will need to complete in order for this support to be forthcoming. For example, under direct mail to membership, place all the tasks that are involved in a direct mail membership effort, such as: preparing copy for the letter; printing letter and enclosures; arranging artwork; arranging for mailing; recording receipts; and sending out thank-you notes. For past renewable institutional sources, place on your calendar not only writing proposals and cover letters but also sending final reports and occasional updates.

You should now have on your calendar all the tasks you will need to complete to elicit funds from your past supporters. Now, turn to your new prospects.

4. Schedule the additional efforts to secure support from individuals that you have decided to undertake. You are choosing here from all the various approaches outlined in Section 2 (face-to-face, direct mail, special events, etc.). In scheduling, you will want to pay particular attention to two major factors: (a) during which months you will need the funds to meet your operating expenses; and (b) the times of the year most appropriate for the activities you are planning.

Try to be as detailed as possible in listing all the tasks inherent in any particular fundraising activity.

5. Finally, plan out your approaches to prospective new institutional supporters. When will people in your organization—staff, board, and volunteers—be free for additional fundraising? Use the calendar and your sense of other organizational priorities to pinpoint the time of year when you can most effectively mount this fundraising effort.

Place on the calendar all the tasks that accompany these approaches to new sources, such as:

(a) identifying prospects through research and networking;

(b) developing program and/or general organizational proposals, including budgets and sample cover letters;

(c) identifying personal contacts as prospects;

(d) making the initial approach, either by telephone or by letter of inquiry, depending on the targeted sources and the nature of the personal relationship;

(e) submitting a formal proposal or application, with back-up supporting materials;

(f) scheduling follow-up appointments and visits with appropriate parties, at either your office or theirs;

(g) submitting any requested additional materials.

6. You can take your planning process one step further by assigning individuals to all the tasks listed. This will aid the organization in defining responsibilities for the individuals involved, as well as ensuring that the timeline and tasks set are realistic. You are anticipating the people power inherent in each step of the way and assigning these responsibilities as the plan unfolds.

7. Next, place conservative income projections for each source on the calendar and the date when you might expect to receive the funds. You should continually keep track of the totals of gross receipts versus gross expenses each month to determine whether you will have sufficient revenues. Don't forget to carry over any unspent revenues from one month to the next. Thus, your calendar will help you project cash flow as well.

8. In listing tasks, don't overlook evaluation of each of your fundraising efforts as part of your list.

You can place all your necessary fundraising activities and tasks on the calendar. Also, note that there is a line for monthly income totals, so you can keep track of your incoming revenues on a regular basis.

Use this calendar as an ongoing tool in your work. Review it at least once a month with all the people who are intimately involved with your organization's fundraising work. Make whatever changes and modifications are warranted. This is the blueprint of your fundraising strategy for the upcoming year.

Worksheet
FUNDRAISING CALENDAR

List on this calendar under the appropriate month, all the tasks and activities inherent in your fundraising plan, and the individuals responsible for their implementation.

September	October	November	December	January	February	March	April	May	June	July	August
Monthly Goal:											
$	$	$	$	$	$	$	$	$	$	$	$

Individual Fundraising

Institutional Fundraising

PHASE 8: MAKING THE APPROACH

For many nonprofit leaders, the moments they dread most in their professional lives arrive when it's time to ask someone for money. At these times, some leaders fall victim to feelings of reluctance and anxiety. Others, of course, face the same task with equanimity, sailing through their meetings with donors without a moment's hesitation. Perhaps these fortunate souls have prepared themselves in earlier careers—as sellers of Girl Scout cookies or UNICEF trick-or-treaters.

Whatever your attitude, making an overture to a prospective supporter should be treated seriously. The well-advised fundraiser makes a number of careful decisions before an approach after asking questions like the following.

Who Should Ask for Financial Support in Behalf of Your Organization?

Frequently, the executive director and the officers of the board of directors are an organization's prime solicitors. They are usually, but not always, the best choice to approach a major prospective supporter. The decision depends on each particular situation. Each and every person associated with a nonprofit can ask others for support: board members, volunteers, constituents, former constituents (i.e., alumni), family members, staff, members, supporters, friends, civic leaders, public officials, contacts, and peers.

Obviously, then, you need not feel alone in your fundraising work. There are many others to call on for assistance. You might even mobilize everyone on your list for a fundraising effort. And there are also instances when the automatic constituencies within an organization can be called on, too, to raise money to fill its coffers. The Girl Scouts, unquestionably the best sales force available, give the best example. Moreover, certain activities—selling raffle or benefit tickets, or recruiting sponsors for walkathons—can be done by anybody and everybody involved with your work, or simply attracted to it.

The leadership of a nonprofit must gauge in advance the most appropriate person or persons to make a particular request, drawing from the list already composed.

Experience shows that people respond most when the request comes from someone they know or respect. Thus, peer-to-peer solicitation is usually very effective: alumni to fellow alumni; students to other students; parents to parents; business people to their counterparts; youth to youth. As a general rule, ask board members to ask their peers for support, staff to ask other staff, volunteers to ask other volunteers, major donors to ask other major donors, and so on. When considering an approach to a particular constituency for the first time, you would do well to ask your prime candidates not only to make a contribution but to join you in asking others for support. In this way, you will be recruiting others who are better suited to ask their peers for assistance than your own current pool of candidates may be.

Unfortunately, some reluctant fundraisers experience their greatest fears when they consider asking their own friends and contacts for money. Yet these individuals are probably the most likely prospects. Personally, they know the value of a particular organization's work, since they have heard first-hand accounts from their friends. You would be overlooking a prime constituency by giving in to such fears. You might pleasantly discover that your friend will not only appreciate being asked but, further, will enjoy joining the life of your organization as a contributor and member.

To reiterate, your prime task is first to identify who should make a particular fundraising request in behalf of your organization, and then to brief that individual or those individuals adequately in preparation for the meeting with your candidate. You, as the executive director or member of the board, may be a member of the team of two or three who might participate in the visit.

Who Should Speak on Your Behalf?

I recall vividly a meeting with David Ramage in Philadelphia in the mid-1970s. At that time, I was co-director of the Philadelphia Clearinghouse for Community Funding Resources, a nonprofit technical assistance organization serving the Delaware Valley, and David was the President of the New World Foundation. He was visiting us with Karl Mathiasen, a member of his board, to assess our work, since we had applied for a grant from his foundation. Representing the Clearinghouse were the two co-directors, Linda Richardson and myself, and two of our board members, Bill Taylor, a finance secretary with the American Friends Service Committee, and Myesha Jackson, co-director of the Tenant Action Group. Bill represented what we referred to as "resource people," those who made their skills available to community-based organizations by serving on our board. Myesha represented a group that had received technical assistance from the Clearinghouse staff. At the close of the meeting, David told us why he had felt that it had been particularly good. He said, "Not only have you demonstrated the importance of your work by Myesha's comments, but you have attested to the quality of your work through Bill's remarks." David had shared with us a valuable insight. And yes we did receive a grant from them as well. The most ironic element of this story is that David Ramage gave significance to something that we were apt to take for granted: organizations found our work valuable, and experts felt that we were providing quality assistance. We had been so busy doing our job that we forgot to take a few steps back to assess it from an outsider's perspective.

Michael Seltzer

What Should You Specifically Ask Support For?

Again, you are matching up your prospective donor's interests with those activities of your organization that the donor would be most interested in supporting. Some people will be willing to give you money simply on the basis of your stated purpose, or to attend a special event you are sponsoring just to have a good time. More often than not, however, they will be more moved to be charitable when they hear or read about the specifics of your work.

Your task, then, is to anticipate which of your projected programs and efforts will have the greatest appeal to your prospects. Phase 3 provided some examples of the ways an organization can present its different needs. In other instances, your research, networking, and other information-gathering activities will provide you with some clues to your prospects' interests.

You may be tempted to present a foundation prospect with a number of choices. This strategy can be useful under certain circumstances, but you would be advised instead to gauge what aspect of your work would most interest a particular prospect and to present only that aspect. This demonstrates not only that you have done your homework but that you are reserving the right to set your own program priorities.

For How Much Should Your Request for Support Be?

Your various prospective supporters can afford to make contributions of varying amounts to support your work. It is your responsibility to give them that opportunity. Some groups choose to suggest an amount in a direct mail solicitation or a proposal.

Certain fundraising approaches, such as direct mail and special events, do lend themselves to a range of gift sizes. A special event, whether a banquet or dinner, is a perfect occasion to offer your contributors a range of options. People can decide to be sponsors, patrons, or benefactors, to mention just some of the traditional terms. You can ascribe a different dollar amount to distinguish between each level of support. That range should reflect the amounts of money you believe your supporters capable of giving. This approach is also helpful when you lack basic information about your prospective donors' giving habits.

In deciding how much you can ask prospective contributors to give, your information gathering and networking can once more be valuable aids. If you are approaching past donors, the simplest approach would be to base the amount you request on the basis of their highest previous gift to your organization. You can ask them either to repeat their past gift or to consider making a larger gift. There are always a number of arguments you can use to provide a rationale to your contributors for increasing their giving, such as increased costs, inflation, greater demand for services, or new threats and challenges to your constituencies. More often than not, you will have a sound rationale for such a request.

What if you are writing a donor who has never given before to your organization? How can you gauge in advance what amount to request? You can turn to other organizations for advice. While some groups may be reluctant to share data on their donors, others will quickly see that it is to their advantage.

After all, you may be able to do the same for them. Development officers at large nonprofits such as hospitals, universities, and museums rely also on a variety of standard reference materials to garner vital facts about prospective major donors. These include *Who's Who in America, The Social Register, Standard and Poor's Register of Corporations,* and *Directors and Executives.*

Since all of these books are standard reference materials, you are certainly not invading anyone's privacy by using them. Building a profile of your prospects will bring you closer to gaining a sense of how much financial support they are capable of providing to your organization. You also will be surprised about the information that is available to you from your local newspapers, which regularly report on philanthropic individuals in your community. Since it is usually desirable for nonprofits to provide some form of public recognition of their strongest supporters, you are also apt to find valuable tidbits about them in an organization's newsletters, annual reports, special event programs, or other publications.

Remember that your financial needs are real. They reflect the costs of programs that you and others value highly. You can assert these needs clearly to your current and prospective supporters, so that they are invited to respond according to their own abilities. By asking them to make contributions, you are extending an invitation to them.

A note about approaching institutional sources: Foundations, corporations, governmental agencies, and religious institutions, as previously indicated, often make information available about their average grant size in their annual reports, guidelines for applicants, requests for proposals, and other literature they publish on their grantmaking programs. It is preferable to approach these sources with requests for targeted amounts that are gauged on the institution's stated financial capabilities. You will, of course, state the entire budget of the project for which you are requesting support, but you want to be clear about what part of that budget you are asking them to underwrite. If you still have doubts about the desirable level of support to request, you can ask the counsel of a sympathetic contact at the institution you are approaching.

To summarize, when approaching either a prospective individual or institutional donor, you should:

1. Decide in advance the specific amount to request.

2. Target that amount to the capacity of the prospect you are approaching.

3. Choose to offer a range of gift options for large mass appeals.

All of the approaches discussed have merit, depending on the specific situation. You have to decide which ones you want to use. The following ladder of communication effectiveness is a useful tool to use in deciding which mix of approaches to individuals you might draw on in making up your fundraising plan.

House Parties

If you decide to throw a house party at a member's home for his or her neighbors, should you charge an admission in advance or at the door, make an appeal once people have congregated, or use the event only to set the stage for a later one-on-one solicitation? *How do you make this decision?*

The safest response is to charge a fixed amount for a ticket, in advance or at the door, or both. You should set your benefit price on the basis of the ability of your audience to pay, the "going rate" for such events in your community, and the entertainment value of your program. You can determine the going rate by checking what other nonprofits charge for similar events. On the basis of these three factors, you can then proceed to set the optimal ticket price.

If you are reaching out to constituents who can afford to make contributions larger than your ticket price, you certainly want to give them the opportunity to do so. In such an instance, you can use the house party to introduce your work to these prospects. Subsequently, approach them individually to elicit a contribution.

If you choose not to use your limited people resources for these follow-up contacts, which usually involve a letter, a phone call, and a visit, you may choose, during the course of the party, to ask individuals to make a contribution. This is referred to as a "pitch." Someone, usually not directly associated as staff with the organization, addresses the gathering at an appropriate moment. He or she makes a testimonial to the value of the work of the organization and asks for contributions. The emcee might start by asking for contributions at a designated high level. Once he or she gets as many pledges as are forthcoming for such sized gifts, the emcee drops to a request for a lower amount, and so on. The atmosphere resembles that of an art auction.

When and Where Can a Request for Financial Support Best Be Made

Institutions usually make decisions about when and where to request support easy for the grantseeker, since they have established procedures that may be printed in their guidelines. Your goal is always to seek as personal a contact as possible with a member of the staff who is engaged in the grant review process. This suggests a visit, to either their office or yours. First, mail an initial letter of inquiry and request a meeting. Since many sources, such as foundations and corporations, are deluged with requests for support, some may request a full proposal prior to meeting. Again, their printed guidelines will usually state such procedures.

If you do your homework well and know that your targeted supporters are strong prospects, you might choose other ways to introduce yourself to them before making a request for funds. You can extend an invitation to activities or programs or special events that you are planning. You can offer to mail them some materials on your work due to *their* stated interest in your field of endeavor. All these ideas will distinguish your approach from those of the legions of grantseekers who are always knocking on the doors of foundations and corporations. If your assumptions about a particular institution's priorities are correct, polite persistence will eventually pay off.

Your choices about when and where to approach individuals for support are more varied. Again, your goal is the same: You want to establish face-to-face contact as soon as possible. You can do that by canvassing door-to-door in your community, or by inviting people to a wine and cheese party, or by staffing a booth at an annual street festival in your town or city, to mention just a few of your options.

On the basis of the time and energy of the people available to you in your fundraising efforts, choose the mix of approaches shown in the chart that you can most effectively mount to reach your constituents.

Ladder of Communication Effectiveness

```
                                                          One-to-one
                                                          conversation
                                                  Small group
                                                  discussion
                                            Large group
                                            discussion
                                      Telephone
                                      conversation
                                Handwritten
                                letter
                          Typewritten
                          letter
                    Mass-produced
                    letter
              Newsletter
        Brochure
    News item
  Advertisement
Handout
```

Reprinted by permission of the *Harvard Business Review*. An exhibit from "What You Need to Know about Fund Raising" by Fisher Howe (March/April 1985). Copyright © 1985 by the President and Fellows of Harvard College; all rights reserved.

PHASE 9: BUILDING THE RELATIONSHIP WITH YOUR SUPPORTERS

On rare occasions, supporters find that they are rewarded for their support with ingratitude. With gift in hand, the nonprofit's leaders simply rush off on their mission and ignore their benefactors.

This is foolhardy. When a contribution is made, it signals the possibility of a long-term relationship taking root between an individual or an institution and the recipient group. Remember that it will always take you more time and effort to find a new donor than to keep an existing donor committed to your organization. The lesson is to value your supporters for the lifeline that they provide to your work.

How can you sustain and strengthen your supporters' interest and involvement in your work?

If you really perceive your supporters as partners in your undertaking, you will have to treat them as such. Some nonprofits actually bestow on their members voting privileges in the governance of their organizations. Their members elect the board of directors of the nonprofit corporation.

Short of this, nonprofit leaders can do many things to heighten the sense of affiliation between their constituents and their organizations. The following chart illustrates the variety of ways in which individuals can choose to become more active in the affairs of a nonprofit.

CHART
The History of John Doe's Participation in the Work of the Bumble Bee Day Care Center

* John makes a modest contribution in response to a request from his neighbor and becomes a member.

* He attends Center's Open House, responding to an invitation.

* He regularly receives newsletters and other publications from the Center.

* He attends special events.

* He becomes a volunteer in response to a call for volunteers in the newsletter.

* He asks others to volunteer their time.

* He asks others to make contributions.

* He receives public recognition for his contributions in a profile article in the newsletter.

* He joins a standing committee of the board.

* He accepts a nomination to the board of directors.

* He steps down from the board after serving two terms.

* He joins the advisory committee.

* He is honored at the annual dinner for his years of service.

The benefits the Center derives from John Doe's contributions are self-evident, but what may be less apparent are those John Doe has personally derived. They may include public recognition, social opportunities, leadership experience, respect from his neighbors and peers, and skill enhancement, to mention a few. In any case, it is safe to assume that both parties have reaped benefits from the association.

Correspondingly, relationships with institutional supporters need not begin and end with the receipt of a grant. There are also ways to increase the participation of institutional representatives in the work and life of your organization. The following chart illustrates some of these ways.

CHART
The History of Joan Swan, Program Officer of the Miracle Foundation, and The Echo Park Job Training Project

* Joan receives an invitation to a reception honoring the first graduating class of Echo Park Job Training Project (EPJTP).

* She chooses to attend after another foundation colleague calls to extend a second invitation.

* She meets the executive director and board president of EPJTP at the ceremony.

* She requests a meeting with them to discuss their work. Subsequently, she invites the submission of a proposal for a new component of their work.

* She receives the proposal and requests additional information.

* Miracle Foundation approves a grant! Joan calls the executive director with the good news.

* She sends out grant agreement and check.

* She receives a thank-you letter, a signed copy of the grant agreement, and a request for a meeting for advice on other prospective funders.

* She sees public acknowledgment of the Foundation's grant in the local newspaper.

* She requests and receives six-month narrative and financial report on the progress of the project.

* She asks EPJTP staff to meet with brand-new job training project in another part of town to provide technical advice.

* She accepts invitation for a site visit.

* She recommends the executive director of EPJTP as a speaker at a local funders' program on "Decreasing Chronic Unemployment."

* She receives final end-of-the-year report on the accomplishments of the project, including a glossy photograph of the program participants.

* She calls an EPJTP executive director for information for a speech she is preparing to give to the Chamber of Commerce.

* She acknowledges request from EPJTP for support for the second year of the project.

The history of Joan Swan and the Echo Park Job Training Project illustrates a key ingredient in a successful partnership between an organization and an institutional supporter: continuity. In this particular example, several things are presumed. The grantee is conducting a program that corresponds to the funder's interests and that is accomplishing its stated objectives. The grantee can choose to decline any request made by the funder that it deems inappropriate or that it cannot fulfill due to pressures of time or other reasons. But in the majority of cases, the grantee will be willing and able to satisfy requests.

These two examples are meant to be neither prescriptive nor exhaustive. They only suggest that the nonprofit organization and its supporters each have something to offer the other. It is the responsibility of the nonprofit to make the first overture and to nurture the relationship. Not every supporter will be interested in ongoing collaborations, but those who are will respond to your initiatives. The reward for both parties will be found in the fruits of an ongoing partnership.

PHASE 10: MONITORING AND EVALUATING YOUR FUNDRAISING EFFORTS: LAYING THE GROUNDWORK FOR NEXT YEAR

As in most aspects of fundraising, common sense is the rule in monitoring and evaluating your efforts. Whether a special event succeeds or fails, find out why. Ask all those involved to participate in an evaluation. Are the mistakes or miscalculations correctable? Did the event require more staff, member, and volunteer time than was warranted in terms of the money it generated? What could be done differently the next time around in order to enhance the event's success? Sometimes burnout or disappointment after a frustrating event are so rampant within an organization that questions such as these never get addressed.

Feedback is vital to other efforts, too. For example, find out why a targeted corporation sends a form rejection letter in response to your letter of inquiry by contacting the corporation. Call or write the charitable contributions officer and ask what might make your organization more attractive to the company for possible future consideration. Gather feedback wherever you can. Such information helps in redefining and refocusing the organization's fundraising strategy.

Most people have a tendency to walk away quickly from both successes and disappointments without reviewing them critically. As part of your planning process, schedule evaluation meetings after every special event and campaign. Ask people who were involved questions such as: What can we learn from this experience for the future? What would we do the same way again? What would we do differently?

Check with others for their perceptions. You can even survey your members, if you are assessing fundraising programs aimed at them.

Finally, be sure to schedule dates for your evaluation meetings as part of your planning process for next year's fundraising efforts. Build on your previous experiences.

FINAL THOUGHTS ON SECURING YOUR ORGANIZATION'S FUTURE

As described in this book, effective fundraising produces two equally important, simultaneous results: (1) you secure funds to support your organization in its immediate work; (2) you lay the financial groundwork for your future endeavors as well, thereby freeing yourself and your organization from reinventing a new fundraising "wheel" each year.

Through building a strong organization (Section 1), choosing appropriate funding partners (Section 2), and crafting a well-thought-out strategy and plan to secure their support (Section 3), you have served your constituents and supporters well. All will derive satisfaction from the knowledge that your nonprofit organization is on the right course.

Now, you are prepared to go out and start your fundraising for the year!

Case Study
THE PEASLEE-FOR-THE-PEOPLE PROJECT

In the summer of 1982 the Cincinnati Board of Education closed the doors of Peaslee School. That corner at 14th and Sycamore in Cincinnati's inner city had served the education of our neighborhood children for more than a hundred years. An old school building had been torn down several years before, leaving a vacant lot and a small, modernly equipped, newer annex we called Peaslee Primary.

My children attended Peaslee Primary and when we heard that the school would be closed we joined with our neighborhood in an effort to keep the school open. Because of the academic achievement and the long emotional attachment people had to the school, losing the fight to keep our school open was a tremendous blow to our community.

The school stood vacant for fourteen months. Walking past the dark, empty windows and seeing the building vandalized instead of alive with children added to the depression of a neighborhood whose low-income residents were being rapidly displaced by gentrification. There was a helpless feeling as our neighborhood was made a National Historic District, and we knew it was a matter of time before rents would be too high for us to afford. We felt the loss of the school was connected with the beginnings of a loss of the neighborhood's fabric.

But our neighborhood, called Over-the-Rhine, had faced losses before and the people who were hit would rebound to fight harder next time. This was such a time. It seemed in those fourteen months we just had time to catch our breath.

In the summer of 1983 a group of young lawyers presented a proposal to the school board to rent the Peaslee property for a day care facility for their children. They asked for a ten-year lease at $35,000 per year. We had heard rumors of this when the school was closed and had approached the young lawyers asking them to join with our community in saving the school. The best they could offer was no offer at all: six slots in their day care center if we could raise the $6,000 per year per child tuition. This would in effect have paid for their rent.

About the same time, our community was approached by an agency which serves low-income people to ask for our support for them purchasing Peaslee School for use as offices. They felt that with our support the school board would turn over the property for $1.00. This proposal was rejected by the school board and they were given two weeks to come back with a sound proposal or the vote would go to the young lawyers. The agency pulled out, leaving us alone.

Parents who had fought for the school, community supporters, our Over-the-Rhine Community Council, and our neighborhood development corporation pulled together to work out a proposal for usage of the school and an offer for purchase. After negotiating back and forth (over six months) with the school board we came up with an agreement that the community would put $15,000 cash down and be given one year to raise the remaining purchase price of $225,000, plus that year's maintenance cost.

We envisioned a building that would belong to the low-income community and be used as an educational and cultural center for our integrated neighborhood. Community control of this building would also help stabilize the low-income housing around it. But the $240,000-plus price tag made that look like an impossible dream. We knew our real work had just begun.

We had only a few days to pull together the $15,000 cash. The city was willing to act as a conduit for the transfer of property so we wouldn't have to bid on the building at public auction. The city would draw up the contract and expect the $15,000 when we signed it.

We tried to look at this as a time to gather community support for the project, knowing our whole neighborhood would have to be behind the effort in order to succeed. We asked everybody for a contribution and people gave knowing it might not be returned, and the $15,000 would be lost if the total purchase price wasn't met a year from now. Many community people gave what they could, from $5 to $10. We asked businesses and churches for $25. Several social workers and religious organizations contributed $100 to $500. Block clubs, the Alcoholic Drop Inn Center, and the Neighborhood Development Corporation contributed larger sums. It was a tremendous vote of confidence to be able to turn over the down payment gathered from our own neighbors.

The next step was to figure out how to raise $225,000 more. What follows is an outline of how we went about it, what some of the ups and downs were, and what kept us going throughout the year.

What we did first was to break into two core groups: a fundraising committee and a development committee. We felt we couldn't raise money without development ideas progressing along simultaneously, and we wanted a group that could set limits and handle larger proposals. This committee would meet every two weeks. We also knew that fundraising would take a lot of nitty-gritty work sessions. This could be more of an open committee meeting weekly to keep our tasks rolling along. Some of the people involved belonged to both committees; several worked with only one committee.

For most of us, this was our first experience raising money. And because our leadership was women without "credentials" in financing, we faced criticism from the male professional establishment from the start. To overcome this we called on people who had done some grassroots fundraising in our community. The Drop Inn Center Shelter House had raised $110,000 in six months to buy their building. They were good about lending us a hand and assuring us that we could do it our way and run a professional, successful campaign without using the typical establishment process. They also gave us respect as women in leadership. We also called on women who were already in the system; there were religious communities, women's groups, and Over-the-Rhine Community Council women who urged us on.

Families in our community have an average annual income of $6,000 per year. One person in our group sat down and figured out how many people would have to donate $10 to achieve our goal. I think that's when the $225,000 price tag really began to hit home and we began to realize that we'd have to go outside our community for financial support, and we would have to explain what Peaslee was and could become for us. We'd have to convince 22,500 people!

One thing that helped was that we picked a chairperson for each of the committees and those two people stayed in close contact and worked on both committees. Another help was that we drew up a tentative time line so that we could see how much we would need to have raised by March, by August, etc. This helped set goals along the way and broke down the enormous sum to smaller attainable amounts. Probably the best thing for me was to know I could count on the other chairwoman if I fell through and that she could count on me. When the goals began to feel overwhelming, she helped me set smaller, closer goals. So instead of "raising a huge amount of money," our goal was just to make it to the next week accomplishing five smaller tasks.

The fundraising committee was made up of about six core members. We decided to meet every week for a business meeting, then follow with a work session. The business meetings were to discuss ideas, divide up tasks, and keep in touch. For the work sessions we'd invite more people and fold brochures, prepare bulk mailings, write thank you notes, and so forth. We wanted to have a large-group meeting inviting more citywide supporters every six to eight weeks. We were able to do this about three times and it was helpful for us to feel the broader support, as well as to have fresh ideas and new contacts.

We did many little fundraisers ourselves from selling balloons at the neighborhood's summer festival to collecting monthly pledges among ourselves. But still we knew our focus had to be on getting the word out. If we could reach other people and convince them to take up the project we'd be better off. So a lot of our time went to contacting groups from schools, social justice classes, community action groups, and church committees. We put together a slide show and made presentations to many different groups. The response was great. One church put on a spaghetti dinner for us, several schools did projects inside their classes to raise donations, and a women's choir arranged a concert on our behalf.

Another aspect of getting the word out was to put together mailings. We developed a brochure and asked different groups or individuals if they would give us their mailing list and a cover letter we could use endorsing our project. Groups like the AFL-CIO endorsed us and sent out our information to their locals and membership. A couple of city council members gave us their campaign lists and support letters. Many work sessions were spent addressing envelopes; the return was quite good.

With the help of the development committee we put together proposals for several foundations. A great breakthrough for us was a grant of $25,000 from the Greater Cincinnati Foundation. This grant legitimized us with the more conservative Cincinnati business community. From there we were able to get a listing from the Chamber of Commerce giving us business addresses and pre-addressed labels. We sent out word about our grant and asked each business to contribute $100. Because we had been able to keep our project in the media—through newspaper editorials and television coverage of events—the businesses began to adopt us as a "community working to improve itself" and that increased their monetary support. There was also "in-kind" support from businesses. One insurance company came forward, donating $5,000 to cover insurance for us. Most of the paper, envelopes, brochures, and copying needs were taken care of by various printing companies.

Some of the larger moneys took a lot of energy from both committees. We were able to get a $50,000 Community Development grant, but only after hours of lobbying city council members and battling with city staff who were opposed to us. A lot of careful paperwork had to be prepared and the case kept on top of or it would have fallen through the cracks along the way before getting to the vote. We were always reminded that the young lawyers, as well as speculators, were out there waiting for our effort to fail.

A major problem with fundraising is that we couldn't find foundations willing to give purchase grants. A lot of groups will support programs or equipment but not the purchase cost. We couldn't commit to renting space at Peaslee until we had money, and it seemed like we couldn't get the money until we could say for certain which groups we'd rent to. We slowly overcame this hurdle by continuing to talk among ourselves, as well being open with the foundation groups. A lot of persistence and determination didn't hurt, either.

During our previous fight to keep the school open, we had met radio, television, and newspaper reporters. We renewed those contacts with the media during this campaign by inviting them to events and press conferences. For example, on Martin Luther King Day we were able to get into the building and hold a "Clean Up/ Fundraising Kick-Off" where we invited neighborhood people to help straighten up and mop down the building and read Martin Luther King's "I Have a Dream" speech.

Film coverage of this and similar events, as well as newspaper articles, served as reminders to the larger Cincinnati community that we were still working toward our goal. People who had never been in our neighborhood began to identify with our struggle just because they saw it mentioned enough. At one point we hung two 8' by 24' signs on the side of the Peaslee building asking for people to contribute and to "Share Our Dream." This gave people who drove by on the way to work or downtown shopping the realization that Peaslee really existed. (Over-the-Rhine sits just north of downtown.)

As our last two months closed in we had to meet and assess where we'd come and how far we had to go. We had kept in mind that we might have to go for a loan and a couple of members of the development committee had taken on getting loan commitments from banks and progressive funding groups if needed. At this meeting we decided to approach the school board and present the details of all we had done toward earning our money, plus all the positive things we had done toward education aside from Peaslee (work in other neighborhood schools, support of a tax levy, development of an Education Task Force at our Community Council). We were able to tell them that we were confident that we would have $200,000 in cash by the deadline. We also related our dreams for Peaslee, and said they could be realized sooner if we didn't have a debt service from a loan. We went forward with our presentation and met with individual board members. Again, because of our hard work and broader community support, we were successful in having the purchase price reduced to $200,000, plus the maintenance costs.

Our last step was to approach the Methodist Union together with a couple of supportive Methodist ministers who work in our community. We told them our story and that with a grant from them for $10,000 we would have the last money needed to buy our building. They came through for us.

On December 14, 1984, we were able to turn over $209,239.13 to the Cincinnati School Board and received the keys for Peaslee School.

by Kathleen Henson

Source: This article appeared in the May/June 1985 issue of *The Grantsmanship Center News.* Copyright © 1985 The Grantsmanship Center, Los Angeles, CA. Reprinted with permission.

Photo: Courtesy of Peaslee for the People Project/OTR, Inc., Cincinnati, OH. Reprinted with permission.

Case Study
THE TIMES OF HARVEY MILK

The Times of Harvey Milk is a powerful eighty-seven-minute film which documents the career of the late San Francisco supervisor—the country's second openly gay elected official—and the aftermath of his assassination in 1978. The film is a testament not only to its subject's belief that gays can come out and build bridges to the larger community but also to the power of grassroots organization. Appropriately enough, these proved to be the key factors in the filmmakers' successful fundraising strategy, giving hundreds of individual donors the opportunity to back what would prove to be an Oscar-winning film.

Filmmaker Rob Epstein was working on a film about the Briggs initiative (which would have prohibited homosexuals from teaching in California public schools) when Harvey Milk was shot. He began raising money for a larger film about Milk, but found fundraising slow-going. Epstein had written to over 100 foundations and corporations in the San Francisco Bay area, including funders who had supported film projects or who had a general interest in San Francisco or the media. Not one responded positively, and government sources of support weren't any more forthcoming. Epstein had been able to get some support from the Harvey Milk United Fund, a community-based fund, and small foundations such as northern California's Pioneer Foundation and the Film Fund, which is specifically dedicated to funding social issue documentaries. He had also had some success with community fundraising events. Vito Russo, a gay film historian and theorist, organized a fifteen-dollar-a-head event in New York at which he showed assorted esoteric film clips (e.g., rare Barbra Streisand footage) and a fifteen-minute sample reel (a sort of trailer for the uncompleted film) of *Harvey Milk* made by Epstein. The organizers of the Gay Film Festival also sponsored a fundraiser in San Francisco. These benefits had shown that individuals would respond to the project, but producing the single events was too labor-intensive to be an efficient fundraising tool.

About the time of these fundraisers—two and half years after Epstein's fundraising had begun—filmmaker Richard Schmiechen joined him. Together, they developed an overall fundraising strategy. They considered the stop-and-go method often used by independent documentarians—in which the filmmakers shoot, stop to raise money, then shoot some more, and stop again to raise more money—the least efficient or desirable method. Their goal was to raise enough money to enable them to work on the film full-time. Because Epstein had had such bad luck with foundations, he and Schmiechen decided to put institutional sources on hold for a while until the project had more momentum and potential funders could be shown concrete evidence, such as a rough cut, that the film was actually going to get made. However, they did target a few institutional sources, which they felt would prove to be more likely supporters than their first choices: the Independent Documentary Fund, a project of New York's public television station WNET, which had once funded Schmiechen for another film; the Corporation for Public Broadcasting, which is the national funding agency associated with public television; the New York State Council on the Arts (NYSCA), which supports independent filmmakers; the National Endowment for the Arts, which is the national counterpart of NYSCA; and the Chicago Resource Center, and the Funding Exchange/National

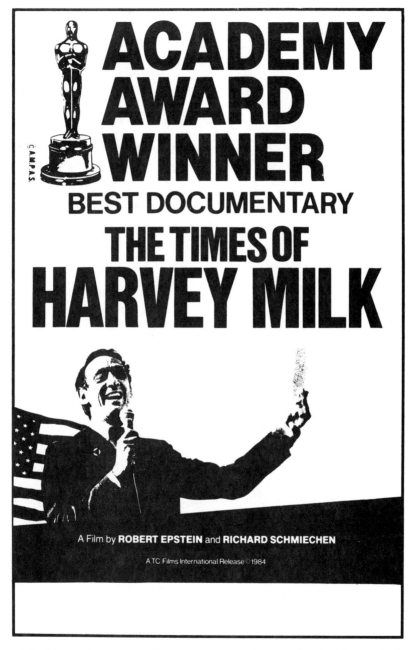

Source: The Times of Harvey Milk, San Francisco, CA. Reprinted with permission.

Community Funds, two national foundations with a particular interest in gay and lesbian initiatives. As their descriptions suggest, each of these choices were natural prospects for *The Times of Harvey Milk.*

After consulting with fundraising specialists, Epstein and Schmiechen decided to get the momentum going with donations from individuals, to be approached via direct mail campaign. But first they had to target their audience. "We asked ourselves, 'Who has the most interest in the subject? Who was the most emotionally attached?,'" Schmiechen recalled. "The answer, obviously, was gay people. San Francisco was clearly a prime target area, as was New York, where I lived. And we targeted politically aware gay people throughout the country." The filmmakers invested money in graphics and printing and came up with a well-designed mailing package consisting of a brochure, a pledge card, a return envelope, an outside envelope, and a cover letter written by Vito Russo. The letter mentioned that the filmmakers' backgrounds included work on *Word Is Out* and *Rosie the Riveter,* two highly respected documentaries that also questioned sexual stereotypes. The filmmakers' track record established their credibility and the professional-looking package backed it up.

"We talked more about the project as a film and its effect than about making Harvey a symbol," Schmiechen said. "We stressed that it would deal with the importance of gays participating openly in the nation's political life and of presenting positive images of gay people. There were strong feelings at the time about bad media images—*Cruising* had just come out," (a controversial film starring Al Pacino in which the depiction of gay men triggered demonstrations). The gay community was still angry about the injustice of the light sentence given to Dan White, Milk's convicted killer, and the prejudice exposed by the Briggs initiative. "We also made it very clear the film would be on PBS and seen by six million people at least," Schmiechen added, "and that it would be shown in educational markets and *maybe* have a theatrical release." Schmiechen was able to predict a PBS showing because, just before the mailing went out, he and Epstein received a grant of $100,000 from the Independent Documentary Fund (IDF), with the stipulation that they had to match $50,000 of it within three months. An additional slip of paper mentioning this new development was included in the direct mailing, giving the appeal an added urgency.

"The direct mail appeal was more efficient than doing events, but it was more complicated than I anticipated," Schmiechen said. The filmmakers investigated which mailing lists were available to them and learned that the best lists are those of people who have sent a check in response to a mailing. They got mailing lists from *Christopher Street* (a national gay magazine), the National Gay Rights Advocates (a legal group), the *Word Is Out* film mailing list, gay businesses found through the Gay Yellow Pages, San Francisco progressive political organizations, and names of friends and contacts. All together, 13,000 pieces of mail went out. The most successful list in terms of response was the list of friends, followed by *Christopher Street* and Gay Rights Advocates lists. The lists that did the worst were the local political organizations. Those people were already giving money, and perhaps they give at meetings—not through the mail. Conventional direct mail wisdom says that if you cover your costs on your first mailing, you're in good shape. The *Harvey Milk* mailing cost around $5,000, which was "borrowed" from a $15,000 production grant the filmmakers had received from NYSCA, and brought in $10,000 in contributions.

Because of the pressure to raise money to make the matching grant, the film makers decided to pursue a second fundraising front. With Schmiechen working in New York and Epstein in San Francisco, they held by-personal-invitation-only screenings of the sample reel for people whom they thought might contribute sizable amounts. "We looked for two kinds of people," Schmiechen said. "People with money and people who knew people with money." The audiences ranged in size from two to twenty. Either Schmiechen or Epstein spoke about the film at each screening, although they were not always the person who gave the pitch itself. And at every screening they collected the names of other people who might be worth inviting to subsequent screenings, as well as pledge cards and checks. Foundation representatives were also invited to the screenings. The most successful screenings were those under the auspices of an interested individual who could then invite his or her friends. For example, one screening that netted $2,500 was held at the home of a gay doctor who invited members of an organization made up of other gay doctors. "Unlike the foundation people, most of the viewers at the screenings were fairly naive in terms of film," Schmiechen recalled, "but they responded to the images they saw. The average giver had donated to gay issues before and most of them were gay professional men or people with inherited wealth who could write a $100 check without cutting into their rent money." Schmiechen and Epstein each did about one screening a week for two months. A higher proportion of the screening audience (at least 50 percent) gave than did the direct mail recipients, and the average contribution was larger than the average gift of twenty-five dollars from the direct mail group. A nonprofit organization had agreed to act as fiscal agent for the filmmakers, so all contributions could be tax-deductible.

Having raised enough money to meet the IDF matching grant, the filmmakers were now able to plunge into production full-time. But they didn't forget about their supporters. Dropping the names of people who had never responded (except for a few targeted, rich potential donors), they culled a pool of 850 donors from the mailing, screenings, and benefits. During the year of production, these donors received four newsletters from the filmmakers, a sort of "family" memo letting them know who the staff was, how the filming was going, and other news about the production. Needless to say, each newsletter contained the ubiquitous pledge card and a business reply envelope. "The response varied with how hard the pitch was," Schmiechen said. "They ranged from 'We still need money' at the end of the newsletter to 'We are desperate' right at the top." All told the donor pool received five appeals from the filmmakers within fifteen months. "Laying the groundwork was the most important thing," Schmiechen said. "We targeted who was most likely to give us money and then really went after them. Having printed materials that communicated effectively and a sample reel that moved and affected people was crucial." Through the screenings and newsletters, the filmmakers gave their supporters a real sense of involvement which paid off handsomely: contributions from individuals came to $115,000. The largest single check was $4,500, but the average contribution was $125.

"The groundwork all paid off at the same time." Schmiechen said. "By the time the IDF grant came in, we had developed a core group of supporters to get names from. Also, we had targeted foundations we could go to for matching funds." With the IDF grant in place, the filmmakers were able to get additional money from the Funding Exchange, the Chicago Resource Center, and the Columbia Foundation (another foundation oriented toward progressive projects). With the contributions from individuals and the $85,000 raised from institutional donors, the filmmakers were able to meet their budget of $220,000. Most of the remaining funds was raised within three months.

Epstein and Schmiechen weren't out of the woods yet, however. While the film was being edited they realized they were going to run out of money, and so began another round of screenings. This time they showed the rough cut (a draft version of the final film) in New York and San Francisco almost weekly for a couple of months, including a screening by Tom O'Horgan, a noted playwright, at his loft. In addition to pledge cards, members of the audience were given response forms to let the filmmakers know their thoughts on the film, thus increasing their sense of participation.

"We depended very much on 'connected giving.' It was very personal, unlike giving to the United Way at the office," Schmiechen said. "Also, our project wasn't a prestige item at that point for potential high donors—we couldn't give our contributors the traditional cachet of giving to, say the Metropolitan Opera." As a result, the filmmakers offered a film credit to entice donations of $500 or more (ultimately numbering sixty). "The credits went on forever," Schmiechen observed. In fact, *everyone* who had contributed found themselves thanked collectively in front of more than a billion people worldwide when Schmiechen and Epstein expressed their appreciation in their acceptance speech during the 1985 Academy Awards telecast. *The Times of Harvey Milk* had won the Oscar for Best Feature Documentary.

Some of the most important contributions had come as volunteer work and in-kind donations. "If we had had to pay for all the labor and services that were donated, our budget would have been $2 million instead of $300,000," Schmiechen said. The filmmakers have continued to correspond with their supporter community now that the film is finished and in distribution. A recent newsletter announced the date of the PBS screening, gave foreign distribution news, and made a pitch for donations to Rob Epstein's documentary on AIDS which is currently in production.

The Times of Harvey Milk is a film about what happens when people emerge from feeling isolated and make links with others to form a community. Personal links proved to be the secret of the film's fundraising. "The fun part for me was meeting interesting people," Schmiechen said. "I also met some people I didn't hit it off with and they never gave us money. I learned it's very important to think of potential donors as potential friends. The people who you like and who respond to you are the ones who will give."

by Ellin Stein

GENERAL
FURTHER READINGS
Books, Articles, Pamphlets

American Association of Fund Raising Counsel, Inc. *Giving USA: <Year> Annual Report.* New York: American Association of Fund Raising Counsel, Inc. Annual. Approx. 104 pp. $30.00. (Order from: American Association of Fund Raising Counsel, Inc., 500 Fifth Ave., New York, NY 10036)

> Annual compilation of the facts and trends of private philanthropy. Includes information on sources of philanthropy and categories of philanthropic activity such as hospitals, educational, religious, etc. Numerous charts and tables.

Basic Grantsmanship Information (Package 1). Los Angeles: The Grantsmanship Center. $19.95. (Order from: The Grantsmanship Center, P.O. Box 6210, 650 S. Spring St., Suite 570, Los Angeles, CA 90014)

> Reprints of 9 articles from *The Grantsmanship Center NEWS* provide basic information on finding foundation, corporate, or government support.

Bauer, David G. *The "How To" Grants Manual: Successful Grantseeking Techniques for Obtaining Public and Private Grants.* New York: Macmillan Publishing Co. 1984. 229 pp. $19.95. (Order from: Macmillan Publishing Co., 866 Third Ave., New York, NY 10022)

> Step-by-step system for success in receiving government, corporate, and foundation grants. Part One focuses on developing a strategy, including organizing ideas, determining priorities, and identifying and evaluating needs. Parts Two and Three provide guidelines for identifying appropriate funding sources, successfully contacting them, submitting a proposal, and following up on it.

Brakeley, George A., Jr. *Tested Ways to Successful Fund Raising.* Hartsdale, NY: Public Service Materials Center. 1980. 171 pp. $19.95. (Order from: Public Service Materials Center, 111 N. Central Ave., Hartsdale, NY 10530)

> Covers all forms of fundraising in a way that is geared primarily to professional fundraisers. Includes useful information on donor motivation and market research.

Breiteneicher, Joe. "Quest for Funds: Insider's Guide to Corporate & Foundation Funding." *Conserve Neighborhoods* no. 29 (March-April 1983): 271–289. $1.50. (Order from: National Trust for Historic Preservation, 1785 Massachusetts Ave., N.W., Washington, DC 20036)

> Overview of private fundraising with discussion of planning, finding the funders, developing market strategies, constructing a case statement, and managing the fundraising program.

Broce, Thomas E. *Fundraising: Guide to Raising Money from Private Sources.* Norman, OK: University of Oklahoma. 1979. 304 pp. $17.50. (Order from: Uni-

versity of Oklahoma Press, 1005 Asp Ave., Norman, OK 73019)
> Overview of fundraising including annual campaigns, club formation, prospect research, case statement development, and planning.

Capital Campaign Resource Guide. San Francisco: Public Management Institute. 1200 pp. $345.00. (Order from: Public Management Institute, 358 Brannan St., San Francisco, CA 94107)
> Five-part directory with (1) "how-to" guide on conducting a capital campaign; (2) directory of foundations and corporations which make capital campaign grants; (3) directory of fundraising consultants who conduct capital campaigns; (4) directory of nonprofit organizations who have recently conducted capital campaigns; and (5) summary of state laws regulating fundraising.

Conrad, Daniel Lynn. *Successful Fund Raising Techniques.* Second Edition. San Francisco: Public Management Institute. 1977. 351 pp. in 3-ring binder. $39.00. (Order from: Public Management Institute, 358 Brannan St., San Francisco, CA 94107)
> Covers a range of proven methods of funding development including direct mail, capital campaigns, grants, endowments, memorial and honor giving, and major gift solicitation. One chapter deals with donor motivations.

Flanagan, Joan. *The Grass Roots Fundraising Book: How to Raise Money in Your Community.* Chicago: Swallow Press. 1982. 344 pp. $11.95 (Order from: Swallow Press, 180 N. Michigan Ave., Chicago, IL 60601)
> One of the most important guides to a wide range of grass roots and community fundraising activities. Provides step by step details on how to set up a fundraising program, how to choose the right strategy for a given group, and how to raise money and build an organization at the same time. Extensive references to other resource materials.

Flanagan, Joan. *The Successful Volunteer Organization: Getting Started and Getting Results in Nonprofit, Charitable, Grass Roots, and Community Groups.* Chicago: Contemporary Books, Inc. 1981. 376 pp. $13.95 (Order from: Contemporary Books, Inc., 180 N. Michigan Ave., Chicago, IL 60601)
> How-to manual for volunteer organizations discusses getting started, getting results, getting organized, and getting advice. Principles for strengthening organizations include how to conduct productive meetings, do fundraising and publicity, and build a stronger membership and board of directors. Includes an annotated bibliography.

Fundraising and Nongrant Support. Los Angeles: The Grantsmanship Center. $19.95. (Order from: The Grantsmanship Center, P.O. Box 6210, 650 S. Spring St., Suite 570, Los Angeles, CA 90014)
> Reprints of 9 articles from *The Grantsmanship Center NEWS* on a variety of sources of support for nonprofit organizations such as profit-making subsidiaries, annual funds, special events, and telephone solicitation. Also includes more general articles on marketing and public relations.

Fund-Raising Research. Volume 1: How to Find Philanthropic Prospects. Volume 2: FRI Prospect-Research Resource Directory. Ambler, PA: Fund-Raising Institute. 1986. Vol. 1, 204 pp.; Vol. 2, 362 pp. $69.95. (Order from: Fund-Raising Institute, Box 365, Ambler, PA 19002)

Volume 1 shows how to identify and evaluate fundraising prospects including individuals, corporations, foundations, associations, and government programs. Volume 2 describes more than 400 resources, including publications, databases, and services, which can be used by nonprofit organizations when researching information on prospects for philanthropic gifts.

Grambs, Marya, and Pam Miller. *Dollars and Sense: A Community Fundraising Manual for Women's Shelters and Other Non-Profit Organizations*. San Francisco: Western States Shelter Network. 1982. 135 pp. $22.00. (Order from: Western States Shelter Network, 870 Market St, Suite 1058, San Francisco, CA 94102)

Discusses a variety of fundraising methods. Examines the politics of fundraising, including the need to help the members of the organization deal with their attitudes about money and asking others for money. Includes a number of practical anecdotes and scenarios to allow people to practice handling sensitive situations.

Grasty, William K., and Kenneth G. Sheinkopf. *Successful Fundraising: A Handbook of Proven Strategies and Techniques*. New York: Charles Scribner's Sons. 1982. 318 pp. $18.75. (Order from: Charles Scribner's Sons, 115 5th Ave., New York, NY 10003)

Covers how to set up a development office, train volunteers, identify and cultivate donors, and manage an annual fund campaign. Includes strategies and examples for such methods as telephone and direct mail, special events, gift clubs, deferred gifts, and capital campaigns.

Gurin, Maurice G. *What Volunteers Should Know for Successful Fund Raising*. Hartsdale, NY: Public Service Materials Center. 1981. 151 pp. $14.95. (Order from: Public Service Materials Center, 111 N. Central Ave., Hartsdale, NY 10530)

Clarifies conventional fundraising practice and introduces new concepts in fundraising in a way that can be used by volunteers as well as professional fundraisers who train volunteers.

Heywood, Ann H., comp. *The Resource Directory for Funding and Managing Nonprofit Organizations*. New York: Edna McConnell Clark Foundation. 1982. 83 pp. Free. (Order from: Edna McConnell Clark Foundation, 250 Park Ave., New York, NY 10017)

Reference book for nonprofit organizations lists publications and technical assistance organizations that will help advise nonprofits.

Hummel, Joan. *Starting and Running a Non-Profit Organization*. Minneapolis: University of Minnesota Press. 1980. 147 pp. $19.95. (Order from: Public Service Materials Center, 111 N. Central Ave., Hartsdale, NY 10530)

Discusses the steps involved in setting up an agency including defining goals, planning programs, creating a board of directors, incorporating, budgeting, and raising funds. Intended for small agencies which are just starting or are under ten years old.

Jackson, Michael R., and Earl W. Anthes. *Nonprofit Management Bibliography. The.* St. Paul: Nonprofit Management Association. 1984. 62 pp. $5.00. (Order from: Nonprofit Management Association, c/o Amherst H. Wilder Foundation, 919 Lafond St., St. Paul, MN 55104)

Lists hundreds of publications under such headings as Fund Raising and Resource Development, Financial Management, Planning and Evaluation, Marketing/Public Relations, and Managing and Developing Human Resources.

Lord, James Gregory. *The Raising of Money: Thirty-five Essentials Every Trustee Should Know.* Cleveland, OH: Third Sector Press. 1984. 17 pp. $34.50. (Order from: Third Sector Press, P.O. Box 18044, Cleveland, OH 44118)

Concise presentations of key ideas of fundraising for trustees and other volunteers of nonprofit organizations. Includes discussion of assessing institutional needs and community desires: getting people involved; setting goals; and following through on the campaign.

Lovelock, Christopher H., and Charles B. Weinberg. *Marketing for Public and Nonprofit Managers.* New York: John Wiley and Sons. 1984. 607 pp. $29.95. (Order from: John Wiley and Sons, One Wiley Dr., Somerset, NJ 08873)

Looks at the role of marketing in improving management practice in the public and nonprofit sectors. Applies a marketing approach to attracting gifts and volunteers.

Mellon Bank Corporation. *Discover Total Resources: A Guide for Nonprofits.* Pittsburgh: Mellon Bank Corporation. 1985. 43 pp. Free. (Order from: Mellon Bank Corporation, Community Affairs Division, One Mellon Bank Center, Pittsburgh, PA 15258)

Resource development guide with a descriptive checklist for boards, staff, and volunteers to assess the degree to which they are tapping all community resources: people, money, goods and services.

Mitiguy, Nancy. *The Rich Get Richer and the Poor Write Proposals.* Amherst, MA: Citizenship Involvement Training Project, 1978. 147 pp. $5.50. (Order from: Citizen Involvement Training Project, 138 Hasbrouck, University of Massachusetts, Amherst, MA 01003)

Quick guide to a variety of fundraising possibilities for nonprofit organizations.

O'Connell, Brian. *Origins, Dimensions and Impact of America's Voluntary Spirit.* Washington, DC: Independent Sector. 1984. 8 pp. $2.00. (Order from: Independent Sector, 1828 L St., N.W., Washington, DC 20036)

Essay on the benefits of voluntary contributions of time and money for the quality of life in America.

Paving the Way for Local Economic Development: A Development and Fundraising Manual for Local Development Corporations. New York: Interface. 1983. 156 pp. $15.00. (Order from: Interface, 666 Broadway, New York, NY 10011)
Manual on program development and fundraising for local economic development organizations. Includes worksheets and checklists.

Pendleton, Neil. *Fundraising: A Guide for Non-Profit Organizations.* Englewood Cliffs, NJ: Prentice-Hall, Inc. 1981. 207 pp. $6.95. (Order from: Prentice-Hall, Inc., Englewood Cliffs, NJ 07632)
Guide to obtaining individual donations for nonprofit organizations including a 16-step procedure for organizing a fundraising campaign. Geared to both volunteers and professionals. Charts, tables and sample letters, many of which are from private schools and colleges.

Setterberg, Fred, and Kary Schulman. *Beyond Profit: The Complete Guide to Managing the Nonprofit Organization.* New York: Harper and Row. 1985. 271 pp. $18.95. (Order from: Harper and Row, 10 E. 53rd St., New York, NY 10022)
Strategies for managing all aspects of nonprofit organizations including long-range planning, publicity and fundraising. In the section on fundraising discusses why and how to ask for money, where the money is and how to get it.

Tenbrunsel, Thomas W. *The Fund Raising Resource Manual: Strategies for Nonprofit Organizations.* Englewood Cliffs, NJ: Prentice-Hall, Inc. 1982. 182 pp. $7.95. (Order from: Prentice-Hall, Inc., Englewood Cliffs, NJ 07632)
Designed in the form of a self-teaching course on fundraising, this manual covers individual and corporate giving, direct mail, government and foundation grants, and special events. Identifies potential fundraising sources and tells how to reach them. Each chapter includes source materials, charts, examples, worksheets and exercises.

Upshur, Carole C. *How to Set Up and Operate a Non-Profit Organization.* Englewood Cliffs, NJ: Prentice-Hall, Inc. 1982. 252 pp. $9.95. (Order from: Prentice-Hall, Inc., Englewood Cliffs, NJ 07632)
Guidelines and procedures for small and medium-sized organizations in such areas as incorporating, raising funds, and writing grant proposals. Provides an annotated bibliography of other resources.

Periodicals

Conserve Neighborhoods. Bimonthly. Washington, DC: National Trust for Historic Preservation. $10.00/yr. (Order from: National Trust for Historic Preservation, 1785 Massachusetts Ave., N.W., Washington, DC 20036)
Practical information to aid community improvement activities including articles on fundraising, nonprofit management, public relations, and current trend analysis.

Foundation News. Bimonthly. Washington, DC: Council on Foundations. $24.00/yr. (Order from: Council on Foundations, 1828 L St., N.W., Washington, DC 20036)

> Primary focus on grantmakers, grantmaking activities and trends with some information on philanthropy in general.

Fund Raising Management. Monthly. Garden City, NY: Hoke Communications. $36.00/yr. (Order from: Hoke Communications, 224 Seventh St., Garden City, NY 11530)

> How-to articles on all aspects of fundraising. Information on successful campaigns and methods.

Fund Raising Review. Bimonthly. New York: American Association of Fund-Raising Counsel, Inc. $25.00. (Order from: American Association of Fund-Raising Counsel, Inc., 25 West 43 St., New York, NY 10036)

> Summary of significant articles, speeches and trends in fundraising. (Available with subscription to *Giving USA* for $55.00)

Government Relations Info and Action. Occasional publication. Washington, DC: Independent Sector. (Available to members of Independent Sector, 1828 L St., N.W., Washington, DC 20036)

> Summary of actions of various branches of the federal government which affect nonprofit organizations, foundations, and corporations which are involved in philanthropy.

Grants Magazine. Quarterly. New York: Plenum Publishing Corporation. $65.00/yr.; $27.00/yr. for individuals. (Order from: Plenum Publishing Corporation, 227 W. 17th St., New York, NY 10011)

> Covers issues in both public and private philanthropy which are of interest to grantmakers and grantseekers. Includes how-to articles and legislative information.

Grassroots Fundraising Journal. Bimonthly. San Francisco: Grassroots Fundraising Journal. $20.00/yr. (Order from: Grassroots Fundraising Journal, 517 Union Ave., Suite 206, Knoxville, TN 37902)

> Each issue features a how-to article on a specific fundraising method or some related issue. Includes ideas submitted by readers. Ideal publication for community-based organizations.

NCRP Bulletin. Monthly. Washington, DC: National Committee for Responsive Philanthropy. (Available to members of NCRP, 2001 S St., N.W., #620, Washington, DC 20009)

> News on issues relevant to the non-profit sector.

NSFRE Journal. Twice a year. Washington, DC: National Society of Fund Raising Executives. (Order from: National Society of Fund Raising Executives, Suite 1000, 1511 K St., Washington, DC 20005)

> How-to articles and reports of successful fundraising activities for professional fundraisers.

Nonprofit Executive, The. Monthly. Washington, DC: The Taft Group. $97.00/ yr. (Order from: The Taft Group, 5130 MacArthur Blvd., N.W., Washington, DC 20016)

Designed to assist nonprofit executives improve their professional development and advance their careers. In addition to news about the nonprofit segment, offers information about management techniques, new techniques and resources.

Nonprofit World Report. Bimonthly. Madison, WI: The Society for Nonprofit Organizations. $59.00/yr.; available at no charge to members. (Order from: The Society for Nonprofit Organizations, 6314 Odana Rd., Suite 1, Madison, WI 53719)

Articles about all issues of interest to those in the nonprofit field including information about pending legislation and successful fundraising approaches and practices.

Update. Monthly. Washington, DC: Independent Sector (Available to members of Independent Sector, 1828 L St., N.W., Washington, DC 20036)

News of interest to voluntary organizations about volunteers and fundraising.

FURTHER READINGS IN
COMMUNICATION, MARKETING
Books, Articles, Pamphlets

Beach, Mark. *Editing Your Newsletter: A Guide to Writing, Design and Production.* Second Edition. Portland, OR: Coast to Coast Books. 1982. 122 pp. $9.95. (Order from: Coast to Coast Books, 2934 N.E. 16th Ave., Portland, OR 97212)

Provides information on writing, editing, graphics, design, and printing for newsletter editors. Tips on both content and appearance to improve newsletters and keep costs low. Many illustrations.

Communication Briefings. Monthly. Blackwood, NJ: Communication Briefings. $49.00/yr. (Order from: Communication Briefings, P.O. Box 587, Glassboro, NJ 08028)

Communication ideas and techniques for a variety of situations and settings.

Detz, Joan. *How to Write and Give a Speech.* New York: St. Martin's Press. 1984. 143 pp. $5.95. (Order from: St. Martin's Press, 175 Fifth Ave., New York, NY 10010)

Practical guide on writing and giving a speech. Includes advice, examples, and tips on focusing the topic, assessing the audience, organizing the material, using humor, etc.

Elbow, Peter. *Writing With Power: Techniques for Mastering the Writing Process.* New York: Oxford University Press. 1981. 384 pp. $8.95. (Order from: Oxford University Press, 200 Madison Ave., New York, NY 10016)

Manual to help those who need to write get control of the writing process. Presents methods for getting started, revising, taking the audience into consideration, and incorporating feedback.

Kotler, Philip. *Marketing for Nonprofit Organizations.* Englewood Cliffs, NJ: Prentice-Hall. 1982. 592 pp. $26.95. (Order from: Prentice-Hall, Englewood Cliffs, NJ 07632)

Introduces marketing concepts and planning for nonprofit organizations. Each of the 22 chapters begins with a vignette related to the topic covered.

Mack, Karin, and Eric Skjei. *Overcoming Writing Blocks.* Boston: Houghton-Mifflin. 1979. 240 pp. $10.00; $6.95 paper. (Order from: Houghton-Mifflin Co., 2 Park St., Boston, MA 02108)

Unblocking techniques to deal with a variety of situations including writing grant proposals. Definition and explanation of writing blocks, analysis of the writing process as it relates to unblocking techniques, and application of techniques to specific situations. Provides stimulation and relaxation exercises to facilitate the process.

Maddelena, Lucille A. *A Communications Manual for Non-profit Organizations.* New York: American Management Association. 1981. 240 pp. $17.95. (Order

from: American Management Association, 135 W. 50th St., New York, NY 10020)
 Guide for marketing and public relations for nonprofit organizations. Covers image building, preparing promotional materials, and media relations. Includes samples and work instruments.

Media Resource Guide: How to Tell Your Story. Los Angeles: Foundation for American Communications. 1981. 40 pp. $5.00. (Order from: Foundation for American Communications, 3383 Barham Blvd., Los Angeles, CA 90068)
 Designed to teach how the news media work and think in order to help an organization become effective in using the news media in getting its story before the public.

Pocket Pal. New York: International Paper Co., 1976. 191 pp. $2.00. (Order from: International Paper Co., 220 E. 42nd St., New York, NY 20027)
 Handbook on various aspects of graphic production such as type and typesetting, copy and art preparation, photography, printing, and paper and inks. Includes a glossary of graphics arts terms.

Rados, David L. *Marketing for Non-Profit Organizations.* Boston: Auburn House Publishing Co. 1981. 572 pp. $24.95. (Order from: Auburn House Publishing Co., 131 Clarendon St., Boston, MA 12116)

Strunk, William Jr., and E. B. White. *The Elements of Style.* Third Edition. New York: Macmillan Publishing Co., Inc. 1979. 85 pp. $6.95; $2.25 paper (Order from: Macmillan Publishing Co., 866 Third Ave., New York, NY 10022)
 Set of suggestions to improve overall writing style plus guidelines and rules for proper usage.

A COMPILATION OF STATE LAWS REGULATING CHARITABLE ORGANIZATIONS

State Laws Regulating Charitable Solicitations
(As of December 1, 1985)

State	Registration or Licensing	Regulatory Agency	Cost Limitations	Charitable Organizations Annual Financial Reporting Requirements	Monetary Exemption Ceiling	Charitable Solicitation Disclosure	Fund-Raising Counsel Registration or Licensing	Bonding Requirement
Arkansas	Registration	Secretary of State Trademarks Department Little Rock, Arkansas 72201 501-371-3622	None	By March 31 or within 90 days after close of fiscal or calendar year *	$1,000 (if all soliciting done by volunteers)	Solicitors must disclose minimum percentage of gross income received by the charity	Registration	$5,000
California	Registration	Registry of Charitable Trust P.O. Box 13447 Sacramento, CA 95813 916-445-2021	None	Annual Financial Reporting Requirements are due at the same time as 990, four and one-half months after the end of the accounting period. Report due May 15. If gross revenue or assets exceed $25,000 during the year the organization must file	None	"Sale for charitable purpose card" must be shown prior to any solicitation	None	None
Connecticut	Registration	Public Charities Unit % Attorney General 30 Trinity St. Hartford, CT 06106 203-566-5836	25% to 50% depending on total raised	In form described by the Department within 5 months of close of fiscal year and must be audited by an independent accountant if public support exceeds $100,000 *	$5,000 (if all soliciting done by volunteers)	Solicitor must disclose true name, that he is a professional solicitor, and, if working for a professional solicitor, the name of the firm. If soliciting on behalf of a charity, but not wholly for a charitable purpose, must disclose percentage of money raised toward the non-charitable purpose	Registration	$10,000
District of Columbia	Licensing	Department of Consumer & Regulatory Affairs 614 H St., N.W. Washington, DC 20001 202-727-7086	None	Within 30 days after the end of a licensing period and 30 days after a demand by the mayor (formerly the commissioner) *	$1,500 (if all soliciting done by volunteers)	Solicitors must present solicitation information card to prospective donor. Card is issued by Department of Consumer and Regulatory Affairs	Licensing	None
Florida	Registration (Names of all fund-raising employees must be registered)	Department of State Division of Licensing The Capitol Tallahassee, FL 32301 904-488-5381	None	With annual registration process on forms audited by an independent public accountant if in excess of $100,000. A review audit can be used if between $50,000 and $100,000. *	$10,000 (if all soliciting done by volunteers)	Organizations must furnish authorization to solicitors which must be exhibited on request	Licensing (Statute refers only to professional solicitors)	$10,000
Georgia	Registration	Secretary of State Office of Special Services 2 Martin Luther King Dr. Atlanta, GA 30334 404-656-2861	30% for administration and fund-raising unless exemption is given	Within 90 days after close of fiscal or calendar year. (Quarterly Reports required in first year of operation. Report must be verified by independent certified accountant if over $50,000.) *	$15,000 if costs are below 30%	Organizations must furnish donor with name of solicitor and purpose for which solicitation is being made	Registration	$10,000 or 50% of total income of PFR for preceding year, whichever is greater

State	Registration or Licensing	Regulatory Agency	Cost Limitations	Annual Financial Reporting Requirements	Monetary Exemption Ceiling	Charitable Solicitation Disclosure	Registration or Licensing	Bonding Requirement
Hawaii	Registration	Department of Commerce & Consumer Affairs P.O. Box 40 Honolulu, HW 96810 808-548-4740	None	With registration statement	$4,000 (if all soliciting is done by volunteers)	Solicitors must furnish authorization on request	Licensing	$5,000
Indiana	None	Consumer Protection Div Attorney General 219 State House Indianapolis, Ind. 46204 317-232-6233	None	None	None	Paid solicitors must disclose percent of contribution going to charity	Registration	None
Illinois	Registration Religious organizations are also required to register.	Attorney General State of Illinois 100 West Randolph 12th fl. Chicago, IL 60601 312-917-2595	At least 75% of gross receipts must be used for charitable purposes and not more than 25% for the cost of un-ordered merchandise	Within six months after end of fiscal or calendar year *	$4,000 (if all soliciting is done by volunteers)	None	Registration	$5,000
Kansas	Registration	Attorney General Judicial Center Topeka, KA 66612 913-296-3751	At least 75% of gross receipts must be used for charitable purposes and not more than 25% for the cost of un-ordered merchandise	Appropriate form pursuant to the Kansas Statutes Annotated Sec. 17-7500 et. seq. as part of registration	$5,000 (if all soliciting is done by volunteers)	None	Registration	$5,000
Kentucky	None	Attorney General Division of Consumer Protection Frankfort, KY 40601 502-564-6607	None	None	None	None	Registration with Attorney General. Division of Consumer Protection	None
Maine	Registration	Attorney General Augusta, ME 04330 207-289-3661	See disclosure	If more than $30,000 raised, within six months after close of fiscal year. Must be audited by independent public accountant *	$10,000 (if all soliciting is done by volunteers)	No professional fund-raiser or solicitor shall solicit funds for a charitable purpose without full disclosure to the prospective donor the estimated cost of solicitation where less than 70% of amount donated will be expended for the specific charitable purpose	Registration	$10,000
Maryland	Registration	Secretary of State State House Annapolis, MD 21404 301-269-3425	None	Most recent completed fiscal year. If in excess of $100,000 an audit is required by an independent certified public accountant according to the standards of accounting and financial reporting of voluntary health and welfare organizations *	$25,000 (if solicitation is not done by profes-sional solicitor. Effective July 1, 1986)	Paid solicitor must disclose his name and that he has been engaged by the charity to raise funds; the name of the organization and the purpose for which contribution is solicited; the percent of donations received by the solicitor percentage which may be deducted for income tax purposes. upon request a copy of organizations finan-cial statement is available	Registration	None

State	Registration or Licensing	Regulatory Agency	Cost Limitations	Annual Financial Reporting Requirements	Monetary Exemption Ceiling	Charitable Solicitation Disclosure	Registration or Licensing	Bonding Requirement
Massachusetts	Licensing	Attorney General Division of Public Charities Boston, MA 02108 617-727-2235	15% to a professional solicitor; 50% overall solicitation expense; unless higher is proven to be in public interest	On or before June 1 or before 60 days following a fiscal year ending in April or May on prescribed forms organizations receiving over $100,000 annually must file audited financial statement *	None	Solicitors must exhibit authorization on request	Licensing	$10,000
Michigan	Licensing	Attorney General Charitable Trust Section 670 Law Building Lansing, MI 48913 517-373-1152	None	Within approximately 6 months of end of fiscal year. Where income from public support is $50,000 or more a certified audit is required *	$8,000 (if all soliciting is done by volunteers and annual report is given to contributions)	None	Licensing	$10,000
Minnesota	Registration	Dept. of Commerce Registration and Licensing Division 500 Metro Square St. Paul, MN 55101 612-296-6324	Expenses of over 30% for administration, general and fund-raising costs is presumed to be unreasonable.	File annual report, financial statement, and copy of IRS 990. (If 990 meets all requirements of financial statement, it can be filed in place of financial statement.) *	$10,000 (if all soliciting is done by volunteers)	Solicitation card must be shown prior to solicitation	Licensing	up to $20,000
Nebraska	Certificate granted on basis of letter of approval obtained from county attorney of home-office county	Secretary of State Lincoln, NE 68509 402-471-2554	None	Can file IRS 990 in lieu of auditor's report *	None	Solicitor must carry and show certificate and issue receipts for donations of more than $2	None	None
Nevada	None	Attorney General Carson City, NE 89701 702-885-4170	None	By July 1 with Secretary of State *	None	None	None	None
New Hampshire	Licensing	Secretary of State Charitable Trust Concord, NH 03301 603-271-4314	85% must be applied to a charitable purpose	When requested by the director of the division *	None	None	None	None
New Jersey	Registration	Charities Registration Sec. 1100 Raymond Blvd. Newark, NJ 07102 201-648-4002	15% to professional fund-raiser and professional solicitor 50% for mail solicitation via unordered merchandise	Within 6 months after close of fiscal or calendar year *	$10,000 (if all fund raising is done by volunteers)	For telephone Solicitations must disclose name and address of organization; state amount as a percentage that will be given to organization; if no tax exempt status, that must be disclosed; must disclose percent that can be deducted as charitable contribution	Registration	$10,000
New Mexico	Registration	Office of the Attorney General Charitable Organization Registry P.O. Drawer 1508 Santa Fe, NM 87504-1508 505-827-6910	None	Within 75 days of the close of the fiscal year. Accompanied by IRS 990.	$2,500	Organization must disclose upon request the percentage of funds solicited spent on fund-raising costs	None	None

State	Registration or Licensing	Regulatory Agency	Cost Limitations	Annual Financial Reporting Requirements	Monetary Exemption Ceiling	Charitable Solicitation Disclosure	Registration or Licensing	Bonding Requirement
New York	Registration	Office of Charities Registration Department of State Albany, NY 12231 518-474-3720	None	Within 90 days after the close of its fiscal year. If in excess of $50,000 for preceding year, report must be accompanied by an opinion signed by an independent public accountant ★	$10,000 (if all fund raising is done by volunteers)	None	Registration	$5,000
North Carolina	Registration	Department of Human Resources Raleigh, NC 27605 919-733-4510	None	With application for registration. CPA Audited Reports are required if more than $250,000 in support and revenue is received. If under $100,000 a report by an independent public accountant is accepted ★	$10,000 (if all soliciting is done by volunteers)	Percent of fund raising expenses and the purpose of the organization must be given in writing upon request	Registration	$10,000
North Dakota	Licensing	Secretary of State Bismarck, ND 58505 701-224-2901	35% re-solicitation of fund-raising expenses	Within 60 days after the close of the fiscal or calendar year.	None	None	Registration	None
Ohio	Registration	Attorney General Columbus, OH 43215 614-466-3180	None	By March 31 if on a calendar year; if on a fiscal year 90 days of close of fiscal year ★	$500	None	Registration	$5,000
Oklahoma	Registration	Revenue Processing Division of Oklahoma Tax Commission 2501 Lincoln Blvd. Oklahoma City, OK 73194-0005 405-521-2617	Payments to professional fund-raisers or solicitors limited to 10% of totals raised	Within 90 days of the end of the fiscal or calendar year	$10,000	Receipts must be given for contributions over $2	Registration	$2,500
Oregon	Registration	Attorney General Portland, OR 97201 503-229-5278	25% for solicitation, 50% overall, unless higher authorized	Within 4 months and 15 days of close of calendar or fiscal year ★	$5,000	Solicitor must disclose name of fund-raising firm, name of the organization for which he is soliciting and the percentage of proceeds beneficiary will receive	None	None
Pennsylvania	Registration	Commission on Charitable Organizations Dept. of State Harrisburg, PA 17120 717-783-1720	35% re-solicitation & fund-raising expenses (including payment to professional solicitor and fund-raiser) (postage is not considered a fund-raising expense) 15% to professional solicitor, unless higher authorized	Organizations receiving less than $15,000 can file signed and notarized short form; over $15,000 and under $50,000 have to accept a review by a registered, independent of organization, public accountant; over $50,000 must have a complete audit ★	None	Solicitor must produce authorization on request	Registration	$10,000
Rhode Island	Registration	Department of Business Regulations Providence, RI 02903 401-277-3048	50% re-solicitation of fund-raising expenses. 25% to professional solicitor, unless higher authorized	Within 90 days after end of fiscal year audited by an independent certified accountant. Organizations receiving less than $100,000 do not require an audit ★	$3,000 (if all soliciting is done by volunteers)	Identification card must be presented for each solicitation and must contain name and address of organization; purpose for which contribution is solicited; tax exempt status; percentage which may be deducted for income tax purposes	Registration	$10,000
South Carolina	Registration	Secretary of State Columbia, SC 29211 803-758-2244	Reasonable percentage to professional solicitor	Within six months of the close of the fiscal year ★	$2,000 (for SC organizations only)	Solicitor must produce authorization on request	Registration	$5,000

State	Registration or Licensing	Regulatory Agency	Cost Limitations	Annual Financial Reporting Requirements	Monetary Exemption Ceiling	Charitable Solicitation Disclosure	Registration or Licensing	Bonding Requirement
Tennessee	Registration	Secretary of State James K. Polk Bldg. Suite 500 Nashville, TN 37219 615-741-2555	25% for fund-raising costs; 15% to professional solicitor, unless higher authorized	Submitted as part of annual registration process, independent public accountant audit required for over $10,000 in annual contributions *	$5,000	None	Registration	$10,000
Virginia	Registration	Director of Consumer Affairs Richmond, VA 23219 804-786-1343	See disclosure	Submitted as part of annual registration process *	$5,000 (if all soliciting is done by volunteers)	Donors must be told minimum percent of donation which will be received by organization for its own use if less than 70% of total donation. Solicitors must produce authorization on request and furnish receipts for contributions of $5 or more	Registration	$20,000
Washington	Registration	Charities Division Office of the Secretary of State Olympia, WA 98504 206-754-1920	None	Must be filed upon request of Attorney General or county prosecutor. If financial information is requested, will accept Federal 990 Form	$10,000 (if all soliciting is done by volunteers)	Solicitor must identify himself, the organization; the purpose of the solicitation and name the organization which will receive contributions. Must disclose upon request the percentage of donations applied to fund-raising costs.	Registration	$5,000
West Virginia	Registration	Secretary of State Capitol Bldg. Charleston, WV 25305 304-345-4000	None	Financial report must accompany annual registration statement and if in excess of $50,000 required to have an audit by an independent public accountant *	$7,500 (if all soliciting is done by volunteers)	None	Registration	$10,000
Wisconsin	Registration	Department of Regulation & Licensing P.O. Box 8935 Madison, WI 53708 608-266-0829	None	Within 6 months of the close of the fiscal or calendar year *	$3,000	Donor must be told the percentage of contribution that will go to charity	Registration	$5,000

*Indicates States which will accept Federal 990 Form in Lieu of Legislatively Mandated Annual Report

Source: AAFRC Trust for Philanthropy Fund Raising Review, 25 West 34th St., Suite 1519, New York, NY 10036.
Note: This compilation is updated annually.

RESOURCE ORGANIZATIONS

RESOURCE ORGANIZATIONS

American Association of Fund -Raising Counsel (AAFRC)
25 West 43rd St.
New York, NY 10036
(212) 354-5799

National membership organization composed of professional fundraising firms which will assist all types of nonprofit agencies to manage and plan fund-raising programs. Committed to the study of economic and social trends in American philanthropy. Publications include *Giving USA*, an annual review of philanthropy, and *The Fund Raising Review*, a bimonthly newsletter.

American Management Association (AMA)
135 W. 50th St.
New York, NY 10020
(212) 586-8100

Membership organization of managers in industry, commerce, government, charitable and non-commercial organizations plus university teachers of management. Provides educational programs including conferences, seminars, courses, briefings, and workshops on various management topics. Publishes a number of periodicals and monographs on various aspects of management.

American Society of Association Executives (ASAE)
1575 Eye St., N.W.
Washington, DC 20005
(202) 626-2723

Professional society of paid executives of national, state and local professional, technical and business associations. Works to promote the proper function of associations and to enhance professional standards of association executives. Conducts referral, résumé, guidance and consultation services. Publications include the monthly journal *Association Management*.

Association for Volunteer Administration (AVA)
P.O. Box 4584
Boulder, CO 80306
(303) 497-0238

Professional association of administrators of volunteer programs, educators, researchers and students, working to stimulate the coordination of community volunteer services. Publishes a monthly *Newsletter/Update* and the quarterly *Journal of Volunteer Administration*.

Center for Community Change
1000 Wisconsin Ave., N.W.
Washington, DC 20007
(202) 342-0519

Center works on-site with local groups, particularly low-income and minority community organizations, to aid in planning, organizational development, public policy analysis, fundraising, and specific program areas such as housing, job development and training, and community crime prevention.

Citizens Forum on Self-Government
55 W. 44th St.
New York, NY 10036
(212) 730-7930 (NY, AK, or HI) or
(800) 223-6004

Nonprofit, non-partisan association of citizens sharing the common goal of making their state and local governments more effective, representative, and responsive. Maintains the CIVITEX database which contains brief descriptions of local problem-solving projects. Also publishes a monthly journal, *National Civic Review.*

Conference Board
845 Third Ave.
New York, NY 10022
(212) 759-0900

Business information service whose purpose is to assist senior executives and other leaders in arriving at sound decisions. The Corporate Relations program group investigates how companies organize for and carry out external relations including those targeted at social groups and studies such factors as corporate contributions and community relations.

Conference on Alternative State and Local Policies
2000 Florida Ave., N.W.
Washington, DC 20007
(202) 387-6030

National public policy center that concentrates on the problems of America's state and local governments. Publishes *Ways and Means,* a quarterly newsletter.

Council on Foundations
1828 L St., N.W.
Washington, DC 20036
(202) 466-6512

National membership organization of independent community, operating, and public foundations, corporate grantmakers, and trust companies. Works to promote responsible and effective grantmaking; develop and maintain a supportive environment for philanthropy; encourage and support collaboration among grantmakers; and promote the formation of new foundations. Publishes a biweekly *Newsletter; Foundation News,* a bimonthly journal; and various handbooks.

The Foundation Center
79 Fifth Ave.
New York, NY 10003
(212) 620-4230

National service organization supported primarily by foundations to provide information to grantseekers. Provides two national libraries and two field offices plus a nationwide library network. Publications provide information on a variety of philanthropic activities.

Funding Exchange
666 Broadway
New York, NY
(212)

National organization of 9 community-based public foundations, all of which have been established to fund grassroots and activist organizations. The Funding Exchange seeks to support and expand these foundations' efforts.

Grantsmanship Center
P.O. Box 6210
650 S. Spring St.
Suite 570
Los Angeles, CA 90014
(213) 689-9222

National training organization. Produces a number of publications and conducts workshops in many cities across the country in such areas as grantsmanship, fundraising, proposal writing, business ventures for nonprofits, and computers in nonprofits.

Independent Sector
1828 L St., N.W.
Washington, DC 20036
(202) 223-8100

Organization of national voluntary organizations, foundations and corporations with major giving programs working together to preserve and enhance the national tradition of giving, volunteering, and not-for-profit initiative. Regular publications for members include *Corporate Philanthropy, Government Relations Information and Action,* and *Update.*

Lutheran Resources Commission-Washington (LRC-W)
1346 Connecticut Ave., N.W., Suite 823
Washington, DC 20036
(202) 872-0110

Grants consultation agency service for participating denominations. Consults with agencies on the development of proposals and guides them to appropriate funding sources. Publishes a monthly resource bulletin, *Newsbriefs,* and conducts semi-annual resource development conferences on grantsmanship and other fundraising techniques for community-based groups, social service agencies and other nonprofits.

National Assembly of National Voluntary Health and Social Welfare
Organizations, Inc.
1346 Connecticut Ave., N.W., Suite 424A
Washington, DC 20036
(202) 296-1515

Association of national, voluntary human service organizations whose purpose is to facilitate communication and cooperation among member agencies. Provides opportunities for its members to develop and share information needed to lead and manage national programs effectively; promotes the implementation of public policies and programs and the development of resources responsive to the needs of human service organizations and those they serve; and works to increase the public visibility, understanding, and acceptance of the member organizations and the issues they represent.

National Black United Fund
2090 Adam Clayton Powell Blvd.
Room 821
New York, NY 10027
(212) 866-5400

National organization encouraging federated fundraising for black causes and activities. Also seeks to act as a catalyst for economic development in black communities.

National Committee for Responsive Philanthropy
2001 S St., N.W., Suite 620
Washington, DC 20009
(202) 387-9177

Membership organization of local and national nonprofits formed to improve the accountability and accessibility of philanthropic institutions and to increase their responsiveness to groups which are working to achieve social justice, equal opportunity and fair representation for disenfranchised people in our economic and governmental systems. Publishes *Responsive Philanthropy*, news bulletins, action alerts, and occasional publications on trends in charitable giving.

National Society of Fund-Raising Executives
1511 K St., N.W.
Washington, DC 20005
(202) 638-1395

Professional organization of fundraising executives. Purpose is to assist its members in their professional efforts by fostering ethical standards for the management, direction, and counseling of fundraising programs for nonprofit organizations and agencies; by providing a forum for the discussion of concerns common to the profession; and by developing and disseminating information relevant to the profession. Publishes the *NSFRE Journal* and *NSFRE News*.

Nonprofit Management Association
Box 2350
Minneapolis, MN 55402
(612) 340-7591

Membership organization for individuals engaged in the improvement of nonprofit management, including employees of management support organizations, consultants, trainers, funders and academicians.

Philanthropic Advisory Service
Council of the Better Business Bureaus Inc.
1515 Wilson Blvd.
Arlington, VA 22209
(703) 276-0133

Evaluates charitable organizations that conduct national or international program services or fundraising activities. Acts as a donor information service to corporations, foundations, local Better Business Bureaus, and members of the general public who have questions about specific charities.

Program on Non-Profit Organizations at Yale University (PONPO)
P.O. Box 154, Yale Station
88 Trumbull St.
New Haven, CT 06520
(203) 432-3864

Interdisciplinary research program based at the Institution for Social and Policy Studies, Yale University. Purpose of the program is to build a substantial body of information, analysis, and theory relating to nonprofit organizations; to enlist the scholarly community in research and teaching about nonprofit organizations; and to generate research that will assist decision makers to address major policy and management dilemmas confronting the nonprofit sector.

United Way of America
701 North Fairfax St.
Alexandria, VA 22314-2045
(703) 836-7100

Provides national, regional and local program support and consultation to local United Ways in the area of fundraising, budgeting, management allocation, planning and communications. Regional United Way offices:

Northeast Regional Office
99 Park Ave., 6th Floor
New York, NY 10016
(212) 661-5666

Western Regional Office
410 Bush St.
San Francisco, CA 94108
(415) 772-4300

Southeast Regional Office
2150 Parklake Dr. - Suite 310
Atlanta, GA 30345
(404) 938-5841

Mid-America Regional Office
10600 West Higgins Rd. - Suite 210
Rosemont, IL 60018
(312) 297-6160

REGIONAL ASSOCIATIONS OF GRANTMAKERS

MULTI-STATE ASSOCIATIONS

Conference of Southwest
  Foundations
  (serves primarily Arizona,
  Arkansas, Nevada, New Mexico,
  Oklahoma, and Texas)

Post Office Box 8832
Corpus Christi, TX 78412
(512) 855-3611

Southeastern Council on
  Foundations
  (Serves primarily Alabama,
  Arkansas, Florida, Georgia,
  Kentucky, Louisiana,
  Mississippi, North Carolina,
  South Carolina, Tennessee and
  Virginia)

134 Peachtree Street, N.W.
Altanta, GA 30303
(404) 524-0911

ASSOCIATIONS CURRENTLY SERVING A STATE OR A MULTI-COUNTY AREA OF A STATE

Pacific Northwest Grantmakers
  Forum

c/o Wyman Youth Trust
304 Pioneer Building
600 First Avenue
Seattle, WA 98104

Council of Michigan
  Foundations
P.O. Box 599
Grand Haven, MI 49417
(616) 842-7080

Donors Forum of Ohio
c/o Kettering Foundation
5335 Far Hills Avenue
Dayton, OH 45429
(513) 434-7300

Foundation Forum of
  Wisconsin
P.O. Box 11978
Milwaukee, WI 53211
(414) 962-6820

Grantmakers of Western
  Pennsylvania
368 One Mellon Bank Center
Pittsburgh, PA 15258
(412) 234-0829

Minnesota Council on
  Foundations
1216 Foshay Tower
9th and Marquette
Minneapolis, MN 55402
(612) 338-1989

Northern California
  Grantmakers
334 Kearny Street
San Francisco, CA 94108
(415) 788-2982

Southern California Association
for Philanthropy
Eastern Columbia Building
849 South Broadway, Suite 815
Los Angeles, CA 90014
(213) 489-7307

GREATER CITY ASSOCIATIONS

Associated Grantmakers of
Massachusetts, Inc.
294 Washington Street
Room 840
Boston, MA 02108
(617) 426-2606

Association of Baltimore Area
Grantmakers
Community Foundation of Greater
Baltimore
6 East Hamilton Street
Baltimore, MD 21202
(301) 332-4171

Clearinghouse for Midcontinent
Foundations
Post Office Box 7215
Kansas City, MO 64113
(816) 276-1176

Co-ordinating Council for
Foundations, Inc.
999 Asylum Avenue
Hartford, CT 06105
(203) 525-5585

Rochester Grantmakers
Forum
Rochester Area Foundation
335 E. Main Street
Suite 402
Rochester, NY 14604
(716) 325-4353

New York Regional Association
Of Grantmakers
505 Eighth Avenue
18th Floor
New York, NY 10018
(212) 714-0699

Metropolitan Association
for Philanthropy
5585 Pershing Avenue
Suite 150
St. Louis, MO 63112
(314) 361-3900

Note: While the principal role of most of these associations is to support grantmakers, many also produce newsletters or sponsor programs for grantseekers as well.

THE FOUNDATION CENTER NATIONAL LIBRARY NETWORK

THE FOUNDATION CENTER is an independent national service organization established by foundations to provide an authoritative source of information on private philanthropic giving. In fulfilling its mission, the Center disseminates information on private giving through public service programs, publications and through a national network of library reference collections for free public use. The New York, Washington, D.C., Cleveland, and San Francisco reference collections operated by The Foundation Center offer a wide variety of services and comprehensive collections of information on foundations and grants. The Cooperating Collections are libraries, community foundations, and other nonprofit agencies that provide a core collection of Foundation Center publications and a variety of supplementary materials and services in subject areas useful to grantseekers.

Over 100 of the network members have sets of private foundation information returns (IRS Form 990-PF) for their states or regions which are available for public use. These collections are indicated by a • next to their names. A complete set of U.S. foundation returns can be found in the New York and Washington, D.C. collections. The Cleveland and San Francisco offices contain IRS returns for those foundations in the midwestern and western states, respectively.

Because the collections vary in their hours, materials, and services, it is recommended that you call each collection in advance. To check on new locations or current information, call toll-free 800-424-9836.

REFERENCE COLLECTIONS OPERATED BY
THE FOUNDATION CENTER

- The Foundation Center
  79 Fifth Avenue
  New York, New York 10003
  212-620-4230

- The Foundation Center
  1001 Connecticut Avenue, NW
  Washington, D.C. 20036
  202-331-1400

- The Foundation Center
  Kent H. Smith Library
  1442 Hanna Building
  1422 Euclid Avenue
  Cleveland, Ohio 44115
  216-861-1933

- The Foundation Center
  312 Sutter Street
  San Francisco, California 94108
  415-397-0902

COOPERATING COLLECTIONS

ALABAMA

- Birmingham Public Library
  2020 Park Place
  Birmingham 35203
  205-226-3600

  Huntsville–Madison County Public
    Library
  108 Fountain Circle
  P.O. Box 443
  Huntsville 35804
  205-536-0021

- Auburn University at Montgomery
    Library
  Montgomery 36193 - 0401
  205-271-9649

ALASKA

- University of Alaska,
    Anchorage Library
  3211 Providence Drive
  Anchorage 99504
  907-786-1848

ARIZONA

- Phoenix Public Library
    Business and Sciences
    Department
  12 East McDowell Road
  Phoenix 85004
  602-262-4782

- Tucson Public Library
    Main Library
  200 South Sixth Avenue
  Tucson 85701
  602-791-4393

ARKANSAS

- Westark Community
    College Library
  Grand Avenue at Waldron Road
  Fort Smith 72913
  501-785-4241

- Little Rock Public Library
    Reference Department

700 Louisiana Street
Little Rock 72201
501-370-5950

CALIFORNIA

Inyo County Library—
Bishop Branch
210 Academy Street
Bishop 93514
619-872-8091

- California Community Foundation
Funding Information Center
3580 Wilshire Blvd., Suite 1660
Los Angeles 90010
213-413-4042

- Community Foundation for
Monterey County
420 Pacific Street
Monterey 93942
408-375-9712

California Community Foundation
4050 Metropolitan Drive
Orange 92668
714-937-9077

Riverside Public Library
3581 7th Street
Riverside 92501
714-787-7201

California State Library
Reference Services, Rm. 309
914 Capital Mall
Sacramento 95814
916-322-0369

- San Diego Community Foundation
625 Broadway, Suite 1015
San Diego 92101
619-239-8815

- The Foundation Center
312 Sutter Street

San Francisco 94108
415-397-0902

Orange County Community
Developmental Council
1440 East First Street, 4th Floor
Santa Ana 92701
714-547-6801

- Penisula Community Foundation
1204 Burlingame Avenue
Burlingame, 94011-0627
415-342-2505

- Santa Barbara Public Library
Reference Section
40 East Anapamu
P.O. Box 1019
Santa Barbara 93102
805-962-7653

Santa Monica Public Library
1343 Sixth Street
Santa Monica 90401-1603
213-458-8603

Tuolomne County Library
465 S. Washington Street
Sonora 95370
209-533-5707

North Coast Opportunities, Inc.
101 West Church Street
Ukiah 95482
707-462-1954

COLORADO

Pikes Peak Library District
20 North Cascade Avenue
Colorado Springs 80901
303-473-2080

- Denver Public Library
Sociology Division
1357 Broadway
Denver 80203
303-571-2190

CONNECTICUT

- Hartford Public Library
  Reference Department
  500 Main Street
  Hartford 06103
  203-525-9121

  D.A.T.A.
  880 Asylum Avenue
  Hartford 06105
  203-278-2477

  D.A.T.A.
  25 Science Park
  Suite 502
  New Haven 06513

DELAWARE

- Hugh Morris Library
  University of Delaware
  Newark 19717-5267
  302-451-2965

FLORIDA

  Volusia County Public Library
  City Island
  Daytona Beach 32014
  904-252-8374

- Jacksonville Public Library
  Business, Science, and Industry
  Department
  122 North Ocean Street
  Jacksonville 32202
  904-633-3926

- Miami–Dade Public Library
  Florida Collection
  One Biscayne Boulevard
  Miami 33132
  305-579-5001

- Orlando Public Library
  10 North Rosalind

  Orlando 32801
  305-425-4694

- University of West Florida
  John C. Pace Library
  Pensacola 32514
  904-474-2412

  Selby Public Library
  1001 Boulevard of the Arts
  Sarasota 33577
  813-366-7303

- Leon County Public Library
  Community Funding Resources
  Center
  1940 North Monroe Street
  Tallahassee 32303
  904-478-2665

  Palm Beach County Community
  Foundation
  324 Datura Street, Suite 311
  West Palm Beach 33401
  305-659-6800

GEORGIA

- Atlanta–Fulton Public Library
  Ivan Allen Department
  1 Margaret Mitchell Square
  Atlanta 30303
  404-688-4636

HAWAII

- Thomas Hale Hamilton Library
  General Reference
  University of Hawaii
  2550 The Mall
  Honolulu 96822
  808-948-7214

  Community Resource Center
  The Hawaiian Foundation
  Financial Plaza of the Pacific

111 South King Street
Honolulu 96813
808-525-8548

IDAHO

* Caldwell Public Library
1010 Dearborn Street
Caldwell 83605
208-459-3242

ILLINOIS

Belleville Public Library
121 East Washington Street
Belleville 62220
618-234-0441

DuPage Township
300 Briarcliff Road
Bolingbrook 60439
312-759-1317

* Donors Forum of Chicago
208 South LaSalle Street
Chicago 60604
312-726-4882

* Evanston Public Library
1703 Orrington Avenue
Evanston 60201
312-866-0305

* Sangamon State University Library
Shepherd Road
Springfield 62708
217-786-6633

INDIANA

Allen County Public Library
900 Webster Street
Fort Wayne 46802
219-424-7241

Indiana University Northwest
Library
3400 Broadway
Gary 46408
219-980-6580

* Indianapolis–Marion County Public
Library
40 East St. Clair Street
Indianapolis 46204
317-269-1733

IOWA

* Public Library of Des Moines
100 Locust Street
Des Moines 50308
515-283-4259

KANSAS

* Topeka Public Library
Adult Services Department
1515 West Tenth Street
Topeka 66604
913-233-2040

* Wichita Public Library
223 South Main
Wichita 67202
316-262-0611

KENTUCKY

Western Kentucky University
Division of Library Services
Helm-Cravens Library
Bowling Green 42101
502-745-3951

* Louisville Free Public Library
Fourth and York Streets
Louisville 40203
503-223-7201

LOUISIANA

- East Baton Rouge Parish Library
  Centroplex Library
  120 St. Louis Street
  Baton Rouge 70821
  504-389-4960

- New Orleans Public Library
  Business and Science Division
  219 Loyola Avenue
  New Orleans 70140
  504-596-2583

- Shreve Memorial Library
  424 Texas Street
  Shreveport 71101
  318-226-5894

MAINE

- University of Southern Maine
  Center for Research and
  Advanced Study
  246 Deering Avenue
  Portland 04102
  207-780-4411

MARYLAND

- Enoch Pratt Free Library
  Special Science and History
  Department
  400 Cathedral Street
  Baltimore 21201
  301-396-5320

MASSACHUSETTS

- Associated Grantmakers of
  Massachusetts
  294 Washington Street
  Suite 501
  Boston 02108
  617-426-2608

- Boston Public Library
  Copley Square
  Boston 02117
  617-536-5400

  Walpole Public Library
  Common Street
  Walpole 02081
  617-668-5497 ext.340

  Western Massachusetts Funding
  Resource Center
  Campaign for Human Development
  Chancery Annex
  73 Chestnut Street
  Springfield 01103
  413-732-3175 ext.67

- Grants Resource Center
  Worcester Public Library
  Salem Square
  Worcester 01608
  617-799-1655

MICHIGAN

- Alpena County Library
  211 North First Avenue
  Alpena 49707
  517-356-6188

  University of Michigan–Ann Arbor
  Reference Department
  209 Hatcher Graduate Library
  Ann Arbor 48109-1205
  313-764-1149

- Henry Ford Centennial Library
  16301 Michigan Avenue
  Dearborn 48126
  313-943-2337

- Purdy Library
  Wayne State University
  Detroit 48202
  313-577-4040

- Michigan State University Libraries
    Reference Library
  East Lansing 48824
  517-353-9184

- Farmington Community Library
  32737 West 12 Mile Road
  Farmington Hills 48018
  313-553-0300

- University of Michigan–Flint
    Library
  Reference Department
  Flint 48503
  313-762-3408

- Grand Rapids Public Library
    Sociology and Education Dept.
  Library Plaza
  Grand Rapids 49502
  616-456-4411

- Michigan Technological University
    Library
  Highway U.S. 41
  Houghton 49931
  906-487-2507

MINNESOTA

- Duluth Public Library
  520 Superior Street
  Duluth 55802
  218-723-3802

- Southwest State University Library
  Marshall 56258
  507-537-7278

- Minneapolis Public Library
  Sociology Department
  300 Nicollet Mall
  Minneapolis 55401
  612-372-6555

  Rochester Public Library
  Broadway at First Street, SE

Rochester 55901
507-285-8002

Saint Paul Public Library
90 West Fourth Street
Saint Paul 55102
612-292-6311

MISSISSIPPI

Jackson Metropolitan Library
301 North State Street
Jackson 39201
601-944-1120

MISSOURI

- Clearinghouse for Midcontinent
    Foundations
  Univ. of Missouri, Kansas City
  Law School, Suite 1-300
  52nd Street and Oak
  Kansas City 64113
  816-276-1176

- Kansas City Public Library
  311 East 12th Street
  Kansas City 64106
  816-221-2685 ·

- Metropolitan Association for
    Philanthropy, Inc.
  5585 Pershing Avenue
  Suite 150
  St. Louis 63112
  314-361-3900

- Springfield–Greene County Library
  397 East Central Street
  Springfield 65801
  417-866-4636

MONTANA

- Eastern Montana College Library
    Reference Department

1500 N. 30th Street
Billings 59101-0298
406-657-2262

- Montana State Library
  Reference Department
  1515 E. 6th Avenue
  Helena 59620
  406-444-3004

NEBRASKA

University of Nebraska, Lincoln
106 Love Library
Lincoln 68588-0410
402-472-2526

- W. Dale Clark Library
  Social Sciences Department
  215 South 15th Street
  Omaha 68102
  402-444-4826

NEVADA

- Las Vegas—Clark County Library
  District
  1401 East Flamingo Road
  Las Vegas 89109
  702-733-7810

- Washoe County Library
  301 South Center Street
  Reno 89505
  702-785-4190

NEW HAMPSHIRE

- The New Hampshire Charitable
  Fund
  One South Street
  Concord 03301
  603-225-6641

Littleton Public Library
109 Main Street

Littleton 03561
603-444-5741

NEW JERSEY

Cumberland County Library
800 E. Commerce Street
Bridgeton 08302
609-455-0080

The Support Center
17 Academy Street, Suite 1101
Newark 07102
201-643-5774

County College of Morris Masten
  Learning
Resource Center
Route 10 and Center Grove Road
Randolph 07869
201-361-5000 x470

- New Jersey State Library
  Governmental Reference
  185 West State Street
  Trenton 08625
  609-292-6220

NEW MEXICO

Albuquerque Community
  Foundation
6400 Uptown Boulevard N.E.
Suite 500-W
Albuquerque 87110
505-883-6240

- New Mexico State Library
  325 Don Gaspar Street
  Santa Fe 87503
  505-827-3824

NEW YORK

- New York State Library
  Cultural Education Center

Humanities Section
Empire State Plaza
Albany 12230
518-474-7645

Bronx Reference Center
New York Public Library
2556 Bainbridge Avenue
Bronx 10458
212-220-6575

Brooklyn in Touch
101 Willoughby Street
Room 1508
Brooklyn 11201
718-237-9300

• Buffalo and Erie County Public
    Library
Lafayette Square
Buffalo 14203
716-856-7525

Huntington Public Library
338 Main Street
Huntington 11743
516-427-5165

• Levittown Public Library
    Reference Department
One Bluegrass Lane
Levittown 11756
516-731-5728

SUNY/College at Old Westbury
    Library
223 Store Hill Road
Old Westbury 11568
516-876-3201

• Plattsburgh Public Library
    Reference Department
15 Oak Street
Plattsburgh 12901
518-563-0921

Adriance Memorial Library
93 Market Street
Poughkeepsie 12601
914-485-4790

Queens Borough Public Library
89-11 Merrick Boulevard
Jamaica 11432
718-990-0700

• Rochester Public Library
Business and Social Sciences
    Division
115 South Avenue
Rochester 14604
716-428-7328

• Onondaga County Public Library
335 Montgomery Street
Syracuse 13202
315-473-4491

• White Plains Public Library
100 Martine Avenue
White Plains 10601
914-682-4488

NORTH CAROLINA

• The Duke Endowment
200 S. Tryon Street, Ste. 1100
Charlotte 28202
704-376-0291

Durham County Library
300 N. Roxboro Street
Durham 27701
919-683-2626

• North Carolina State Library
109 East Jones Street
Raleigh 27611
919-733-3270

• The Winston-Salem Foundation
229 First Union National Bank
    Building

Winston-Salem 27101
919-725-2382

NORTH DAKOTA

Western Dakota Grants Resource
    Center
Bismarck Junior College Library
Bismarck 58501
701-224-5450

- The Library
North Dakota State University
Fargo 58105
701-237-8876

OHIO

- Public Library of Cincinnati and
    Hamilton County
Education Department
800 Vine Street
Cincinnati 45202
513-369-6940

- The Foundation Center
1442 Hanna Building
1422 Euclid Avenue
Cleveland 44115
216-861-1933

CALLVAC Services, Inc.
370 South Fifth Street
Suite 1
Columbus 43215
614-221-6766

Lima-Allen County Regional
    Planning Commission
212 N. Elizabeth Street
Lima 45801
419-228-1836

- Toledo-Lucas County Public
    Library

Social Science Department
325 Michigan Street
Toledo 43624
419-255-7055 ext.221

Ohio University-Zanesville
Community Education and
    Development
1425 Newark Road
Zanesville 43701
614-453-0762

OKLAHOMA

- Oklahoma City University Library
NW 23rd at North Blackwelder
Oklahoma City 73106
405-521-5072

- The Support Center
525 NW Thirteenth Street
Oklahoma City 73103
405-236-8133

- Tulsa City-County Library System
400 Civic Center
Tulsa 74103
918-592-7944

OREGON

- Library Association of Portland
    Government Documents Room
801 S.W. Tenth Avenue
Portland 97205
503-223-7201

Oregon State Library
State Library Building
Salem 97310
503-378-4243

PENNSYLVANIA

Northampton County Area
    Community College

Learning Resources Center
3835 Green Pond Road
Bethlehem 18017
215-865-5358

- Erie County Public Library
3 South Perry Square
Erie 16501
814-452-2333 ext.54

- Dauphin County Library System
Central Library
101 Walnut Street
Harrisburg 17101
717-234-4961

Lancaster County Public Library
125 North Duke Street
Lancaster 17602
717-394-2651

- The Free Library of Philadelphia
Logan Square
Philadelphia 19103
215-686-5423

- Hillman Library
University of Pittsburgh
Pittsburgh 15260
412-624-4423

- Economic Development Council of
Northeastern Pennsylvania
1151 Oak Street
Pittston 18640
717-655-5581

James V. Brown Library
12 E. 4th Street
Williamsport 17701
717-326-0536

RHODE ISLAND

- Providence Public Library
Reference Department
150 Empire Street
Providence 02903
401-521-7722

SOUTH CAROLINA

- Charleston County Public Library
404 King Street
Charleston 29403
803-723-1645

- South Carolina State Library
Reader Services Department
1500 Senate Street
Columbia 29201
803-758-3138

SOUTH DAKOTA

- South Dakota State Library
State Library Building
800 North Illinois Street
Pierre 57501
605-773-3131

Sioux Falls Area Foundation
404 Boyce Greeley Building
321 South Phillips Avenue
Sioux Falls 57102-0781
605-336-7055

TENNESSEE

- Knoxville–Knox County Public
Library
500 West Church Avenue
Knoxville 37902
615-523-0781

- Memphis Shelby County Public
Library
1850 Peabody Avenue
Memphis 38104
901-725-8876

- Public Library of Nashville and
Davidson County
8th Avenue, North and Union Street
Nashville 37203
615-244-4700

TEXAS

Amarillo Area Foundation
1000 Polk
P. O. Box 25569
Amarillo 79105-269
806-376-4521

- The Hogg Foundation for Mental
    Health
  The University of Texas
  Austin 78712
  512-471-5041

- Corpus Christi State University
    Library
  6300 Ocean Drive
  Corpus Christi 78412
  512-991-6810

- Dallas Public Library
    Grants Information Service
  1515 Young Street
  Dallas 75201
  214-749-4100

- Pan American University
    Learning Resource Center
  1201 W. University Drive
  Edinburg 78539
  512-381-3304

- El Paso Community Foundation
  El Paso National Bank Building
  Suite 1616
  El Paso 79901
  915-533-4020

- Funding Information Center
  Texas Christian University Library
  Ft. Worth 76129
  817-921-7664

- Houston Public Library
  Bibliographic & Information Center
  500 McKinney Avenue
  Houston 77002
  713-224-5441 ext.265

- Funding Information Library
  507 Brooklyn
  San Antonio 78215
  512-227-4333

UTAH

- Salt Lake City Public Library
  Business and Science Department
  209 East Fifth South
  Salt Lake City 84111
  801-363-5733

VERMONT

- State of Vermont Department of
    Libraries
  Reference Services Unit
  111 State Street
  Montpelier 05602
  802-828-3261

VIRGINIA

- Grants Resources Library
  Hampton City Hall
  22 Lincoln Street, Ninth Floor
  Hampton 23669
  804-727-6496

- Richmond Public Library
  Business, Science, & Technology
    Department
  101 East Franklin Street
  Richmond 23219
  804-780-8223

WASHINGTON

- Seattle Public Library
  1000 Fourth Avenue
  Seattle 98104
  206-625-4881

- Spokane Public Library
    Funding Information Center

West 906 Main Avenue
Spokane 99201
509-838-3361

WEST VIRGINIA

- Kanawha County Public Library
  123 Capital Street
  Charleston 25301
  304-343-4646

WISCONSIN

- Marquette University Memorial
  Library
  1415 West Wisconsin Avenue
  Milwaukee 53233
  414-224-1515

- University of Wisconsin–Madison
  Memorial Library
  728 State Street
  Madison 53706
  608-262-3647

  Society for Nonprofit Organizations
  6314 Odana Road
  Suite One
  Madison 53719
  608-274-9777

WYOMING

- Laramie County Community
  College Library
  1400 East College Drive
  Cheyenne 82007
  307-634-5853

CANADA

Canadian Center for Philanthropy
3080 Yonge Street
Suite 4080
Toronto, Ontario M4N3N1
416-484-4118

ENGLAND

Charities Aid Foundation
14 Bloomsbury Square
London WCIA 2LP
01-430-1798

MARIANNA ISLANDS

Northern Marianas College
P.O. Box 1250 CK
Saipan, GM 96950

MEXICO

Biblioteca Benjamin Franklin
Londres 16
Mexico City 6, D.F.
525-591-0244

PUERTO RICO

Universidad Del Sagrado Corazon
M.M.T. Guevarra Library
Correo Calle Loiza
Santurce 00914
809-728-1515 ext.274

VIRGIN ISLANDS

College of the Virgin Islands Library
Saint Thomas
U.S. Virgin Islands 00801
809-774-9200 ext. 487

1986
GRAMMAR HOTLINE DIRECTORY

ALABAMA

AUBURN 36830
  (205) 826-5749—Writing Center
    Hotline
  Monday through Thursday, 9:00
    a.m. to noon and 1:00 p.m. to
    4:00 p.m.; Friday, 9:00 a.m. to
    noon; reduced hours during
    summer
  Auburn University
  Mike Moyle

ARKANSAS

LITTLE ROCK 72204
  (501) 569-3162—The Writer's
    Hotline
  Monday through Friday, 8:00
    a.m. to noon
  University of Arkansas at Little
    Rock
  Marilynn Keys

CALIFORNIA

MOORPARK 93021
  (805) 529-2321—National
    Grammar Hotline
  Monday through Friday, 8:00
    a.m. to noon, September
    through June
  Moorpark College
  Michael Strumpf

COLORADO

PUEBLO 81001
  (303) 549-2787—USC Grammar
    Hotline
  Monday through Friday, 9:30
    a.m. to 3:30 p.m.; reduced
    hours May 15 to August 25
  University of Southern Colorado
  Margaret Senatore and
    Ralph Dille

FLORIDA

FT. LAUDERDALE 33314
  (305) 475-7697—Grammar
    Hotline
  Monday through Thursday, 8:00
    a.m. to 4:00 p.m.; Friday,
    8:00 a.m. to 1:00 p.m.
  University School of Nova
    University
  Dr. S. Solomon

GEORGIA

ATLANTA 30303
  (404) 658-2904—Writing Center
  Monday through Thursday, 8:30
    a.m. to 4:00 p.m.; Friday, 8:30
    a.m. to noon; evening hours vary
  Georgia State University
  Dabney Hart

ILLINOIS

CHARLESTON 61920
(217) 581-5929—Grammar
Hotline
Monday through Friday, 10:00
a.m. to 3:00 p.m.; summer
hours vary
Eastern Illinois University
Jeanne Simpson

NORMAL 61761
(309) 438-2345—Grammar
Hotline
Monday through Friday, 8:00
a.m. to 4:30 p.m.
Illinois State University
Janice Neuleib and
Maurice Scharton

RIVER GROVE 60171
(312) 456-0300, ext. 254—
Grammarphone
Monday through Thursday, 8:30
a.m. to 9:00 p.m.; Friday,
8:30 a.m. to 5:30 p.m.;
Saturday, 10:00 a.m. to
1:00 p.m.
Triton College
Marie Saeli

INDIANA

WEST LAFAYETTE 47907
(317) 494-3723—Grammar
Hotline
Monday through Friday, 9:30
a.m. to 3:00 p.m.; when a
writing instructor is available;
closed late April through mid-
June and closed August
Purdue University
Muriel Harris

KANSAS

EMPORIA 66801
(316) 343-1200, ext. 380—
Writer's Hotline

Monday through Thursday,
11:30 a.m. to 4:30 p.m.;
Tuesday night, 7:00 p.m. to
9:30 p.m. during spring and
fall semesters; summer hours
vary
Emporia State University
Linda Palmer

see KANSAS CITY, MISSOURI

LOUISIANA

LAFAYETTE 70504
(318) 231-5224—English Hotline
Monday through Thursday,
8:00 a.m. to 4:00 p.m.; Friday
8:00 a.m. to 1:00 p.m.
University of Southwestern
Louisiana
Sylvia Iskander, Writing Center,
English Department

MARYLAND

FROSTBURG 21532
(301) 687-4327—
Grammarphone (patented
trademark)
Monday through Friday, 10:00
a.m. to noon (accepts long-
distance-calls—funded by
Maryland Committee for the
Humanities, Frostburg State
College Foundation, C&P
Telephone Company)
Frostburg State College
A. Franklin Parks

MASSACHUSETTS

BOSTON 02115
(617) 437-2512—Grammar
Hotline
Monday through Friday, 8:30
a.m. to 4:30 p.m.;
Northeastern University
Stuart Peterfreund, English
Department

MISSOURI

JOPLIN 64801
(417) 624-0171—Gammar
Hotline
Monday through Friday, 9:00
a.m. to 2:00 p.m.
Missouri Southern State College
Dale W. Simpson

KANSAS CITY 64110-2499
(816) 276-2244—Writer's
Hotline
Monday through Friday, 9:00 a.m.
to 4:00 p.m., September through
May; summer hours vary
University of Missouri at Kansas
City
Judy McCormick and
David Foster

NEW YORK

JAMAICA 11451
(718) 739-7483—Rewrite
Monday through Friday, 1:00
p.m. to 4:00 p.m.
York College of the City
University of New York
Joan Baum and Alan Cooper

OHIO

CINCINNATI 45236
(513) 745-4312—Dial-A-
Grammar
Tapes requests—returns call
(long-distance calls returned
collect)
Raymond Walters College
Dr. Phyllis A. Sherwood

CINCINNATI 45221
(513) 475-2493—Writer's
Remedies
Monday through Friday, noon
to 1:00 p.m. and 2:00 p.m. to
3:00 p.m.
University of Cincinnati

Jay A. Yarmove and
Jim Crocker-Lakness

CINCINNATI 45223
(513) 559-1520, ext. 133 or 202—
Writing Center Hotline
Monday and Wednesday, 9:00
a.m. to 8:00 p.m.; Tuesday,
Thursday, and Friday, 9:00
a.m. to 4:15 p.m.
Cincinnati Technical College
Cathy Wiesner and
John Battistone

DELAWARE 43015
(614) 369-4431, ext. 301—
Writing Resource Center
Monday through Friday, 9:00
a.m. to noon and 1:00 p.m. to
4:00 p.m., September through
May
Ohio Wesleyan University
Dr. Ulle Lewes and
Mrs. Jean Hopper

PENNSYLVANIA

ALLENTOWN 18104
(215) 437-4471—Academic
Support Center, Writing
Center Hotline
Monday through Friday, 9:00
a.m. to 4:00 p.m., September
through May
Cedar Crest College
Karen Coleman and Bea Meyer

LINCOLN UNIVERSITY 19352
(215) 932-8300, ext. 460—
Grammar Hotline
Monday through Friday, fall
semester, 8:00 a.m. to 5:00
p.m.; spring semester, 9:00
a.m. to 5:00 p.m.; summer
hours vary
Lincoln University
Dr. Annabelle Linneman

SOUTH CAROLINA

CHARLESTON 29409
  (803) 792-3194—Grammar
    Hotline
  Monday through Friday, 8:00
    a.m. to 4:00 p.m.; Sunday
    through Thursday, 6:00 p.m.
    to 10:00 p.m.
  The Citadel
  Angela W. Williams

COLUMBIA 29208
  (803) 777-7020—Writer's
    Hotline
  Monday through Thursday, 8:30
    a.m. to 5:00 p.m.; Friday,
    8:30 a.m. to 1:00 p.m.
  University of South Carolina
  Marian Rhame

TEXAS

HOUSTON 77002
  (713) 221-8670—University of
    Houston Downtown Grammar
    Hotline
  Monday through Thursday,
    9:00 a.m. to 4:00 p.m.; Friday,
    9:00 a.m. to 1:00 p.m.
  University of Houston
    Downtown
  Barbara G. Bartholomew

SAN ANTONIO 78284
  (512) 733-2503—Learning Line
  Monday through Thursday, 8:00
    a.m. to 9:45 p.m.; Friday, 8:00
    a.m. to 4:00 p.m.
  San Antonio College
  Vivian Rudisil

VIRGINIA

VIRGINIA BEACH 23456
  (804) 427-7170—Grammar
    Hotline
  Monday through Thursday,
    10:00 a.m. to 12:30 p.m. and
    1:30 p.m. to 2:00 p.m.; Friday
    10:00 a.m. to noon; reduced
    hours during summer
  Tidewater Community College
  Donna Friedman

WISCONSIN

GREEN BAY 54307-9042
  (414) 498-5427—Grammar
    Hotline
  Monday through Thursday, 8:30
    a.m. to 9:00 p.m.; Friday 8:00
    a.m. to 4:00 p.m.
  Northeast Wisconsin Technical
    Institute
  Rose Marie Mastricola and
    Joanne Rathburn

CANADA

EDMONTON, ALBERTA T5J2P2
  (403) 483-4393—Grammar
    Hotline
  Monday through Friday, 10:00
    a.m. to 2:00 p.m.
  Grant MacEwan Community
    College
  Karl Homann

FREDERICTON,
NEW BRUNSWICK E3B5A3
  (506) 453-4666—Grammar
    Hotline
  Variable hours
  University of New Brunswick
  A. M. Kinloch

Many of the services reduce hours during the summer, and most close during college breaks. One, Frostburg State College, Maryland, accepts collect calls.

Source: Reprinted with the permission of Tidewater Community College, Virginia Beach, VA. Annual updates are available every October from Tidewater Community College for those sending a stamped, self-addressed envelope.

INDEX

510